# Learning Maya7 | Foundation

Alias | LearningTools

# ACKNOWLEDGEMENTS

**Artwork from *Blue*:**
Christopher Mullins and Aaron Webster

**Cover design:**
Louis Fishauf

**Cover image and interior book design:**
Ian McFadyen

**Editorial services:**
Erica Fyvie

**Technical Editor:**
Cathy McGinnis

**DVD production:**
Roark Andrade and Julio Lopez

**Production Coordinator:**
Lenni Rodrigues

**Project Manager:**
Carla Sharkey

**Product Manager, Learning Tools and Training:**
Danielle Lamothe

**Director, Learning Tools and Training:**
Michael Stamler

**Primary Author:** Marc-André Guindon

Marc-André Guindon is the founder of Realities Studio (www.RealitiesStudio.com), a Montreal-based production facility. An advanced user of both Maya and Alias MotionBuilder, Marc-André and Realities have partnered with Alias on several projects, including The *Art of Maya*, *Learning Maya 6 | MEL Fundamentals*, and the series *Learning Maya 7*. Realities Studio was also the driving force behind Pipeline Technique DVDs, such as *How to Integrate Quadrupeds into a Production Pipeline* and *Maya and MotionBuilder Pipeline*. Realities also created the *Maya Quick Reference Sheets* and contributed to *Creating Striking Graphics with Maya & Photoshop*.

Marc-André has established complex pipelines and developed numerous plug-ins and tools for a variety of projects in both the film and games industries. His latest projects include the integration of motion capture for the Outlaw Game Series (*Outlaw Volleyball*, *Outlaw Golf 1* and *2* and *Outlaw Tennis*). He served as Technical Director on *XXX2*, *State of the Union* (Revolution Studios), *ScoobyDoo 2* (Warner Bros. Pictures), and *Dawn of the Dead* (Universal Pictures).

Marc-André is also an Alias MasterClass™ presenter. Marc-André continues to seek additional challenges for himself, Realities and his crew.

**Contributing author:** Cathy McGinnis

Cathy McGinnis is an Alias Certified Instructor teaching at the Media Design School in Auckland, New Zealand. Prior to moving down under, Cathy was a Technical Product Specialist for Alias, specializing in rendering in both Maya and mental ray for Maya. Cathy has been a Maya trainer since the birth of the software and has been a contributor to several Alias publications including *Learning Maya | Rendering*, and *Learning Maya 6 | Foundation*.

**Contributing author *Sketchbook*:** Roark Andrade

Roark Andrade has been a video producer with Alias since 2002. Roark is a multi-media artist and graduate of the Ontario College of Art. Roark has been teaching animation and video to children at the Art Gallery of Ontario since 2000. He has been working with Alias Sketchbook Pro since the launch of the software and enjoys the flexibility this technology permits. He likens using Sketchbook to "painting with light".

**A special thanks goes out to:**

Carmela Bourassa, Sylvana Chan, Deion Green, Rachael Jackson, David Haapalehto, James Christopher, Colin Smith, Anthony Nehme, Paula Suitor, Jill Ramsay, Shai Hinitz, and Maria Oliveira.

# FOREWARD

Danielle Lamothe | Product Manager, Learning Tools and Training

From its first printing, at the birth of Maya® 1.0, *Learning Maya | Foundation* has been the resource of choice for those who want to learn to use the world's most powerful 3D modeling and animation software. Legions of users have started the path to Maya mastery with the familiar projects that have been the core of *Learning Maya* - from the bouncing ball to Salty the Seal. Now in its seventh edition, the Learning Tools team at Alias® decided it was time to shake things up. It wasn't an easy decision to retire Salty to the place where digital animals go, however, it was with great excitement and enthusiasm that we set about producing *Learning Maya 7 | Foundation*.

While we've made some dramatic changes to the look and feel of *Learning Maya 7 | Foundation*, we've stayed true to its core philosophy – that the best way to learn is to do. While readers who've worked through previous versions won't recognize the projects in this latest edition, they will be familiar with the opportunity this book provides to model, animate, render and add dynamic effects to the scenes they create. In seeking to provide the best possible learning experience for users of Maya software, we've made some key changes that we feel are certain to improve your learning experience:

## Real-world Productions

Create production quality images from the award-winning short film *Blue* by Christopher Mullins – every *Learning Maya 7 | Foundation* project is based on the theme and artwork of the film.

Gain a stronger understanding of the entire production pipeline by exploring the creative process from storyboarding to final rendering. Get insight into the challenges of an independent production with an interview and comments by Aaron Webster, one of the core contributors on the film.

## Alias Authored

Benefit directly from the makers of Maya with "Alias Tips" notes and pointers from Alias developers, application engineers and product specialists.

We've also included a free copy of Alias Sketchbook™ Pro as an introduction to complementary Alias technology!

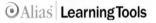

We believe these changes will improve your learning experience and make *Learning Maya 7 | Foundation* the definitive resource for everyone wishing to learn Maya. Enjoy!

# ABOUT *BLUE*

Christopher Mullins | Xenobi Studios

Grand Prize Best Animated Short Rhode Island Film Festival 2004

Best Professional Animation — Real to Reel Film Festival 2004

Official Selection CINEME International Animation Festival 2004

Golden Lion Best Professional Animation George Lindsey Festival 2004

Animation 2nd Place — Forest Film Festival 2004

I developed my idea for *Blue* as a short animated film in December 2000. In February of 2001, I hired professional artist and friend, Aaron Webster, to help with the modeling, texturing and rendering aspects of the film. I traveled to Canada to work with him on concept illustrations and storyboards. In March, I traveled back to the States and we began production via the Internet, large file transfers, and painful long-distance phone bills.

The very talented Australian composer, James Anderson (*JelloKnee*), joined the small team to create the score and handle sound design.

From the outset, this has been a very ambitious project. All of us have put our hearts into it 110%. The film was officially released on September 21, 2003, and entered the international film festival circuit. To date, we've been fortunate enough to have our efforts rewarded with several awards and honors.

Creating *Blue* was truly a learning experience for us so it's wonderful to have our artwork used to help you learn Maya. Being an artist is a lot of hard work, but the reward of seeing your completed film up on the big screen is worth every painful moment.

# Table of Contents

## Introduction

## Project01

## Project02

## Project03

**Project**04

**Project**05

**Project** One

**Project** Two

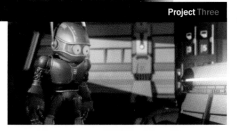

**Project** Three

**Project** Four

Maya is a character animation and visual effects system designed for the professional animator. Built on a procedural architecture called the *Dependency Graph*, Maya offers incredible power and flexibility for generating digital images of animated characters and scenes.

This tutorial book gives you hands-on experience with Maya as you complete a series of project-focused lessons. In each project you will model, animate, texture map, add visual effects and render.

Shown to the left are the five projects you will be creating throughout this book.

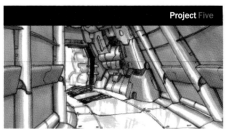

**Project** Five

## How to use this book

How you use this book will depend on your experience with computer graphics and 3D animation. This book moves at a fast pace and is designed to help both the novice and the expert as outlined below:

**Beginner** - If this is your first experience with 3D software, we suggest that you glance over each lesson before you complete it. This will give you a better understanding of what is going to happen before you tackle the software directly.

**Intermediate** - If you are already familiar with the world of 3D animation, you can dive in and complete the lessons as written. You may want to keep the *Getting Started with Maya 7* manual handy to help give you a more complete understanding of each tool.

**Expert** - Experts can run through the exercises in this book at a quicker pace. The location of the tools and the terminology found in Maya surrounding its use will be the most helpful aspect of this book for experts.

## Updates to this book

In an effort to ensure your continued success through the lessons in this book, please visit our web site for the latest updates available:

*www.alias.com/learningtools_updates/*

## Windows and Macintosh

This book is written to cover Windows® and Macintosh® platforms. Graphics and text have been modified where applicable. You may notice that your screen varies slightly from the illustrations depending on the platform you are using.

**Things to watch for:**

Window focus may differ. For example, if you are on Windows, you have to click in the panels with your middle mouse button to make it active.

To select multiple attributes in Windows, use the **Ctrl** key. On Macintosh, use the **Command** key. To modify pivot position in Windows, use the **Insert** key. On Macintosh, use the **Home** key.

Introduction

## Maya packaging

This book can be used with **Maya Complete**, **Maya Unlimited**, or **Maya Personal Learning Software** as the lessons included here focus on functionality shared among the three packages. Each of the Maya versions listed above include all of the tools you'll need to complete the exercises within this book.

## *Learning Maya* **DVD-ROM**

The Learning Maya DVD-ROM contains several resources to accelerate your learning experience including:

- *Learning Maya* tutorial files

- *Blue*: a short film

- An interview with Aaron Webster on the making of the film

- Three hours of instructor-led overviews to guide you through the projects in the book.

- Alias SketchBook Pro software

If you are new to 3D, it is recommended that you watch this DVD-ROM before proceeding with the *Learning Maya book tutorials*.

**Installing tutorial files** - Before beginning the lessons in this book, you will need to install the lesson support files. Copy the project directories found in the *support_files* folder on the DVD disc to the *maya\projects* directory on your computer. Launch Maya and set the project by going to **File** → **Project** → **Set...** and selecting the appropriate project.

**Windows**: *C:\Documents and Settings\username\My Documents\maya\projects*

**Macintosh**: *Macintosh HD:Users:username:Documents:maya:projects*

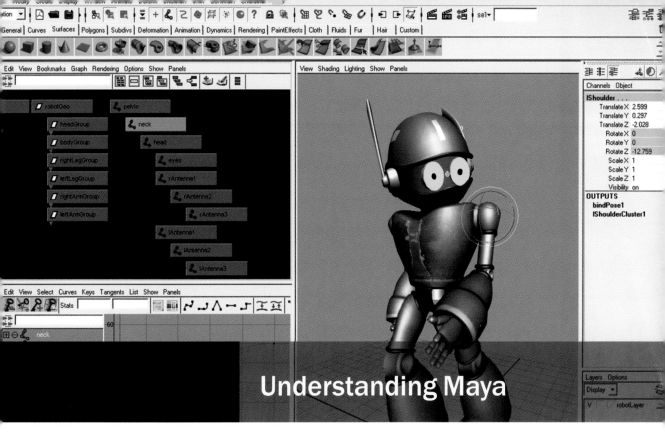

# Understanding Maya

To understand Maya Software, it helps to understand how Maya works at a conceptual level. This introduction is designed to give you the story of Maya. In other words, the focus of this introduction will be on how different Maya concepts are woven together to create an integrated workspace.

While this book teaches you how to model, animate and render in Maya, these concepts are taught with a particular focus on how the underlying architecture of Maya supports the creation of animated sequences.

You will soon learn how the Maya architecture can be explained by a single line – *nodes with attributes that are connected*. As you work through this book, the meaning of that statement becomes clearer and you will learn to appreciate how the Maya interface lets you focus on the act of creation, while giving you access to the power inherent in the underlying architecture.

# The user interface (UI)

The Maya user interface (UI) includes a number of tools, editors and controls. You can access these using the main menus or special context-sensitive Marking Menus™. You can also use *shelves* to store important icons or hotkeys to speed up workflow. Maya is designed to let you configure the UI as you see fit.

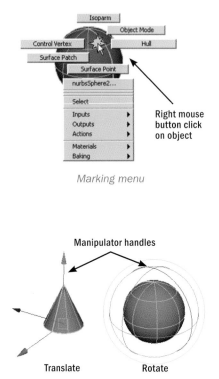

*Marking menu*

To work with objects, you can enter values using coordinate entry or you can use more interactive 3D manipulators. Manipulator handles let you edit your objects with a simple click+drag.

The Maya UI supports multiple levels of *undo* and *redo* and includes a drag+drop paradigm for accessing many parts of the workspace.

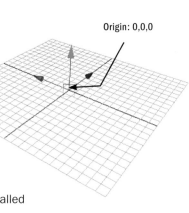

*Maya manipulators*

# Working in 3D

In Maya, you will build and animate objects in three dimensions. These dimensions are defined by the cardinal axes that are labeled as X, Y and Z. These represent the length (X), height (Y) and depth (Z) of your scene. These axes are represented by colors – red for X, green for Y and blue for Z.

In Maya, the Y-axis is pointing up (also referred to as *Y-up)*.

As you position, scale and rotate your objects, these three axes will serve as your main points of reference. The center of this coordinate system is called the *origin* and has a value of 0, 0, 0.

*The cardinal axes*

## UV coordinate space

As you build surfaces in Maya, they are created with their own coordinate space that is defined by U in one direction and V in another. You can use these coordinates when you are working with *curve-on-surface* objects or when you are positioning textures on a surface.

One corner of the surface acts as the origin of the system and all coordinates lie directly on the surface.

You can make surfaces *live* in order to work directly in the UV coordinate space. You will also encounter U and V attributes when you place textures onto surfaces.

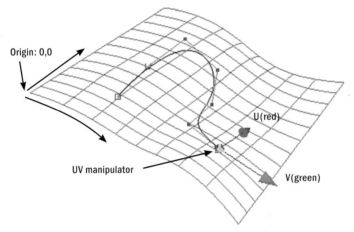

Origin: 0,0

U (red)

UV manipulator

V (green)

*UV coordinates on a live surface*

## Views

In Maya, you visualize your scenes using view panels that let you see into the 3D world.

**Perspective** views let you see your scene as if you are looking at it with your own eyes or through the lens of a camera.

**Orthographic** views are parallel to the scene and offer a more objective view. They focus on two axes at a time and are referred to as the *top*, *side* and *front* views.

In many cases, you will require several views to help you define the proper location of your objects. An object's position that looks good in the top view may not make sense in a side view. Maya lets you view multiple views at one time to help coordinate what you see.

Introduction

Perspective view ⎯⎯⎯

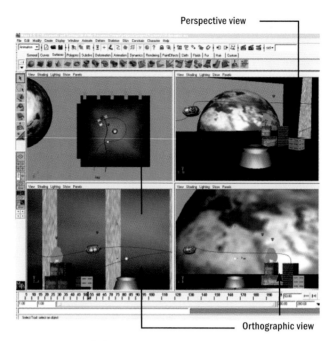

Orthographic view

*Orthographic and Perspective views*

# Cameras

To achieve a particular view, you look through a virtual camera. An Orthographic camera defines the view using a parallel plane and a direction while a Perspective camera uses an *eye point*, a *look at point* and a *focal length*.

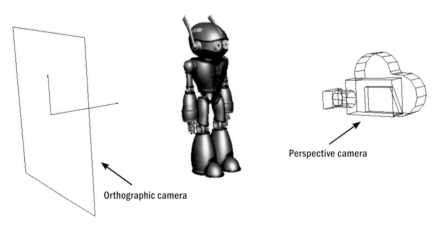

Perspective camera

Orthographic camera

*Perspective and Orthographic cameras*

## Image planes

When you work with cameras, it is possible to place special backdrop objects called *image planes* onto the camera. An image plane can be placed onto the camera so that as the camera moves, the plane stays aligned.

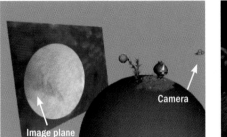

*Image plane attached to a camera*

*Image plane seen looking through the camera*

The image plane has several attributes that allow you to track and scale the image. These attributes can be animated to give the appearance that the plane is moving.

# THE DEPENDENCY GRAPH

The system architecture in Maya uses a procedural paradigm that lets you integrate traditional keyframe animation, inverse kinematics, dynamics and scripting on top of a node-based architecture that is called the **Dependency Graph**. If you wanted to reduce this graph to its bare essentials, you could describe it as *nodes with attributes that are connected*. This node-based architecture gives Maya its flexible procedural qualities.

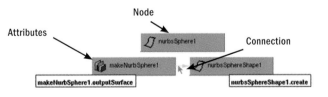

*The Dependency Graph*

Above is a diagram showing a primitive sphere's Dependency Graph. A procedural input node defines the shape of the sphere by connecting attributes on each node.

# Nodes

Every element in Maya, whether it is a curve, surface, deformer, light, texture, expression, modeling operation or animation curve, is described by either a single node or a series of connected nodes.

A *node* is a generic object type in Maya. Different nodes are designed with specific attributes so that the node can accomplish a specific task. Nodes define all object types in Maya including geometry, shading and lighting.

Shown below are three typical node types as they appear on a primitive sphere:

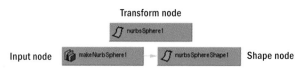

*Node types on a sphere*

### Transform node

Transform nodes contain positioning information for your objects. When you move, rotate or scale, this is the node you are affecting.

### Shape node

The shape node contains all the component information that represents the actual look of the sphere.

### Input node

The input node represents options that drive the creation of your sphere's shape, such as Radius or End Sweep. This is sometimes referred to as it's DNA.

The Maya UI presents these nodes to you in many ways. To the right is an image of the Channel Box, where you can edit and animate node attributes.

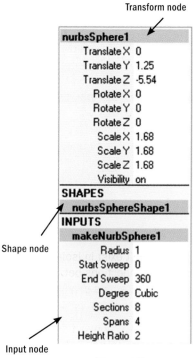

*Channel Box*

Introduction

Node tabs

*Attribute Editor*

## Attributes

Each node is defined by a series of attributes that relate to what the node is designed to accomplish. In the case of a transform node, *X Translate* is an attribute. In the case of a shader node, *Color Red* is an attribute. It is possible for you to assign values to the attributes. You can work with attributes in a number of UI windows including the *Attribute Editor*, the *Channel Box* and the *Spread Sheet Editor*.

One important feature in Maya is that you can animate virtually every attribute on any node. This helps give Maya its animation power. You should note that attributes are also referred to as *channels*.

## Connections

Nodes don't exist in isolation. A finished animation results when you begin making connections between attributes on different nodes. These connections are also known as *dependencies*. In modeling, these connections are sometimes referred to as *construction history*.

Most of these connections are created automatically by the Maya UI as a result of using commands or tools. If you desire, you can also build and edit these connections explicitly using the *Connection Editor*, by entering *MEL*™ (Maya Embedded Language) commands, or by writing MEL-based expressions.

# Pivots

Transform nodes are all built with a special component known as the *pivot point*. Just like your arm pivots around your elbow, the pivot helps you rotate a transform node. By changing the location of the pivot point, you get different results.

Pivots are basically the stationary point from which you rotate or scale objects. When animating, you sometimes need to build hierarchies where one transform node rotates the object and a second transform node scales. Each node can have its own pivot location to help you get the effect you want.

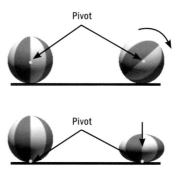

*Rotation and scaling pivots*

# Hierarchies

When you are building scenes in Maya, you have learned that you can build dependency connections to link node attributes. When working with transform nodes or joint nodes, you can also build hierarchies which create a different kind of relationship between your objects.

In a hierarchy, one transform node is *parented* to another. When Maya works with these nodes, Maya looks first at the top node, or *root* node, then down the hierarchy. Therefore, motion from the upper nodes is transferred down into the lower nodes. In the diagram below, if the *group1* node is rotated, then the two lower nodes will rotate with it. If the *nurbsCone1* node is rotated, the upper nodes are not affected.

*Object and joint hierarchy nodes*          *Object and joint hierarchies*

Joint hierarchies are used when you are building characters. When you create joints, the joint pivots act as limb joints while bones are drawn between them to help visualize the joint chain. By default, these hierarchies work just like object hierarchies. Rotating one node rotates all of the lower nodes at the same time.

You will learn more about joint hierarchies later in this introduction (see "Skeleton and Joints"), where you will also learn how *inverse kinematics* can reverse the flow of the hierarchy.

## MEL scripting

MEL stands for Maya Embedded Language. In Maya, every time you use a tool or open a window, you are using MEL. MEL can be used to execute simple commands, write expressions or build scripts that will extend the existing functionality in Maya. The Script Editor displays commands and feedback generated by scripts and tools. Simple MEL commands can be typed in the Command Line, while more complex MEL scripts can be typed in the Script Editor.

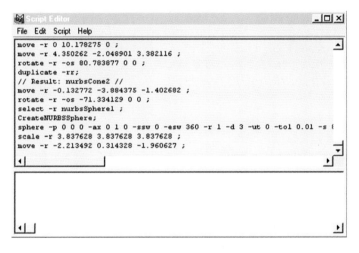

*The Script Editor*

MEL is the perfect tool for technical directors who are looking to customize Maya to suit the needs of a particular production environment. Animators can also use MEL to create simple macros that will help speed up more difficult or tedious workflows.

# ANIMATING IN MAYA

When you animate, you bring objects to life. In Maya, there are several different ways in which you can animate your scenes and the characters who inhabit them.

Animation in Maya is generally measured using frames that mimic the frames you would find on a film reel. You can play these frames at different speeds to achieve an animated effect. By default, Maya plays at 24 frames per second.

## Keyframe animation

The most familiar method of animating is called *keyframe animation*. Using this technique, you determine how you want the parts of your objects to look at a particular frame, then save the important attributes as keys. After you set several keys, the animation can be played back with Maya filling motion in-between the keys.

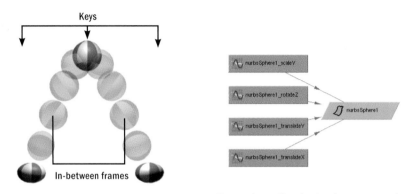

*Keys and in-between frames*

*Dependency Graph showing curve nodes*

When keys are set on a particular attribute, the keyed values are stored in special nodes called *animation curve* nodes.

These curves are defined by the keys that map the value of the attribute against time. The following is an example of several animation curve nodes connected to a transform node. One node is created for every attribute that is animated.

Once you have a curve, you can begin to control the tangency at each key to tweak the motion in-between the main keys. You can make your objects speed up or slow down by editing the shape of these animation curves.

Generally, the slope of the graph curve tells you the speed of the motion. A steep slope in the curve means fast motion while a flat curve equals no motion. Think of a skier going down a hill. Steep slopes increase speed while flatter sections slow things down.

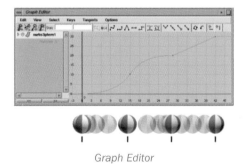

*Graph Editor*

## Path animation

*Path animation* is already defined by its name. You can assign one or more objects so they move along a path that has been drawn as a curve in 3D space. You can then use the shape of the curve and special path markers to edit and tweak the resulting motion.

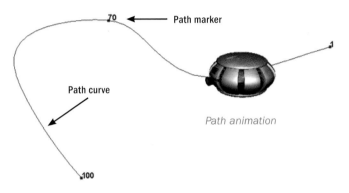

*Path animation*

## Non-linear animation

Non-linear animation is a way to layer and mix character animation sequences non-linearly - independently of time. You can layer and blend any type of keyed animation, including motion capture and path animation. This is accomplished through the Maya Trax Editor™.

*Trax Editor*

## Reactive animation

*Reactive animation* is a term used to describe animation in which one object's animation is based on the animation of another object.

An example of this technique would be moving gears when the rotation of one gear is linked to the rotation of other gears. You can set keys on the first gear and all the others will animate automatically. Later, when you want to edit or tweak the keys, only one object needs to be worked on and the others update reactively.

In Maya, you can set up reactive animation using a number of tools including those outlined below:

**Set Driven Key**

This tool lets you interactively set up an attribute on one object to drive one or more attributes onto another.

**Expressions**

Expressions are scripts that let you connect different attributes on different nodes.

**Constraints**

Constraints let you set up an object to point at, orient to or look at another object.

**Connections**

Attributes can be directly linked to another attribute using dependency node connections. You can create this kind of direct connection using the Connection Editor.

*Diagram of
animated gears*

## Dynamics

Another animation technique involves *dynamics*. You can set up objects in your Maya scene that animate based on physical effects such as collisions, gravity and wind. Different variables are *bounciness, friction* or *initial velocity*. When you playback the scene, you run a simulation to see how all the parts react to the variables.

This technique gives you natural motion that would be difficult to keyframe. You can use dynamics with rigid body objects, particles or soft body objects.

*Rigid body objects* are objects that don't deform. You can further edit the rigid body by setting it as either *active* or *passive*. Active bodies react to the dynamics, whereas passive bodies don't.

To simulate effects such as wind or gravity, you add *fields* to your dynamic objects.

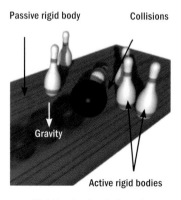

*Rigid body simulation of
bowling ball and pins*

Particles are tiny points that can be used to create effects such as smoke, fire or explosions. These points are emitted into the scene where they are also affected by the dynamic fields.

Soft bodies are surfaces that you deform during a simulation. To create a soft body, create an object and turn it's points into particles. The particles react to the dynamic forces which in turn, deform the surface.

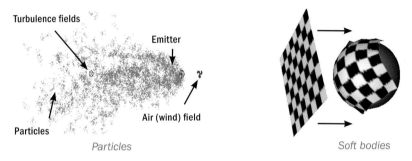

*Particles*          *Soft bodies*

# MODELING IN MAYA

The objects you want to animate in Maya are usually built using either NURBS surfaces or polygonal meshes. Maya offers you both of these geometry types so that you can choose the method best suited to your work.

## NURBS curves

NURBS stands for *non-uniform rational b-spline,* which is a technical term for a spline curve. By modeling with NURBS curves, you lay down control points and smooth geometry will be created using the points as guides.

Shown below is a typical NURBS curve with important parts labelled:

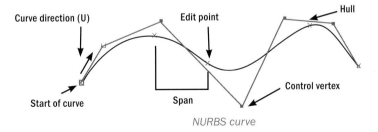

*NURBS curve*

These key components define important aspects of how a curve works.
The flexibility and power of NURBS geometry comes from your ability to edit the shape of the geometry using these controls.

As your geometry becomes more complex, you may need more of these controls. For this reason, it is usually better to start out with simpler geometry so that you can more easily control the shape. If you need more complex geometry, then controls can be inserted later.

## NURBS surfaces

Surfaces are defined using the same mathematics as curves except now they're in two dimensions – U and V. You learned about this earlier when you learned about UV coordinate space.

Below are some of the component elements of a typical NURBS surface:

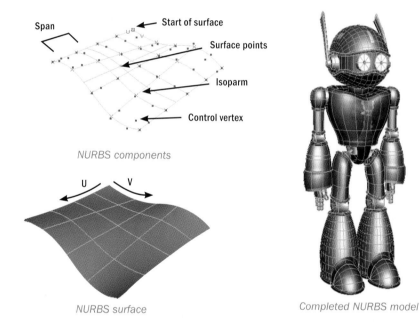

*NURBS components*

*NURBS surface*

*Completed NURBS model*

Complex shapes can be, in essence, sculpted using this surface type as you push and pull the controls to shape the surface.

## Subdivision Surfaces

Subdivision surfaces exhibit characteristics of both polygon and NURBS surfaces, allowing you to model smooth forms using comparatively few control vertices. They will enable you to create levels of detail exactly where you want.

# Polygons

Polygons are another geometry type available in Maya. Whereas NURBS surfaces interpolate the shape of the geometry interactively, polygonal meshes draw the geometry directly to the control vertices.

Below are some of the components found on a polygonal mesh:

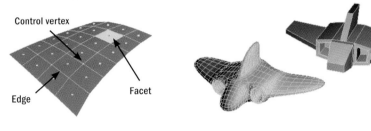

*Polygon components*              *Polygonal model before and after smoothing*

You can build up poly meshes by extruding, scaling and positioning polygonal facets to build shapes. You can then smooth the shape to get a more organic look for your model.

# Construction history

When you create models in Maya, the various steps are recorded as dependency nodes that remain connected to your surface.

In the example to the right, a curve has been used to create a revolved surface. Maya keeps the history by creating dependencies between the curve, a revolve node and the shape node. Edits made to the curve or the revolve node will update the final shape.

Many of these nodes come with special manipulators that make it easier to update the node attributes. In the case of the revolve, manipulators are available for the axis line and for the revolve's sweep angle.

*Revolve surface with dependencies*

It is possible to later delete history so that you are only working with the shape node. Don't forget though, the dependency nodes have attributes that can be animated. Therefore, you lose some power if you delete history.

# DEFORMATIONS

Deformers are special object types that can be used to reshape other objects. By using deformers, you can model different shapes, or give animations more of a squash and stretch quality.

A powerful feature of Maya are the deformers; they can be layered for more subtle effects. You can also bind deformers into skeletons or affect them with soft body dynamics.

The following lists some of the key deformer types available in Maya:

## Lattices

Lattices are external frames that can be applied to your objects. If you then reshape the frame, the object is deformed in response.

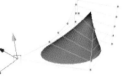

*Lattice deformer*

## Sculpt object

Sculpt object lets you deform a surface by pushing it with the object. By animating the position of the sculpt object, you can achieve animated surface deformations.

*Sculpt object deformer*

## Clusters

Clusters are groups of CVs or lattice points that are built into a single set. The cluster is given its own pivot point and can be used to manipulate the clustered points. You can weight the CVs in a cluster for more control over a deformation.

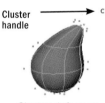

*Cluster deformer*

# CHARACTER ANIMATION

In Maya, character animation typically involves the animation of surfaces using skeleton joint chains and inverse kinematic handles to help drive the motion.

## Skeletons and joints

As you have already learned, skeleton joint chains are actually hierarchies. A skeleton is made of joint nodes that are connected visually by bone icons. Binding geometry to these hierarchies lets you create surface deformations when the joints are rotated.

# Inverse kinematics

By default, joint hierarchies work like any other hierarchy. The rotation of one joint is transferred to the lower joint nodes. This is known as *forward kinematics*. While this method is powerful, it makes it hard to plant a character's feet or move a hand to control the arm.

Inverse kinematics lets you work with the hierarchy in the opposite direction. By placing an IK handle at the end of the joint chain, Maya will solve all rotations within that joint chain. This is a lot quicker than animating every single joint in the hierarchy. There are three kinds of inverse kinematic solvers in Maya – the IK spline, the IK single chain and the IK rotate plane.

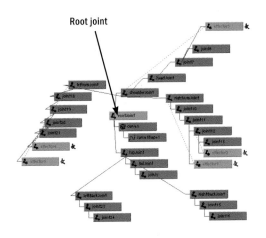

*Character joint hierarchy*

*Joints and bones*

Each of these solvers is designed to help you control the joint rotations with the use of an IK handle. As the IK handle is moved, the solver solves joint rotations that allow the end joint to properly move to the IK handle position.

The individual solvers have their own unique controls. Some of these are outlined below:

# Single chain solver

The *single chain solver* provides a straightforward mechanism for posing and animating a chain.

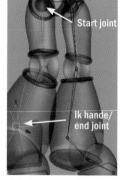

*IK single chain solver*

# Rotate plane solver

The *rotate plane solver* gives you more control. With this solver, the plane that acts as the goal for all joints can be moved by rotating the plane using a *twist attribute* or by moving the *pole vector handle*.

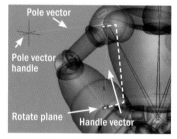

*IK rotate plane solver*

# IK spline solver

The *IK spline* solver lets you control the chain using a spline curve. You can edit the CVs on the spline to influence the rotation of the joints in the chain.

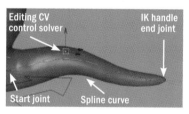

*IK spline solver*

# Skinning your characters

Once you have a skeleton built, you can *bind skin* the surfaces of your character so that they deform with the rotation of the joints. In Maya you can use either *soft skinning* or *hard skinning*. Soft skinning uses weighted clusters while hard skinning does not.

*Surface deformations*

**Introduction**

## Flexors

In some cases, skinning a character does not yield realistic deformations in the character's joint areas. You can use *flexors* to add this secondary level of deformations to help control the tucking and bulging of your character.

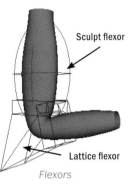

Sculpt flexor

Lattice flexor

*Flexors*

# RENDERING

Once your characters are set up, you can apply color and texture, then render with realistic lighting.

## Shading networks

In Maya, you add texture maps and other rendering nodes to create shading networks. At the end of every shading network is a shading group node. This node has specific attributes on it such as displacement maps and mental ray® for Maya ports, but more importantly, it contains a list of objects that are to be shaded by that network at render time. Without this node at the end of the network, the shader won't render.

Materials

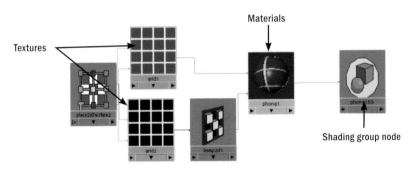

Textures

Shading group node

*Shading group dependencies*

Think of a shading network as a bucket into which you place all the color, texture and material qualities that you want for your surface. Add a light or two and your effect is achieved.

## Texture maps

To add detail to your shading groups, you can *texture map* different attributes. Some of these include bump, transparency and color.

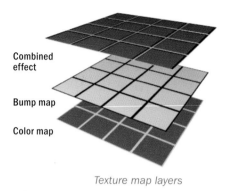

Combined effect

Bump map

Color map

*Texture map layers*

## Lighting

You can light your scenes using any number of lights. These lights let you add mood and atmosphere to a scene in much the same way as lighting is used by a photographer. Maya lets you preview your lights interactively as you model, or you can render to see the final effect.

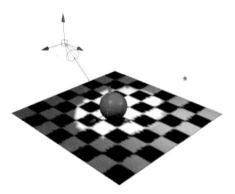

*Light manipulator*

## Motion blur

When a real-life camera takes a shot of a moving object, the final image is often blurred. This *motion blur* adds to the animated look of a scene and can be used in Maya. Maya contains two types of motion blur – a 2 1/2 D solution and a 3D solution. You will use both these types of motion blur in this book.

No motion blur

Motion blur

*Motion blur*

Introduction

# Hardware rendering

Maya includes *hardware rendering* that uses the power of your graphics card to render an image. This is a quick way to render, as the quality can be very good or it can be used to preview animations. You will need to use the hardware renderer to render most particle effects. These effects can be composited in later with software rendered images of your geometry.

Hardware rendering

# A-buffer rendering

The Maya rendering architecture is a hybrid renderer. It uses an EAS (Exact Area Sampling) or A-buffer algorithm for primary visibility from the eye (camera), and then raytraces any secondary rays.

A-buffer rendering

## Raytrace rendering

Raytracing lets you include reflections, refractions and raytrace shadows into your scenes. Only objects that have their raytrace options turned on will use this renderer. Raytracing is slower than the A-buffer algorithm and should only be used when necessary.

*Raytrace rendering*

## How the renderer works

The Maya renderer works by looking through the camera at the scene. It then takes a section (or tile) and analyzes whether or not it can render that section. If it can, it will combine the information found in the shading group (geometry, lights and shading network) with the Render Settings information, and the whole tile is rendered.

As the renderer moves on to the next section, it again analyzes the situation. If it hits a tile where there is more information than it wants to handle at one time, it breaks down the tile into a smaller tile and renders.

When you use raytracing, each tile is first rendered with the A-buffer, then the renderer looks for items that require raytracing. If it finds any, it layers in the raytraced sections. When it finishes, you have your finished image, or if you are rendering an animation, a sequence of images.

*Rendering of A-buffer tiles in progress*

## IPR

Maya includes an Interactive Photorealistic Renderer (IPR) that gives you fast feedback for texturing and lighting updates. You will use IPR throughout this book.

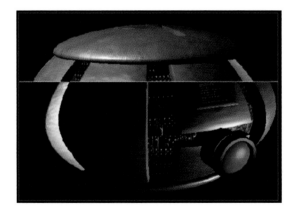

*IPR rendering in progress*

## Conclusion

Now that you have a basic understanding of what Maya is designed to do, it is time for you to start working with the application directly. The concepts outlined in this introduction will be clearer when you experience them first-hand.

# Project One

## Lessons

In Project One, you are going to learn the basics of object creation, along with the basics of animation, textures, lights, particles and Maya Paint Effects™. This will give you the chance to explore the Maya workspace while building your scene.

You will start by creating a room and filling it with objects in order to learn about building models. Then you will explore the rudiments of hierarchies and animation by creating a solar system. After that, you will experiment with shaders, textures and lights, which will allow you to render your scene. You will also explore the basics of the Maya particle system, along with some Paint Effects.

These lessons offer you a good look at some of the key concepts and workflows that drive Maya. Once this project is finalized, you will have a better understanding of the Maya user interface and its various modules.

*This lesson teaches you how to build and transform primitives in 3D space in order to create a spaceship warehouse. You will explore the Maya user interface (UI) as you learn how to build and develop your scene.*

**In this lesson you will learn the following:**

- How to set a new Maya project;

- How to create primitive objects;

- How to move objects in 3D space;

- How to duplicate objects;

- How to change the shape of objects;

- How to use the Maya view tools;

- How to change the display of your objects;

- How to name your objects;

- How to save your scene.

# Setting up Maya

The first step is to install Maya. Then, copy the Learning Maya support files to your *Maya* projects directory. Support files are found in the *support_files* directory on the DVD-ROM included with this book.

In order to find your Maya projects directory, you need to launch Maya at least once so that it creates your user directory structure. Here is typically where the Maya projects directory is located on your machine:

> **Windows**: *Drive:\Documents and Settings\username\My Documents\maya\projects*

> **Mac OS X**: *Users/username/Library/Preferences/Alias/maya/projects*

**Note:** *To avoid the* **Cannot Save Workspace** *error, ensure that the support files are not read-only after you copy them from the DVD-ROM.*

When Maya is launched for the first time and you have other Maya versions installed, Maya will ask if you want to copy your preferences or create the default preferences. In order to follow the exercises in this book, you should be using default preferences. If you have been working with Maya and changed any of your user interface settings, you may want to delete your preferences in order to start with the default Maya configuration.

# Creating a new project

Maya uses a project directory to store and organize all files (scenes, images, materials, textures, etc.) related to a particular scene. When building a scene, you create and work with a variety of file types and formats. The project directory allows you to keep these different file types in their unique sub-directory locations within the project directory.

## 1 Launch Maya

## 2 Set the project

To manage your files, you can set a project directory that contains sub-directories for different types of files that relate to your project.

- Go to the **File** menu and select **Project** → **Set…**

A window opens that directs you to the *Maya* projects directory.

- Open the folder *support_files*.

- Click on the folder named *project1* to select it.

- Click on the **OK** button.

- This sets *project1* of the *learningMaya* directory as your current project.

- Go to the **File** menu and select **Project → Edit Current...**

*Make sure that the project directories are set up as shown below.*
*This ensures that Maya is looking into the proper sub-directories when*
*it opens up scene files.*

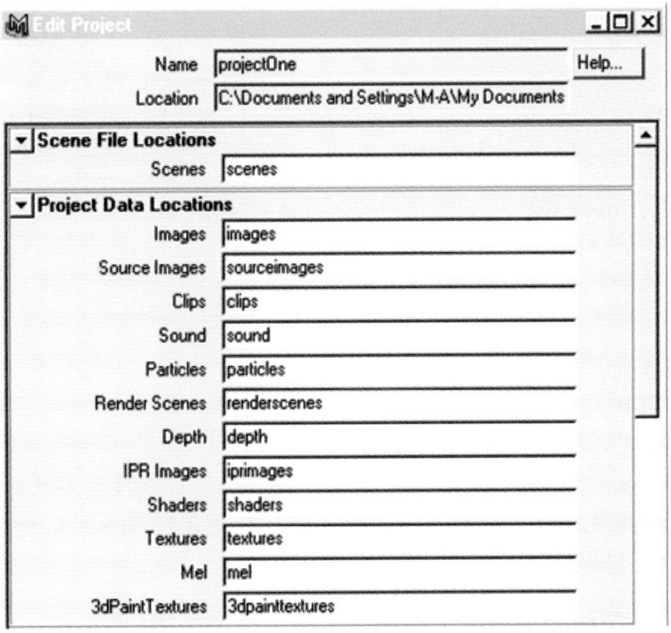

| | |
|---|---|
| **Edit Project** | _ □ × |

| Name | projectOne | | Help... |
|---|---|---|---|
| Location | C:\Documents and Settings\M-A\My Documents | | |

**▼ Scene File Locations**

| Scenes | scenes |
|---|---|

**▼ Project Data Locations**

| Images | images |
|---|---|
| Source Images | sourceimages |
| Clips | clips |
| Sound | sound |
| Particles | particles |
| Render Scenes | renderscenes |
| Depth | depth |
| IPR Images | iprimages |
| Shaders | shaders |
| Textures | textures |
| Mel | mel |
| 3dPaintTextures | 3dpainttextures |

*Edit Project window*

### 3   Make a new scene

- Select **File → New Scene**.

*This will create a new scene in the current directory when it's saved.*

# BUILDING OBJECTS

Every scene you create in Maya will most likely contain objects, like surfaces, deformers, skeleton joints or particle emitters. For this scene, you will build a room, several boxes and wires.

## Creating the room

To start, you will build a big cube, which will be the room itself with a floor, ceiling and walls. That first object will be a primitive polygonal cube. To reference the finished file before you start, open the file *01-room.ma*.

### 1 Change menu sets

There are four main menu sets in Maya: *Animation, Modeling, Dynamics* and *Rendering*. These menu sets are used to access related tool sets.

- From the drop-down menu at the left edge of the Status Line (Toolbar), select **Modeling**.

*As you change menu sets, the first six menus along the top of the viewport remain the same while the remaining menus change to reflect the chosen menu set.*

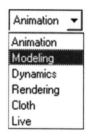

*Menu set drop-down menu*

### 2 Create a polygonal cube

A primitive cube will be used as a large surrounding room. It will be built using polygonal geometry. Throughout this lesson and in the next project, you will learn more about this geometry type.

- From the **Create** menu, select **Polygon Primitives** → **Cube**.

*A cube is placed at the origin.*

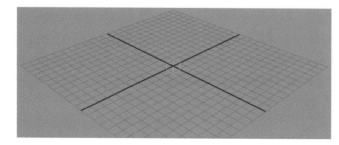

*Perspective view of pCube1*

## 3   Change the cube's dimensions

The cube is a procedural model. This means that it is broken down into parts called *nodes*. One node contains its positioning information, one contains its shape information and another contains input information that defines the cube's construction history using attributes such as width, height and depth. You can edit this input node's attributes in the Channel Box in order to edit the cube's shape.

The Channel Box is found at the right side of the screen and lets you make changes to key attributes very easily.

- From the Channel Box's **Inputs** section, click on *polyCube1*.

*This will make several new attributes available for editing.*

- Type **25** in the **Width** entry field and press the **Enter** key.

- Type **10** in the **Height** entry field and press the **Enter** key.

- Type **25** in the **Depth** entry field and press the **Enter** key.

*Now the cube is shaped like a room in the Perspective view.*

Channels  Object

Current → **pCube1**
object
| | | |
|---|---|---|
| | Translate X | 0 |
| | Translate Y | 0 |
| | Translate Z | 0 |
| | Rotate X | 0 |
| | Rotate Y | 0 |
| | Rotate Z | 0 |
| | Scale X | 1 |
| | Scale Y | 1 |
| | Scale Z | 1 |
| | Visibility | on |

**SHAPES**
  **pCubeShape1**
**INPUTS**
  **polyCube1**

Inputs
section
| | | |
|---|---|---|
| | Width | 25 |
| | Height | 10 |
| | Depth | 25 |
| | Subdivisions Width | 1 |
| | Subdivisions Height | 1 |
| | Subdivisions Depth | 1 |

*Channel Box*

**Note:** *If your Channel Box is not along the right side of the screen, you can access it by selecting* **Display** → **UI Elements** → **Channel Box/Layer Editor.**

**Note:** *Another method for increasing the size of the cube would be to scale it. In Maya, you can often achieve the same visual results using many different methods. Over time, you will begin to choose the techniques that best suit a particular situation.*

## 4   Rename the cube node

You should rename the existing transform node
to make it easier to find later.

| Channels   Object |
| --- |
| room |

|   | | |
| --- | --- | --- |
| Translate X | 0 |
| Translate Y | 0 |

*Renaming the node in
the Channel Box*

- Click on the *pCube1* name at the top of the
  Channel Box to highlight it.

- Type the name *room,* and press the **Enter** key.

## Moving the room

You will now use the Move Tool to reposition the room. This will involve the use of
manipulator handles that let you control where you move your object.

## 1   Position the room

You can now use the **Move Tool** to reposition the cube's floor above the
working grid.

- Select the **Move Tool**.

*A transform manipulator appears centered on the object.*

- **Click+drag** on the **green** manipulator handle to move the cube along the
  **Y-axis** until the bottom of the room is flush with the grid.

*You'll notice that the manipulator handle turns **yellow** to indicate that it is active.*

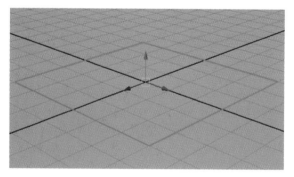

*Manipulator handle*

> **Tip:** The transform manipulator has three handles that let you constrain your
> motion along the X, Y and Z-axes. These are labeled using red for the X-axis,
> green for the Y-axis and blue for the Z-axis. In Maya, the Y-axis points up by
> default. This means that Maya is "Y-up" by default.

## 2 Create four view panels

By default, a single Perspective window is shown in the workspace. To see other views of the scene, you can change your panel layout.

- At the top of the Perspective view panel, go to the **Panels** menu and select **Saved Layouts** → **Four View**.

*You can now see the cube using three Orthographic views – top, side, and front – that show's you the model from a projected view. You can also see it in a Perspective view that is more like the 3D world we see every day. This multiple view setup is very useful when positioning objects in 3D space.*

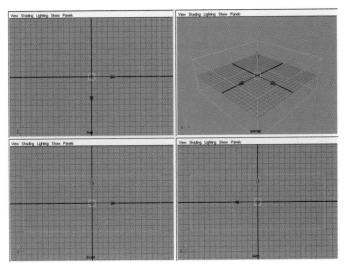

*Four view panels*

**Tip:** *Quickly pressing and releasing the keyboard spacebar will switch from a single view panel to a four view panel.*

## 3 Reposition the room

When moving in an Orthographic view, you can work in two axes at once by dragging on the center of the manipulator or constraining the motion along a single axis using the handles.

- In the front view, **click+drag** on the square center of the manipulator to move the cube along both the **X** and **Y-axes**.

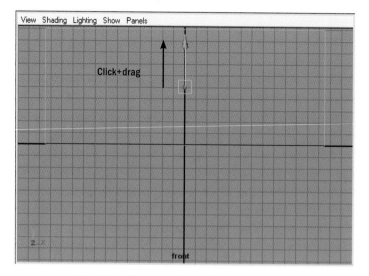

*Front view & appropriate position of the room*

- Use the manipulator in the various view windows to position the cube's lower face on the ground plane, as shown.

*Be sure to refer to all four view windows to verify that the object is positioned properly.*

**Note:** *If you click+drag on the center of the manipulator in the Perspective view, you will notice that it doesn't move along any particular axis. It is actually moving along the camera's view plane.*

## Viewing the scene

When you work in 3D space, it is important to see your work from different angles. The different view panels let you see your work from the front, top, side and Perspective angles.

You can also use the Maya view tools to change the views in order to reposition how you see your scene. In some cases, a view change is like panning a camera around a room, while in other cases a view change might be like rotating an object around in your hand to see all the sides. These view tools can be accessed using the **Alt** key in combination with various mouse buttons.

## 1 Edit the Perspective view

You can use the **Alt** key with either your left mouse button (LMB), your middle mouse button (MMB) or the two together to tumble, track and dolly in your Perspective view.

- Change your view using the following key combinations:

    **Alt + LMB** to tumble;

    **Alt + MMB** to track;

    **Alt + LMB + MMB** to dolly.

You can also combine these with the **Ctrl** key to create a bounding box dolly where the view adjusts based on a bounding box. This is useful when you want to dolly on a precise section of the view or quickly dolly out to get a general look of the scene.

    **Ctrl + Alt + LMB** to box dolly.

*Click+drag to the right to dolly in and to the left to dolly out.*

*You can also undo and redo view changes using the following keys:*

    To undo views use [

    To redo views use ]

- Alter your Perspective window until it appears as shown below:

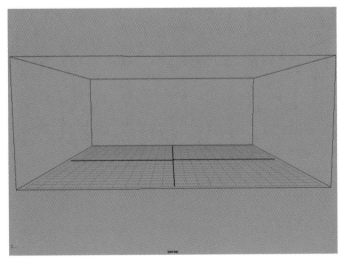

*New view*

## 2    Edit the view in the side view

Orthographic views use similar hotkeys – except that you cannot tumble by default in an Orthographic view.

- In the side view, change your view using the following key combinations:

    **Alt + MMB** to track;

    **Alt + LMB + MMB** to dolly.

- Keep working with the *Orthographic* views until they are set up as shown:

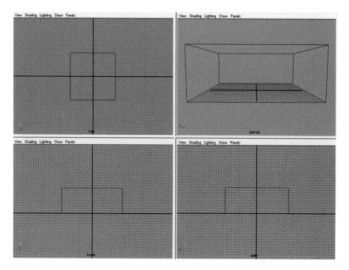

*New Orthographic views*

## 3    Frame Selected and Frame All

Another quick way to navigate in the different views is to use the Frame Selected or Frame All hotkeys for the active view.

- Select the room.

- While in the four view panels, move your mouse over a view.

- Press the **f** hotkey to frame the selected geometry in the view under your mouse.

- Press the **a** hotkey to frame everything visible in the view where your mouse is.

## Setting display options

The view panels let you interactively view your scene. By default, this means viewing your scene as a wireframe model. To better evaluate the form of your objects, you can activate hardware shading.

### 1  Turn on hardware shading

To help visualize your objects, you can use hardware rendering to display a shaded view within any panel.

- From the Perspective view's **Shading** menu, select **Smooth Shade All**.

*This setting affects all of the objects within the current view panel.*

*Smooth shaded view*

**Tip:**   You can also turn on Smooth Shading by moving your cursor over the desired panel, clicking with your middle mouse button and pressing the **5** key. The **4** key can be used to return the panel to a wireframe view.

## 2 Hide the grid

You can hide the grid to simplify your view using one of two options:

- From the Perspective view panel's **Show** menu, select **Grid** to hide the grid for that view only,

**Or**

- From the **Display** menu, deselect **Grid** to hide the grid for all views.

# Moving inside the room

In order to have the feeling of being inside the room in the Perspective view, you need to move the perspective camera inside the cube geometry. You will soon realize that even if you can see inside the cube, sometimes one of its sides will appear in front of the camera while moving, thus hiding the inside. The following steps will prevent this from happening:

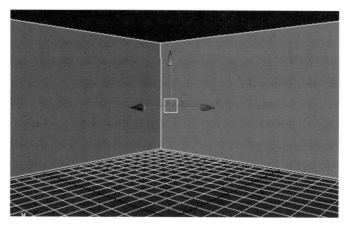

*Perspective inside the cube*

## 1 Change the room's display

To simplify your scene interaction, Maya can let you see inside the cube even when the camera is outside of it. To do so, you will have to change the way Maya displays the cube. The following actions are somewhat more advanced than what you will undertake in this project, but they will allow you to see inside the room more easily.

- Select the cube.

- In the Modeling menu set, select **Edit Polygons** → **Normals** → **Reverse**.

*This tells Maya that you want to turn the cube inside out. This is good in our case since we want to be inside the room.*

- With the cube still selected, while in the main Maya menu, select **Display** → **Component Display** → **Backfaces**.

*This tells Maya to hide the sides of the cube facing away from the camera.*

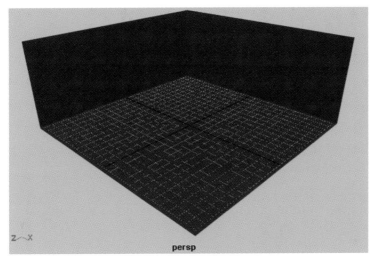

*Seeing inside the room without backfaces*

## Create boxes

To create a box, follow the same steps as you did to create the primitive cube for the room. You can use the hotbox as an alternative method for accessing tools.

### 1 Create another polygonal cube

- Press and hold the spacebar anywhere over the Maya interface to display the hotbox.

- In the hotbox, select **Create** → **Polygon Primitives** → **Cube**.

*Another cube is placed at the origin.*

> **Tip:** You can access all functions in Maya using either the main menus or the hotbox. As you become more familiar with the hotbox, you can use the user interface options found in the **Display** menu to turn off the panel menus and therefore reduce screen clutter.

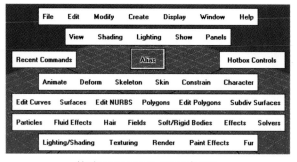

*Hotbox access to menu items*

## 2    Rename the cube node

It is a good idea to rename the existing transform node to make it easier to find later.

- Click on the pCube1 node's name in the top of the Channel Box.

- Enter the name *box*.

## 3    Transform the cube

Instead of using the cube's input node to change its size, try using the scale manipulator. You can also experiment by translating and rotating the cube into a proper position on the floor surface.

- Select the **Scale Tool** in the toolbox on the left side of the Maya interface.

- Using the different axes of the **Scale Tool**, change the shape of the cube.

- Switch to the **Translate Tool** by pressing the **w** hotkey and move the box above the floor.

- Switch to the **Rotate Tool** by pressing the **e** hotkey and offset the box on its Y-axis.

*Toolbox*
- You can switch back to the **Scale Tool** by pressing the **r** hotkey.

## 4   Make more cubes

Instead of always creating a default primitive cube, you can duplicate an existing one, preserving its position and shape.

- Select your first box and select **Edit** → **Duplicate**.

- Create a stack of boxes.

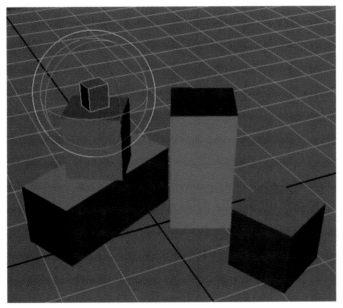

*Stack of boxes*

**Tip:**   *You can use the* **Ctrl+d** *hotkey to duplicate the selected geometry without going into the menu each time.*

# Adding pillars, wires and a pedestal

Now that you know how to place objects and interact with the Perspective view, you will add some details to the room. You will start by creating a bunch of pillars that hold the ceiling, then you will add a wire running on the ground, and finally, you will add a pedestal to the middle of the room.

*Lesson 01*
*Adding pillars, wires and a pedestal*

## 1 Making pillars

The Duplicate Tool has options allowing you to duplicate multiple copies of the same object, separated by a fixed translation or rotation value. For example, if you make one pillar, you can make four other copies separated by five units, all in one easy step.

• Create a polygonal cube and place it against a wall.

*You'll need to rotate it slightly and then scale and translate it back so that it rests partially inside and outside the room.*

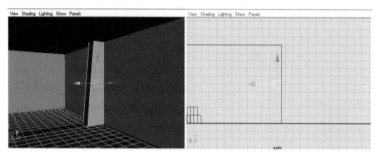

*Placement of one pillar*

• Rename the cube *pillar*.

• Place the pillar in a corner of the room as shown:

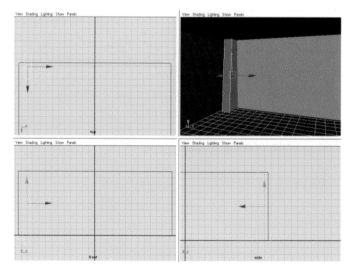

*Translate the pillar in a corner of the room*

Project One

- Select **Edit** → **Duplicate** → ☐.

- Set the **Number of Copies** to **4**.

In order to determine the good translation axis, look at the view axis located at the bottom left corner of each view. If you want the copies to be created along the positive X-axis, enter a positive value in the first field of the translation vector.

- Set the appropriate **Translate** value to **5** and leave the others at **0**.

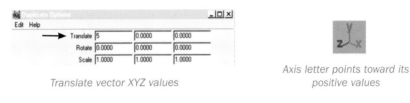

*Translate vector XYZ values*

*Axis letter points toward its positive values*

- Click on the **Duplicate** button to execute the command.

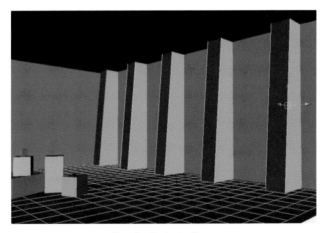

*The duplicated pillars*

- Hit **Edit** → **Undo** for any errors and try again.

## 2  Electrical wire on the floor

You now want to create another type of primitive geometry. In this step, you will create a NURBS cylinder. NURBS stands for *Non-uniform Rational B-spline*, which means that it is made out of curves instead of straight edges like polygons. NURBS geometry looks much smoother than polygons.

- If your stack of boxes is still in the middle of the room, click on one cube, then hold down the **Shift** key and click all the remaining cubes to select them.

- **Translate** them all together in a corner of the room.

- Select **Create** → **NURBS Primitives** → **Cylinder**.

*A cylinder will appear at the origin.*

- Set the **X rotation** to **90**.

- Click on *makenurbsCylinder1* in the Channel Box to display the construction history of the cylinder.

    Set **Radius** to **0.2**.

    Set **Spans** to **6**.

    Set **Height Ratio** to **10**.

- **Move** the cylinder above the ground.

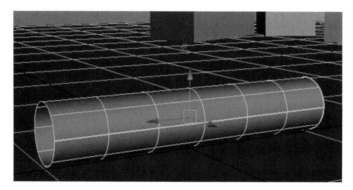

*The base shape of an electrical wire*

- If the radius of the cylinder is too wide, you can scale it down using the **Scale Tool**.

**Tip:**  *When scaling an object, you can hold down the **Ctrl** key and click+drag one of the axes to proportionally scale the other two axes.*

- Select the **Component** icon located in the Status Line at the top of the interface. Once clicked, make sure the **Vertices** button next to it is also enabled as follows:

*Going into Component mode with Vertices enabled*

*Working in this mode will display the components of the currently selected geometry. You can then select and transform the points defining a surface's shape. Polygon points are called* **vertex/vertices** *and NURBS points are called* **control vertices** *or* **CVs**.

- Go to the top view and select a row of CVs and move them. Select the next row of CVs and move them. Continue moving the CVs apart and out to lengthen the cylinder and create a snakelike wire.

**Tip:**   *When selecting components, hold down* **Shift** *to toggle the new selection, hold down* **Ctrl** *to deselect the new selection and hold down* **Ctrl+Shift** *to add the new selection to the currently selected group of components.*

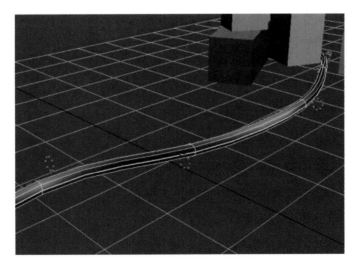

*The final shape of the wire*

- Go back in Object mode and move the object towards the back of the wall.

File   Edit   Modify   Create   Display   Window   Edit Curves   Surfaces   Edit NURBS   Polygons   Edit Polygons

*Selecting Object mode*

- **Rename** the cylinder *wire*.

## 3   Adjust NURBS smoothness

To better display a NURBS surface in a viewport, you can increase/decrease its smoothness.

- Select the wire.

- From the main **Display** menu, select **NURBS Smoothness**.

*These settings will affect how selected NURBS objects are displayed in all view panels.*

---

**Tip:**   *A NURBS object can have its smoothness set using the following hotkeys:*

   **1** – *rough*      **2** – *medium*      **3** - *fine*

---

## 4   Pedestal

In this step, you will make a pedestal from a polygonal cone.

- Select **Create** → **Polygon Primitives** → **Cone**.

- **Move** the *cone* above the floor.

- Change it's **Subdivision Height** value to **5** so that the cone looks like the image to the right.

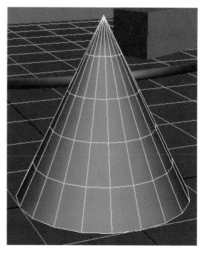

*Modified cone primitive*

*Project One*

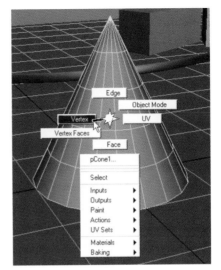

- **RMB** on the cone to display its contextual radial menu, and select **Vertex**.

- Edit the cone vertices to get the following pedestal shape. Select each row of vertices and translate them up or down and scale them slightly where needed. For the top of the pedestal, select the group of vertices at the top of the cone and move them down into the center.

*Context menu*

**Tip:** *You might want to go in wireframe (hotkey 4), in order to select components more easily.*

*Pedestal*

- **Rename** the cone *pedestal*.

Lesson 01

*Project One*

## 5   Save your work

- From the **File** menu, select **Save Scene As...**

- Enter the name *01-room*.

- Click the **Save** button or press the **Enter** key.

*Windows Save As dialog box*

*Make sure you save this file since you will be continuing with it in the next lesson.*

**Note:** *Throughout this book, you will be using the final saved file from one lesson as the start file for the next, unless specified otherwise. Save your work at the end of each lesson to make sure that you have the start file ready.*

## Conclusion

Congratulations. You have completed your first exercise using Maya. You should now be able to easily navigate the different views and change the basic hardware display settings. You should also be confident in creating, duplicating, transforming and renaming objects, along with using the translation, rotation, and scale manipulators. Before pursuing your work, make sure you understand the principles of this Maya project. As well, be careful to save scene files.

In the next lesson, you will animate a holographic solar system floating over the room's pedestal.

# Making a solar system

*In the last lesson, you built a room using various primitive objects. You will now learn about hierarchies by creating a holographic solar system in the center of the room. You will then animate several objects in your scene, which should liven up the room.*

**In this lesson you will learn the following:**

- How to group and parent objects;

- How to understand parent inheritance;

- How to traverse a hierarchy;

- How to set keyframes;

- How to use the Graph Editor;

- How to change the infinity of an animation;

- How to use the Time Slider.

# Working with a good file

Use the scene that you saved in the previous lesson or use the one provided in your scenes directory, *01-room.ma*.

## 1   Open a scene

There are several ways to open a scene in Maya. Following are two easy options:

- From the **File** menu, select **Open Scene**.

Or

- Click on the **Open** button located in the top menu bar.

*File Open button*

## 2   Find your scene

In the **File Open** dialog box, if you cannot immediately locate *01-room.ma*, it might be because your project is not set correctly or that Maya did not direct you into the *scenes* directory.

- At the top of the dialog box, if the path is not pointing into the project created in the last lesson, click the **Set Project...** button at the bottom of the window and browse to find the correct project directory. When you find it, click **OK**.

- When you open a scene now, it should automatically take you to your current project's *scenes* directory. If it doesn't, open the combo box located at the top of the dialog box and select **Current scenes**.

Current location →

Set Project button →

*File Open dialog*

- Select *01-room.ma* and click **Open**.

**3   Save Scene As**

Since you will be modifying this scene, it is a good idea to save this file under a new name now. Doing so will allow you to keep a copy of the previous lesson in case you would like to start this lesson over.

- Select **File** → **Save Scene As...**.

- Type *02-solarSystem* in the **File name** field.

- Select *MayaASCII (*.ma)* in the **Files of type** field.

*Maya can save its files in two different types of formats:*

**Maya ASCII (.ma)** *saves your scene into a text file which is editable in a Text Editor. Though this format takes more space on your drive, it is possible to review and modify its content without opening it in Maya. Experienced users find this very useful.*

**Maya Binary (.mb)** *saves your scene into a binary file which is compiled into computer language. This format is faster to save and load, and takes less space on your drive.*

## Creating a sun and planets

You will begin by creating spheres in your scene that will represent the solar system. Then you will create a hierarchy in order to get ready to animate. To do so, you will learn how to group and parent objects together and learn how to use the Outliner.

**1   Create a sun**

Every solar system has a sun as its center, so that is a good starting point. To build a good working space, start by hiding all the scene's geometry.

- Select **Display** → **Hide** → **All**.

- Click **Create** → **NURBS Primitives** → **Sphere**.

- Select the sphere's scaling attributes through the Channel Box by clicking on the **Scale X** value and dragging to the **Scale Z** value.

*Doing so will highlight all three scaling values, allowing you to enter a single value to change all of them at once.*

**nurbsSphere1**

| | |
|---|---|
| Translate X | 0 |
| Translate Y | 0 |
| Translate Z | 0 |
| Rotate X | 0 |
| Rotate Y | 0 |
| Rotate Z | 0 |
| Scale X | 1 |
| Scale Y | 1 |
| Scale Z | 1 |
| Visibility | on |

Click+drag

*Click+drag on the scale values*

- Enter **0.5** and press **Enter**.

*Make sure all three scaling values changed simultaneously.*

- **Rename** the sphere *sun*.

## 2  Making planets

Next, you will create four planets of various sizes, along with a moon and a ring.

- Duplicate the *sun* and rename it *planet*.

**Tip:** Make sure that you go into **Duplicate** options and reset the options back to their default values.

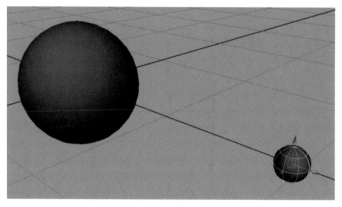

*The birth of your solar system*

- **Translate** the *planet* on the **X-axis** by about **2** units.

- **Scale** the *planet* down to **0.1**.

- **Duplicate**, **translate** and **scale** the *planet* in order to create three other planets.

- Add a tiny sphere next to one of the planets and **rename** it *moon*.

- Make a ring by creating a torus. Go to **Create** → **NURBS primitives** → **Torus**.

- In the Channel Box, change the **Height Ratio** of the torus construction history to **0.2**.

- Flatten the *torus* by scaling the **Y-axis** to **0.2**.

- **Rename** the torus *ring* and place it over one of the planets.

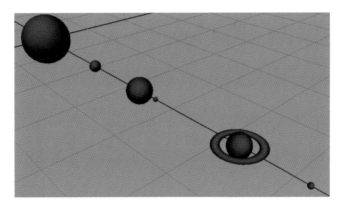

*The completed system*

## 3  Hierarchy

It is very important for a Maya user to understand the concept of a hierarchy. A hierarchy consists of the grouping of child nodes under parent nodes. When transforming a parent node, all of its children will inherit its transformation. The following steps explain how to create a hierarchy of objects.

- To better visualize what you are about to do, open the Outliner by selecting **Window** → **Outliner…**.

*The Outliner lists all the nodes in your scene along with their hierarchies. Currently, in your scene, you can see the default Maya cameras, all of the prior lesson objects, every component of your solar system and at the very bottom, two default sets.*

**Outliner**

Display   Show   Help

| | |
|---|---|
| persp | |
| top | |
| front | |
| side | |
| room | |
| box | |
| box1 | |
| box2 | |
| box3 | |
| box4 | |
| box5 | |
| box6 | |
| box7 | |
| box8 | |

*Outliner*

- Scroll down in the Outliner and click on the first *planet* object.

*Doing so selects the geometry (just like when selecting in a viewport).*

- Press and hold your **MMB** over the *planet* object and drag it over the *sun* object.

*As you can see in the following images, dragging a node will set it as the child of the object it was dragged on to.*

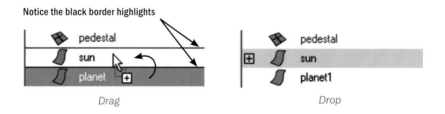

Notice the black border highlights

*Drag*                                    *Drop*

- Expand the newly created hierarchy by clicking on the **plus** sign next to the *sun* object.

*Notice the green highlight on the sun object, which means one of its children is currently selected.*

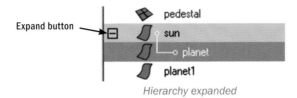

Expand button →

pedestal
sun
planet
planet1

*Hierarchy expanded*

**Tip:** *Another way of parenting objects together is through the main Maya menu or with the* **parent** *hotkey.*

## 4 Completing the hierarchy

- In the Outliner or in a viewport, select one of the unparented planets.

- Hold **Ctrl**, then select the *sun*.

- From the **Edit** menu, select **Parent**.

Or

- Press **p** on your keyboard.

- Organize the hierarchy so that it looks like the image to the right.

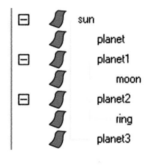

sun
planet
planet1
moon
planet2
ring
planet3

*The completed hierarchy*

# Understanding inheritance

If you rotate the sun object, all of its children will follow that rotation. Also, when rotating one of the planets, its children, for instance a moon, will also inherit that rotation.

## 1 Child values

When you transform a parent object, none of its children's values change.

- Select the *sun* and rotate its **Y-axis**.

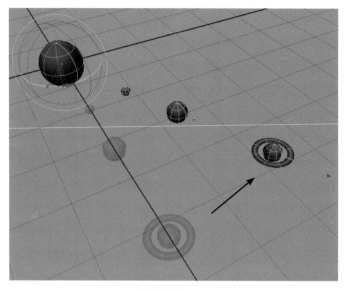

*Rotate the sun*

- Select any of its children and notice that all of their rotation values are still zero.

- Select *planet1* and rotate it.

*Notice the moon's rotation values did not change.*

- Select the *sun* and scale it down.

*All of its children follow the parent scaling, but none of their values are changing.*

**Note:** A child inherits its transformations from the parent. If you reset the translation and rotation values to zero, the child will end up positioned exactly at its parent's position. For instance, if you zero the moon's translation and rotation values, the moon will move exactly on the pivot of its parent planet.

## Animating the planets

Your solar system is now ready to be animated. Once you keyframe your planets, you will have a greater understanding of how to use inheritance to your advantage.

## 1 The timeline

The first step with animation is to determine how long you would like your animation to be. By default, Maya is playing animation at a rate of 24 frames per seconds (24FPS), which is a standard rate used for films. So if you want your animation to last one second, you need to animate 24 frames.

- In the Time Slider and Range Slider portion of the Maya interface, change **Playback End Time** to **100**.

*The frames in the Time Slider now go from 1 to 100. One hundred frames is just above four seconds of animation in 24FPS.*

Start time              End time

Playback start time      *Time Slider and Range Slider*      Playback end time

## 2 Setting keyframes

Luckily, you do not need to animate every single frame in your animation. When you set keyframes, Maya will interpolate the values between the keyframes, thus giving you animation.

- Press the **First Frame** button from the playback controls to make the current frame **1**.

- Select the sun.

- Set all of its rotation values to **0**.

- At the top of the Maya interface, change the current menu set to **Animation**.

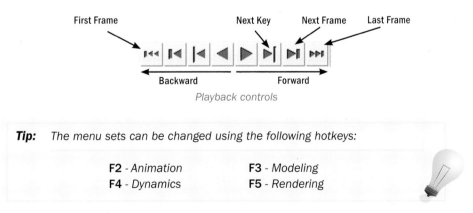

First Frame         Next Key     Next Frame    Last Frame

Backward           Forward

*Playback controls*

**Tip:**    *The menu sets can be changed using the following hotkeys:*

         **F2** - *Animation*         **F3** - *Modeling*
         **F4** - *Dynamics*         **F5** - *Rendering*

- With the *sun* still selected, select **Animate** → **Set Key**.

**Set Key** *can also be executed by pressing the* **s** *hotkey.*

- In the current frame field on the left of the rewind button, type **100** and hit **Enter**.

*Notice the position of the current frame mark in the Time Slider.*

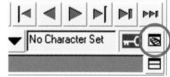

Current frame mark    Current frame field

*The current frame mark*

- Type **360** in the **Rotate Y** field of the *sun* and hit **Enter**.

- **MMB** click into the viewport in order to remove focus from the Y-axis field, then hit the **s** hotkey to **Set Key**.

## 3   Playback speed

Before you play your animation, you need to set the Maya playback properly.

- Click the **Animation preferences** button found at the far right side of the Range Slider.

*The Animation preferences button*

*This opens a window that lets you set various animation and playback options. Currently, the scene is playing back as fast as it can. Since you only have a couple of objects in your scene, playback will be a little too fast.*

*In the* **Timeline** *section, set the following:*

- **Playback Speed** to **Real-time**.

- Click the **Save** button.

- Press the **Play** button in the playback controls area to see your animation.

- To stop the playback of the animation, press the **Play** button again or hit **Esc**.

- You can drag the current frame by **click+dragging** in the Time Slider area.

*Click+drag in the Time Slider*

*Notice the red tick at frame 1 and frame 100, specifying keyframes on the currently selected objects.*

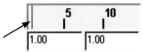

*A keyframe tick in the Time Slider*

Now you will set up the planet. You have a partially animated solar system, but you have probably noticed that all of the planets follow the same orbit around the sun, which is not appropriate. Each planet should be orbiting at their own speed. In order to do that, a bit of set up is required.

- Go to frame **1** by pressing the **Rewind** button.

- Select the *sun*.

- Remove all its animation by clicking **Edit** → **Delete by Type** → **Channels**.

Doing so removes all keyframes on the selected objects.

- Select *planet* and click on **Edit** → **Group**.

*If you look in the Outliner, you can see that group1 is now the parent of planet.*

*A newly created group's transformations are always set to its default. This means translation and rotation are zero, and scale is one.*

- Make sure the group is selected and press **w** to select the **Translate Tool**.

*Notice the pivot of* group1 *is located on its parent* sun *pivot (where the manipulator is).*

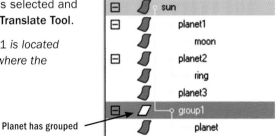

Planet has grouped

*The newly created group*

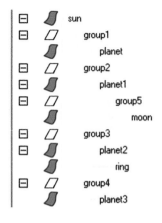

- Press **e** to select the **Rotate Tool** and rotate the group on its Y-axis.

*The group's pivot is perfect to animate an orbit around the sun.*

- Select another planet and press the **g** hotkey to **group** it.

- Repeat for the other planets and the moon.

*The final setup*

## 4   Finalize the animation

Now you can animate each group to have all the planets and the moon orbit at their own speeds. On top of that, you can animate the planets to spin on themselves.

- Select all the groups, the planets and the moon.

- Select the **Rotate Y** attribute in the Channel Box by clicking its name.

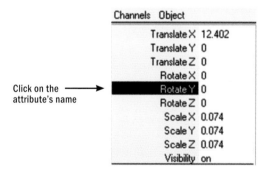

*Select only the Rotate Y attribute*

- Click and hold the **RMB** over that same attribute.

*This will pop the attribute context menu.*

- Select **Key Selected**.

*Doing so will set a keyframe on that attribute for every selected object.*

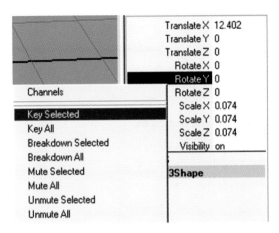

*Select Key Selected from the attribute menu*

- Go to frame **20**.

- Rotate the **Y-axis** of each group, planet and moon by approximately **10** to **50** units.

*Do not rotate them all the same amount, or they will not have different orbit speeds.*

- Again select all the groups, the planets and the moon.

- Choose Key Selected from the **Rotate Y** attribute again, but this time at frame **20**.

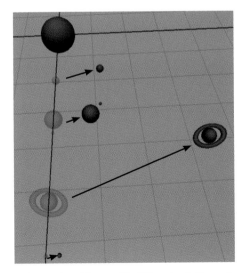

*Keyframe the objects with different rotation values*

## 5  Graph Editor

The Graph Editor is the place in Maya where you can look at all the keyframes on an object and see their interpolations as curves (*function curves* or *fcurves*).

- Select one of the groups you've just animated.

- Select **Window** → **Animation Editors** → **Graph Editor**.

- Press the **Alt** key and click+drag with the left and middle mouse buttons to dolly into the graph.

- Press the **Shift+Alt** keys and click+drag up and down with the left and middle mouse buttons to dolly only along the **Y-axis**.

- Press the **Shift+Alt** keys and click+drag up and down with the middle mouse button to track along the **Y-axis**.

- Select **View** → **Frame All** to frame the entire curve.

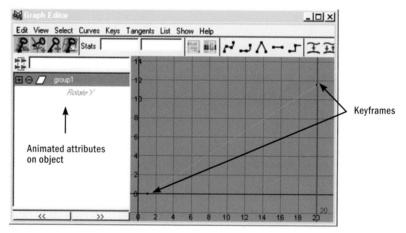

*The Rotate Y fcurve*

*The two keyframes you have set on the Y-axis are represented by black dots.*

**Tip:**  *The same view tools used in the modeling views apply to other panel types. The* **Shift** *key constraint works in all view panels and with tumbling and tracking.*

## 6 Infinity

You can set the infinity of a curve to be linear. That means even if the current time is outside of your fcurve, Maya will keep interpolating the fcurve in a linear way.

- With the **Rotate Y** fcurve still selected, select **View** → **Infinity**.

- Dolly out to see the infinity.

*Dotted lines represent the infinity*

- Select **Curves** → **Pre Infinity** → **Linear**.
- Select **Curves** → **Post Infinity** → **Linear**.

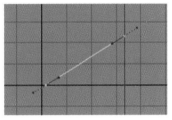

*The linear infinity*

- Select all the remaining animated objects.

- Repeat the above steps to change their **Rotate Y** fcurves infinity to **Linear**.

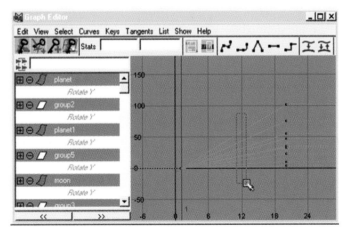

*Select all the fcurves at the same time*

- Close the Graph Editor.
- **Play** your animation.

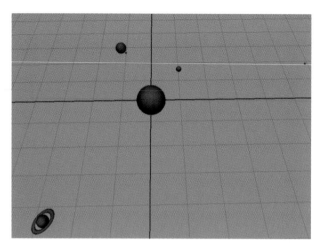

*The final animation*

## 7 Traversing a hierarchy

Now we can place the solar system over the pedestal from the first lesson. First, we need to show everything that was hidden at the beginning of this lesson, then place the parent of the solar system at the right position. Since objects might be overlapping each other, it could be dificult to select them directly in the viewports.

- From the main menu, select **Display** → **Show** → **All**.

*The room is made visible in the viewports.*

- Select any of the planets.
- Press the **Up arrow** to change the selection to the parent of the current selection.
- Press the **Up arrow** again until the selection is on the *sun*.

**Tip:** *You can use the arrows on your keyboard to traverse a hierarchy:*

**Up arrow** - *Parent*          **Down arrow** - *First child*
**Right arrow** - *Next child*          **Left arrow** - *Previous child*

- Translate, rotate and scale the *sun* above the pedestal.

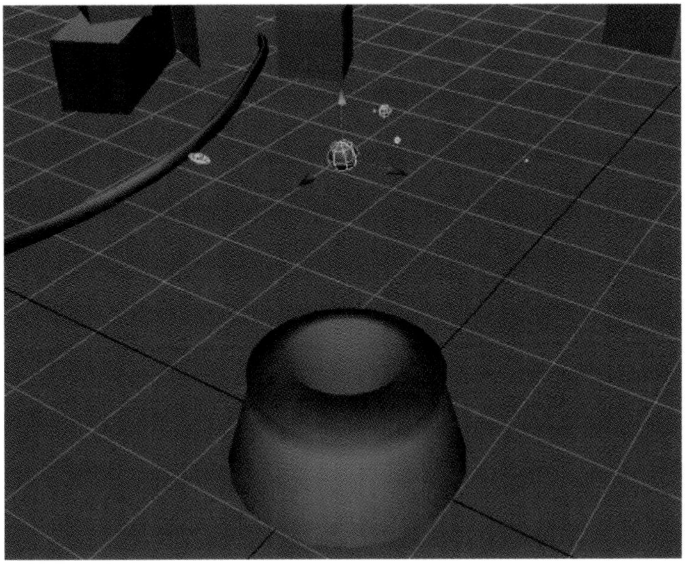

*The placed solar system*

## 8    Save your work

- From the **File** menu, select **Save**.

## Conclusion

You have now touched upon some of the basic concepts in hierarchies and animation. Maya gathers much more powerful tools to help you bring your scenes to life, but these basic principles represent a great step forward. As well as learning how to group and parent objects together, you also learned about inheritance of transformation and animation and worked with two of the most useful editors: the Outliner and the Graph Editor.

In the next lesson, you will bring colors into your scene by assigning shaders and textures to your objects.

**Lesson 02**

# Lesson 03 Shaders and textures

*Now that you have created an environment and animated several objects, you are ready to render your scene. The rendering process involves the preparation of materials and textures for objects.*

**In this lesson you will learn the following:**

- How to work with a menu-less UI;

- How to work with the Hypershade;

- How to create shading groups;

- How to texture map an object;

- How to render a single frame;

# Hiding the general UI

In the last two lessons, you used menus, numeric input fields and other UI elements to work with your scene. In this lesson, you will hide most of the user interface and rely more on the hotbox and other hotkeys that let you access the UI without actually seeing it on screen. Feel free to continue using the file you created from the last lesson, or open *02-solarsystem.ma* from the scenes directory.

## 1   Turn off all menus

- Move your cursor over the Perspective view panel, then press the spacebar quickly to pop this panel to full screen.

- Press and hold on the spacebar to evoke the hotbox.

> **Tip:**   *Tapping and holding down the spacebar, can be used to both toggle between window panes and bring up the hotbox.*

- Click on the **Hotbox Controls**.

- From the marking menu, go down to **Window Options** and set the following:

    **Show Main Menubar** to **Off** (Windows only);

    **Show Pane Menubars** to **Off**.

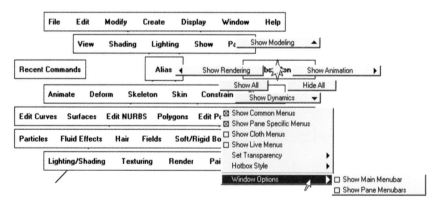

*Marking menu*

Now the various menus are hidden and you must rely on the hotbox to access tools.

**Project One**

## 2 Turn off all of the workspace options

- From the hotbox, select **Display** → **UI Elements** → **Hide UI Elements**.

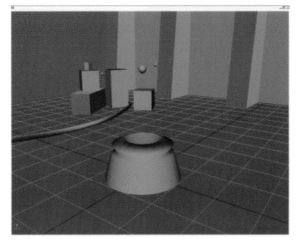

*Simplified UI*

You now have a much larger working area, which will let you focus more on your work.

## 3 Change the panel organization

- Press and hold on the spacebar to evoke the hotbox.

- Click in the area above the menus to invoke a marking menu.

- Select **Hypershade**/**Render**/**Persp** from this marking menu.

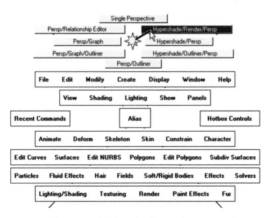

*Hypershade/Render/Persp layout*

Lesson 03

**Tip:** Each of the four quadrants surrounding the hotbox and the hotbox's center all contain their own marking menu set. You can edit the contents of these menus using **Window** → **Settings/Preferences** → **Marking Menus...**

This saved layout puts a Hypershade panel above a Perspective panel and a Render view panel.

The Hypershade is where you will build shading networks and the Render view is where you will test the results in your scene.

## 4 Open the Attribute Editor

- From the hotbox, select **Display** → **UI Elements** → **Attribute Editor**.

Now you also have an Attribute Editor panel on the right side of the workspace. This will make it easy to update shading network attributes.

Increase/
decrease
panel size
buttons

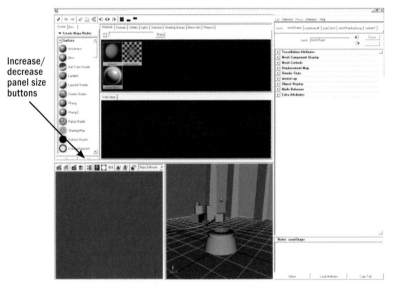

*New UI layout*

# Hotkeys

When working with a minimal UI, you will rely on the hotbox and hotkeys for your work. The following is a list of relevant hotkeys that you may need to use as you work:

| | | |
|---|---|---|
| **spacebar** | – | Hotbox/window popping |
| **Ctrl + a** | – | Show/hide Attribute Editor |
| **Alt + v** | – | Start/stop playback |
| **Alt + Shift + v** | – | Go to first frame |
| **Alt + .** | – | Move one frame forward |
| **Alt + ,** | – | Move one frame back |
| **k** | – | Click+drag to scrub animation |

For a complete listing of available hotkeys, go to **Window → Settings/ Preferences → Hotkeys...**

> **Alias Tip:** *Gestural menus are my favourite feature in Maya. Watching a trained Maya expert use the menu system in Maya is truly poetry in motion. They fly through the actions and seem to really be communicating with Maya at a higher level. The workflow is streamlined and effective.*
>
> *Shai Hinitz | Sr. Product Manager*

# SHADING GROUPS

To prepare the room and objects for rendering, you need to add color and texture. In Maya, this is accomplished using *shading networks* that bring together material qualities, textures, lights and geometry to define the desired look.

## The Hypershade panel

The Hypershade panel is made up of three sections - the Create bar, the Hypershade tabs and the Work Area. The Create bar allows you to create any rendering nodes required for your scene. The Hypershade tabs list all nodes that make up the current scene while the Work Area allows you to look more closely and alter any part of the shading network that is used to create a shading network.

> **Tip:** *Note that you can use all the same mouse and key combinations that you use in the viewports for maneuvering in the Hypershade work area.*

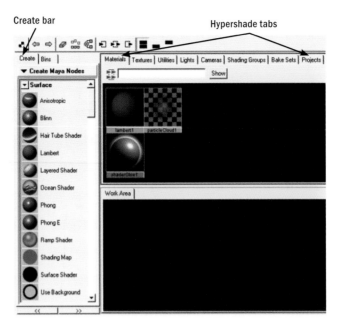

*Close-up of Hypershade*

# Creating shading networks

A shading network consists of a series of nodes that input into a *shading group*. In the following examples, you will create several nodes that define the material qualities of the room, boxes and planets.

## 1    Create a material for the pedestal

To build a material for the pedestal, you will use the Hypershade and Attribute Editor.

- Click with your **RMB** in the Work Area and select **Graph** → **Clear Graph**.

*This clears the workspace so that you can begin working on a new shading network.*

- At the top of the Create bar section, click on the tab **Create**.

- Click on the **down arrow** just below the **Create** tab, then select **Create Maya Nodes** from the pop-up.

*This offers you a series of icons that represent new Maya nodes, such as Surface materials.*

- Click on **Blinn**.

*This adds a new Blinn material under the materials Hypershade tab and in the Work Area. You will also see the Attribute Editor update to show the new node's information.*

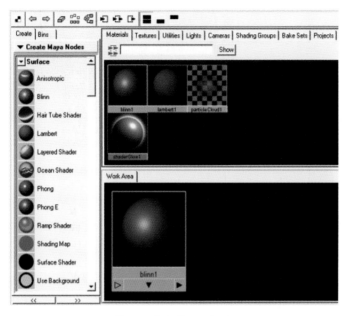

*New node in Hypershade*

*Blinn is a particular type of shading model that defines how the material will look. The Blinn model gives you control over the look of the materials' highlights using special attributes.*

## 2 Rename the material node

- In the Attribute Editor, change the name of the material node to *pedestalM*.

*The M designation is to remind you that this node is a material node.*

## 3 Edit the material's color

To define how the material will render, you will need to set several key material attributes, such as color.

- In the Attribute Editor, click on the color swatch next to the **Color** attribute.

Click here

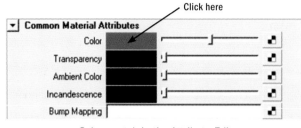

*Color swatch in the Attribute Editor*

*This opens the Color Chooser. This window lets you set color by clicking in a color wheel and editing HSV (hue, saturation, value) or RGB (red, green, blue) values.*

- Choose any color you want and click the **Accept** button.

### 4   Assign the material

- With your **MMB**, **click+drag** on the *pedestalM* node, drag it from the Hypershade panel into the Perspective view and drop it on the *pedestal*.

*This assigns the material to the object.*

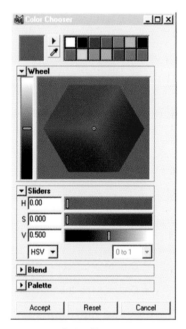

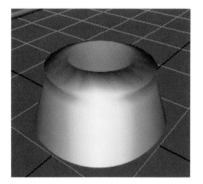

*Assigned shader*

*Color Chooser*

**Tip:**   *It is a good idea to be in Hardware Texture mode to make sure that the assignment is correct. The hotkey is **5** on your keyboard.*

## 5    More materials

- From the Create bar section, create a **Phong** material with a black color.

*Phong materials have an intense specular that looks more like plastic.*

- In the Attribute Editor, change the name of the material node to *wireM*.

- Select the *wire*, then **RMB** on your material *wireM* and select **Assign Material To Selection**.

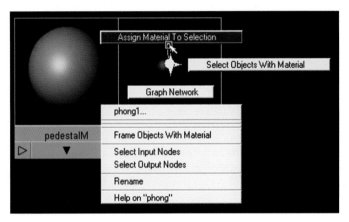

*Assign to selection*

**Tip:**    *This method of assigning materials works better than the click+drag method when you want to assign a material to multiple objects.*

- Create a **Lambert** material with a *bright yellow* color and rename it *sunM*.

- Change the **Incandescence** color to *dark yellow*.

*Lambert does not have any specular component and is matte compared to the other material you just created. Adding incandescence tends to flatten the material out as well as give the illusion that it is illuminating light.*

- Assign this new material to the sun.

*Since the sun node has children, Maya automatically assigns the sunM material to all the children.*

# Creating a procedural texture map

To give one of the boxes a pattern, a grid procedural texture will be added to the *box* material's color. A procedural texture means the look of the texture is driven by attributes and drawn by mathematical functions. You will also experiment with the drag + drop capabilities of the Hypershade.

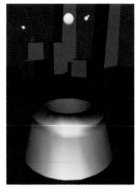

*The latest materials*

## 1 Create a material for the boxes

To build a textured material for the box, you will use the Hypershade panel to build up the material using a grid texture.

- In the Hypershade, clear the Work Area by holding down the right mouse button and selecting **Graph → Clear Graph** or press the **Clear Graph** button at the top of the Hypershade.

- Create a **Lambert** material and name it *boxM*.

*The Clear Graph button*

## 2 Create a grid texture

- In the **Create bar** section, scroll down to the **2D Textures** section.

*This section allows you to create new textures.*

- **MMB**-drag a **Grid** from the menu anywhere into the work area.

- In the Work Area of the Hypershade, click with your **MMB** on the **Grid** icon and drag it onto the *boxM* material node.

*When you release the mouse button, a pop-up menu appears offering you a number of attributes that can be mapped by the grid texture.*

*MMB drag from the grid onto the material*

- Select **color** from the menu to map the grid to the material node's Color attribute.

- Click on the **Rearrange Graph** button at the top of the Hypergraph panel.

*The Rearrange Graph button*

*Rearranging the Work Area will organize the view so connections appear from left to right. This is very useful for following the flow of connections.*

## 3   Assigning the material

You will assign the texture map to one of the boxes and then use hardware shading to preview it.

- With your **MMB**, click on the *boxM* material node and drag it on to one of the box surfaces in the Perspective view.

- Over the Perspective window, click with your **MMB** to make it the active window.

- Evoke the hotbox and select **Shading** → **Hardware Texturing**.

*Hardware texturing*

**Tip:**   *You can also turn on hardware texturing by making the desired panel active and pressing the **6** key.*

## 4 Edit the grid attributes

- In the Hypershade, click on the *grid* node.

- In the Attribute Editor, click on the color swatch next to the **Line Color** attribute.

- Choose any color you want and click the **Accept** button.

- Click on the color swatch next to the **Filler Color** attribute.

- Choose any color you want and click the **Accept** button.

- Change the grid's width attributes as shown below:

     **U Width** to **0.3**;

     **V Width** to **0.9**.

*The Attribute Editor allows you to easily update the look of a procedural texture.*

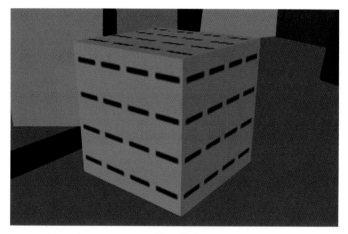

*New grid*

## 5 Display the whole shading group

- With the *grid* texture selected in the Hypershade, click on **Input and Output Connections**.

*This displays some other nodes that help define this shading group.*

*Input and Output Connections button*

- Press the **Alt** key and click+drag with your left and middle mouse button to zoom out.

- Press the **a** hotkey to frame everything in the view.

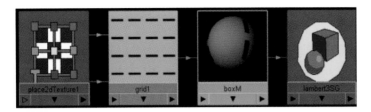

*Complete shading network*

## 6 Edit the texture's positioning

The placement of a texture on a surface is defined by the *place2DTexture* node.

- Select the *place2dTexture* node by clicking on it.

- In the Attribute Editor, change the following attributes:

> Repeat **U** to **2**;
>
> Repeat **V** to **3**.

*Updated texture placement*

# Creating a texture map

You will create a material for one of the boxes that uses a file texture instead of a procedural texture. Many digital artists like to create textures in a 2D paint package. For the box, you will use a crate texture.

## 1 Create a material for the box

- From the Hypershade panel's work area **RMB** click and select **Graph → Clear Graph**.

- Scroll to the **Surface** section in the **Create bar** and select **Phong**.

- **Rename** this node *crateM*.

*Crate texture*

**Lesson 03**

## 2 Create a file texture node

To load an external texture, you need to start with a file texture node.

- In the Attribute Editor, click on the **Map** button next to **Color**. The map button is shown with a small checker icon.

*Map button*

*This opens the Create Render Node window.*

- Click on the **Textures** tab.

- In the **2D Textures** section, click on **File**.

*A file node is added to the Phong material. The appropriate connections have already been made.*

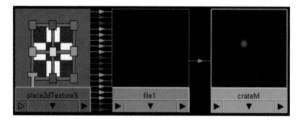

*New file texture node*

## 3 Import the file texture

- In the Attribute Editor for the file node, click on the **File folder** icon next to **Image name**.

- Select the file named *crate.tif* from your project *textures* directory, then click on the **Open** button.

*The file texture is now loaded into the shading network.*

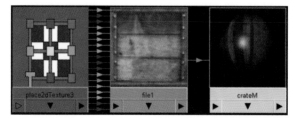

*Imported file texture*

**Note:** *This file will be available only if your project is set to current, as indicated at the beginning of Lesson 1.*

## 4   Apply textured materials to the boxes

- Select some of the boxes in the Perspective view.

- In the Hypershade, click on the *crateM* node with your right mouse button and choose **Assign Material to Selection** from the pop-up menu.

*The texture is assigned to the boxes.*

*Boxes with texture*

## 5   Complete the scene

Before continuing with the next lesson, it is a good idea to assign materials to the remaining objects in your scene.

- Experiment with the fractal, ramp and cloth procedural textures.

- Planet textures can be found in the project's *textures* directory.

**Note:** *Remember to pay attention to which planets are selected when assigning textures. If you select from the parent, then all the children are selected as well.*

Lesson 03

# Test render the scene

Now that you have materials and textures assigned, it is a good time to
do a test render. The following is an example of the completed room:

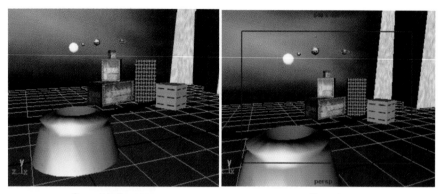

Completed room          New view

Render view panel          Close-up of rendering

## 1   Display Resolution Gate

Your current view panel may not be displaying the actual proportions that will
be rendered. You can display the camera's Resolution Gate to see how the
scene will actually render.

- Make the Perspective view the active panel.

- Use the hotbox to select **View** → **Camera Settings** → **Resolution Gate**.

*The view is adjusted to show a bounding box that defines how the default
render resolution of 640x480 pixels relates to the current view.*

- Dolly into the view so that it is well composed within the Resolution Gate.
  Try to set up a view where the planets are in the view's foreground, looking
  toward the boxes in the other corner of the room.

*Keep in mind that only objects within the green surrounding line will
be rendered.*

## 2  Your first render

- In the Render view panel, click with your **RMB** and select
  **Render** → **Render** → **persp** from the pop-up menu.

*You can now see a rendered image of your scene. However, because you
have not created any lights the image renders using a default light.*

## 3  Zoom into the rendering

You can view the rendering using the **Alt** key and the dolly and track hotkeys.

- Use the **Alt** key and the left and middle mouse buttons to zoom
  into the view.

*Now you can evaluate in more detail how your rendering looks at
the pixel level.*

- In the Render View panel, click with your **RMB** and choose
  **View** → **Real Size**.

## 4  Save your work

- Through the hotbox, select **Save Scene As...** from the **File** menu.

- Enter the name *03-textures.ma*, then press the **Save** button.

## Conclusion

You have now been introduced to some of the basic concepts in texturing and
rendering a 3D scene. The Maya shading networks offer a lot of depth for
creating the look of your objects. You have learned how to create materials,
procedural textures and file textures, and rendered a single frame to preview the
look of your shaders with default lighting. In the next lesson, you will add light
and shader effects which will only be visible at render time.

# Lesson 04  Lights and effects

*In the real world, it is light that allows us to see the surfaces and objects around us. In computer graphics, digital lights play the same role. They help define the space within a scene, and in many cases help to set the mood or atmosphere. As well, several other effects can be added to the final image in order to have it look more realistic. This lesson explores and explains some of the basic Maya effects.*

## In this lesson you will learn the following:

- How to add lighting to your scene;

- How to enable shadows;

- How to add light fog and lens flare;

- How to add shader glow;

- How to set up motion blur;

- How to software render an animation;

- How to use fcheck.

# Placing a point light

To create the primary light source in the scene, you will use a point light. This light type works exactly like a light bulb, with attributes such as color and intensity. Continue using the file saved in the previous lesson, or open *03-textures.ma* from the *scenes* directory.

## 1 Create a point light

- Put your mouse in the Perspective view panel and press the spacebar quickly to pop to a full view.

- From the hotbox, select **Create** → **Lights** → **Point Light**.

*This places a point light at the origin.*

- With the light still selected, use the hotkey **W** to translate the point light above the floor.

## 2 Turn on hardware lighting

One step beyond hardware texturing is *hardware lighting*. This lets you see how the light is affecting the surface that it is shining on.

- From the hotbox, select **Lighting** → **Use All Lights**. You could also use the **7** key.

*You may not see much lighting on the room surface. To see better lighting in the room, you need to increase the room's subdivisions.*

- In the Perspective window, click and hold with the **RMB** on the *room* object.

- From the marking menu, select **Inputs** → **PolyCube** → ❑.

*This node now displays in the Attribute Editor.*

- Set the following attributes:

  **Subdivisions Width** to **20**;

  **Subdivisions Height** to **20**;

  **Subdivisions Depth** to **20**.

*The point light's illumination area can now be seen on the surface of the floor.*

**Note:** *If your graphics card is unqualified, you may not be able to turn on hardware lighting. To ensure your hardware meets Alias requirements, visit www.alias.com/qual_charts.*

Project One

*Increased Subdivisions for the room*

**Note:** *You only need to increase the Subdivisions for a hardware texturing preview of the scene. If you are software rendering, then one Subdivision in each direction should work fine.*

## 3 Change the light attributes

- Select the point light from either the viewport or from the **Lights** tab in the Hypershade.

- In the Attribute Editor, expand the **Shadows** section.

- Enable shadow casting by checking the **Use Depth Map Shadows** attribute.

- Test render the shadows casted by the objects.

- Since we want a moody room, change the light's **Intensity** to **0.3**.

*Shadows section in the Attribute Editor*

*Shadow render*

## Placing a spot light

As a second light source in the scene, you will use a spot light. This light type lets you define the same attributes as the point light, as well as others including the light's cone angle.

### 1 Create a spot light

- From the hotbox, select **Create → Lights → Spot Light**.

*This places a spot light at the origin.*

### 2 Edit the spot light's position

The Show Manipulator Tool provides a manipulator for the light's *look at point* and *eye point*. You can edit these using the same method as you would with a typical transform manipulator.

- Press the **t** key to access the **Show Manipulator Tool**.

- **Click+drag** on the manipulator handles to reposition the light.

- **Move** the manipulators until they appear as shown below:

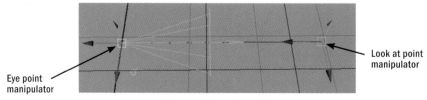

*Show Manipulator Tool*

Eye point manipulator

Look at point manipulator

## 3   Edit the spot light's cone angle

You can now edit some of the light's attributes to control its effect. You will reveal other light manipulators to let you edit this attribute interactively.

- With the spot light still selected, press **t** to select the **Show Manipulator Tool**.

Next to the light is a small icon that displays a circle with a small line pointing up and to the right. This icon is the cycling index and is used to cycle between different types of light manipulators.

- Click two times on the manipulator's cycle index.

*The cycling index rotates to show that you are accessing new manipulators. The chosen manipulator consists of a little blue dot just outside of the light cone. The new manipulator lets you edit the cone angle of the spot light.*

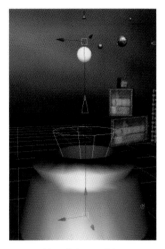

*New light position*

- **Click+drag** on the cone angle manipulator to fit the pedestal center hole. It's the yellow square along the rim of the spot light.

*In the Attribute Editor, you can watch the **Cone Angle** attribute update as you drag the manipulator.*

## 4   Adjust the Penumbra Angle

For softness at the edge of the spot light, you can adjust the light's penumbra.

- In the Attribute Editor, set the **Penumbra Angle** to **30**.

- Click one more time on the manipulator's cycle index.

*You can now see a second circular line inside the cone angle icon that indicates the area where the light will be soft.*

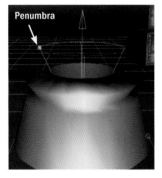

*Penumbra manipulator*

## 5   Adding light fog

To actually see the light beam when you render, you need to add light fog. Light fog mimics light bouncing off microscopic particles in the air, thus displaying the light beam.

- In the Attribute Editor, set the light's **Color** to a pale blue.

- Set the light's **Decay Rate** to **Quadratic**.

*The decay rate controls how fast the light fades as it is traveling through space. A quadratic decay rate simply tells Maya to fade off the light faster so that it doesn't light up the ceiling.*

*Penumbra manipulator*

- Open the **Light Effects** section of the light's attributes in the Attribute Editor.

- Set the **Fog Intensity** attribute to **5**.

- Click on the **Map** button on the right of the **Light Fog** attribute.

*Doing so will automatically create a lightFog node and it will also display a fog cone in the viewports. The lightFog node is automatically selected and displayed in the Attribute Editor.*

- Set the *lightFog*'s color to blue.

- Quickly press the **spacebar** to come back to the *Hypershade/ Render/Persp* layout.

- Test render your scene by pressing on the **Render** button.

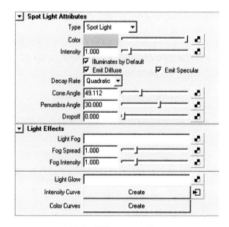

*Light Effects section*

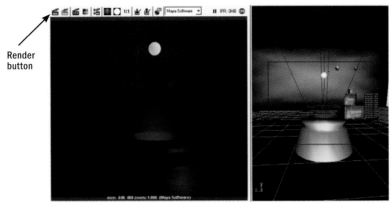

| Light fog render | Lighting view in Maya |

# Refining the solar system

Your solar system looks a little dull in the latest render. You will remedy this by adding glow and lens flare so that your scene looks more realistic.

## 1 Adding shader glow

Most Maya surface shaders have the ability to give the illusion that the object they are assigned to is glowing. This works especially well if an object has some kind of incandescence added to it. Here you will enable glow on the *sun* material.

- Select the *sun* object.

- At the top of the Hypershade, click on the **Graph Materials on Selected Objects** button.

*Graph Materials on Selected Objects button*

*This should display the sunM material in the workspace area of the Hypershade.*

- Select the *sunM* material.

- In the Attribute Editor, open the **Special Effects** section.

- Set **Glow Intensity** to **0.5**.

- Test render your scene.

*Special Effects section*

*The glowing sun render*

*The Maya glow is rendered in a second pass. This means you will not see the glow until the render is completely finished.*

## 2 Creating another point light

The Maya glow does not actually cast lights into your scene, so the planets are not lit by sunlight. Add one more point light exactly at the sun's position.

- Create a point light.

- With the light selected, **Shift-select** the *sun*.

- Press **p** to parent the light to the *sun*.

- Press **Ctrl+a** to close the Attribute Editor.

- In the Channel Box, reset the light's transformation to its default values.

*The point light should move exactly in the center of its parent.*

- From the Light's Attribute Editor, set the point light's attributes as follows:

    **Color** to a light yellow;

    **Decay Rate** to **Quadratic**.

*Sunlight on planets*

## 3   Adding light glow

Since the rendered camera is looking directly at bright sunlight, adding lens flare would add realism to your renders.

- With the Attribute Editor still open, click on the **Map** button next to the **Light Glow** attribute in the **Light Effects** section.

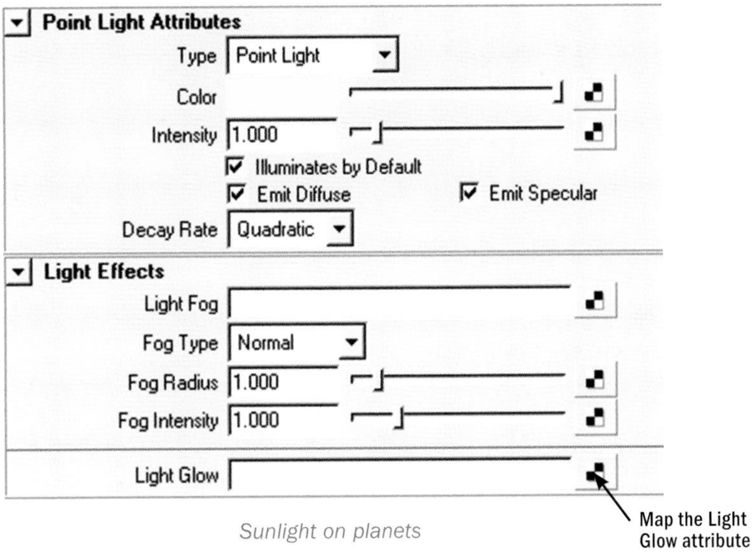

Sunlight on planets

Map the Light Glow attribute

Maya will automatically create, select and display an opticalFX node in the Attribute Editor.

- Set the *opticalFX1* attributes as follows:

  **Lens flare** to **Enabled**;

  **Glow Type** to **None**;

  **Halo Type** to **None**.

Since the sun material already has glow enabled, it would not be relevant to also have a light glow.

- Test render your scene to see the lens flare.

> **Tip:** If you find it difficult to see, darken some of your lights and/or increase
> the **Lens Flare Intensity** *found on the lights Optical F/X node.*

*Sun lens flare*

## Render an animation

Now that you have defined the lighting in your scene and you are happy with your
test rendering, it is time to render an animation. This is accomplished using the
*batch renderer* in Maya. In preparation, you will add motion blur to your scene to
simulate the blur generated in live action film and video work.

### 1   Render Settings

Render Settings are a group of attributes that you can set to define how
your scene will render. To set up the quality of the rendering, you need to
set the Render Settings.

- Quickly tap the spacebar if you are not in the Persp/Hypershade/Render
  View layout.

- In the Render View panel, click with your **RMB** and choose
  **Options → Render Settings.**

- Select the **Maya Software** tab.

- Open the **Anti-aliasing Quality** section if it is not already opened.

- Set the **Quality** presets to **Intermediate Quality**.

*Anti-aliasing is a visual smoothing of edge lines in the final rendered image.
Because bitmaps are made up of square pixels, a diagonal line would appear
jagged unless it was somehow anti-aliased.*

## 2   Set the image output

To render an animation, you must set up the scene's file extensions to indicate a rendered sequence. You must also set up the Start and End Frames.

- Select the **Common** tab in the **Render Settings** window.

- From the **Image File Output** section, set the following:

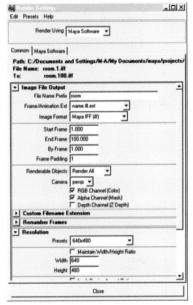

*Render Settings*

> **File Name Prefix** to *room*.

*This sets the name of the animated sequence.*

**Frame/Animation Ext** *to:*

> **name.#.ext** (for Windows, Mac);

*This sets up Maya to render a numbered sequence of images.*

> **Start Frame** to **1**;

> **End Frame** to **100**;

> **By Frame** to **1**.

*This tells Maya to render every frame from 1 to 100.*

## 3   Turn on motion blur

- Select the **Maya Software** tab.

- Under the **Motion Blur** section, click on the **Motion Blur** button to turn it on.

- Set the **Motion Blur Type** to be **2D**.

*This type of motion blur renders the fastest.*

*Motion Blur check box*

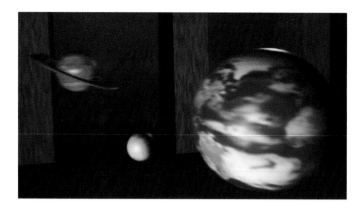

*Motion Blur render*

## 4 Save your work

- From the **File** menu, select **Save Scene As...**

- Enter the name *04-lighting.ma*.

- Press the **Save** button or press the **Enter** key.

## 5 Batch render the scene

- Press **F5** to change to the **Rendering** menu set.

- Use the hotbox to select **Render** → **Batch Render**.

- If for any reason you want to cancel the current batch render, select **Render** → **Cancel Batch Render** from the hotbox.

## 6 Watch the render progress

The sequence will be rendered as a series of frames.

- Use the hotbox to select **Window** → **General Editors** → **Script Editor**.

In this window you can watch a series of status entries about the current rendering process.

## 7 View the resulting animation

After the rendering is complete, you can preview the results using the *fcheck* utility.

**On Windows, Mac**

- Open the fcheck utility by clicking on its icon. In Windows, click on **Start** and select **Programs**. From there go to **Alias** → **Maya 7.0** → **FCheck**.

- Select **File** → **Open Animation**.

- Navigate to the *project1\images* folder.

- Select the file *room.1.iff* and click **Open**.

*This is the first frame of your rendered animation.*

*Animation previewed with fcheck utility*

**Tip:** *To learn more about the capabilities of fcheck for previewing your animations, enter* `fcheck -h` *in a shell window or select the Help menu.*

## Conclusion

You are now familiar with the basic concepts of lighting and rendering a scene. You began by enabling various light options such as color, shadows, light fog and light glow. Then you added material glow and 2D motion blur, just before launching your first animation batch render. Once your render was complete, you viewed it in the fcheck utility.

In the next lesson, you will add basic particle systems to your scene.

# Lesson 05    Particles

*Particles are small object types that can be animated using dynamic forces instead of traditional keyframes. These effects are, in essence, simulations of physical effects such as water, smoke and fire.*

*To experiment with particle effects, you will add fire to your scene. The flames will be generated using the default particle fire effect found in Maya. You will then create sparks that will collide against the boxes and floor.*

**In this lesson you will learn the following:**

- How to add a fire effect to an object;

- How to set the particle's initial state;

- How to add an emitter;

- How to define a particle attribute using a ramp;

- How to collide particles against geometry;

- How to add gravity fields;

- How to software render a particle animation;

- How to hardware render a particle animation.

# Project set up

If you are continuing from the last lesson, you can begin working right away.
If not, open the Maya file you saved in that lesson or *04-lighting.ma* in the *scenes* directory. You will continue to  explore the use of hotkeys and the hotbox.

### 1    Set up your Perspective panel

To simplify the workspace, you will focus on a single Perspective view. You will also turn off the Resolution Gate to focus on the particles.

- Use the spacebar to make the Perspective view panel full screen.

- Select **View** → **Camera Settings** → **No Gate** to turn off the Resolution Gate.

### 2    Change menu sets

- Press **h** and click with the **LMB**. Choose **Dynamics** from the marking menu.

**Note:** *You can also use the* **F4** *hotkey to change to the Dynamics menu set.*

# Start a fire

Using one of the preset particle effects, you will add fire to your scene.
This preset creates everything needed to make the particles act and look like fire.

### 1    Adding the fire effect

- Select the highest *box* from the box stack.

- Select **Effects** → **Create Fire**.

### 2    Playback the simulation

- Select **Display** → **UI Elements** → **Range Slider and Time Slider**.

- Click the **Animation preferences** button found at the right side of the Range Slider.

**Alias**  *Because the Maya dynamics solvers are relatively easy, even users*
**Tip:**  *with little or no knowledge of physics and dynamics can produce some*
  *interesting and realistic simulations in a very short amount of time.*

*Julio Lopez | Sr. Multimedia Specialist*

- In the **Timeline** section,
  set the following:

  **Playback Speed** to **Play
  every frame**.

*When working with particles it is very
important that the playback speed is
set to play every frame. Otherwise, your
simulations may act unpredictably.*

- Click the **Save** button.

- Rewind to frame **1** and playback
  the simulation.

*The particles are generated from the box
but their attributes are not adequate.*

*Default fire particles*

*The fire effect is the result of a particle object that is controlled by several
dynamic fields, such as gravity and turbulence. The fire preset added these
elements to your scene and lets you easily control them.*

**Note:** *When working with dynamics, it's important that you always use the rewind
button to move to the beginning of your simulation. Never scrub through a
scene that has dynamics in it unless you cache the particles to disk.*

## 3   Editing the fire attributes

To control various parts of the fire effect, you can simply edit attributes that
are designed specifically for this effect.

- Playback the simulation to a point where particles are visible, then stop.

- Select the fire particles.

- In the Attribute Editor, make sure that the *particle1* tab is selected.

- Rename the particles *flame*.

*When renaming the transform node, the shape node automatically
gets renamed.*

- Change tab to the *flameShape*.

- Scroll down to the bottom and open the **Extra Attributes** section.

- Set the following attributes:

   **Fire Scale** to **0.4**;

   **Fire Turbulence** to **10**;

   **Fire Density** to **1000**;

   **Fire Intensity** to **1**;

   **Fire Lifespan** to **0.5**.

- Go back to frame **1** and playback the simulation.

*Now there are more fire particles and their scale is more appropriate.*

*Updated fire particles*

## 4 Setting the initial state

One thing you may notice with the simulation is that there are no particles when the animation starts. If you want the fire to be visible right from the beginning, you must set the particle's initial state.

- Playback the scene until around frame **30**, then stop playback.

- Select the particles.

- From the **Solvers** menu, select **Initial State** → **Set for Selected**.

- Go back to frame **1** and playback the simulation.

*By setting the initial state for the particles, you can see that at frame 1, the particles are already created.*

**Note:** *The flame's shadows don't look very convincing because the depth map shadows don't work well with the fire's volumetric shader. Also, there might be a strange halo around the fire that is caused by the 2D motion blur. You will fix these problems later in the lesson.*

*Software rendering*

## 5   Test render the particles

- Press **F5** to go to the **Rendering** menu set.

- From the **Render** menu, select **Render Current Frame...**

*The scene is now rendered with the fire particles included. Some particles can be rendered using the software renderer, which allows them to be automatically integrated into the scene.*

**Tip:**   *For a faster rendering, lower the anti-aliasing setting to Preview and turn off the 2D motion blur option in the Render Settings. Do this from the Render View window, by selecting the clipboard icon beside the IPR button to open the Render Settings window.*

# Sparks

As an added effect, you will set up more particles that will represent emitted sparks from the blaze. To create particles that look like sparks, you need to adjust various particle attributes. In this case, you will create streak particles that will die fairly quickly after being emitted. Their color will start out yellow, and then turn to red and finally black. You will also set up those sparks to collide with the surrounding geometry.

## 1   Add an emitter

In order to have new particles in your scene, you must first create a particle emitter.

- Select the fire particles and press **Ctrl+h** to hide them.

- Press **F4** to go back to the **Dynamics** menu set, then from the **Particles** menu, select **Create Emitter**.

*An emitter will appear at the origin.*

- Select the new emitter, then **Shift-select** the *box*.

- Press **p** to parent the emitter to the *box*.

- Select **Modify** → **Reset Transformations**.

*This resets the emitter's transformations so that it gets centered at its parent's position.*

- Playback your scene to see the new default particles being emitted.

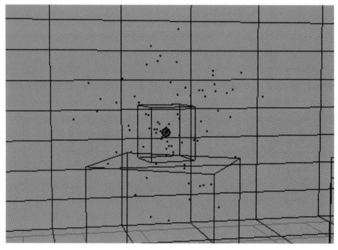

*Default particles*

## 2   Change render type to streak

Particles can have their render type set from a list of possible looks. You can switch between the different types until you get one that suits your needs.

- Select the new particles.

- Rename them *sparks*.

- In the Attribute Editor, go to the **Render Attributes** section of the *sparksShape* node and set **Particle Render Type** to **Streak**.

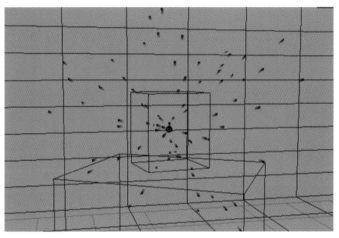

*Render Attributes*

This render type is designed to work with hardware rendering. This means that later, you will have to composite the final hardware rendered particles with software rendered scenes.

*Streak particles*

### 3   Add and edit render attributes

- Click on the **Current Render Type** button.

- Set the **Render Attributes** as follows:

  **Line Width** to **4**;

  **Tail Fade** to **0**;

  **Tail Size** to **2**.

This gives the sparks a much stronger presence. The higher tail size value lengthens the sparks.

**Lesson 05**

*Streak particles*

## 4 Add color per particle

The particle node has the ability to have new attributes added to it as needed. This lets you add complexity to a particle node when necessary.

You can use this technique to add color to the particles individually (per particle or PP), instead of as an entire group.

- In the **Add Dynamic Attributes** section of the Attribute Editor, click on the **Color** button.

- From the Particle Color window, select **Add Per Particle Attribute**, then click the **Add Attribute** button.

*This adds an rgbPP line to the **Per Particle Attributes** section.*

- Click on the **rgbPP** field with your **RMB** and select **Create Ramp**.

- Click again on the **rgbPP** field with your **RMB** and select **<-arrayMapper. outColorPP** → **Edit Ramp.**

*In the Ramp window, you will find three markers, each with a square and a circular icon.*

- Click on the circle icon at the bottom of the ramp, then click on the color swatch next to **Selected Color**.

- Change the color to yellow.

- Complete the same steps to change the middle marker to red and the top marker to black.

- **Click+drag** the circle to change its position in the ramp as follows:

*Particle color ramp*

- Press **6** to go into hardware texturing mode.

- Playback the simulation.

*Now the particles start out yellow, then red, then go black over time.*

## 5   Particle lifespan and randomness

The **Lifespan** attribute lets you determine how long the particle will remain in the scene before it disappears or dies. You will add a slight randomness to the lifespan of the particles.

- With *sparks* selected, go to the **Lifespan Attributes** section in the Attribute Editor.

- Change **Lifespan Mode** to **Random range**.

- Change the **Lifespan** to **1**.

- Change the **Lifespan Random** to **0.5**.

*The lifespan is uniformly distributed with **Lifespan** as the mean and **Lifespan Random** as the width of the distribution.*

*The particles in this case have a lifespan between 0.5 and 1.5. This gives the sparks a more random look.*

## 6   Change the settings of the emitter

Some attributes on the emitter should be changed to get a better sparks simulation. The rate at which the emitter creates particles should be decreased and the emitting speed should be increased.

- From the Outliner, select *emitter2*. This should be the child of the *box*.
- Go to the **Basic Emitter Attributes** section in the Attribute Editor.
- Set the **Rate (Particles/Sec)** attribute to **10**.
- Go to the **Basic Emission Speed Attributes** section lower in the Attribute Editor.
- Set the **Speed** attribute to **2**.
- Set the **Speed Random** attribute to **0.5**.

## Fine-tuning the sparks

The current particles don't quite move like real sparks. They should react to gravity and collide with the surrounding surfaces.

## 1   Add gravity to the particles

- Select *sparks*.
- From the **Fields** menu, select **Gravity**.

*A gravity field appears at the origin.*

- In the Attribute Editor, make sure the **Magnitude** is set to **9.8**.

*A magnitude of 9.8 mimics the earth's gravity.*

- Playback the simulation.

*Now the particles drop straight to the ground without collisions. The gravity field is pulling them down.*

## 2   Set up particle collisions

To make the particles collide against the boxes and the floor, you must define them as colliding objects.

- Select the *sparks* particles.
- Press the **Shift** key and select the *room*.

**Note:** *The room should be selected last.*

- From the **Particles** menu, select **Make Collide**.

- Repeat these steps for all the surrounding objects in the range of your particles.

*Do not set collisions on the box emitting the sparks; the sparks would collide and stay inside the box.*

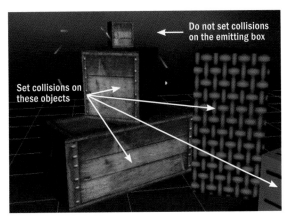

*Particle collision*

## 3 Adding friction

As you playback the scene, the sparks seem to bounce too much off the colliding objects. To fix this, you must change the resilience and friction attributes for each surface.

- Select the sparks particles on their own.

- At the top of the Attribute Editor, click on the first *geoConnector* tab.

- Set the following attributes:

> **Resilience** to **0.1**;
>
> **Friction** to **0.6**.

- Repeat for all the remaining *geoConnector* tabs.

*The geoConnector objects have been created for the collision objects specified.*

- Playback the simulation.

*Now the sparks react more realistically when colliding with the objects. Resilience is used to calculate the bounciness of a surface and friction is used to slow down the particles when they touch a surface.*

Lesson 05

## 4 Create a particle event

Use the **Collision Event Tool** to emit a new smoke particle upon collision.

- Select the *sparks*.

- From the **Particles** menu, select **Particle Collision Events...**

- In the **Particle Collision Events** window, go to the **Event Type** section and set the following:

> **Type** to **Emit**;
>
> **Num particles** to **1**;
>
> **Spread** to **1**;
>
> **Inherit Velocity** to **1**.

- Click **Create Event** and close the **Particle Collision Events** window.

- Playback the simulation.

*Several small particles are emitted after the sparks collide. These particles float around based on the momentum they gained from the collision. Now you will adjust how they react and look.*

- Stop at a frame where the new particles are visible.

## 5 Set the new particles as smoke

- Select the new particles.

- Rename them *smoke*.

- In the Attribute Editor, set the **Particle Render Type** to **Cloud**.

*The (s/w) beside the Cloud particle type means it is a software particle type.*

*Particle collision event*

- Click on the **Current Render Type** button.

- Set the **Radius** attribute to **0.05**.

- In the **Lifespan Attributes** section, set the **Lifespan** to **0.5**.

- In the **Add Dynamic Attributes** section, click on the **Opacity** button and select **Add Per Particle Attribute**.

- In the **Per Particle Attributes** section, **RMB** on the **OpacityPP** field and select **Create Ramp**.

*The default opacity ramp should turn from white (opaque) to black (transparent).*

## 6   Smoke goes up

- Select the smoke particles.

- Click on **Fields** → **Gravity**.

- Change the **Magnitude** of the new gravity field to **-1**.

*Reversing the gravity's magnitude will push the particles up instead of pulling them down.*

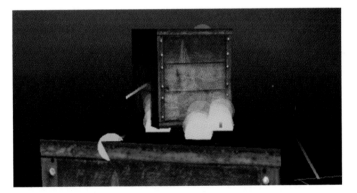

*Smoke particles*

## 7   Save your work

- From the **File** menu, select **Save Scene As...**

- Enter the name *05-particles.ma*.

- Press the **Save** button or the **Enter** key.

# Rendering particles

It was mentioned earlier that the sparks used a particle type that could only be rendered using hardware rendering, while the fire and smoke used software rendering. The question, therefore, is how do you bring hardware rendered particles together with a software rendered scene?

The answer is to render them separately, and then bring them together using a compositing package.

To composite the spark particles with the rest of the scene, you will need to render the top layer (in this case the sparks) with a matte, or *mask*.

The mask is a grayscale channel that defines which areas of the color image are going to be transparent when brought into a compositing package. In this scene, the background contains all the scene's geometry.

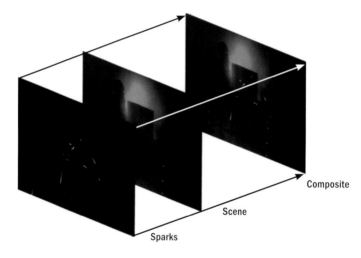

Composite

Scene

Sparks

*Diagram of compositing layers*

# Software rendering

The flames created using the Fire effect and the smoke can be rendered using software rendering. This means creating another batch rendering of your scene. This will represent the first render pass that can be later composited together with the sparks.

## 1  Change your motion blur type

Since the 2D motion blur used in the last lesson doesn't render well with the flame particles, you will switch to the 3D motion blur type.

- Select **Window** → **Rendering Editors** → **Render Settings**...

- Open the **Motion Blur** section and change the **Motion Blur Type** to **3D**.

*This type of motion blur renders more slowly but is more accurate and works better with software rendered particles.*

## 2    Fix the flame and smoke shadows

Earlier it was noted that the shadows generated from the particles didn't look correct. The depth map shadows cannot recognize the subtleties of the volumetric shader used by the particles. Raytrace shadows are needed.

- Select the point light that is illuminating and casting shadows in the scene.

- In the Attribute Editor, open the **Shadows** section, scroll down to **Raytrace Shadow Attributes** and set **Use Ray Trace Shadows** to **On**.

- Set the **Ray Depth Limit** to **2**.

*This sets up the light, but to use raytraced shadows, you will need to turn on raytracing itself.*

- Open the **Render Settings**.

- Open the **Raytracing Quality** section and turn **Raytracing** to **On**.

**Note:** *Maya uses a selective raytracer and only objects that require reflections, refractions or raytraced shadows will use this technique.*

## 3    Limiting the reflections

When raytracing is turned on, any shader that has a reflectivity value will render with reflections. If the object is not required to be reflective, then it's a good idea to turn Reflectivity off.

- Go into the Material node and set it's **Reflectivity** to **0**.

Or

- Select the geometry that you don't want involved in raytracing.

- Under its **Render Stats** section, turn **Visible in Reflections** to **Off**.

*When you do this, the object will not reflect and won't be calculated in the raytrace.*

- Repeat for each object in the scene with a shader that has the **Reflectivity** attribute.

**Note:** *Lambert shaders do not have a reflectivity attribute.*

## 4    Batch render the scene

- Select **File** → **Save Scene As...**

- Enter the file name *background* and click **Save**.

- Press **F5** to change to the **Rendering** menu set.

- Use the hotbox to select **Render** → **Batch Render**.

*This will create a render pass that includes the geometry and software particles. You will now render the sparks using hardware rendering.*

**Tip:**    *From now until the end of this lesson, do not move the rendered camera, or the software and hardware renders won't match.*

## Hardware rendering

You have been using hardware rendering in the Perspective view panel to help preview the scene. You can also use hardware rendering to render the spark particles so that they match the rendered scene.

## 1    Hide the software particles

Since you only want the sparks to appear in the hardware rendering, you will need to hide the flames and smoke particles.

- Select the *flame* particles and **Shift-select** the *smoke* particles.

- Press **Ctrl+h** to hide them.

*Now the particles will not be visible in the hardware rendering.*

## 2   Set the hardware render attributes

- Select **Window** → **Rendering Editors** → **Render Settings.**

- Open the **Render Settings** window and change **Render Using** to **Maya Hardware.**

- In the Attribute Editor, set the following attributes:

  **Filename Prefix** to **sparks**;

  **Extension** to **name.#.ext** (Windows, Mac);

  *To match the extension setting you chose for your software rendering set:*

  **Start Frame** to **1**;

  **End Frame** to **100**;

  **Resolution** to **640x480.**

- Go to the **Maya Hardware** tab and set:

  **Enable Geometry Mask** to **On.**

  *This will use the geometry as mask objects to hide particles falling behind them. An alpha channel, also known as a matte channel, is important for layering images in a compositing package.*

  Set **Motion Blur** to **On** and leave **Number of Exposures** to **3**.

---

**Note:** *These attributes only affect hardware rendering.*

---

## 3   Test a frame

- Playback the simulation until you hit a frame where some of the sparks appear.

- Click on the **Test** button in the middle of the Render Buffer's time controls.

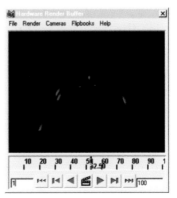

*Hardware render buffer*

## 4  Render a sequence

You can now render an entire animation using this window. Compared to software rendering, it lets you use the speed of hardware rendering to generate animations quickly.

- Select **Render** → **Render Sequence**.

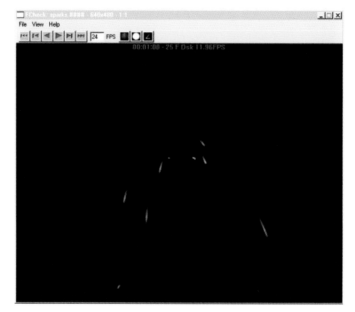

*Animation flipbook*

## 5  Preview the resulting animation using FCheck

## 6  Composite rendered animations

You currently have a software rendered animation of fire and smoke and a hardware rendered sequence of sparks with an embedded alpha channel. You can now use your compositing software to layer all these elements together.

*Final composite*

There are several advantages to compositing your layers instead of rendering all of them into one scene:

- By separating background and foreground elements and rendering them individually, rendering times can be greatly reduced;

- By rendering different elements on different layers, it is easier to make revisions later to one layer without having to re-render the whole scene;

- By compositing hardware and software rendered particles, you can achieve interesting effects; and

- By using different layers, your compositing software can adjust the color for one particular layer without affecting other layers.

## Conclusion

You now have a better understanding of Maya hardware and software particles. You created and modified the preset fire effect and added your own effect by customizing emitter and particle attributes. The lesson also covered some of the most important aspects of particle simulations, including per particle attributes, gravity, collisions and collision events.

In the next lesson you will experiment with polygonal components, light linking and explore the Paint Effects Tool.

# Lesson 06    Adding details

*In this lesson you will change the shape of the room to include a large window facing the outer space. This is a good time to experiment with basic polygonal tools and light tools. You will also use one of the most awesome Maya tools: Paint Effects.*

## In this lesson you will learn the following:

- How to extrude polygonal faces;

- How to assign shaders to polygonal faces;

- How to duplicate a shading network;

- How to create directional lights;

- How to use light linking;

- How to use Paint Effects.

## Big front window

To see outside the room into the outer space, you will create a large glass window, changing the room's geometry. That window will use raytracing from the last lesson for its reflection.

### 1 Change the resolution of the room

In Lesson 4, you increased the room's Subdivisions to see the effect of your lighting on the floor. Since that is no longer required, you will change the room back to its simplest form. You can open the previously saved file or *05-particles.ma*.

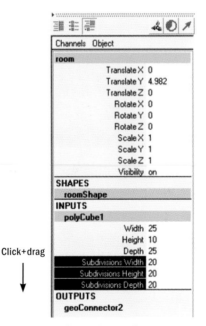

- Instead of using the Attribute Editor, display the Channel Box by selecting **Display** → **UI Elements** → **Channel Box / Layer Editor**.

- Select the *room* object.

- In the **Inputs** section of the Channel Box, click on *polyCube1*.

- Select all three **Subdivisions** attributes by click+dragging over their names.

- In the Perspective view, **MMB** drag to the left to decrease the attributes' value to **1**.

Click+drag

*When attributes are highlighted in the Channel Box, middle mouse dragging in a viewport invokes a virtual slider that changes the attributes' values.*

*Select the attribute names*

### 2 Extrude a polygon face

Extruding polygons is a very common action for Maya users. To do an extrusion, you first need to pick polygon components, then execute the tool that will display a useful all-in-one manipulator to move around the new polygons.

- With the *room* still selected, press the **F11** hotkey to go into Component mode with the polygonal faces enabled.

> **Tip:** There are several hotkeys for going into Component and Object modes. The more you use Maya, the better you will know the difference between those modes. The polygon related hotkeys are listed here:
>
> **F8** – Toggle between Object mode and the last Component mode
>
> **F9** – Display vertices
>
> **F10** – Display edges
>
> **F11** – Display faces
>
> **F12** – Display UVs

- With your **LMB**, select the dot at the center of the front wall.

*The face will be highlighted in orange to show that it's currently selected.*

*Pick the center of the face to select it*

> **Tip:** You can also do a **click+drag** square selection of the face centers to highlight faces.

- Press **F3** to change the menu set to Modeling.
- Select **Edit Polygons** → **Extrude Face**.

*A manipulator is displayed at the selection. This manipulator has all translation, rotation and scale manipulators integrated.*

- **LMB** on an arrow to display the translation manipulator.
- **LMB** on the outer circle to display the rotation manipulator.
- **LMB** on a square to display the scale manipulator.

*Toggle between local and global transformation by clicking on the round icon.*

- **LMB** on a square of the manipulator to use its scale function.
- **LMB** drag on the center square to uniformly scale the extruded face as follows:

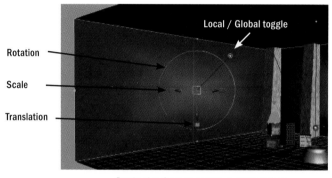

*Scale the face to make a large window*

- **LMB** on an arrow of the manipulator to use its translate function.
- **LMB** translate the face toward the center of the room to create a window border.
- Select **Edit Polygons** → **Extrude Face**.
- **LMB** translate the new face toward the outside of the room to create the window pane itself.

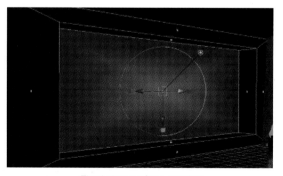

*Final shape of the window*

- Press **F8** to return to Object mode.

### 3   Assign a glass material

Once the window geometry is established, it is time to assign a glass material to that last extruded face in order to see the outer space.

- Select **Window** → **Rendering Editors** → **Hypershade**...

- Create a new **Phong** material.

- Press **Ctrl+a** to display the Attribute Editor.

- Rename the *phong* material *glassM*.

- Click+drag the **Transparency** slider all the way to the right to change it to white.

*A white transparency means it is completely transparent.*

- Bring the **Reflectivity** down to **0.3**.

- Close the Attribute Editor.

- Select the window's face component.

- In the Hypershade, **RMB** on the *glassM* material and select **Assign Material to Selection**.

*This will assign the glassM to the room's face component. In Maya, it is possible to assign multiple shaders to different faces on the same polygonal object.*


## Outer space

It would be great to see something outside the window. Here, you will add a planet slowly revolving on itself.

### 1   Add a big planet

- Select **Create** → **NURBS primitives** → **Sphere**.

- Rename it *bigPlanet*.

- Translate, scale and tilt the sphere so it looks like the following:

*The planet outside the window*

- In the Hypershade, select your favorite planet shader from the previously created shaders for the solar system. In our case, it is the earth shader.

- **RMB** in the Work Area and select **Edit** → **Duplicate** → **Shading Network**.

*This will duplicate the selected shader along with all of its related nodes; in this case, the texture file and its placement node. The duplicated network automatically appears in the Work Area.*

- Rename the new shader *bigPlanetM*.

- Assign *bigPlanetM* shader to the *bigPlanet*.

- Select **Window** → **Rendering Editors** → **Render View...**

- Test render your scene.

*Test render*

**Note:** *Notice the nice reflection in the glass when raytracing is enabled in the Render Settings.*

## 2   Fine-tuning the lighting

One thing that is not accurate in this render, is that the lights from the room are lighting the big planet. The room light should not have any influence on such a big object. You will need to create a directional light and then use light linking to prevent the planet from being lit by any other lights.

- Select **Create** → **Lights** → **Directional Light**.

*The light directionalLight1 appears at the origin.*

*Directional light mimics real sunlight, where all the rays are parallel and seem to come from a distant source.*

- Move the directional light next to the *bigPlanet* as follows:

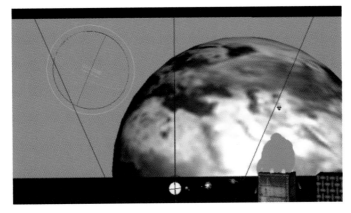

*The new directional light*

- Select **Window** → **Relationship Editors** → **Light Linking** → **Light-Centric**.

*The following Relationship Editor will open, letting you select a light on the left side, and select or deselect affected objects on the right side.*

*Relationship Editor*

- Select *directionalLight1* on the left side.

*Every object affected by that light gets highlighted on the right side.*

- Deselect everything but *bigPlanet* and its shading group, *bigPlanetMSG*.

> **Note:** *If you cannot find bigPlanetMSG, it is because you assigned the shader before renaming it and the shading group has its default name. To find the planet's shading group name, select bigPlanetM in the Hypergraph, then select* **Graph → Output Connections**.

- For all the other lights on the left side of the Relationship Editor, select the light and deselect *bigPlanet* on the right side.

*Doing so will prevent bigPlanet from being lit by any of the room's lighting.*

*Good lighting*

> **Note:** *In this render, the light in the room reflects in the window due to the window's specular light.*

## 3   Adding planet details

At the moment, the planet doesn't look to have an atmosphere. To simulate that effect, you will be using the glow attribute on the planet's shader. Also, in the case of the earth texture, there should be some bump mapping to simulate the mountains and clouds.

- Select the *bigPlanetM* material.

- In the Attribute Editor, scroll down to the **Special Effects** section of *bigPlanetM*.

- Enter **0.2** as the **Glow Intensity**.

- Graph the whole shading group by selecting **Graph** → **Input Connections** in the Work Area of the Hypershade.

- Reuse the texture map of the **color** channel for the bump by **MMB+dragging** the file texture onto *bigPlanetM*.

*This will display a context menu.*

- Select **bump map** for the context menu.

*By dropping the texture in the bump map, Maya will automatically create a bump2d node which is used to specify the depth of the bumps on the geometry. In our case, the bump depth should be very subtle.*

- Select the newly created *bump2d1* node.

- In the Attribute Editor, change **Bump Depth** to **0.1**.

*This will decrease the amount of bump.*

- Test render your scene.

*The final render*

**Lesson 06**

> **Tip:** If the specular light of the planet looks too strong in your test render, you can tone down the **Specular Color** of the bigPlanetM shader. Also, you can change the **Bump Depth** to increase or decrease the bumps.

### 4   Animate the planet

A nice effect in your final render would be to have the planet slowly revolving.

- If the Time Slider is hidden, press the spacebar to invoke the hotbox, then select **Display** → **UI Elements** → **Time Slider**.
- Select *bigPlanet*.
- Go to frame **1**.

> **Tip:** Remember to use the **Rewind** button and not scrub in the timeline as the scene contains uncached particles.

- Press the **s** hotkey to **Set Key**.
- Go to the last frame.
- Using the **Rotate Tool**, rotate the planet slightly on its **Y-axis**.
- Set another keyframe by pressing **s**.

## Paint Effects

The Paint Effects Tool lets you select brushes to draw special effects directly in your scene. Brushes can be almost anything you want. Included in Maya is a group of default brushes such as grass, trees, lightings, fur, and even stars. To keep this lesson simple, you will draw default stars, which will be perfect for your outer space scene.

### 1   Paint stars

First, you need to have something to paint on, and for that, you will create a very large sphere. Once that is done, you will paint on it with the star brush. Finally, you will hide the sphere.

- Select **Create** → **NURBS primitives** → **Sphere**.

- Rename the sphere *drawSphere*.

- In the Channel Box, set the new sphere's scaling in **X**, **Y** and **Z** to **100**.

- Press **F5** to activate the **Rendering** menu set.

- With the drawing sphere still selected, press the spacebar to access the hotbox and select **Paint Effects** → **Make Paintable**.

*Doing so simply tells Maya that you will be drawing on that sphere.*

- Again in the hotbox, select **Paint Effects** → **Get Brushes**.

*The Visor window will pop open, letting you choose a default library brush.*

- Make sure the **Paint Effects** tab is selected at the top of the Visor.

- On the left side, select the **galactic** folder.

- **LMB** click on the *space.mel* brush to set it as the current brush.

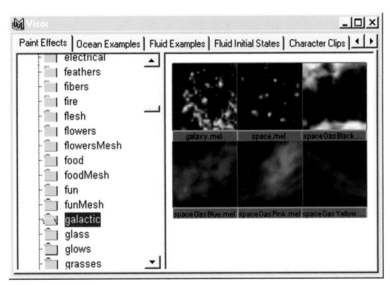

*Visor window*

**Note:** *Clicking on a Paint Effects brush will automatically activate the Paint Effects Tool.*

- In one continuous movement, **LMB** draw in your Perspective viewport to cover the entire outer space area as follows:

*Paint in the viewport*

> **Tip:** Drawing the entire *Paint Effects* stroke in one continuous move will make it simpler for you to continue with the lesson. Every time you release the mouse button and draw again, a new stroke object will be created. Use **Edit** → **Undo** if you want to redraw your stroke.

- Press **Ctrl+a** to show the Attribute Editor for your new stroke.

- Select the *space1* tab at the top of the Attribute Editor.

- Change the **Global Scale** of the stroke to **5**.

*Since the stroke was drawn so far away, the stars would have rendered barely visible. Boosting up their scaling will make the stroke more present in your render.*

- Zoom out and select the *drawSphere*.

- Press **Ctrl+h** to hide it since it is not required in the scene render.

- Open the hotbox and select **Render** → **Render Current Frame** to do a test render.

# Conclusion

Congratulations! You now have a complete scene that includes objects, shaders and visual effects. You have begun to develop skills that you will continue to use throughout your work with Maya.

The next lesson is a more in-depth look into most of the tools that you have been using since the beginning of this project. Also, once you have read this lesson, you will be able to make your own decisions on how to configure the UI for your needs.

In the projects that follow, the instructions will not specify whether or not you should use the hotbox or menus to complete an action. The choice will be yours.

**Alias** *Don't be afraid to start small. Maya is a large and complex program with*
**Tip:** *many features and can be intimidating for the beginner. To make the interface less daunting, try hiding some of the UI elements you don't use by going to the **Display** → **UI** menu and unchecking the elements you don't want. Once you have mastered the basics, you can go back to the default layout and further explore Maya.*

*Julio Lopez | Sr. Multimedia Specialist*

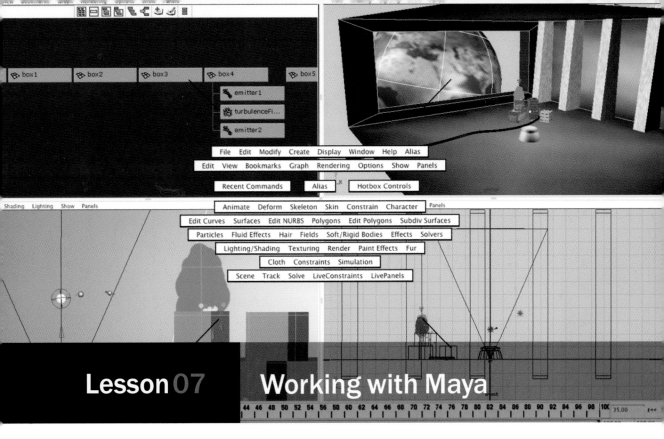

box1    box2    box3    box4    box5

emitter1
turbulenceFi...
emitter2

File   Edit   Modify   Create   Display   Window   Help   Alias

Edit   View   Bookmarks   Graph   Rendering   Options   Show   Panels

Recent Commands          Alias          Hotbox Controls

Shading   Lighting   Show   Panels

Animate   Deform   Skeleton   Skin   Constrain   Character   Panels

Edit Curves   Surfaces   Edit NURBS   Polygons   Edit Polygons   Subdiv Surfaces

Particles   Fluid Effects   Hair   Fields   Soft/Rigid Bodies   Effects   Solvers

Lighting/Shading   Texturing   Render   Paint Effects   Fur

Cloth   Constraints   Simulation

Scene   Track   Solve   LiveConstraints   LivePanels

# Lesson 07     Working with Maya

44  46  48  50  52  54  56  58  60  62  64  66  68  70  72  74  76  78  80  82  84  86  88  90  92  94  96  98  100  35.00

*If you completed the first six lessons, then you worked with Maya from modeling and animating to rendering and particles. Now is a good time to review some of the UI concepts that you worked with to provide a more complete overview of how Maya works.*

*It is recommended that you work through this lesson before proceeding with the remaining lessons in the book. This lesson explores the basic UI actions that you will use in your day-to-day work.*

## In this lesson you will learn the following:

- About the Maya interface;

- About the different UI parts;

- About view tools;

- About the different hardware displays;

- About menus and hotkeys;

- About the manipulators and the Channel Box;

- About selection and selection masks;

- About the difference between tools and actions.

# The workspace

You learned how to build and animate scenes using different view panels and UI tools. The panels offer various points of view for evaluating your work – such as Perspective views, Orthographic views, graphs and Outliners – while the tools offer you different methods for interacting with the objects in your scene.

Shown below is the workspace and its key elements:

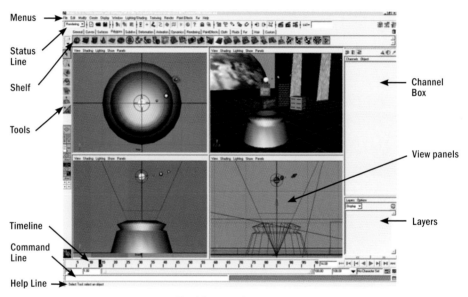

*The Maya workspace*

## Layouts

When Maya is first launched, you are presented with a single Perspective view panel. As you work, you may want to change to other view layouts.

**To change your view layouts:**

- Go to the view panel's **Panels** menu and select a new layout option from the **Layouts** pop-up.

*The Layouts pop-up menu*

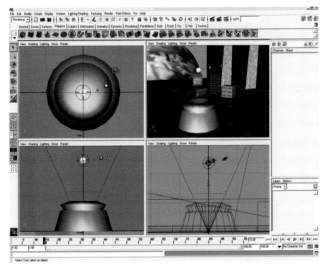

*The default layout*

*A four-view layout*

You can set up various types of layouts ranging from two to four panels.

**Tip:** *If you are looking at several view panels simultaneously and want to focus on one of them, put your cursor in that view and tap the spacebar. The view will become full-screen. Tap the spacebar again and the panels will return to the previous layout.*

# View panels

As you begin to build and animate objects, you will want to view the results from various points of view. In Maya, you can place either Perspective or Orthographic views in each panel.

**To change the content of a view panel:**

- Go to the view panel's **Panels** menu and select a view type from either the **Perspective** or **Orthographic** pop-ups.

# View tools

When you are working with Perspective and Orthographic views, you can change your view point by using hotkey view tools.

**To tumble in a Perspective view:**

- Press the **Alt** key and **click+drag** with the **LMB**.

*Tip:* *The ability to tumble an Orthographic view is locked by default. To unlock this feature, you need to select the desired Orthographic view and under View, go to Camera Tools and unlock it in the Tumble Tool Attribute Editor.*

**To track in any view panel:**

- Press the **Alt** key and **click+drag** with the **MMB**.

**To dolly in or out of any view panel:**

- Press the **Alt** key and **click+drag** with both the **LMB** and **MMB**.

*These view tools allow you to quickly work in 3D space using a simple hotkey.*

*Tip:* *You can also track and dolly in other view panels, such as the Hypergraph, the Graph Editor, Visor, Hypershade, and even the Render View window. The same view tools work for most panel types.*

**Project One**

## View Compass

The View Compass appears in the top right corner of the scene's Perspective view and shows your current camera view; such as Perspective, top, bottom, left, right, front, or back.

*The View Compass*

You can move between views by clicking parts of the View Compass. Clicking any of the six cones rotates the current camera view to an Orthographic view. Clicking the central cube moves the camera back to Perspective view.

To turn the View Compass on and off per camera:

- Select **View** → **Camera Settings** → **View Compass**.

## Other panel types

As well, you can change the content of the view panel to display other types of information, such as the Hypershade or the Graph Editor.

To change the content of a view panel:

- Go to the view panel's **Panels** menu and select a panel type from the **Panel** pop-up.

*In the workspace below, you can see a Hypershade panel for helping you organize your shading groups and a Graph Editor for working with animation curves.*

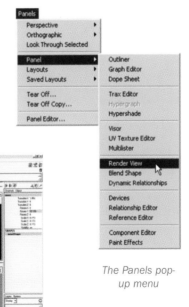

*The Panels pop-up menu*

*The workspace with various panel types*

## Saved layouts

As you become more familiar with Maya, you may want to set up an arrangement of panels to suit a particular workflow. For example, you may want a Dope Sheet, a Perspective view, a top view and a Hypergraph view all set up in a particular manner.

**To add a new layout of your own:**

- Go to the view panel's **Panels** menu and select **Saved Layouts → Edit → Layouts...**

  *In the Edit window, you can add a new saved layout and edit the various aspects of the layout.*

**To add a new layout to the list:**

- Select the **Layouts** tab and click on **New → Layout**.

- Select and edit the layout's name.

- Press the **Enter** key.

*Layout toolbox*

**To edit the configuration of a saved layout:**

- Press the **Edit Layouts** tab.

- Choose a configuration, then **click+drag** on the separator bars to edit the layout's composition.

- Press the **Contents** tab.

- Choose a panel type for each of the panels set up in the configuration section.

Panels

Help

Panels | New Panel | Layouts | Edit Layouts | History |

Configurations | Contents |

Configuration | Three Panes Split Left ▾ |

1

2

3

Current Layout

Close

*Layout Editor*

**Tip:** *There is quick access to preset layouts, panel types and layout configuration through the toolbox on the left side of the Maya UI.*

## Display options

Using the **Shading** menu on each view panel, you can choose which kind of display you want for your geometry.

**To change your panel display:**

- Go to the panel's **Shading** menu and select one of the options.

**Or**

- **MMB** in a panel to set it as the active panel and use one of the following hotkeys to switch display types:

    **4** for wireframe;

    **5** for smooth shaded.

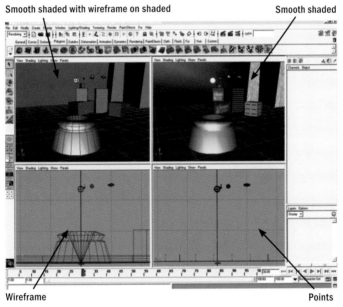

Smooth shaded with wireframe on shaded     Smooth shaded

Wireframe     Points

*Various display styles*

## Texturing and lighting

Another important option found on this menu is hardware texturing. This option allows you to visualize textures and lighting interactively in the view panels.

**To use Hardware Texturing:**

- Build a shader that uses textures.

- Go to the panel's **Shading** menu and select **Hardware Texturing**.

Or

- Press the following hotkey:

    **6** for hardware texturing.

**To display different textures:**

It is possible to display different texture maps on your surface during hardware texturing. For example, you could display the color map or the bump map if those channels are mapped with a texture.

- Select the material that is assigned to your objects.

- In the Attribute Editor, scroll down to the **Hardware Texturing** section and set the **Textured channel** to the desired channel.

- You can also set the **Texture quality** for each material node so that you can see the texture more clearly in your viewport.

**To add hardware lighting to your scene:**

- Add a light into your scene.

- Go to the panel's **Lighting** menu and select one of the options.

Or

- Press the following hotkey:

    **7** for all lighting.

*Hardware lighting and texturing*

## High Quality Rendering

When high quality interactive shading is turned on, the scene views are drawn in high quality by the hardware renderer. This lets you see a very good representation of the look of the final render without having to software render the scene.

**To turn on High Quality Rendering:**
- Go to the panel's **Shading** menu and enable **High Quality Rendering**.

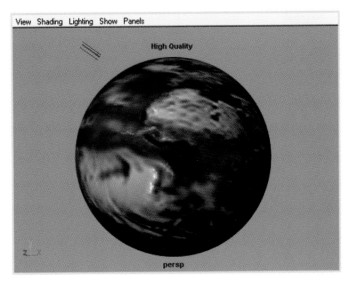

*High Quality Rendering*

## Display smoothness

By default, NURBS surfaces are displayed using a fine smoothness setting. If you want to enhance playback and interactivity, you can have them drawn in a lower quality.

**To change NURBS smoothness:**
- Go to the **Display** menu and under **NURBS Smoothness** choose one of the options.

**Or**
- Use one of the following hotkeys to switch display types:

   **1** — for rough;

   **2** — for medium;

   **3** — for fine.

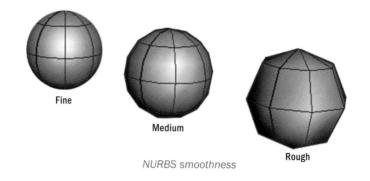

Fine

Medium

Rough

*NURBS smoothness*

**Tip:** *To speed up camera movement in a scene with heavy NURBS geometry, go
to the* **Window** → **Settings/Preferences** → **Preferences...** *Under* **Categories**,
*select the* **Display** *option. Then enable* **Fast Interaction** *by clicking the* **On**
*option. This option shows the rough NURBS smoothness any time a camera
is moving.*

## Show menu

The **Show** menu is an important tool found on each view panel's menu. This menu
lets you restrict or filter what each panel can show on a panel-by-panel basis.

Restricting what each panel shows lets you display curves in one window and
surfaces in another to help edit construction history. Or, you can hide curves when
playing back a motion path animation while editing the same curve in another panel.

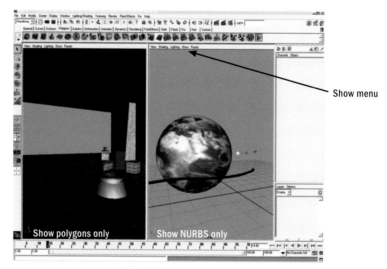

Show menu

Show polygons only     Show NURBS only

*The Show menu*

# UI preferences

The Maya workspace is made up of various UI elements that assist you in your day-to-day work. The default Maya workspace shows all of them on screen for easy access.

**To reduce the UI to only view panels and menus:**

- Go to the **Display** menu and select **UI Elements** → **Hide UI Elements**.

*With less UI clutter, you can rely more on hotkeys and other UI methods for accessing tools while conserving screen real estate.*

**To return to a full UI:**

- Go to the **Display** menu and select **UI Elements** → **Restore UI Elements**.

# Menus

Most of the tools and actions you will use in Maya are found in the main menus. The first six menus are always visible, while the next few menus change depending on which UI mode you are in.

Menus and menu pop-ups that display a double line at the top can be *torn off* for easier access.

**To tear off a menu:**

- Open the desired menu, then select the double line at the top of the menu.

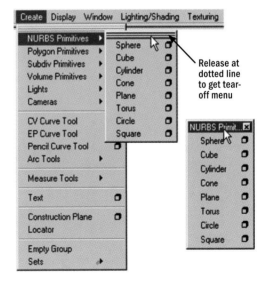

*A tearoff menu*

**Project One**

# Menu sets

There are four menu sets in Maya Complete: *Animation, Modeling, Dynamics* and *Rendering*. Each menu set allows you to focus on tools appropriate to a particular workflow.

**To choose a menu set:**

- Select the menu set from the pop-up menu found at the left of the Status Line bar.

**To choose a menu set using hotkeys:**

- Press the **h** key and choose the desired UI mode from the radial marking menu.

**To choose a menu set using function keys:**

- Press **F1** — to invoke the **Help**;

- Press **F2** — for **Animation**;

- Press **F3** — for **Modeling**;

- Press **F4** — for **Dynamics**;

- Press **F5** — for **Rendering**.

# Shelves

Another way of accessing tools and actions is using the shelves. You can move items from a menu to a shelf to begin combining tools into groups based on your personal workflow needs.

**To add a menu item to a shelf:**

- Press **Ctrl+Shift** and select the menu item. It will appear on the active shelf.

**To edit the shelf contents and tabs:**

- Go to the **Window** menu and select **Settings/Preferences** → **Shelves...**

Or

- Select the **Shelf Editor** from the arrow menu located to the left of the shelves.

**To remove a menu item from a shelf:**

- **MMB click+drag** the shelf icon to the trash icon located at the far right of the shelves.

# Status Line

The Status Line, located just under the Maya main menu, provides feedback on settings that affect the way the tools behave. The display information consists of:

- The current menu set;

- Icons that allow you to create a new scene, open a saved one, or save the current one;

- The selection mode and selectable items;

- The snap modes;

- The history of the selected lead object (visible by pressing the input and output buttons);

- The construction history flag;

- Render into new window and IPR button;

- Quick selection field and Numeric Input field.

**To collapse part of shelf buttons:**

- Press the small handle bar next to a button set.

*Select modes before collapsing*

*Select modes button collapsed*

# Hotbox

As you learned, tapping the spacebar quickly pops a pane between full screen and its regular size, but if you press and hold the spacebar, you gain access to the hotbox.

The hotbox is a UI tool that gives you access to as much or as little of the Maya UI as you want. It appears where your cursor is located and offers the fastest access to tools and actions.

**To access the hotbox:**
- Press and hold the spacebar.

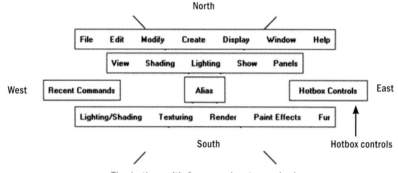

*The hotbox with four quadrants marked*

The hotbox offers a fully customizable UI element that provides you with access to all of the main menus, as well as your own set of marking menus. Use the **Hotbox Controls** to display or show as many or as few menus as you need.

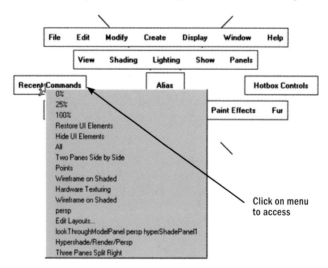

# Hotbox marking menus

You can access marking menus in five areas of the hotbox. Since each of these areas can have a marking menu for each mouse button, it is possible to have fifteen menus in total. You can edit the content of the marking menus by going to the **Window** menu and selecting **Settings/Preferences** → **Marking Menus...**

**To access the center marking menu:**

- Press the spacebar.

- **Click+drag** in the center area to access the desired menu.

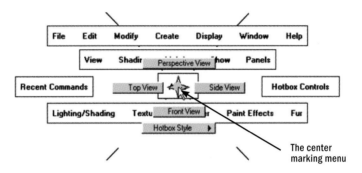

The center marking menu

**To access the edge marking menus:**

- Press the spacebar.

- **Click+drag** in the top quadrant to access the desired menu.

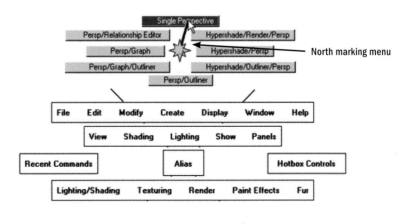

North marking menu

# Customizing the hotbox

You can customize the hotbox to make it as simple or complex as you need. You can choose which menus are available and which are not.

If you want, you can reduce the hotbox to its essentials and focus on its marking menu capabilities.

*A reduced hotbox layout*

Alternatively, you could hide the other UI elements, such as panel menus, and use the hotbox for access to everything. You get to choose which method works best for you.

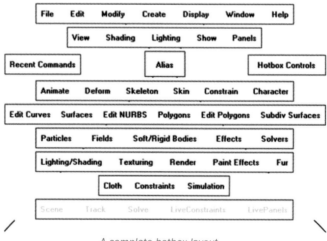

*A complete hotbox layout*

**To customize the hotbox:**

- Use the **Hotbox Controls**.

**Or**

- Use the center marking menu.

- Choose an option from the **Hotbox Styles** menu.

## Tool manipulators

To the left of the workspace you have access to important tools. These include the **Select**, **Move**, **Rotate**, **Scale** and **Show Manipulator** tools. Each of these is designed to correspond to a related hotkey that can be easily remembered using the **QWERTY** keys on your keyboard.

These tools will be used for your most common tool-based actions, like selecting and transforming.

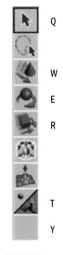

*QWERTY tool layout*

**Note:** *The Y key drives the last spot on the QWERTY palette, which is for the last tool used. The advantages of this will be discussed under the heading Tools and Actions.*

## Universal Manipulator

The **Universal Manipulator** lets you transform geometry in translation, rotation or scaling, both manually or numerically. A single click on any of the manipulators will display a numeric field allowing you to type in a specific value.

*Universal manipulator*

## Soft Modification Tool

The **Soft Modification Tool** lets you push and pull geometry as a sculptor would on a sculpture. The amount of deformation is greatest at the center of the push/pull, and gradually falls off further away from the center. The Soft Modification Tool is located in the tool box, although it is not associated with the **QWERTY** keys. The corresponding action is **Deform → Soft Modification**.

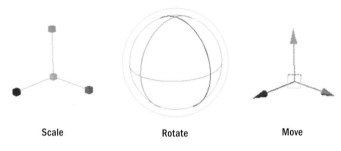

| Scale | Rotate | Move |

*Transform manipulators*

## Transform manipulators

One of the most basic node types in Maya is the *transform node*. This node contains attributes focused on the position, orientation and scale of an object. To help you interactively manipulate these nodes, there are three transform manipulators that make it easy to constrain along the main axes.

Each of the manipulators uses a color to indicate their axes. RGB is used to correspond to X, Y, Z. Therefore, red is for X, green for Y and blue for Z. Selected handles are displayed in yellow.

To explore some of the options available with manipulators, you will use the transform manipulator.

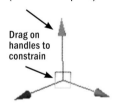

Drag in center for all axes
(based on view plane)

Drag on
handles to
constrain

*The move manipulator*

**To use a transform manipulator in view plane:**

- **Click+drag** on the center of the manipulator to move freely along all axes.

**To constrain a manipulator along one axis:**

- **Click+drag** on one of the manipulator handles.

**To constrain a manipulator along two axes:**

- Hold the **Ctrl** key and **click+drag** on the axis that is aligned with the desired plane of motion.

*This now fixes the center on the desired plane, thereby letting you click+drag on the center so that you can move along the two axes. The icon at the center of the manipulator changes to reflect the new state.*

**To go back to the default view plane center:**

- Press the **Ctrl** key and click on the center of the transform manipulator.

*Working along two axes*

**Note:** *The ability to constrain in two axes at one time is available for the move and scale manipulators.*

## Using the mouse buttons

You can interact directly with manipulators by using the left mouse button to select objects.

The **MMB** is for the active manipulator and lets you **click+drag** without direct manipulation.

**To select objects:**

- Set up selection masks.
- Click with the **LMB**.

**To select multiple objects:**

- Use the **LMB** and **click+drag** a bounding box around objects.

**To add objects to the selection:**

- Press **Ctrl+Shift** while you select one or multiple objects.

**To manipulate objects directly:**

- **Click+drag** on a manipulator handle.

**To manipulate objects indirectly:**

- Activate a manipulator handle;
- **Click+drag** with the **MMB**.

# Shift gesture

The manipulators allow you to work effectively in a Perspective view panel when transforming objects.

If you want to work more quickly when changing axes for your manipulators, there are several solutions available.

**To change axis focus using hotkeys:**

- Press and hold on the transform keys:

    **w** — for move;

    **e** — for rotate;

    **r** — for scale.

- Choose an axis handle for constraining from the marking menu.

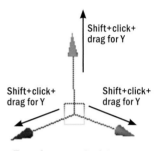

Shift+click+ drag for Y

Shift+click+ drag for Y

Shift+click+ drag for Y

*Transform manipulators*

**To change axis focus using Shift key:**

- Press the **Shift** key.

- **Click+drag** with the **MMB** in the direction of the desired axis.

# Set pivot

The ability to change the pivot location on a transform node is very important for certain types of animation.

**To change your pivot point:**

- Select one of the manipulator tools;

- Press the **Insert** key (**Home** on Macintosh);

- **Click+drag** on the manipulator to move its pivot;

- Press **Insert** to return to the manipulator tool (**Home** on Macintosh).

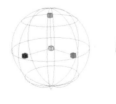

Press Insert or Home      Drag on manip      Press Insert or Home

## Channel Box

Another way of entering accurate values is through the Channel Box. This powerful panel gives you access to an object's Transform node and any associated Input nodes.

If you have multiple objects selected, your changes to a channel will affect every node sharing that attribute.

To put one of the selected objects at the top of the Channel Box so that it is visible, choose the desired node from the Channel Box's **Object** menu.

If you want to work with a particular channel, you can use the **Channels** menu to set keys, add expressions and complete other useful tasks. You can also change the display of Channel Box names to short MEL-based names.

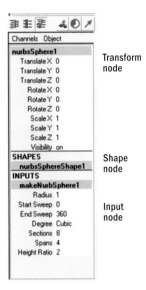

*The Channel Box*

**Note:** *To control what channels are shown in the Channel Box, go to the* **Window** *menu, and choose* **General Editors** → **Channel Control...**

## Channel Box and manipulators

One of the features of the Channel Box is the way in which you can use it to access manipulators at the transform level.

By default, the Channel Box is set to show manipulators every time you tab into a new Channel Box field. You will notice that as you select the channel names such as *Translate Z* or *Rotate X*, the manipulator switches from translate to rotate.

One fast way to edit an attribute is to invoke the virtual slider by selecting the name of the desired channel in the Channel Box, then use the **MMB+drag** in a view panel to change its value.

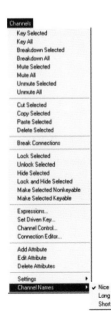

There are three options for the Channel Box manipulator setting:

**Default manipulator setting**

This setting lets you activate the appropriate field in the Channel Box, and then modify the values with either the left or the middle mouse button.

To use the default method, complete the following steps:

- Click on the desired channel name or input field then **click+drag** directly on the active manipulator with the **LMB**.

Or

- Click on the desired channel name or input field, then **click+drag** in open space with the **MMB**.

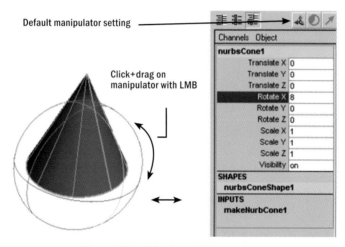

Default manipulator setting

Click+drag on
manipulator with LMB

*Channel Box default manipulator setting*

**No-manipulator setting**

You can click on the manipulator icon over the Channel Box to turn manipulation off, which leaves the Channel Box focused on coordinate input. With this setting, you cannot use the middle or left mouse button for manipulation. To manipulate objects in this mode, you must do one of the following:

- Click in the channel's entry field and type the exact value.

Or

- Use one of the normal transform tools such as **move**, **rotate** and **scale**.

No-manipulator setting

No interactive
manipulation
possible unless you
use a Transform Tool

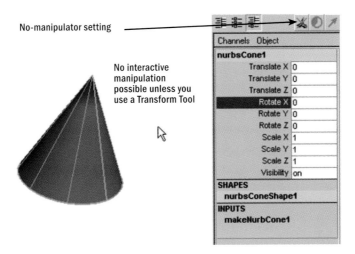

*Channel Box no-manipulator setting*

## No-visual manipulator setting

A third option found on this manip button returns manipulator capability to the
Channel Box – but now you won't see the manipulator on the screen,
as shown in the icon at the bottom of the Channel Box.

- Click on the desired channel name or within the channel's input field.

- **Click+drag** in open space with the **MMB**.

*You can now use the two new buttons that let you edit the speed and dropoff
of the manipulations.*

No-Visual manip setting

Click+drag in
open space with
mouse button

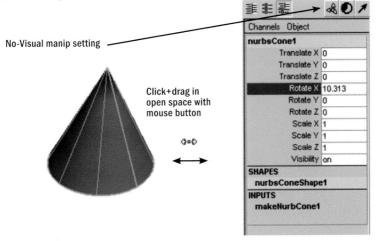

*Channel Box no-visual manipulator setting*

The first button that becomes available with the *No-visual* setting is the **speed** button which lets you click+drag with your **MMB** either slow, medium or fast.

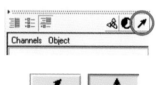

*Channel speed controls*

The second button is the **drop-off** button which lets you choose between a linear motion, as you **click+drag** with the **MMB**, or a click+drag that is slow at first and faster as you drag further.

*Channel drop-off options*

## Attribute Editor

If the Channel Box lets you focus on attributes that are keyable using **Set Key**, then the Attribute Editor gives you access to all the other attributes/channels.

The Attribute Editor is used for all nodes in Maya. This means that shaders, textures, surfaces, lattices, Render Globals, etc. can all be displayed in this one type of window.

**To open the Attribute Editor window:**

- Select a node.

- Go to the **Window** menu and select **Attribute Editor**.

**To open the Attribute Editor panel:**

- Select a node.

- Go to the **Display** menu and select **UI Elements** → **Attribute Editor**. The Channel Box is now replaced by an Attribute Editor panel.

*A typical Attribute Editor*

When you open up the Attribute Editor, you get not only the active node, but also related nodes based on dependency relationships. In the example below, a sphere's transform, shape and *makeNurbSphere* nodes are all present. These are the same input and shape nodes shown in the Channel Box.

**Tip:** *You can also press the **Ctrl+a** hotkey to open the Attribute Editor. You can set your preference for having the Attribute Editor in a panel or in its own window through the **Window** → **Settings/Preferences** → **Preferences...** and click on the **Interface** section to modify the **Open Attribute Editor** option.*

## Numeric input

To add values to your transformations using accurate values, you can use the numeric input box. This allows you to apply exact values to the attributes associated with the current manipulator. You can use the Help Line to confirm your results.

**To display the Help Line:**

- From the **Display** menu, select **UI Elements** → **Help Line**.

*Numeric input field*

**To change all values at once:**

- Enter three values in a row, with spaces in-between.

**Note:** *Beside the coordinate box is a button to toggle between absolute and relative values. Depending on which mode you are in, your transformation will happen either relative to your current object or absolute.*

**To enter a value for the active manipulator:**

- Click on the desired handle. (e.g. – Translate Z arrow)

- Enter a single value.

*Inputting active manipulator value*

**Note:** *If no manipulator handle is active, the single value will be applied to X.*

**To enter a value while preserving others:**

- Type in periods [.] for channels that you want to stay the same. Remember to add spaces in-between.

*Entering periods to keep values constant*

- Enter a numeric value for the channels that will change.

*The example to the right would keep the X and Y values constant and change only the Z information.*

# SELECTING IN MAYA

One of the most important tasks when working in Maya is your ability to select different types of nodes and their key components.

For instance, you need to be able to select a sphere and move it, or you need to select the sphere's control vertices and move them. You also need to distinguish between different types of objects so that you can select only surfaces or only deformers.

## Selection masks

To make selecting work in Maya, you have a series of selection masks available to you. This allows you to have one select tool that is then *masked* so that it can only select certain kinds of objects and components.

The *selection mask* concept is very powerful because it allows you to create whatever combination of selecting types that you desire. Sometimes, you only want to select joints and selection handles, or maybe you want to select anything but joints. With selection masks, you get to set up and choose the select options.

# The selection UI

The UI for selecting offers several types of access to the selection masks. You can learn all of them now and then choose which best suits your way of working down the line.

## Grouping and parenting

When working with transform nodes, you can create more complex structures by building hierarchies of these node types.

To build these structures, you can choose to *group* the nodes under a new transform node or you can *parent* one of the nodes under the other so that the lower node inherits the motion of the top node.

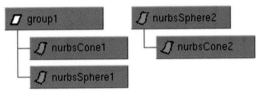

*Grouped and parented nodes*

## Selection modes

At the top of the workspace, you have several selection mask tools available. These are all organized under three main types of select modes. Each type gives you access to either the hierarchy, object type or components.

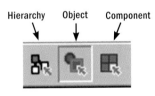

*The select modes*

## Scene hierarchy mode

Hierarchy mode gives you access to different parts of the scene hierarchy structure. In the example shown below, the leaf node and the root node are highlighted. This mode lets you access each of these parts of the hierarchy. You can select root nodes, leaf nodes and template nodes using the selection masks.

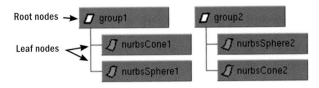

*Hierarchy types*

# Object mode

Object mode lets you perform selections based on the object type. Selection masks are available as icons that encompass related types of objects.

With your **RMB**, you can access more detailed options that are listed under each mask group. If you create a partial list, the mask icon is highlighted in orange.

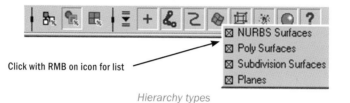

*Hierarchy types*

> **Tip:** *Once you choose selection masks, Maya gives priority to different object types. For instance, joints are selected before surfaces. You will need to use the* **Shift** *key to select these two object types together. To reset the priorities, select* **Window → Settings/Preferences → Preferences...** *and click on the* **Selection** *section to modify the* **Priority.**

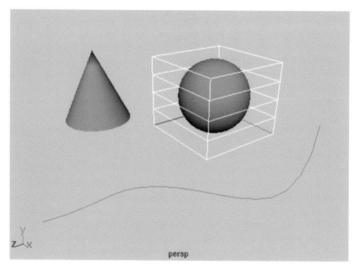

*A lattice object and a curve object selected*

## Pop-up menu selection

When objects overlap in a view, the pop-up menu selection lets you display a pop-up list of the objects to select. **LMB** click the overlap area to display the menu. Your selection is highlighted in the scene viewports as you select an item in the list.

- This option is disabled by default. To turn it on, select **Window** → **Settings/Preferences** → **Preferences...** and click on the **Selection** section to enable **Popup Menu Selection**.

*Selection pop-up menu*

## Component mode

The shape nodes of an object contain various components, such as control vertices or isoparms. To access these, you need to be in Component mode.

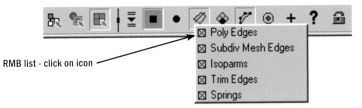

*Component selection mask*

When you select an object in this mode, it first highlights the object and shows you the chosen component type; you can then select the actual component.

Once you go back to Object mode, the object is selected and you can work with it. Toggling between Object and Component modes allows you to reshape and position objects quickly and easily.

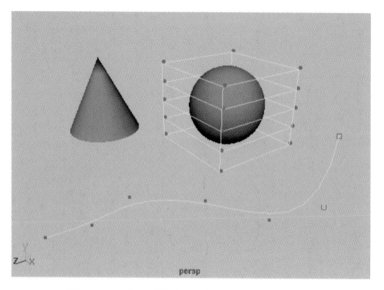

*CV components and lattice point components*

**Tip:** *To toggle between Object and Component modes, press the **F8** key.*

## RMB select

Another way of accessing the components of an object is to select an object, then press the **RMB**. This brings up a marking menu that lets you choose from the various components available for that object.

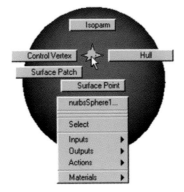

If you select another object, you return to your previous select mask selection. This is a very fast way of selecting components when in hierarchy mode, or for components that are not in the current selection mask.

*The right mouse button select menu*

## Combined select modes

In front of the selection mask mode icons is a pop-up menu that gives you different preset mask options. These presets let you combine different object and component level select options.

An example would be the NURBS option. This allows you to select various NURBS-based mask types such as surfaces, curves, CVs, curve control points and isoparms.

> **Note:** *In this mode, if you want to select CVs that are not visible by default, you must make them visible by going to the* **Display** *menu and selecting* **NURBS Components → CVs.**

When using a combined select mode, objects and components are selected differently. Objects are selected by click+dragging a select box around a part of the object while components can be selected with direct clicking.

> **Note:** *If you have CVs shown on an object and the select box touches any of them, you will select these components instead of the object. To select the object, you must drag the select box over part of the surface where there are no CVs.*

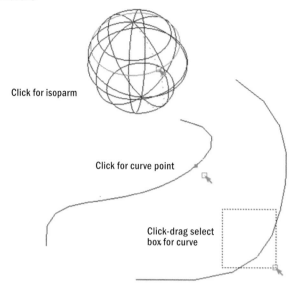

Click for isoparm

Click for curve point

Click-drag select
box for curve

*NURBS select options*

# TOOLS AND ACTIONS

In Maya, a large group of menu items lets you act on your scenes in a number of ways. These menu items can be broken down into two types of commands: *tools* and *actions*, each working in their own particular way. Almost every function in Maya can be set as a tool or action.

**Tip:** *If a menu item says "Curve Tool", it uses tool interaction. If the word "tool" is not mentioned, the menu item is set as an action.*

## Tools

Tools are designed to remain active until you have finished using them. You select a tool, use it to complete a series of steps, then press the **Select Tool**, or another tool. In most cases, the Help Line at the bottom of the workspace can be used to prompt your actions when using the tool.

Earlier you were introduced to the **Y** key on the **QWERTY** toolbox. By default, this button is blank because it represents the last tool used. When you pick a tool from the menus, its icon inserts itself into the **QWERTY** menu.

Project One

**As tool option:**

- Pick a menu item and go to the options.

- Under the **Edit** menu, select **As Tool**.

*By default you will remain in this tool until you pick the select tool, or another tool. There is also a setting that will remove you from the tool after the first completion.*

**To return to the last tool used:**

- Press the **y** key.

# Actions

Actions follow a selection-action paradigm. This means that you have to first pick something and then act on it. In Maya, this allows you to choose an action, return to editing your work, and refine the results immediately.

Actions require that you have something selected before acting on it. This means that you must first find out what is required to complete the action.

**To find out selection requirements of an action:**

- Move your cursor over the menu item.

- Look at the Help Line at the bottom-left of your workspace.

*The selection requirements are displayed. For instance, a **Loft** requires curves, isoparms or curves on surfaces while **Insert Isoparm** requires that isoparms be picked.*

**To complete the action:**

- If the tool is not already set as an action, select **Edit → As Action** from the menu items' options.

- Use either pick modes or the **RMB** pick menu to make the required selections.

- Choose the action using either the hotbox, shelf or menus.

*The action is complete and your focus returns to your last Transform Tool.*

## A typical action: 2D fillet

A good example of a typical action is a 2D fillet. As with all actions, you must start with an understanding of what the tool needs before beginning to execute the action.

### 1    Draw the first curve

- Select **Create** → **CV Curve Tool**.

- Place several points for one curve.

- Press **Enter** to complete.

- Press the **y** key to refocus on Curve Tool.

### 2    Draw the second curve

- Draw the second curve so that it crosses the first.

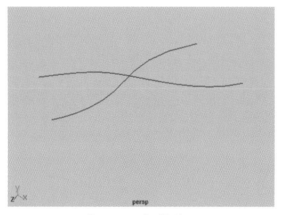

*Two curves for filleting*

- Press the **Enter** key to complete.

- In the Modeling menu set, move your cursor over the **Edit Curves** → **Curve Fillet** menu item.

- Look in the Help Line to determine what kind of pick is required.

*The Help Line is asking for curve parameter points.*

### 3    Pick the first curve point

- Click on the first curve with the **RMB**.

- Pick **Curve Point** from the selection marking menu.

- Click on the curve to place the point on the side you want to keep.

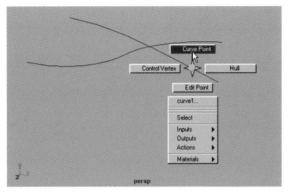

*RMB pick of curve parameter point*

## 4 Pick the second curve point

- Click on the second curve with the right mouse button.

- Pick **Curve Point** from the selection marking menu.

- Press the **Shift** key and click on the curve to place the point on the side of the curve you want to keep.

*The* **Shift** *key lets you add a second point to the selection list without losing the first curve point.*

**Note:** *You must first use the marking menu and then the* **Shift** *key to add a second point to the selection list, otherwise the selection menu will not appear.*

*Two curve points in place*

## 5   Fillet the curves

- Select **Modeling** → **Edit Curves** → **Curve Fillet** → ❑ to open the tool options.

- Turn the **Trim** option **On**.

- Click on the **Fillet** button.

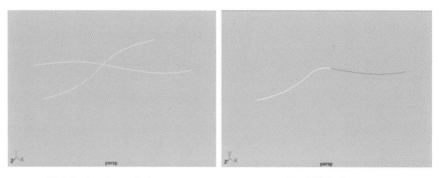

*Fillet Tool options window*                     *Final filleted curves*

# A typical tool: 2D fillet

With this example you will use the menu item as a tool rather than an action.

## 1   Draw two curves

- In a new scene, draw two curves as in the last example.

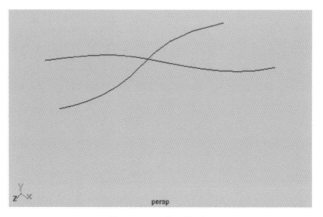

*Two curves for filleting*

## 2   Change curve fillet to tool

- Select **Edit Curves** → **Curve Fillet** → ◻.

- Select **Edit** → **As Tool** from the options window.

- Set **Trim** to **On**.

- Press the **Fillet Tool** button.

## 3   Pick the first curve

- Click with the **LMB** on the first curve.

## 4   Pick the second curve

- Click with the **LMB** on the second curve.

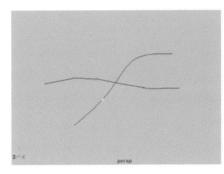
*First curve selected*

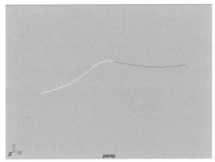
*Final filleted curves*

## Conclusion

You now know how to navigate the Maya UI and how tools and actions work. The skills you learned here will be applied throughout the rest of this book. You have the knowledge now to determine how you want to use the interface. Experiment with the different techniques taught here as you work through the *Learning Maya* projects.

In the next lesson, you will explore the Dependency Graph. You will learn about the different Maya nodes and how to build them into hierarchies and procedural animations.

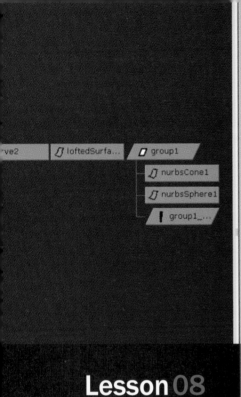

# Lesson 08    The Dependency Graph

*In the first six lessons of this book, you encountered many nodes that helped you animate and render your scene. You were introduced to input nodes, hierarchy nodes, shading networks and texture nodes, as well as emitter, particle and stroke nodes. These nodes represent key elements within Maya – each node containing important attributes that help you define and animate your scenes.*

*This lesson might seem a bit abstract at first, but in the end you will see how the various nodes contribute to an animated scene that will help you in later lessons.*

**In this lesson you will learn the following:**

- About hierarchies and dependencies;

- About connections;

- About construction history.

The Maya architecture is defined by this node-based system, known as the *Dependency Graph*. Each of your nodes contains attributes which can be connected to other nodes. If you wanted to reduce Maya to its bare essentials, you could describe it as *nodes with attributes that are connected*. This node-based approach gives Maya its open and flexible procedural characteristics.

In this lesson, you are going to explore nodes, attributes and connections by animating objects at various levels. You will explore how attributes are connected by Maya and how you can connect them yourself. You will also learn how to distinguish scene hierarchies from object dependencies.

# Hierarchies and dependencies

If you understand the idea of *nodes with attributes that are connected,* you will understand the Dependency Graph. By building a simple primitive sphere, you can see what this means in Maya.

## 1 Set up your view panels

To view nodes and connections in a diagrammatic format, the Hypergraph panel is required along with a Perspective view.

- Select **Panels → Layouts → 2 Panes Side by Side**.

- Set up a Perspective view in the first panel and a Hypergraph view in the second panel.

- Dolly into the Perspective view to get closer to the grid.

## 2 Create a primitive sphere

- Select **Create → NURBS Primitives → Sphere**.

- Press **5** to turn on smooth shading.

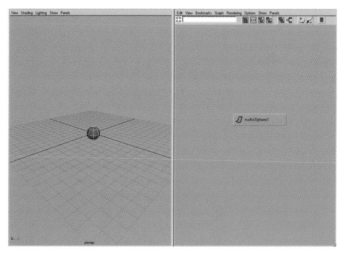

*New sphere*

## 3 View the Shape node

In the Hypergraph panel, you are currently looking at the scene view. The scene view is focused on *Transform nodes.* This type of node lets you set the position and orientation of your objects.

Right now, only a lone *nurbsSphere* node is visible. In actual fact, there are two nodes in this hierarchy but the second is hidden by default. At the bottom of most hierarchies, you will find a *Shape node* which contains the information about the object itself.

- In the Hypergraph, select **Options** → **Display** → **Shape nodes**.

*You can now see the Transform node which is, in effect, the positioning node, and the Shape node which contains information about the actual surface of the sphere. The Transform node defines the position of the shape below:*

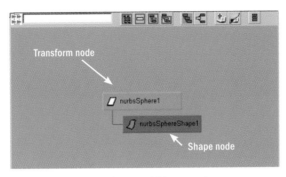

*Transform and Shape nodes*

- In the Hypergraph panel, select **Options** → **Display** → **Shape nodes** to turn these **Off**.

*Notice that when these nodes are expanded, the Shape node and the Transform node have different icons.*

*When collapsed, the Transform node takes on the Shape node's icon to help you understand what is going on underneath.*

*Transform node on its own*

## 4   View the dependencies

To view the dependencies that exist with a primitive sphere, you need to take a look at the up and downstream connections.

- In the Hypergraph panel, click on the **Input and Output Connections** button.

*The original Transform node is now separated from the Shape node. While the Transform node has a hierarchical relationship to the Shape node, their attributes are not dependent on each other.*

*The Input node called makeNurbSphere is a result of the original creation of the sphere. The options set in the sphere's tool option window have been placed into a node that feeds into the Shape node. The Shape node is dependent on the Input node. If you change values in the Input node, then the shape of the sphere changes.*

*You will also see the initial shading group connected to the sphere. This is the default gray lambert that is applied to all new objects.*

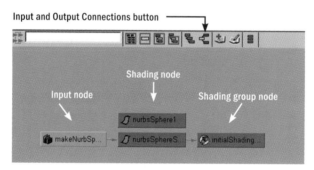

*Sphere dependencies*

## 5   Edit attributes in the Channel Box

In the Channel Box, you can edit attributes belonging to the various nodes. Every node type can be found in the Channel Box. This lets you affect both hierarchical relationships and dependencies.

If you edit an attribute belonging to the *makeNurbSphere* node, then the shape of the sphere will be affected. If you change an attribute belonging to the *nurbSphere* Transform node, then the positioning will be altered. Use the Channel Box to help you work with the nodes.

- For the Transform node, change the **Rotate Y** value to **45**.

- For the *makeNurbSphere* Input node, change the **Radius** to **3**.

**Note:** *You can set attribute values to affect either the scene hierarchy or the Dependency Graph.*

# Shading group nodes

In earlier lessons, the word *node* was used a great deal when working with shading groups. In fact, shading group nodes create dependency networks that work the same way as Shape nodes.

## 1   Create a shading network

When you create a material, it automatically has a Shading Group connected to it.

- Select **Window** → **Rendering Editors** → **Hypershade...**

- In the Hypershade window, select **Create** → **Materials** → **Phong**. Assign this material to the sphere.

- Select the sphere in the Perspective panel and click on the **Input and Output Connections** button.

*In the Hypergraph view, you will notice how the Input node is connected to the Shape node which relates to the phong shading group.*

*A line is now drawn between the sphere's Shape node and shading group node. This is because the shading group is dependent on the surface in order to render.*

*Every time you assign a shading network to an object you make a Dependency Graph connection.*

- Select the *nurbSphere1* node and the *phong1SG* node in the Hypergraph.

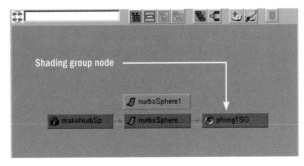

*Shading group dependencies*

- Again, click on the **Input and Output Connections** button.

*You can now see how the phong material node and the sphere's Shape node both feed the shading group. You can move your cursor over any of the connecting lines to see the attributes that are being connected.*

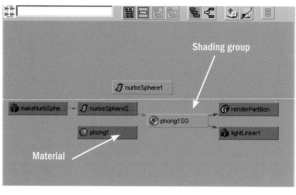

*Assigned shading group*

**Alias**   *Take the time to understand the Maya architecture. If you understand the*
**Tip:**   *Maya architecture, you will get all the power to free your creativity.*

*Patrice Paradis | Application Engineer*

## 2   Open the Attribute Editor

You have seen how the nodes in the Hypergraph and Channel Box have been used to view and edit attributes on connected nodes. Now you will see how the Attribute Editor displays nodes, attributes and connections.

- Click on the **Scene Hierarchy** button in the Hypergraph panel to go back to a scene view.

- Select the sphere's Transform node.

- Press **Ctrl+a** to open the Attribute Editor.

*In this integral window, you will see several tabs each containing groups of attributes. Each tab represents a different node. All the tabs displayed represent parts of the selected node's Dependency Graph that are related to the chosen node. By bringing up several connected nodes, you have easier access to particular parts of the graph.*

**Note:** In Maya, the Dependency Graph lets you focus on one part of
the graph at a time.

Nodes and attributes in Attribute Editor

## Making your own connections

To help you understand what a Dependency Graph connection is, you are
going to make your own connection and see how it affects the graph.

### 1 Open the Connection Editor

- Select **Window** → **General Editors** → **Connection Editor...**

- Click on the **Reload Left** button.

*The selected Transform node is loaded into the left column. All of the*
*attributes belonging to this node are listed.*

**Note:** There are more nodes here than you saw earlier in the Channel Box.
The Channel Box only shows attributes that have been set as keyable.
Other nodes can be found in the Attribute Editor.

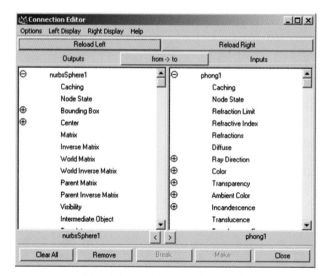

*Transform node in Connection Editor*

## 2 Add phong as the output node

- In the Hypergraph, select **Rendering** → **Show Materials**.

- Select the *phong1* material node.

- In the Connection Editor, click on the **Reload Right** button.

*Material node in Connection Editor*

## 3 Make connections

You will now connect some attributes in from the Transform node to the material node.

- In the left-hand column, scroll down until you find the *Translate* attributes.

- Click on the plus (+) sign to expand this multiple attribute and see the *Translate X, Y,* and *Z* attributes. Be sure not to click on the name.

- In the right-hand column, scroll down until you find the *Color* attribute.

- Click on the plus (+) sign to expand this multiple attribute and see the *Color R, G* and *B* attributes.

- Click on the **Translate X** attribute in the left-hand column.

- Click on the **Color R** in the right-hand column.

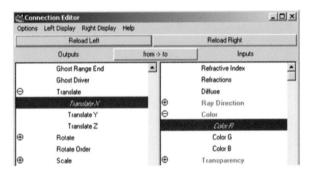

*Connected attributes*

- Use the same method to connect:

    **Translate Y** to **Color G**;

    **Translate Z** to **Color B**.

## 4 View the connections

- In the Hypergraph panel, select the *phong1* node and click on the **Input and Output Connections** button.

- Move your cursor over one of the arrow connections between the Transform node and the material node.

*The arrow is highlighted and the connected attributes are displayed. You now see the diagrammatic results of your action. You should see the effect in the Perspective view.*

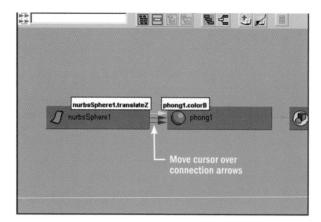

*Viewing attribute connections*

## 5   Move the sphere

- In the Perspective view, select the sphere.

- **Move** the sphere along the **X-axis**.

*The color of the sphere changes to red. By increasing the value of the translation along X, you add red to the color.*

- Try moving the sphere along each of the three main axes to see the colors change.

## Adding a texture node

While it is a fun and educational exercise to see the material node's color dependent on the position of the ball, it may not be very realistic. You will now break the existing connections and map a texture node in their place.

## 1   Delete connections

You can delete the connections in the Hypergraph view.

- In the Hypergraph view panel, select one of the three connection arrows between the Transform node and the material node.

- Press the **Backspace** or **Delete** key to delete the connection.

- Repeat for the other two connections between these nodes.

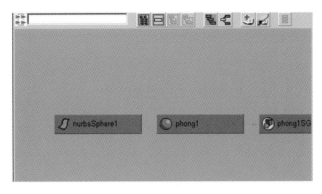

*Broken connections*

## 2    Add a checker texture map

You will now use the Attribute Editor to help add a texture to the existing shading group.

- Click on the *phong1* material node.

- Press **Ctrl+a** to open the Attribute Editor.

- Click on the **Map** button next to **Color**.

- Choose a *Checker* texture from the **Create Render Node** window.

- **MMB** in the Perspective view to make it active and press **6**.

*In the Hypergraph, you can see the dependencies building up for the shading group. The texture is built using two nodes: the checker node, which contains the procedural texture attributes, and the placement node, which contains attributes that define the placement of the texture on the assigned surfaces.*

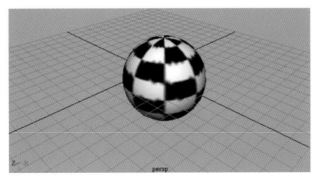

*Shading group network*

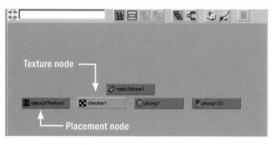

*Shading group network*

## Animating the sphere

When you animate in Maya, you are changing the value of an attribute over time. Using keys, you set these values at important points in time, then use tangent properties to determine how the attribute value changes in-between the keys.

The key and tangent information is placed in a separate animation curve node that is then connected to the animated attribute.

### 1 Select the sphere

- In the Hypergraph panel, click on the **Scene Hierarchy** button.

- Select the *nurbsSphere* Transform node.

### 2 Return the sphere to the origin

Since you earlier moved the sphere along the three axes, it's a good time to set it back to the origin.

- In the Channel Box, set the **Translate X**, **Y** and **Z** to **0, 0, 0**.

- In the Channel Box, change the **Rotate Y** attribute to **0**.

### 3 Animate the sphere's rotation

- In the Time Slider, set the playback range to **120** frames.

- In the Time Slider, go to frame **1**.

- Click on the **Rotate Y** channel name in the Channel Box.

- Click with your **RMB** and select **Key Selected** from the pop-up menu.

*This sets a key at the chosen time.*

- In the Time Slider, go to frame **120**.

- In the Channel Box, change the **Rotate Y** attribute to **720**.

- Click with your **RMB** and select **Key Selected** from the pop-up menu.

- Playback the results.

*The sphere is now spinning.*

## 4   View the dependencies

- In the Hypergraph panel, click on the **Input and Output Connections** button.

*You see that an animation curve node has been created and then connected to the Transform node. The Transform node is shown as a trapezoid to indicate that it is now connected to the animation curve node. If you move the mouse cursor over the connection arrow, you will see that the connection is to Rotate Y.*

*If you select the animation curve node and open the Attribute Editor, you will see that each key has been recorded along with value, time and tangent information. You can actually edit this information here, or use the Graph Editor where you get more visual feedback.*

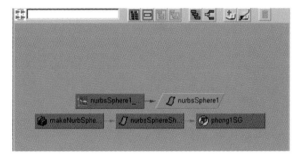

*Connected animation curve node*

## Procedural animation

If the procedural nature in Maya is defined as *nodes with attributes that are connected*, then a procedural animation would be set up by animating attributes at various levels of a Dependency Graph network.

You will now build a series of animated events that build on each other to create the final result.

## 1   Create an edit point curve

- Hide everything in your scene by selecting **Display → Hide → All**.

- Select **Create → EP Curve Tool**.

- Press and hold the **x** hotkey to turn on grid snap.
- Draw a curve as shown below:

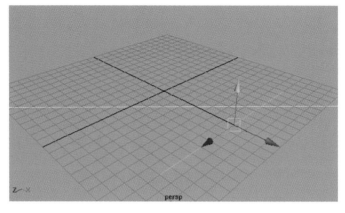

*New curve*

- When you are finished, press **Enter** to finalize the curve.
- Select **Modify** → **Center Pivot**.

**Note:** *The pivot of a new curve is centered to the origin by default.*

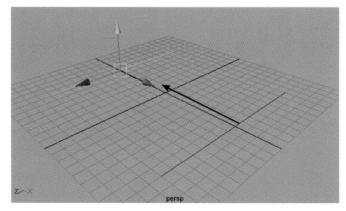

*Moved curve*

## 2    Duplicate the curve

- Select **Edit** → **Duplicate**.

- Move the new curve to the opposite side of the grid.

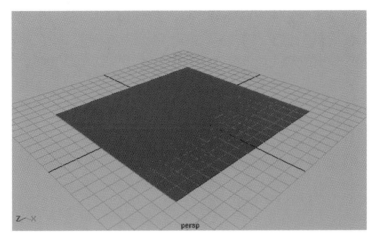

*Lofted surface*

## 3    Create a lofted surface

A lofted surface can be created using two or more profile curves.

- **Click+drag** a selection box around both of the curves.

- Select **Surfaces** → **Loft**.

## 4    Change your panel display

- In the Hypergraph panel, select **Panels** → **Perspective** → **persp**.

- In the Perspective panel, select **Show** → **None then Show** → **NURBS Curves**.

*Now you have two Perspective views. One shows the surface in shaded mode and the second shows only the curves. This makes it easier to pick and edit the curves in isolation from the surface itself.*

## 5 Edit CVs on the original curves

- Select the first curve.

- Click with your **RMB** to bring up the selection marking menu and select **Control Vertex**.

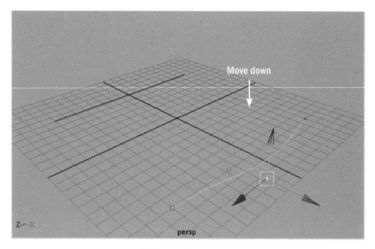

*Edited profile curve*

- **Click+drag** a selection box over one of the CVs and move it down.

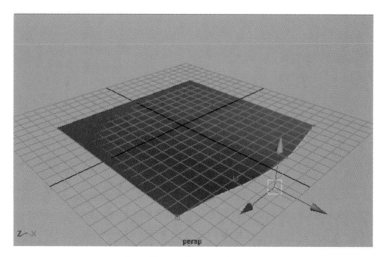

*Resulting surface update*

In the original Perspective view, you can see the effect on the lofted surface. Since the surface was dependent on the shape of the curve, you again took advantage of the Dependency Graph.

**Note:** *The dependencies associated with models are sometimes referred to as construction history. By updating the input shape, you have, in effect, updated the history of the lofted surface.*

## Creating a curve on surface

You will now build a curve directly onto the surface. This curve will become dependent on the shape of the surface for its own shape.

The surface was built as a grid of surface lines called *isoparms*. These lines help define a separate coordinate system specific to each surface. Whereas world space coordinates are defined by X, Y and Z, surface coordinates are defined by U and V.

### 1    Make the surface live

So far, you have drawn curves into the world space coordinate system. You can also make any surface in Maya into a *live* surface and draw into the UV space of the surface.

- Select the lofted surface.

*New curve on surface*

*The CVs on the curve disappear and you are able to focus on the surface.*

- Select **Modify** → **Make Live**.

*Live surface display changes to a green wireframe.*

- Select **Display** → **Grid** to turn off the ground grid.

## 2 Draw a curve on the surface

- Select **Create** → **EP Curve Tool**.

- Draw a curve on the live surface.

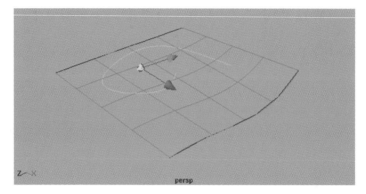

*Moving the curve on surface*

## 3 Move the curve on surface

- Press the **Enter** key to complete the curve.

- Select the **Move Tool**.

*The move manipulator looks a little different this time. Rather than three manipulator handles, there are only two. One is for the U direction of the surface and the other is for the V direction.*

- **Click+drag** on the manipulator handles to move the curve around the surface space.

**Tip:**  *This UV space is the same one used by texture maps when using 2D placement nodes.*

**Project One**

## 4    Revert live surface

- Click in empty space to clear the selection.

- Select **Modify** → **Make Not Live**.

*With nothing selected, any live surfaces are reverted back to normal surfaces.*

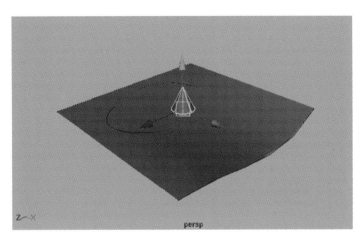

*New primitive cone*

**Tip:**    *You can also use the **Make Live** button on the right of the snap icons in the Status bar.*

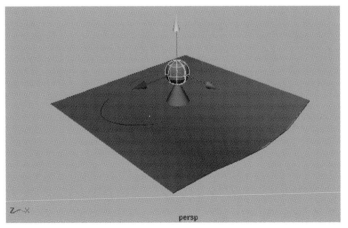

*Second primitive object*

# Create group hierarchy

You are now going to build a hierarchy by grouping two primitives, then animating the group along the curve on surface using path animation.

## 1 Create a primitive cone

- Select **Create** → **NURBS Primitives** → **Cone**.

## 2 Create a primitive sphere

- Select **Create** → **NURBS Primitives** → **Sphere**.

- Move the sphere above the cone.

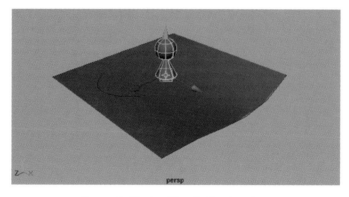

*Grouped objects with selection handle*

## 3 Group the two objects

- Select the cone and the sphere.

- Select **Edit** → **Group** or use the **Ctrl+g** hotkey.

- Select **Display** → **Component Display** → **Selection Handles**.

*The selection handle is a special marker that will make it easier to pick the group in object selection mode.*

**Note:** *Selection handles have higher selection priority than curves and surfaces.*

# Create a path animation

To animate the new group, you will attach it to the curve on surface. You can use the curve on surface to define the group's position over time.

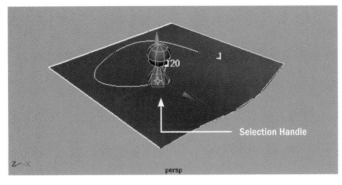

*Path animation*

## 1   Attach to the curve on surface

- With the group still selected, press the **Shift** key and select the curve on surface.

- Go to the **Animation** menu set.

- Select **Animate** → **Motion Paths** → **Attach to Motion Path** → ❑.
  In the Option window, make sure that the **Follow** option is turned **Off**.

- Click **Attach**.

- Playback the results.

*As the group moves along the path curve, you will notice that it is always standing straight up.*

## 2   Constrain to the surface normal

You will now constrain the orientation of the group to the normal direction of the lofted surface. The normal is like the third dimension of the surface's UV space.

- Click on the loft surface to select it on its own.

- Press the **Shift** key and select the grouped primitives using the selection handle.

- Select **Constrain** → **Normal** → ❑.

*In the Option window, set the following:*

    **Aim Vector** to **0**, **1**, **0**;

    **Up Vector** to **1**, **0**, **0**.

- Click **Add** to create the constraint.
- Playback the results.

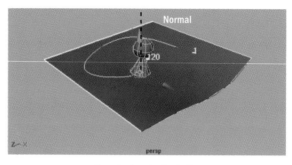

*Constrained orientation*

**Note:** *If your group is upside down, it could be because the surface normals are reversed. To fix this, select your plane and select* **Edit NURBS** → **Reverse Surface Direction**.

Now the group is orienting itself based on the normal direction of the surface. The group is dependent on the surface in two ways. Firstly, its position is dependent on the path curve, which is dependent on the surface for its shape. Secondly, its orientation is directly dependent on the surface's shape.

## Layer the animation

In Maya, the various parts of the Dependency Graph can all be animated to create exciting results. To see the Dependency Graph in motion, you will animate different nodes within the network to see how the dependencies react.

### 1 Edit the loft curve shape

Since the shape of the surface is dependent on the original loft curves, you will start by animating the shape of the second curve.

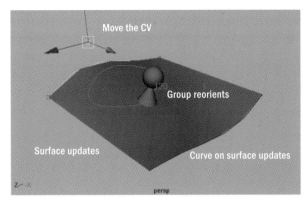

*Updating the dependencies*

- Select the second loft curve. You may want to use the second Perspective panel which is only displaying curves.

- Click with your **RMB** to bring up the selection marking menu and select **Control Vertex**.

*Control vertices define the shape of the curve. By editing these, you are editing the curve's Shape node.*

- **Click+drag** a selection box over one of the CVs and move it up to a new position.

*As you move the CV, the surface updates its shape, which in turn redefines the curve on surface and the orientation of the group. All the dependencies are being updated.*

## 2 Set keys on the CV position

- Go to frame **1** in the Time Slider.

- Press **s** to set key.

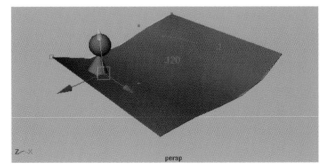

*Animated history*

- Go to frame **120** in the Time Slider.
- Press **s** to set key.
- Go to frame **60** in the Time Slider.
- Move the CV down to a new position.
- Press **s** to set key.
- Playback the results.

*You can see how the dependency updates are maintained as the CV is animated. You are animating the construction history of the lofted surface and the connected path animation.*

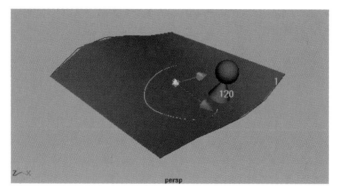

*Animated curve on surface*

## 3    Animate the curve on surface

To add another layer of animation, you will key the position of the curve on surface.

- Select the curve on surface.
- Go to frame **1** in the Time Slider.
- Press **s** to set key.
- Go to frame **120** in the Time Slider.
- Move the curve on surface to another position on the lofted surface.
- Press **s** to set key.

## 4   Assign the phong shading group

To make it easier to see the animating objects, apply the checker shading group created earlier to the primitive group.

- Select the primitive group using its selection handle.

- Go to the **Rendering** menu set.

- Select **Lighting/Shading** → **Assign Existing Material** → **phong1**.

- Playback the scene.

## 5   View the dependencies

Of course, you can view the dependency network that results from all these connections in the Hypergraph view, which will probably be a bit more complex than anything you have seen so far.

- Select the primitive group that is attached to the motion path.

- Open the Hypergraph panel and click on the **Input and Output Connections** button.

*The resulting network contains the various dependencies that you built during this example.*

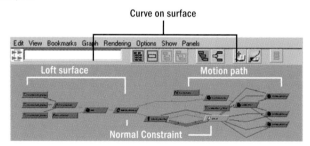

*The dependency network*

# Conclusion

The procedural qualities in Maya are tied to how the Dependency Graph uses nodes, attributes and connections. You can see how deep these connections can go and how they are maintained throughout the animation process. Similar techniques can be used on other node types throughout Maya.

Obviously, you don't have to use the Hypergraph and the Connection Editor to build, animate and texture map your objects. In most cases, you will be thinking more about the motion of your character's walk or the color of their cheeks. In this way, it is a good idea to know that the Dependency Graph supports everything you do and can always be used to your advantage.

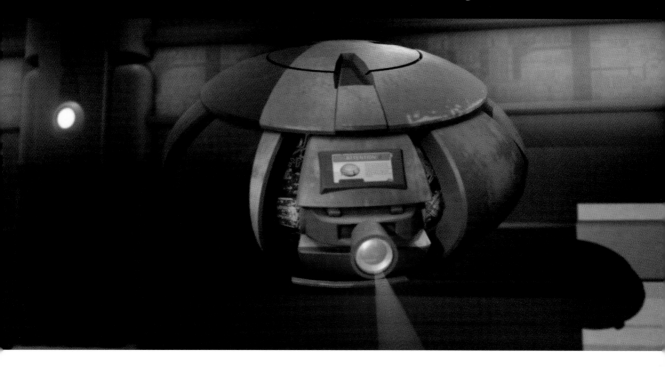

# Project Two

## Lessons

In this project, you will animate and crash a flying orb. You will begin by modeling the robot using several polygonal modeling tools. Once that is done, you will texture and test-render the orb. Finally, you will set up the robot to be animated.

To animate the scene, you will use a motion path and keyframes, mixed with some dynamic simulation toward the end. Deformations will also be used to add subtle details to the scene.

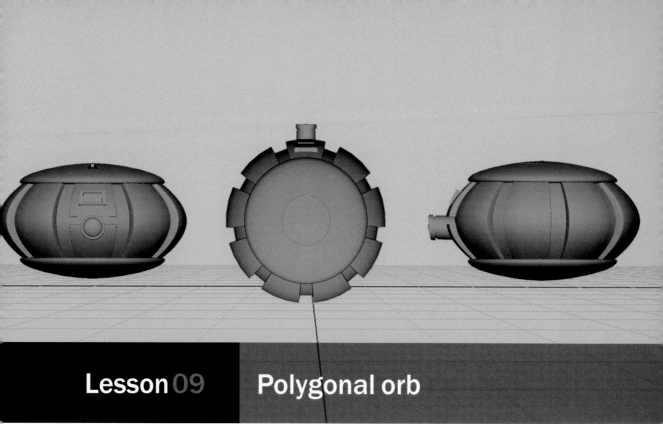

# Lesson 09    Polygonal orb

*In this lesson, you will build a polygonal orb. The robot will be created from primitives, starting with a polygonal cylinder for the body. You will use many polygonal tools and deformers until the desired shape is achieved. You will be able to edit the construction history of the modeling actions to update the model and edit the results throughout the lesson.*

## In this lesson you will learn the following:

- How to model using polygons;

- How to use a squash nonlinear deformer;

- How to select contiguous edges;

- How to bevel polygonal edges;

- How to manually change edge normals;

- How to revolve a profile curve;

- How to work with procedural modeling attributes;

- How to use a lattice deformer;

- How to delete history when needed.

# Set up your project

Since this is a new project, you must set a new directory as your current project directory. This will let you separate the files generated in this lesson from other lessons. If you have trouble working through this lesson, you can refer to the scene *09-polyOrb.ma* for reference.

## 1   Set the project

As you have already learned, it is easier to manage your files if you set a project directory that contains subdirectories for different types of files that relate to your project.

- Go to the **File** menu and select **Project** → **Set...**

*A window opens pointing you to the Maya projects directory.*

- Open the folder named *support_files*.

- Click on the folder named *project2* to select it.

- Click on the **OK** button.

*This sets the support_files directory as your current project.*

## 2   Make a new scene

- Select **File** → **New Scene**.

## 3   Restore all UI settings

Before beginning this lesson, you should restore all UI settings.

- Select **Display** → **UI Elements** → **Restore UI Elements**.

## 4   Set up the modeling panels

- In the view panel menu bar, select **Panels** → **Saved Layouts** → **Edit Layouts...**

- In the **Panels** window, open the **Edit Layouts** tab.

- Set the **Configuration** to **4 Panes Split Left**.

- Set the large panel to the Perspective view with the top, front and side view panels along the side.

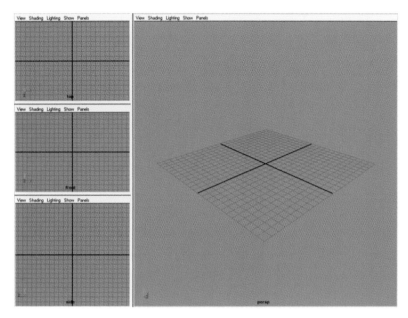

*Recommended layout for this tutorial section*

## Starting the orb

Build the orb starting with a polygonal cylinder. The facets will then be extruded to create a more complex shape.

### 1    Create a primitive cylinder

- Select **Create** → **Polygon Primitives** → **Cylinder**.

- Press **5** to **Smooth Shade All**.

- Rename the surface to *body*.

- Edit the *polyCylinder*'s construction history as follows:

    **Subdivisions Axis** to **36**;

    **Subdivisions Height** to **20**;

    **Subdivisions Cap** to **0**.

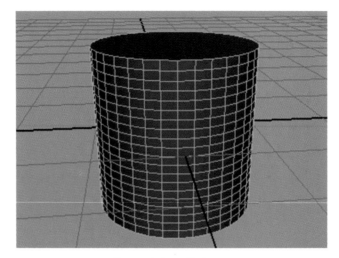

*Base polygon cylinder*

## 2   Main frame selection

- With the *body* selected, press **F11** to go into Component mode to display the faces.

- From the top view, select every three faces with the selection box as shown to the right.

*Selecting in the top view will select the entire column of facets.*

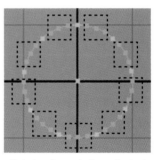

*Polygon faces to be selected*

> **Tip:**   While selecting, remember to use **Shift** to toggle the new selection, **Ctrl** to deselect and **Ctrl+Shift** to add the new selection.

- In the side view, hold **Ctrl** and deselect the six faces intended for the front camera of the orb.

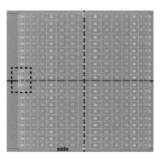

*Polygon facet to be deselected*

Project Two

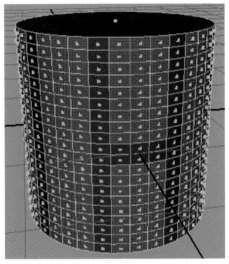

*Current selection*

**Note:** *During the process of modeling the orb, make sure that you do not accidentally select, deselect or modify facets that are on the opposite side of the object. If you do, use Ctrl to deselect unwanted components.*

## 3   Extrude faces

Before extruding the faces, you will make sure that the **Keep Faces Together** option is enabled. When this option is on, it extrudes chunks of facets instead of each facet individually. Following is an example of **Keep Faces Together** both on and off:

- Turn on **Polygons** → **Tool Options** → **Keep Faces Together** if it is not on already.

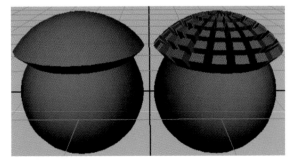

*Keep New Faces Together both on and off*

- Select **Edit Polygons** → **Extrude Face**.

*A manipulator appears that gives you access to simultaneous translation, rotation and scaling.*

- **Click+drag** on the blue translation handle to extrude new faces.

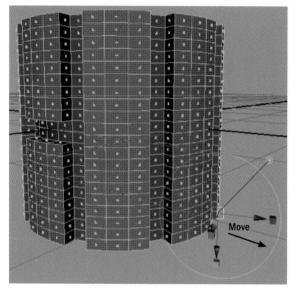

*Extruded facets*

**Note:** *When you manipulate the handle associated with one face, the other face reacts equally. Extrusions work according to the normals of the original faces. Normals are lines perpendicular to the surface. To view polygon surface normals, select* **Display** → **Polygon Components** → **Normals**.

## 4   Squash deformer

- Press **F8** to go into Object mode.
- From the **Animation** menu set, select **Deform** → **Create Nonlinear** → **Squash**.

*A nonlinear deformer handle appears inside the body geometry.*

- In the Channel Box, highlight the *squash1* input construction history.

*All the attributes for controlling the deformer are listed there.*

- Set the *squash1*'s **Factor** attribute to **-0.5**.

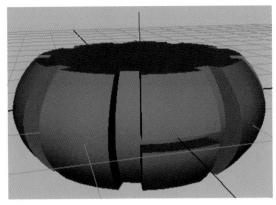

*The squashed geometry*

## 5   Editing the history

You are almost done with the basic frame of the orb, but before you go on, you need to edit the history for the extrusion.

- Select the *body*.

- In the Input section of the Channel Box, highlight the *polyExtrudeFace* history node.

- Set the **Local Translate Z** attribute to **0.1**.

*Doing so will modify the extrusion done earlier. The construction history is still available for you to modify.*

## Bevel the hard edges

The edges of the extrusion on the frame of the orb look very hard at the moment. Hard edges mean that you can clearly see a crisp line between two polygon faces. By doing a bevel on those edges, you will reinforce the metal aspect of the geometry.

*Example of soft and hard edges*

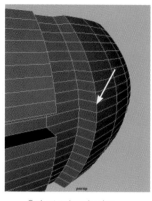
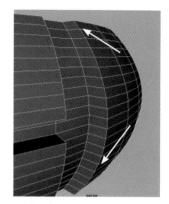

Select a hard edge                    Contiguous edges selected

## 1  Select contiguous edges

- With the *body* selected, press **F10** to go in Component mode to display the polygon edges.

- **LMB+click** any of the hard edges to select it.

- In the Modeling menu set, select **Edit Polygons** → **Selection** → **Select Contiguous Edges**.

*Doing this will select all contiguous edges, which are essentially adjacent or bordering edges.*

- To speed up the selection of hard edges, **Shift-select** one edge per hard extruded edge.

- Execute **Edit Polygons** → **Selection** → **Select Contiguous Edges** to select the contiguous edges all at once.

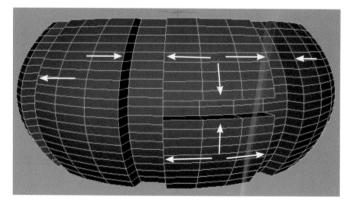

*All contiguous edges selected*

## 2    Bevel the edges

- With the edges from the previous step still selected, select **Edit Polygons** → **Bevel**.

*The selected hard edges now have a nice bevel with history attached.*

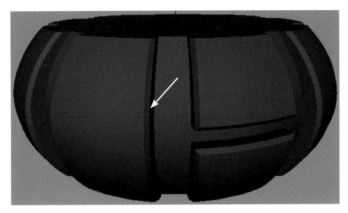

*The bevelled body*

- Adjust the bevels by highlighting the *polyBevel* history node in the Channel Box, as follows:

> **Offset** to **0.2**;
>
> **Segments** to **2**.

*These settings will narrow the bevels and smooth them nicely.*

## 3    Delete history

Once a piece of geometry is final and no longer needs all of its construction history, you can dispose of the history input nodes with a single command.

- Press **F8** to go back in Object mode.

- With the geometry selected, select **Edit** → **Delete by Type** → **History**.

*Notice that all the input nodes are gone from the Channel Box.*

---

**Tip:**    *You could delete all the history for the entire scene by selecting* **Edit** → **Delete All by Type** → **History**. *Be careful; sometimes you want to keep certain history nodes, such as binding or deformers.*

# Top and bottom caps

You will now create the top and bottom caps of the orb by revolving a profile curve around the Y-axis. To do so, you will first draw a profile curve, and then revolve it specifying polygonal quads as the output of the operation. You will then be able to modify the newly created polygonal surface to complete the caps.

## 1  Draw the profile curve

- Select **Create** → **EP Curve Tool**.

- Frame the orb in the front view.

- Hold down **x** to open **Snap to Grid** and **LMB+click** to draw the first curve point centered on the Y-axis.

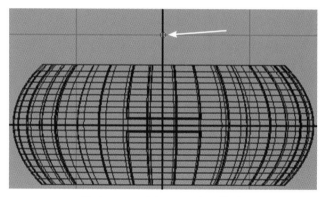

*First curve point snapped on Y-axis*

- Release **x**, then draw the remaining curve points as follows:

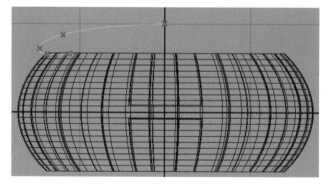

*The completed curve*

- Hit **Enter** to complete the curve.

## 2   Revolve

- With the curve selected, choose **Surfaces** → **Revolve** → ❐.

- Set the revolve options as follows:

    **Output Geometry** to **Polygons**;

    **Type** to **Quads**.

- Click the **Revolve** button to execute the action.

- Rename the surface to *topCap*.

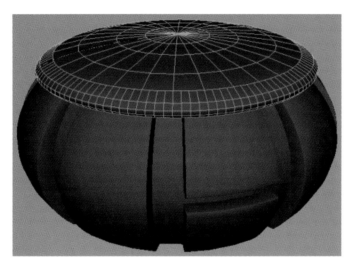

*The top cap*

**Tip:**   *Since the revolvedSurface still has history attached, you can continue to tweak the profile curve's components to change the shape of the geometry.*

## 3   Duplicate the geometry

- With the *cap* selected, press **Ctrl+d** to duplicate it.

- In the Channel Box, set **Scale Y** to **-1**.

*This will mirror the geometry on the Y-axis, thus creating the bottom cap.*

- Rename the surface *bottomCap*.

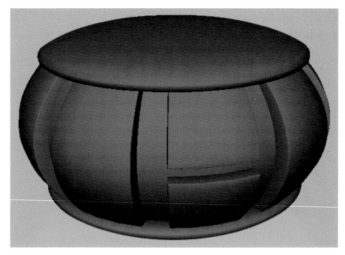

*The orb with a top and bottom cap*

## Adding details

At this point, you might be thinking that this will be a very simplistic looking orb. You will now add details that will greatly improve the look of the orb.

### 1    Tweaking the top cap

- Select the top *cap*.

- Press **F11** to display its faces.

- Select the following two faces:

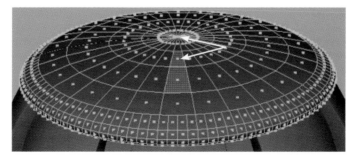

*Face to select on the top cap*

- **Extrude** the faces and push them down.

## 2   Making a groove

- Press **F10** to enable the edges selection mask.

- Using **Select Contiguous Edges**, select the center ring of edges on the *topCap*.

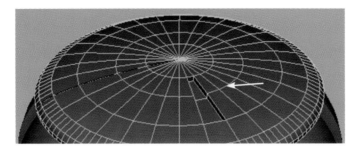

*Face to select on the top cap*

- Select **Edit Polygons** → **Bevel**, and change the **Segments** attribute to **2** in the *polyBevel* history node.

- Use **Select Contiguous Edges** once again to select the ring of edges between the new bevel.

- Move the edges down as follows:

*The new groove*

**Note:** Notice how the topCap shading seems to change as you move the edges to create the groove. This is due to the normals orientation change.

## 3   Change edge normals by hand

- Select the three rings of edges used for the groove.

- Select **Edit Polygons** → **Normals** → **Soften/Harden** → ❑.

*The* **Soften/Harden** *window pops up.*

- Click on the **All Hard** button to change the **Angle** to **0**.
- Click the **Soft/Hard** button to apply and close the window.

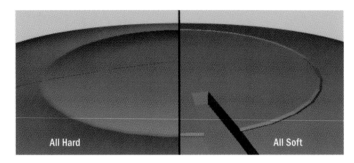

*Difference between soft and hard groove*

## 4    Finishing the details

Using what you have learned up to this point in this lesson, add the remaining details on the orb. Starting from a polygonal cube, make a small display area, and then make a camera lens from a polygonal cylinder and sphere.

## Adjusting proportions

Sometimes when modeling, you sit back and look at your work thinking you could improve the proportions of the model. An easy way to change the proportions of a model is to create and modify a lattice box deformer. A lattice surrounds a deformable object with a structure of points that can be manipulated to change the object's shape. Once you are happy with the new proportions, you can simply delete the history, thus freezing the deformations on the models.

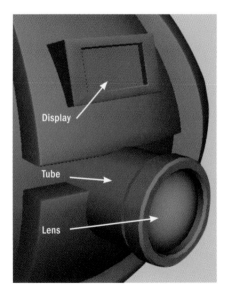

## 1   Create a lattice box

- Select all the orb's geometry and go to the Animation menu set

- Select **Deform** → **Create Lattice**.

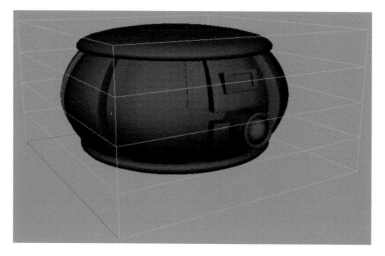

*The surrounding lattice deformer*

- In the Channel Box, change the *ffd1LatticeShape* to the following:

    **S Divisions** to **3**;

    **T Divisions** to **3**;

    **U Divisions** to **3**.

*Doing so will change the amount of subdivisions in the lattice deformer, which in turn adds more lattice points to deform the surface with. This will allow more control over the deformations.*

## 2   Deform the lattice box

- **RMB** on the lattice object in the viewport to bring up the lattice context menu and select **Lattice Point**.

- In the front view, select all the lattice points along the top and **Shift-select** all the ones along the bottom.

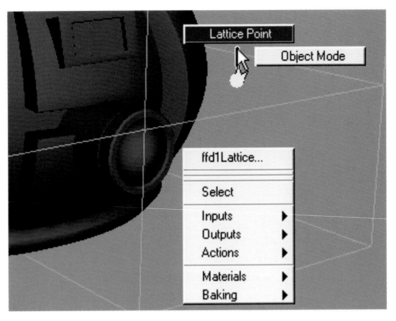

*The lattice menu*

- In the top view, press **Ctrl** to deselect the lattice points in the middle of the orb.

- Using the **Scale Tool**, hold **Ctrl** and then **LMB** scale down on the **Y-axis**. This will proportionate scale on the X and Z-axes.

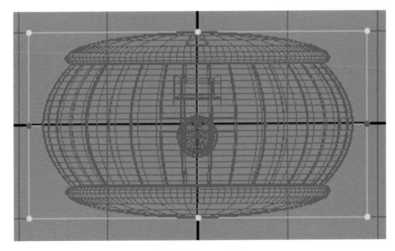

*Select those points*

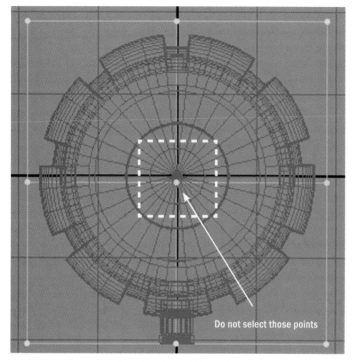

Do not select those points

*Deselect the middle points*

## 3    Lattice influence

Right now, the lattice box deforms the orb using only one section defined by
the lattice points. This means that if a geometry vertex is in a section of the
lattice, none of the surrounding sections will affect it. If you want a smoother
deformation across the lattice, you need to increase the lattice influences.

- In the Channel Box, highlight the *ffd1* output node.

- Change the following attributes:

    **Local Influence S** to **3**;

    **Local Influence T** to **3**;

    **Local Influence U** to **3**;

- Continue tweaking the lattice until you are happy with the
resulting proportions.

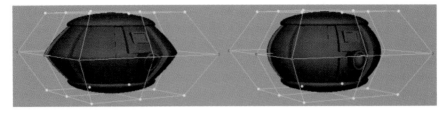

*The difference between the ffd1 influences*

## 4  Delete history

- Select all the orb geometry.

- Select **Edit** → **Delete by Type** → **History**.

*The lattice box is now gone and the geometry maintained its correct proportions.*

**Note:** *If you delete the lattice box, the geometry it was influencing will pop to its undeformed state.*

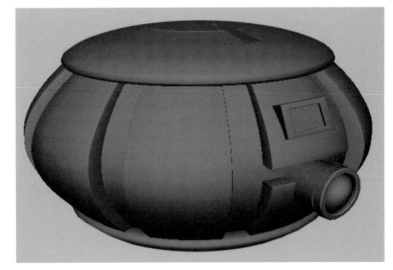

*The final orb geometry*

Project Two

## 5    Save the file

- Select **File** → **Save Scene As...**

- Save the file as *09-polyOrb.ma*.


# Conclusion

In this lesson, you learned how to model a complete orb robot out of basic polygonal primitives. In the process, you used polygon modeling tools to create the shape and details. Each tool created an input node that you were able to edit later to change the construction history of the orb. You also used the squash nonlinear deformer and the lattice deformer.

In the next lesson, you will texture and test render the orb. This will allow you to experiment with polygonal texture tools and new rendering techniques.

# Lesson 10

# Texturing the orb

*You now have a polygonal mesh that requires texturing. Even though polygons have a default setting for UV parameters onto which textures can be applied, you will need to adjust these settings for each specific application. You can use special polygon tools to assign and modify these kinds of values on the orb.*

*You will first apply texture projections in order to create UV coordinates on the polymesh. Then you will texture map the orb using a series of texture maps imported as file textures.*

## In this lesson you will learn the following:

- How to project textures on polygons;

- How to manipulate projections;

- How to use the Texture Editor;

- How to use the Paint Selection Tool;

- How to manipulate UVs;

- How to animate a texture.

# Planar mapping

The orb will be textured using multiple shading groups and texture maps. You will start by texturing the top and bottom caps at the same time. The method of positioning the texture on the surface will be accomplished using useful polygon texturing tools. Feel free to continue using your own file or start with *09-polyOrb.ma*.

## 1 Create and assign a new shader

- Open the Hypershade window.

- Create a *Blinn* material node.

Blinn *is the material that looks the most like metal.*

- Assign the *Blinn* material to both the *topCap* and the *bottomCap* objects.

- Rename the material node to *metalBlinn*.

- Turn on hardware texturing in your view panel(s) for the upcoming steps.

## 2 Map an image file to the color

- Open the Attribute Editor for the *metalBlinn* node.

- Map the **Color** attribute with a **File** texture node. Make sure that the **Normal** option is selected at the top of the Create Render Node window.

- Rename the *file1* node *metalFile.*

- Click on the **Folder Icon** button next to **Image Name.**

- In the *sourceimages* directory of the *project2* project, locate the *metal.tif* image file.

- Click **Open.**

*The texture has been placed on the polymesh surface using the default UV mapping inherited from the original revolved surface.*

*Bitmap file to be used as color texture map*

*Applied texture using default UVs*

Notice the pinching of the texture at the center of the cap. That pinch is due
to the points of the revolved surface that meet at that location. Also notice
the hash lines at the groove location. This is a visual cue to show that no UVs
were created by the Bevel Tool.

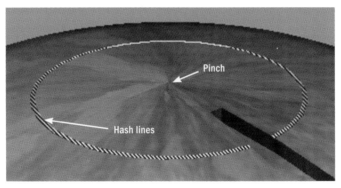

*Incorrect UVs*

## 3   Planar mapping

You will be using the polygon planar projection method to create correct UV
coordinates on the orb's caps.

- Select the *topCap* and *bottomCap*.

- Select **Polygon UVs** → **Planar Mapping** → ❑.

- Enable the **Fit to Bounding Box** option and enable the **Y-axis** option, which
  tells Maya to do the UV projection along the world Y-axis.

- Click the **Project** button.

*A large projection plane icon surrounding both objects appears, which projects the texture map along the Y-axis. You can see the texture mapped onto the surface with hardware texturing.*

*Projection plane manipulator and texture*

## 4 Projection manipulators

The projection manipulator allows you to transform the projection to better suit your geometry.

You can toggle the manipulator type for a conventional all-in-one manipulator by **LMB+clicking** on the *red T*.

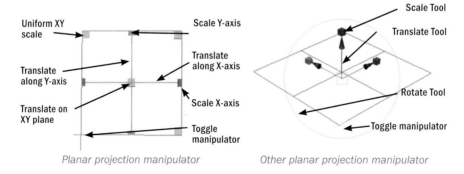

*Planar projection manipulator*          *Other planar projection manipulator*

**Note:** *If the projection manipulator disappears, reselect the geometry, click on the polyPlanProj input node in the Channel Box, and select the Show Manipulator Tool or press the* **t** *hotkey.*

## 5    Open the Texture Editor

- Select **Window** → **UV Texture Editor...**

*The window opens displaying the mapped UVs of the cap geometry, shown from the view of the texture projection.*

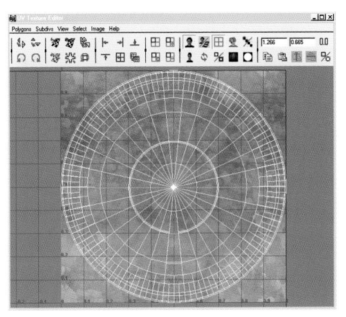

*UV Texture Editor*

**Note:** *The view of the object and the loaded texture are both initially displayed in the Texture Editor with a square proportion – regardless of the proportion of the planar projection positioned in the 3D space of the model and the proportion of the texture image file.*

## Spherical mapping

The body geometry of the orb will be textured using a spherical projection. A spherical projection works just like the planar projection, except that the texture is wrapped around your model on a sphere, like a wrapper on a candy.

## 1  Apply a spherical projection

- Assign the *metalBlinn* material to the *body*.

- With the *body* mesh selected, select **Polygon UVs** → **Spherical Mapping**.

*A large spherical manipulator is positioned around the selected geometry, defining the way the texture is wrapped around the object.*

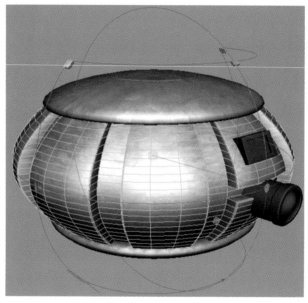

*Spherical projection*

## 2  Tweak the spherical projection

By default, the texture does not cover the entire projection sphere. For the entire sphere to be covered, the texture is tiled and repeated. In this case, you want the texture to completely wrap the object.

- **Click+drag** the **red** manipulator handle all the way to the back of the sphere until the projection joins together.

## 3  Cover the projection sphere

- **Click+drag** the **green** manipulator handle and move it all the way up to completely cover the projection sphere.

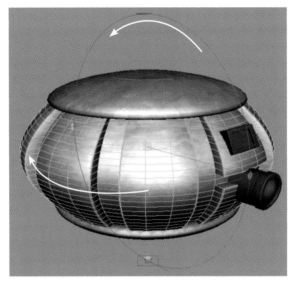

*Full spherical projection*

**Note:** *Keep the Texture Editor open to see the effect of the placement on the geometry as you move the manipulators.*

## 4    Relaxing UVs

When using projections, you often get texture stretching on faces perpendicular to the projection's direction. The following is a polygonal texture operation that can help solve that problem:

- With *body* selected, select **Edit Polygons** → **Selection** → **Convert Selection to Faces**.

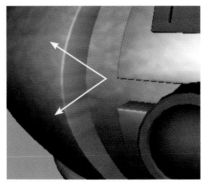

*This will take your currently selected components and covert them into face components.*

- Select **Polygon UVs** → **Relax UVs**.

*UVs relaxed*

> **Note:** *Notice the relax operation's result in the UV Texture Editor.*

## 5 Create a new shader

- Create another *Blinn* material node and rename it *circuitsBlinn*.

- Map the **Color** attribute with a **File** texture node.

- Rename the *file1* node *circuitsFile*.

- Click on the **Folder Icon** button and select the circuits.*tif* image file from the textures folder.

## 6 Using the Paint Selection Tool

In order to select faces to assign the new circuit's shader, you will use the Paint Selection Tool. This tool allows you to select components on an object by simply painting on the surface.

- With the *body* selected, press **F11** to display the polygonal faces.

- Select **Edit** → **Paint Selection Tool** → ❐.

*The tool's window appears.*

- Set the brush **Radius(U)** to **0.05**.

**Tip:** *Hold* **b** *while* **click+dragging** *in the viewport to dynamically change the brush size.*

*Paint select the grooves on the body*

- Paint on the grooves of the *body* geometry to prepare the selection for the *circuitsBlinn* material.

**Tip:** *If you select unwanted faces by mistake, you can change the* **Paint Operation** *in the Paint Selection window to* **Unselect** *or hold down* **Ctrl**, *just like selecting components.*

- Once all the faces are selected, assign the *circuitsBlinn* to the selection.

## 7  Using another spherical projection

The faces you just assigned with *circuitsBlinn* don't need to be relaxed as in the previous step. You can use another spherical projection to correct this, but this time only on the selected components.

- Still with the groove faces of *body* selected, select **Polygon UVs** → **Spherical Mapping**.
- Use the spherical manipulator to place the texture correctly on the surface.

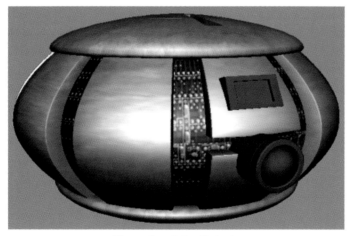

*The assigned circuit shader*

**Note:** *Note that the two spherical projections are still accessible in the construction history through the Channel Box. To make any refinements to the texture positioning, select the polySphProj input node and the Show Manipulators Tool.*

# Finish mapping the orb

Now that the main frame of the orb is textured, the remaining objects can be textured using cylindrical mapping and automatic mapping. Cylindrical projection works just like the planar and spherical projections, but the texture is wrapped around a cylinder. Automatic projection will let Maya decide how to texture an object from multiple planar projections. For example, Maya will use six planar projections (top, bottom, left, right, front and back), to generate a UV map on an object.

## 1   Make a darker metal shader

- Select the *metalBlinn* shader.

- In the Hypershade, select **Edit** → **Duplicate** → **Shading Network**.

- Select the duplicated *metalBlinn1*.

- In the Attribute Editor, click on the mapping arrow at the right of the **Color** attribute to follow the connection to the *metalFile1* texture.

- In the **Color Balance** section, set the **Color Gain** slider to gray.

*Doing so will darken the metal file texture.*

- Assign the new darker shader to the *tube* and the *display* objects.

- Create a new red *Phong* material and assign it to the *lens* object.

*The darker shader*

## 2   Cylindrical mapping

- With the *tube* selected, select **Polygon UVs** → **Cylindrical Mapping**.

- Set the projection as follows:

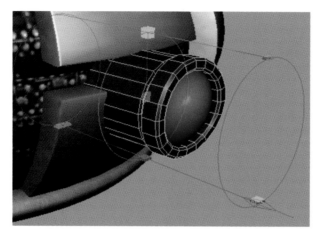

*Cylindrical projection*

**Tip:**   *Use the red T on the manipulator to toggle manipulator types and gain access to the Rotate Tool.*

## 3   Automatic mapping

- Select the *display* object.

- Select **Polygon UVs** → **Automatic Mapping** → ❒.

*The automatic mapping options are displayed.*

- Set the options as follows:

  > **Planes** to **6**;
  >
  > **Optimize** to **Fewer Pieces**;
  >
  > **Layout** to **Into Square**;
  >
  > **Scale** to **Uniform**.

*This specifies that you want to project with six planes (like a cube), and have Maya make as few pieces as possible.*

- Open the UV Texture Editor to see the results of the automatic mapping.

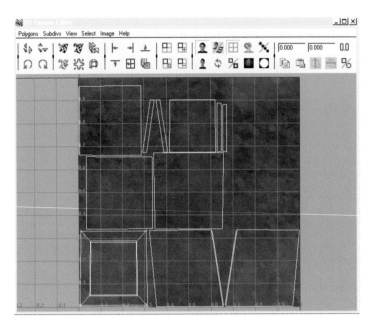

*Result of the automatic mapping action*

# Animated texture

The only thing left to do on the orb is to set up an animated texture on the center face of the *display* object. To do so, you will first tweak the UVs of that single face to place them into a square to cover the entire texture area. Once that is done, you will be able to set up an animated texture using the support files.

## 1   Tweaking UVs

The center face of the *display* object should have its UVs in a perfect square so that you can use an animated texture on it. There are two simple ways to achieve this. In this step, you will do it manually, using the UV Texture Editor and the **Snap to Grid** option.

- Select the center face of the *display* object.

- In the UV Texture Editor, **RMB** and select **UV** from the marking menu.

*This enables the UV selection mask.*

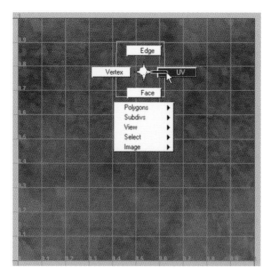

*Selecting UVs in the Texture Editor*

- **Click+drag** a selection box over the selected face to select its UVs components.

*You should now see the four UV components that you need to snap to each corner of the grid.*

- Select each UV, then hold **x** to turn on Snap to Grid and translate them to their respective corners.

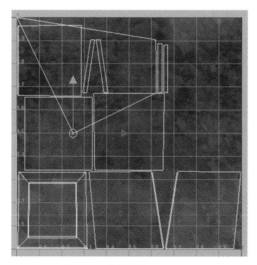

*Snap each UV into a square*

## 2 Unitize UVs

Another easy way is to use the Unitize UVs operation, which will reset the selected UVs into a perfect square.

- Select the center face of the *display* object.
- Select **Polygon UVs** → **Unitize UVs**.

**Note:** *If the entire object is selected instead of only a single face, every polygon will be reset into a square.*

## 3 Create a new shader

- Create a *newLambert* material and assign it to the *display*'s center face.
- Rename the lambert *animTxtLambert*.
- Map a **File** texture to the **Color** attribute of *animTxtLambert*.
- Rename the File texture *animTxtFile*.
- Browse for the *text.tif* texture file.

*The texture to be animated*

## 4 Animate the texture

- Select the *place2DTexture* node for the *animTxtFile* you have just created.
- Go to frame **1** in the Time Slider.
- **LMB+click** in the second **Offset** field (Offset V) in the Attribute Editor, and select **Set Key**.

*This will set a keyframe for the V parameter of the Offset attribute.*

- Go to frame **10** in the Time Slider.
- Set the same **Offset** attribute to **-1**.
- **LMB+click** and **Set Key** again.

- In the Graph Editor, select the curve and set **Pre Infinity** and **Post Infinity** to **Linear**.

*This will ensure the texture plays constantly throughout the animation.*

- Playback your scene to see the texture being animated.

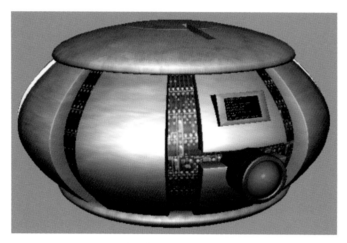

*The final textured orb*

## 5   Save your work

- Save this file as *10-texturedOrb.ma*.

## Conclusion

You now have a good understanding of texturing polygons in Maya. You have experimented with all the projection types and several other essential tools and actions.

In the next lesson, you will refine the model's shading groups using the Interactive Photorealistic Rendering (IPR) and other rendering tools.

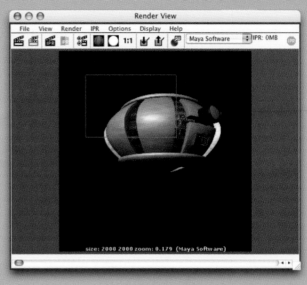

# Rendering features

In this lesson, you will set up materials and textures for the orb. You will explore the makeup of a typical shading network, including its material node and any texture maps.

This lesson will make extensive use of the Interactive Photorealistic Renderer (IPR) found in Maya. This tool allows you to create a rendering of the scene that can then be used to interactively update changes to the scene's lighting and texturing. You will see how fast and intuitive it is to texture in Maya using IPR.

**In this lesson you will learn the following:**

- How to render a region;

- How to display snapshots;

- How to open and save your rendered images;

- How to display an image's alpha channel;

- How to set up the IPR;

- How to make connections in the Hypershade;

- How to enable High Quality Rendering in a viewport.

# Render View features

You are now ready to test render the orb. In this section, you will experiment with the Render View features, such as snapshots, image storage and region rendering. You can continue with the file you were using previously, or open *11-texturedOrb.ma*.

## 1   Panel set up

- In the Perspective view, select **Panels** → **Saved Layouts** → **Hypershade/ Render/Persp**.

- **RMB+click** in the Render View and select **Render** → **Render** → **Persp**.

> **Note:** *You can change the size of the panels by* **click+dragging** *on their separators.*

## 2   Keep and remove image

When test rendering a scene, it is good to be able to keep previously rendered images for comparison with the changes you implement.

- To keep the current render for reference, select **File** → **Keep Image in Render View** or click the **Keep Image** button.

*Notice a slider bar appears at the bottom of the Render View.*

- In the Hypershade, **MMB-drag** the *animTxtLambert* shader into the Work Area and graph its connections.

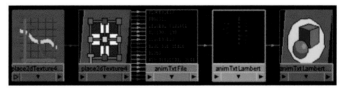

*The animTxt shading group*

- **MMB+drag** the *animTxtFile* over the *animTxtLambert* material.

- Choose **Incandescence** from the context menu to map the file in the incandescence of the material.

*This will reuse that same texture file but for incandescence. Incandescence will give the illusion that the numbers of the texture are glowing.*

- In the Render View, render the model again.

- Once the rendering is done, scroll the image bar at the bottom of the Render View to compare the previous render results.

- Scroll the image bar to the right (the older image), and select **File** →
**Remove Image from Render View** or click the **Remove Image** button.

*This will remove the currently displayed image stored earlier.*

**Note:** *You can keep as many images as you want in the Render View. The images will be kept even if you close and reopen the Render View window.*

## 3  Region rendering

You might think it is a waste of time to render the entire image again just for the small portion of the image that changed. With the Render View, you can render only a region of the current image.

- Select a region of the current image by **click+dragging** a square straight on the rendered image.

*Select a region of the rendered image*

- Click on the **Render Region** button to render the selected region.

- To automatically render a selected region, enable the **Options** → **Auto Render Region**.

*With this option, every time you select a region on the rendered image, Maya will automatically render it.*

## 4  Snapshots

If your scene is long to render, you might not want to wait for a complete render before selecting a region to render. The Render View allows you to take a wireframe snapshot of the image to render so that you can easily select the region you want.

- **RMB** in the Render View and select **Render** → **Snapshot** → **Perps.**

*A wireframe image is placed in the Render View for reference.*

- Select the region you would like to render.

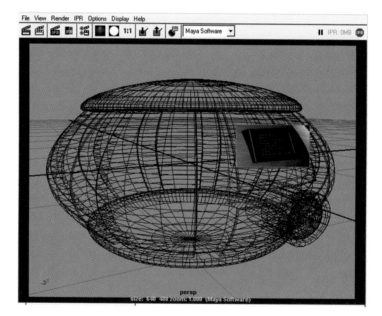

*A snapshot in the Render View*

## 5  Open and save images

You can open renders or reference images directly in the Render View.

- To open a reference image, select **File** → **Open Image**.
- Browse to the reference image *orbReference.tif* located in the *images* folder of the current project.

You can also save your renders to disk from the Render View.

▪ To save your current Render View image, select **File** → **Save Image**.

## 6    Display the alpha channel

When rendering, you often want to display the image's alpha channel to see if it will composite well onto another image.

▪ Once you have rendered your scene, click on the **Display Alpha Channel** button located at the top of the Render View.

▪ To go back to the colored images, click on the **Display RGB Channels** in the Render View.

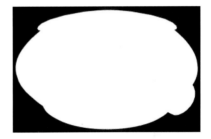

*The orb's alpha channel*

# IPR

To give you access to interactive updating capabilities, you will set up an IPR rendering. An IPR rendering creates a special image file that stores not only the pixel information about an image but also data about the surface normals, materials and objects associated with each of these pixels. This information is then updated as you make changes to your scene's shading.

## 1   IPR set up

- From the Render View panel, click on the **Render Globals** button.

- Click on the **Maya Software** tab.

- From the **Anti-aliasing Quality** section, set **Quality** to **Production Quality**.

*For IPR, you can use the best settings if desired. Your initial IPR rendering will be slower but the interactive updates will still be fast.*

- Close the Render Globals window.

## 2   IPR render

- From your Render View panel, select **IPR** → **IPR Render** → **persp**.

*Now what seems to be a regular rendering of the scene appears. Notice the message at the bottom of the Render View saying "Select a region to begin tuning".*

- Click+drag to select an area of the IPR rendering that will cover the entire orb. This is the area that will be updated as you make changes.

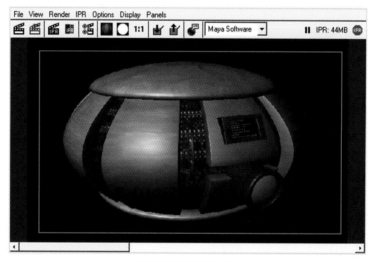

*Initial IPR rendering*

**Note:** *You can still change the region by click+dragging again in the Render View.*

## 3 Tweak your materials

- In your Hypershade panel, graph the *metalBlinn* shader group.

- Drag the *metalFile* onto the *metalBlinn* material and drop it in the **specularColor** attribute.

- Drag the *metalFile* onto the *metalBlinn* material and drop it in the **bump map** attribute.

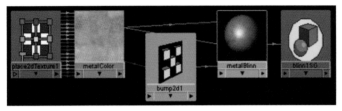

*The updated shading group*

*Notice how the IPR updates every time you bring a change to the shading group.*

- Select the *bump2D* node and change the **Bump Depth** to **0.1**.

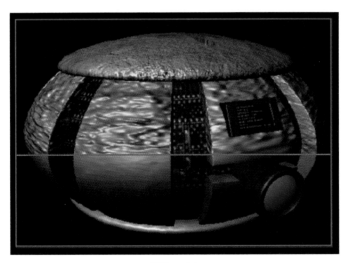

*IPR update*

- Graph the *circuitsBlinn* shader in the Hypershade and map the *circuitsFile* into the **bump map** attribute for this material as well.

**Note:** *To clear the Hypershade Work Area, click on the* **Eraser** *button.*

## 4 Drag and drop feature

- Create a new Phong material.

- With your **MMB**, drag the new Phong in the Render View and drop it on the *tube*.

*Dropping a material directly in the IPR has the same effect as dropping it on a model in a viewport.*

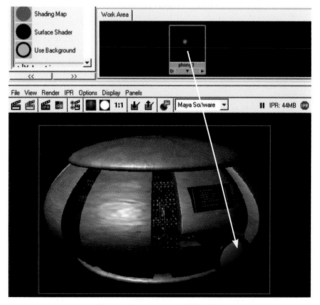

*Dropping a material in IPR*

## 5 IPR and the Attribute Editor

- Open the Attribute Editor.

- Click on an object in the IPR image and see the Attribute Editor update to show its shader.

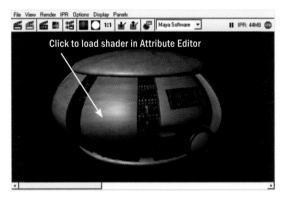

*Initial IPR rendering*

## 6 Refresh the IPR image

When you have models outside the IPR region, you can refresh the entire image without losing your selected region.

- To refresh the entire image, click on the **Refresh the IPR Image** button.

*The entire image gets redrawn and your original region is maintained.*

## 7 IPR lighting

You can also use the IPR window to explore different lighting scenarios. By default when you don't have any lights in your scene, the IPR creates a directional light for you. Changing the light direction will cause the IPR to redraw accordingly.

- Using the Outliner, select the *defaultLight* node.

- In the Perspective view, rotate the light to see the IPR update with the new lighting.

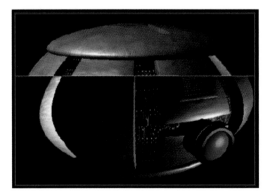

*New lighting direction in IPR*

**Note:** *You can also change the light color and intensity interactively.*

## 8    IPR shadows

- Set the *defaultLight* **Use Depth Map Shadows** to **On**.

*You will notice the IPR did update the render but the shadows did not appear.*

- Select **IPR → Update Shadow Maps**.

*Now the IPR updates and the shadows are visible.*

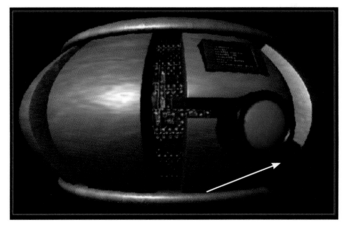

*IPR with shadows*

**Note:** *The defaultLight node gets deleted when you stop an IPR rendering.*

## 9    Stop the IPR

- If you would like to pause or stop the IPR, click on the buttons located at the top right of the Render View.

Pause    File size    Stop

# High Quality Rendering

When High Quality Rendering is turned on, the scene views are drawn in high quality by the hardware renderer. This lets you see a very good representation of the final render's look without having to software render the scene.

## 1 Enabling High Quality Rendering

- In the Perspective view, make sure to press **5**, **6** or **7**.

*High Quality Rendering is not available while in wireframe.*

- Select **Shading** → **High Quality Rendering**.

**Tip:** *If you require faster playback or camera tumbling while using High Quality Rendering, turn on* **Shading** → **Interactive Shading**.

*High Quality Rendering*

# Conclusion

The Maya IPR helps speed up the creative process and allows you to explore fast shading, lighting and texturing possibilities.

In the next lesson you will prepare the orb for animation.

*In this lesson, you will prepare the orb for animation. First, you will create a blend shape deformer, which is a type of deformer that blends between two different geometry shapes. Then, you will establish a hierarchy to be used with an animation path in the next lesson. You will also add your own custom attributes and Set Driven Keys.*

**In this lesson you will learn the following:**

- How to freeze transformations;

- How to sculpt surfaces by painting with Artisan;

- How to use different brush operations;

- How to create blend shapes;

- How to add custom attributes;

- How to create locators;

- How to use Set Driven Keys.

# Start sculpting the surface

You will now test the Artisan Sculpt Tool. You will use the tool on a sphere to get a feel for it. Once you are more familiar with the tool, you will apply brush strokes to the orb geometry.

## 1 Make a test sphere

- Create a polygonal primitive sphere.

- Set its construction history for both **Subdivisions Axis** and **Subdivisions Height** to **60**.

- To better see the effect of your painting in the viewport, assign a new Phong material to the sphere by selecting **Lighting/Shading** → **Assign New Material** → **Phong**.

## 2 Open the Sculpt Polygons Tool

- With the *pSphere* selected, select **Edit Polygons** → **Sculpt Polygons Tool** → ❒.

*This opens the* **Tool Settings** *window which includes every Artisan sculpting option.*

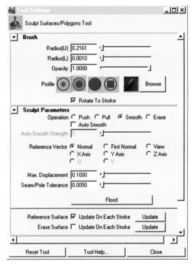

- Click on the **Reset Tool** button to make sure that you are starting with Artisan's default settings.

- Set the following attributes:

*Under* **Brush**:

    **Radius (U)** to **0.2**.

*Under* **Sculpt Parameters**:

    **Max Displacement** to **0.1**.

- Place the Tool Settings window to the right of the sphere.

*Tool Settings window*

---

**Alias Tip:** *The brush paradigm in Artisan is so natural for users. Having the ability to select, paint, edit and animate attributes as well as add, remove and sculpt geometry with a brush is a powerful high-level interface to what would otherwise require tedious and error prone manipulation of many individual elements.*

*Shai Hinitz | Sr. Product Manager*

## 3 Paint on the surface

- Move your cursor over the *pSphere* geometry.

*The cursor icon changes to show an arrow surrounded by a red circular outline. The arrow indicates how much the surface will be pushed or pulled while the outline indicates the brush radius. The Artisan brush icon is context sensitive. It changes as you choose different tool settings.*

- **Click+drag** on the sphere.

*You are now painting on the surface, pushing it toward the inside.*

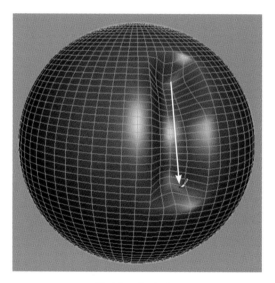

*First brush stroke*

**Tip:** *Artisan works more intuitively with a tablet and stylus, since the input device mimics the use of an actual paintbrush.*

## 4 Change the Artisan display

- Click the **Display** tab in the Tool Settings window.
- Click on **Show Wireframe** to turn this option **Off**.

*Now you can focus on the surface without displaying the wireframe lines.*

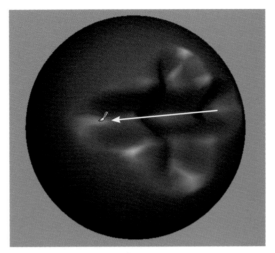

*Second brush stroke*

## 5 Paint another stroke

- Paint a second stroke across the mask surface.

*Now it is easier to see the results of your sculpting.*

## The sculpting tools

You will now explore some of the Artisan sculpting operations to see how they work. So far, you have been pushing on the surface. Now you will learn how to pull, smooth and erase.

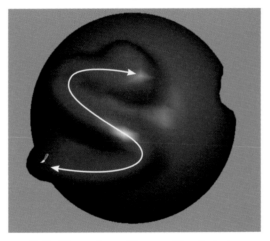

*Pulling the surface with several brush strokes*

## 1 Pull on the surface

- In the Tool Settings window, scroll to the **Sculpt Parameters** section.

- Under **Operation**, click on **Pull**.

- Tumble around to the other side of the sphere.

- Paint on the surface to create a few strokes that pull out.

## 2 Smooth out the results

- Under **Operation**, click on **Smooth**.

- Under **Brush**, change the **Radius (U)** to **0.6**.

*This increases the size of your brush. You can see that the red outline has increased in size. This is the brush feedback icon.*

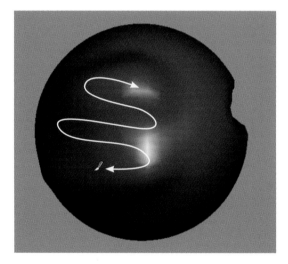

*Smoothing the brush strokes*

**Tip:** You can hold the **b** hotkey and **click+drag** in the viewport to interactively change the brush size.

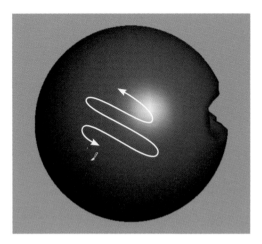

*Erasing the brush strokes*

- Paint all of the strokes to smooth the details. If you stroke over an area more than once, the smoothing becomes more evident.

## 3  Erase some of the brush strokes

- Under **Operation**, click on the **Erase** option.

- Paint along the surface to begin erasing the last sculpt edits.

## 4  Flood erase the surface

- Under **Operation**, click on the **Pull** option.

- In the **Sculpt Parameters** section, click on the **Flood** button.

*Fully erased surface*

*This uses the current operation and applies it to the entire surface using the current opacity setting.*

- Under **Operation**, click on the **Erase** option.

- In the **Sculpt Parameters** section, click on the **Flood** button.

*The sphere comes back to its orginal shape.*

## Updating the reference surface

When you paint in Artisan, you paint in relation to a *reference surface*. By default, the reference surface updates after every stroke so that you can build your strokes on top of one another. You can also keep the reference surface untouched until you decide to update it manually.

### 1 Change the brush attributes

- Under **Operation**, click on **Pull**.

- Set the following attributes:

*Under* **Brush***:*

  **Radius (U)** to **0.2**.

*Under* **Sculpt Parameters***:*

  **Max Displacement** to **0.2**.

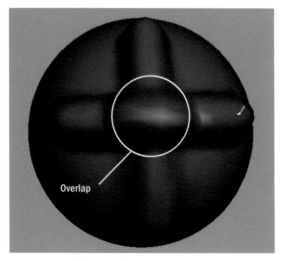

*Painting with reference update*

## 2  Pull the surface with two strokes

- Paint on the surface to create two crossing strokes that pull out.

*The second stroke built on top of the first stroke. Therefore, the height of the pull is higher where the two strokes intersect.*

## 3  Change the reference update

- In the Tool Settings window, scroll down in the **Sculpt Parameters** section, and turn **Off** the **Reference Surface: Update On Each Stroke**.

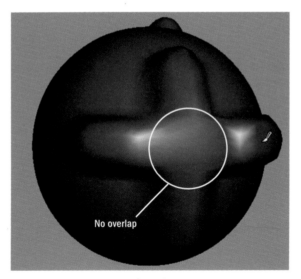

No overlap

*Painting with no reference update*

## 4  Paint more overlapping strokes

- Paint on the surface to create a few strokes that pull out. This time, the strokes do not overlap. The reference surface does not update, therefore the strokes can only displace to the **Maximum Displacement** value. You cannot displace beyond that value until you update the reference surface.

## 5  Update the reference layer

- Still in the **Sculpt Parameters** section, click on the **Update** button next to **Reference Surface**.

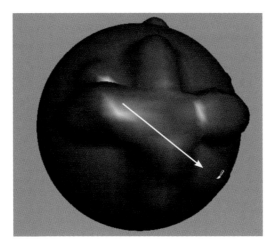

*Painting on updated reference layer*

## 6  Paint on the surface

- Paint another stroke over the last set of strokes.

*The overlapping strokes are again building on top of each other.*

## 7  Flood erase the surface

- Under **Operation**, click on the **Erase** option.

- Click on the **Flood** button.

# Sculpting the orb

You will now use the Artisan Sculpt Tool to create a crashed looking orb. You will first group and duplicate the orb in order to have two copies to use later for the blend shape deformer. Feel free to use your previously saved orb or continue with *10-texturedOrb.ma*.

## 1  Before starting the orb set up

It is recommended to establish a good scaling for the orb and freeze its transformations before establishing a final set up. Since the modeling and texturing construction history is no longer required, make sure to also delete all the history.

- Select all the orb geometry.

- Press **Ctrl+g** to group it together.

- Rename the group *orbGroup*.

- Scale the *orbGroup* to **0.4** in all directions.

- Still with the *orbGroup* selected, select **Modify** → **Freeze Transformations**.

*When freezing transformations, all the translation, rotation and scaling attributes for the selected nodes and their children are frozen and set to their default values.*

- Select **Edit** → **Delete All by Type** → **History**.

**Note:** *If you wait too long before deleting unwanted construction history, you might eventually get stuck with it, which will slow down your scene. Since the blend shape deformer will be part of the construction history, deleting the history after this point will also get rid of the deformer.*

## 2  Duplicate the orb

Later in this lesson, you will be using the blend shape deformer which will require one untouched orb and another one to deform.

- Select the group *orbGroup*.

- Press **Ctrl+d** to **Duplicate** the *orb*.

- Move the second *orbGroup* next to the original one.

- Rename the new *orbGroup* to *orbCrashGroup*.

## 3  Sculpt the orb

You will use Artisan to paint and deform the selected geometry. Since the orb is made of multiple objects, you must select the *orbCrashGroup* before entering the Sculpt Tool.

- With the *orbCrashGroup* selected, select **Edit Polygons** → **Sculpt Polygons Tool** → ❏.

- Click on the **Reset Tool** button to make sure that you are starting with Artisan's default settings.

- Set the following attributes:

*Under* **Brush***:*

      **Radius (U)** to **0.2**.

Under **Sculpt Parameters**, set the following:

**Operation** to **Pull**;

**Reference Vector** to **Y-axis**;

**Max Displacement** to **0.1**.

**Note:** *In the previous test sphere example, you were painting using the normals of the surface as the direction to be pushed and pulled. In this case, you will pull along the Y-axis, which will move the vertices up.*

- Paint directly on the model to get a shape similar to the following:

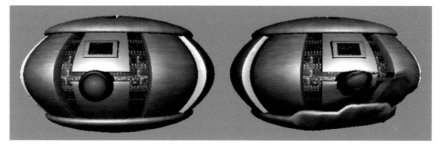

*Original and crashed orb shapes*

## Blend shape deformer

In the next lesson, you will animate the orb colliding with the ground. To make it more realistic, you will need a deformer that will blend between the original orb geometry and the crashed one. That kind of deformer is called *blend shape*. Blend shapes are very useful in 3D, especially to animate facial expressions on characters, but for this project, blend shapes will be used to deform the orb.

### 1 Creating the deformer

- Select the *orbCrashGroup*, then **Shift-select** the *orbGroup*.

- It is important to select the original object last.

- From the Animation menu set, select **Deform** → **Create Blend Shape** → ❑.

- In the **Blend Shape Options** window, make sure to set **Origin** to **Local**.

- Click the **Create** button.

## 2 Testing the deformer

- Select any piece of geometry on the original orb. In the Channel Box, you should see a *blendShape1* node in its construction history.

- Click on the *blendShape1* node to make it active.

*Notice the orbCrashGroup attribute. It will control the blending of the orb's shape between the original and crashed one.*

- Click on the *orbCrashGroup* attribute's name to make it active.

- **MMB click+drag** from left to right to invoke the virtual slider and see the effect of the deformer on the geometry.

## 3 Tweaking the blend shape

Since construction history still links the blend shape with the deformed surface, you can still tweak the *orbCrashGroup* geometry.

- Make modifications on the *orbCrashGroup* geometry with the **Artisan Sculpting Tool**.

**Tip:** *Make your changes on the orbCrashGroup and not on the original orb.*

## 4 Delete targets

- Select the *orbCrashGroup*.

- Press **Backspace** or **Delete** to dispose of the second orb.

**Note:** *When you delete blend shape targets, Maya keeps the blend values in the blend shape node instead of using the geometry in the scene.*

# Animation set up

The only thing missing before you can begin animating is a proper hierarchy for the intended animation. Since the orb will fly in your scene using a motion path, you will need a node only for that purpose. You will also need another node to keyframe the floating of the orb. Lastly, you will add custom attributes and connections to simplify your keyframing task.

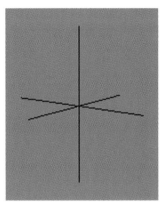

*A locator*

## 1 Making a proper hierarchy

- Create a locator by selecting **Create → Locator**.

  *A locator is similar to a group, but it has a visual representation that does not render.*

- Rename the locator *pathLocator*.

- Create another locator and rename it *animLocator*.

- Select *animLocator,* **Shift-select** the *pathLocator* and press **p** to parent them together.

- Parent the *orbGroup* to the *animLocator*.

```
⊟   ✳   pathLocator
⊟   ✳      animLocator
⊟   ▱         orbGroup
    ◈            body
    ◈            topCap
    ◈            bottomCap
    ◈            display
    ◈            tube
    ◈            lens
```

*The hierarchy*

**Note:** *The last selected object will become the parent of the hierarchy.*

## 2  Add a custom attribute

Since the blend shape attribute is hidden in the setup, you will add and connect an attribute for it on the *animLocator*.

- Select the *animLocator*.

- Select **Modify** → **Add Attribute**.

*This will open the Add Attribute option window.*

- Enter *crashShape* as the new **Attribute Name**.

- Make sure the **Keyable** checkbox is turned **On**.

*A keyable attribute means that it will be displayed in the Channel Box.*

- Make sure the **Data Type** is set to **Float**.

- In the **Numeric Attribute Properties**, set the following:

    **Minimum** to **0**;

    **Maximum** to **1**;

    **Default** to **0**.

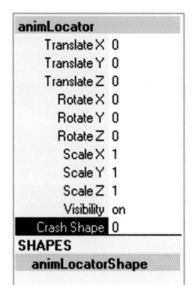

*The custom attribute*

- Press the **OK** button to add the attribute.

*Notice the new crashShape attribute is now displayed in the Channel Box when animLocator is selected.*

## 3  Connecting attributes

- Select **Window** → **General Editors** → **Connection Editor**.

- Select the *animLocator* and click on the **Reload Left** button.

- Select any geometry object of the orb, then highlight the *blendShape1* node in the Channel Box.

- Click on the **Reload Right** button.

- On the left side, scroll down to our custom **Crash Shape** attribute.

- Click on the **Crash Shape** attribute to select it.

- On the right side, find and expand the **Weight** attribute to reveal the *orbCrashGroup* attribute.

- Click on the *orbCrashGroup* to make the connection between the two attributes.

- Test the **Crash Shape** attribute on the *animLocator*.


## Set Driven Keys

The logic behind Set Driven Keys is that one attribute (the *driver*) drives another attribute (the *driven*) based on manually set keyframes.

A typical example would be an *Open* custom attribute which would drive the rotation of a door. You would only need to keyframe the door closed when the *Open* attribute is at zero, and set a second keyframe where the door is opened when the *Open* attribute is set to one.

It would be nice to have a custom attribute to control the lens of the orb to go in and out rather than keyframing both the *tube* and the *lens* objects manually. Set Driven Keys can be used for that purpose.

---

**Alias** With the Set Driven Key, you have the power to build action/reaction.
**Tip:** You can build the causal relations between anything. It is very simple to use. Simple and efficient.

*Patrice Paradis | Application Engineer*

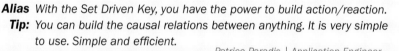

---

### 1 Add a second custom attribute

- Select the *animLocator*.

- Select **Modify** → **Add Attribute**.

- Set the following:

> **Attribute Name** to *lensControl*;
>
> **Keyable** to **On**;
>
> **Data Type** to **Float**;
>
> **Minimum** to **0**;
>
> **Maximum** to **1**;
>
> **Default** to **0**.

- Press the **OK** button to add the new attribute.

*The Set Driven Key window*

## 2 Define the driven keys

- From the Animation menu set, select **Animate** → **Set Driven Key** → **Set** → ☐.

*The Set Driven Key window is displayed.*

- Select the *animLocator* and click on the **Load Driver** button.

*The animLocator object and its keyable attributes are displayed in the **Driver** section.*

- Highlight the *lensControl* attribute to specify it as the driver.

- Select the *lens* and *tube* objects and click on the **Load Driven** button.

*Both objects are displayed in the **Driven** section.*

- **Click+drag** to highlight *lens* and *tube* objects in the **Driven** section to display their common attributes.

- Highlight all of the **Translate** attributes to specify them as **Driven**.

## 3  Set the driven keys

- Make sure the *lensControl* attribute is set to **0**.

- Press the **Key** button.

*This will define the current position of the lens and tube objects as the wanted position when the* **lensControl** *is at* **0**.

- Set the **lensControl** attribute to **1**.

- Translate the *lens* and *tube* objects together toward the inside of the orb.

- Press the **Key** button to set the second driven key.

- Test the *lensControl* attribute to see if it affects the *lens* and *tube* as desired.

- Press the **Close** button.

## 4  Save your work

- Save this scene as *12-orbSetup.ma*.

## Conclusion

You are now more familiar with the very useful blend shape deformer as well as the Artisan Sculpting Tool. You also learned about locators, custom attributes, connections and Set Driven Keys, which are essential to understanding any basic animation setup.

In the next lesson, you will use the animation locators to animate the orb into your scene.

# Lesson 13    Orb animation

*Now that your orb is ready for animation, you will explore the basics of character animation. You will fly the orb around the room and crash into a stack of boxes. To do so, you will use a motion path to determine the trajectory of the orb, then keyframe some secondary animation to refine the motion. Finally, you will generate a playblast, which will allow you to preview your animation and make final modifications if required.*

## In this lesson you will learn the following:

- How to import a scene;

- How to create layers;

- How to define a motion path;

- How to shape the path to edit the animation;

- How to update the path markers;

- How to keyframe secondary animation;

- How to use the auto keyframe option;

- How to make a playblast.

**Project Two**

## Scene set up

Before you can begin animating the orb, you need both the orb and the room from the previous project in the same scene. All you have to do is open one of the two scenes and import the other one, thus merging them together. When that is done, you can save the new merged scene under a new name.

### 1    Merge the scenes

- If the latest orb scene is not already open, select **File** → **Open** and select the file *12-orbSetup.ma*.

- Once the scene is loaded, select **File** → **Import** → ❐.

*This will display the import options.*

- Set the **Group** checkbox to **On**.

*The **Group** option will group the objects of the imported scene together.*

- Click on the **Import** button.

- Select the file *06-details.ma* from the *project1* folder.

**Note:** *Maya will find the textures automatically.*

- Save the new scene as *13-orbAnimation.ma*.

### 2    Double check the Outliner

When merging files together, it is always a good idea to open the Outliner and make sure that your new scene is well organized. Notice that since you enabled the **Group** checkbox in the import options, the room's objects were grouped all together. This is a good way to keep your scene well organized.

- Open the Outliner.

- Rename the new group *roomGroup*.

### 3    Layers

When a scene grows more complex, working in the viewport becomes complicated since there are many overlapping objects. A layer is a tool that you can use to hide parts of a scene.

- Click on the **Create a new layer** button located on the right of the Layer Editor, just under the Channel Box.

Create new layer button

- Double-click on the new layer and enter the name *roomLayer* in the option window.

- Click the **Save** button to confirm the new name.

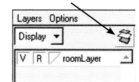

*The new layer*

## 4 Assign objects to the layer

- Select the *roomGroup*.

- **RMB+click** on the *roomLayer* and select **Add Selected Objects** from the pop-up menu.

- Click on the **V** on the left of the *roomLayer* to set the layer visibility to **Off**.

*The entire room gets hidden.*

## 5 Display selection handles

- Select the *pathLocator*.

- Select **Display** → **Component Display** → **Selection Handles**.

*A small selection handle appears at the pathLocator's position, which makes it easier to select the locator in the viewport.*

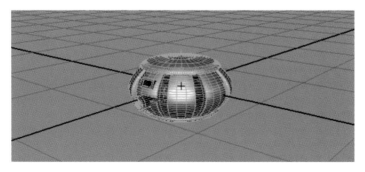

*The orb and its selection handle*

## 6 Change the roomLayer attributes

- For the *roomLayer*, click in the leftmost layer box to display a **V** which will make the layer visible.

**Note:** *Toggle this on and off so that all objects in that layer become visible or invisible.*

- Make the *roomLayer* unselectable by clicking in the layer box right beside the **V** until an **R** appears.

*When clicking in the second layer box, it will first change to **T**, which stands for **Template**. Here, all the geometry in the layer is displayed as grey wireframe and is unselectable. When you click again in the layer box, an **R** will appear which stands for **Reference**, where all the geometry in the layer is displayed normally, but is unselectable.*

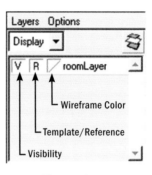

*The new layer*

**Note:** *Use Reference to do things like Snap to Points onto unselectable geometry.*

## Path animation

Path animations are created by assigning an object or series of objects to a path. This creates a special *motionPath* node that allows you to key its motion along the path.

### 1 Draw a path animation curve

- Change the viewport for the top view.

- Select **Create → EP Curve Tool**.

- Click to draw a curve around the pedestal, as shown in the image on the top of the following page.

**Note:** *Notice that the curve passes right through the box stack. The curve will be used in the next lesson for dynamic simulation.*

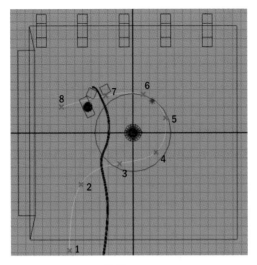

*Path curve*

## 2   Attach the orb to the path

- Change the **Time Slider** range to **100** frames.

- Select the *pathLocator* using its selection handle, press **Shift** and select the path.

**Note:** *In order to create a path animation, the path must be picked last. The last object picked is indicated in green.*

- Go to the **Animation** menu set.

- Select Animate → **Motion Paths** → **Attach to Motion Path** → ❐.

- Set **Time Range** to **Time Slider**.

- Click the **Attach** button and playback the results.

*Orb attached to path*

**Note:** *If you want to preview the correct playback timing, remember to set your playback speed to normal in the General Preferences window.*

## 3 Edit the motion path input node

The orb is moving down the path but it is not aimed in the correct direction. You can change this using the *motionPath* input node.

- With the *pathLocator* selected, open the Attribute Editor.

- Click the tab for *motionPath1* and set the following:

  **Follow** to **On**;

  **Front Axis** to **Z**;

  **Up Axis** to **Y**;

  **Bank** to **On**.

- Playback the results and see how the orb points in the direction it is traveling. As well, notice the effect of the **Bank** attribute, which specifies that the object should lean into the curve of the motion path.

**Tip:** *If the orb does not face the right direction while moving down the path, change the* **Front Axis** *or turn* **On** *the* **Inverse Front** *checkbox.*

## 4 Edit the path's shape

You can edit the shape of the path using the curve's control vertices and the object will follow the path.

- Select the path curve.

- **RMB+click** on the path curve and select **Control Vertices** from the context menu.

- Move the CVs along the Y-axis so that the orb flies above the ground and into the box stack.

- Playback the results.

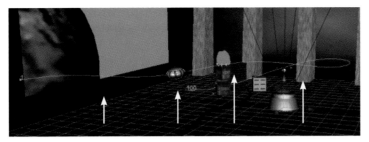

*Edited path curve*

**Tip:** You can press the **Alt** key and tumble in the Perspective window as the animation is playing back. This lets you preview the shape of the path from different angles.

## 5 Key the path's U value

Notice the start and end markers on the path. They tell you the start and end frame of the animation along the path. You can set a key on the *motionPath's* U value to add more markers to the path.

- Go to frame **50**.

- Select the *pathLocator* using its selection handle.

- In the Channel Box, click on the *motionPath1* input node.

- Still in the Channel Box, click on the **U Value** channel name to highlight it.

- With your **RMB**, select **Key Selected** from the pop-up menu.

*A new marker is placed where the new key is set. You are setting a key on the position of the orb along the U direction of the curve. The value represents the parameter of the curve.*

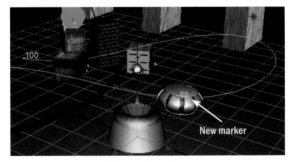

New marker

*New path markers*

## 6 Key a second value

This time you will key the U value using the Show Manipulator Tool and Auto Key. When the Auto Key button is enabled, any attributes that already have a keyframe are being keyed as soon as you change the attribute's value. This is a very handy feature when animating.

- Go to frame **60**.

- Click on the **Auto Key** button at the right end of the Time Slider to turn it **On**.

- Select the **Show Manipulator Tool**.

*A manipulator appears with handles for positioning and twisting the object along the path. You will use the middle yellow handle to move the orb along the path.*

*Auto Key button*

- **Click+drag** on the yellow manipulator handle to drag the orb back a little.

- Another path marker is placed on the curve.

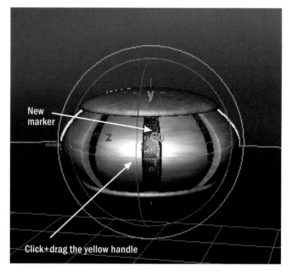

New
marker

Click+drag the yellow handle

*New path marker*

**Tip:** *It is always good to remember that input nodes may have manipulators that you can access using the Show Manipulator Tool.*

## 7 Edit the path marker's position

The position of the markers can be moved to edit the animation of the ship.

- Click on the **Auto Key** button to turn it **Off**.

- Select the **Move Tool**.

- To select the path marker that is labelled as **50**, click on the number without touching the curve to select the marker on its own.

*When selected, the marker is yellow.*

- Move the marker past the marker labelled as **60**.

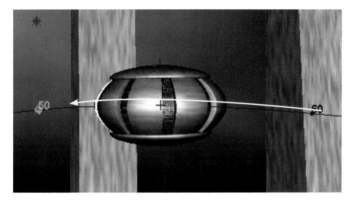

*Edited path curve*

*The marker is constrained to the curve as you move it.*

- Playback the results.

*The orb animates up to the **50** marker, then goes backwards to the **60** marker, and then forward to the end of the curve. The position of the orb at these keyframes can be set using the marker manipulator.*

## 8 Edit the timing

Since the marker points are simply keys set on the U Value of the *motionPath* node, you can edit the timing of the keys in the Graph Editor.

- Select the *pathLocator* using its selection handle, and then click on the *motionPath* input node in the Channel Box.

- Open the Graph Editor panel.

- Move your cursor into the Graph Editor window and press **a** to frame all into the panel.

*The position of the attached object in the U direction of the curve is mapped against time. You can see that a key has been set for each of the path markers.*

- Select the key at frame **60**.

- In the Graph Editor's **Stats** area, change the time from **60** to **80**.

- In the Graph Editor, select **Tangents** → **Flat**.

*You can edit the effect of the path keys' in-between frames using the same techniques used for set keys.*

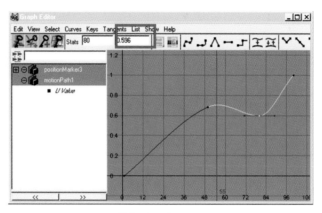

*Edited path curve*

*You can see that the path marker is now labelled as **80** in the view panel.*

## 9  Remove the middle two markers

While the markers have shown you how to make the orb move back and forth, this is not how you want the orb to animate. You will remove the middle markers to return to a two-marker path.

- Select the markers that are labelled as **50** and **80**. Make sure that no other objects are selected.

- Press the **Backspace** or **Delete** key on your keyboard.

**Tip:**   *You can select the keyframes from the Graph Editor to delete them as well.*

## 10  Finalize the path animation

You will require only one keyframe on the motion path in order to have the orb gain speed before crashing into the box stack.

- Go to frame **70**.

- Select the *pathLocator* using its selection handle.

- In the Channel Box, for the *motionPath1* node, highlight the **U Value** attribute.

- With your **MMB**, invoke the virtual slider to move the orb near the middle of the path.

*Doing so will have the orb move slower at the beginning of the animation and faster towards the end.*

**Tip:**   *If the virtual slider changes the value too fast, hold down* **Ctrl** *which will change the attribute with smaller increments.*

## Secondary animation

Now that you have a basic animation for your orb, you can keyframe secondary animation on top of what you already have. Secondary animation usually adds life to an animation, making the scene more natural. For the orb, you will keyframe some rotations and offsets. You will also animate the *crashShape* and *lensControl* attributes created in the previous lesson.

## 1  Looking around

- Select the *animLocator*, which is the child of *pathLocator*.

*This is the node that you will use to keyframe any secondary animation since it is already inheriting animation from the motion path.*

- Make sure to turn **On** the **Auto Key** option.

- Go to frame **10**.

- Press **Shift+e** to keyframe only the rotation of the locator.

- Go to frame **20** and rotate the orb so that it faces the right.

*The Auto Key option has automatically added a keyframe for you on the changed rotation attribute.*

- Go to frame **30** and rotate the orb so that it faces the left.

- Go to frame **50** and reset the rotation of the orb to **0** in all directions.

**Note:** *If you don't set another keyframe at zero for the rotation, the offset will be kept until the end of the animation.*

## 2   Orb malfunction

- Go to frame **60**.

- With the *animLocator* still selected, press **Shift+w** to set a keyframe only for the translation.

- Go to frame **65**.

- Move the orb up.

- Go to frame **70**.

*Linear tangent from the Time Slider*

- Bring the translation of the orb back to **0** in all directions.

- Go back to frame **65**.

- In the Time Slider, **RMB-click** for the keyframe context menu.

- Select **Tangents** → **Linear**.

*This will cause the orb's malfunction keyframe to look steeper.*

## 3   Crash blend shape

- Go to the frame just before the orb collides with the boxes.

- Keyframe the **Crash Shape** attribute on the *animLocator* at **0**.

- Step forward by **2** frames.

- Set another keyframe on **Crash Shape** at **1**.

*This will blend the orb into its crashed shape exactly as it collides with the boxes and the ground.*

## 4   Animate the lens

- Keyframe secondary animation on the **Lens Control** attribute of the *animLocator*.

## 5   Save your work

## 6    Playblast the animation

When making a playblast, Maya generates the animation by grabbing the image directly from the active viewport, so make sure to display only what you want in your playblast.

- Frame the scene in the Perspective view to see it in its entirety.

- From the **Show** menu in the Perspective window, hide objects that you do not want in your playblast, such as the **Grid**, **NURBS curves**, **Lights**, **Locators**, **Handles** and **Strokes**.

- Press **6** if you want the textures to appear in your playblast.

- Select **Window** → **Playblast...**

- The playblast will appear in your default movie player.

**Note:** *For more options on the playblast, select* **Window** → **Playblast** → □.

*Playblast preview*

# Conclusion

You are now more familiar with merging files, creating layers, attaching objects to a motion path and keyframing secondary animation. You have also learned how to playblast a sequence, which is an essential tool for animators.

As a result of your work, the orb now appears to malfunction and crashes right into a stack of boxes.

In the next lesson, you will implement a dynamic simulation so that the orb and boxes collide and crumble to the floor.

# Lesson 14　Rigid bodies

*In this lesson, you will experiment with the basics of rigid bodies, an example of dynamic simulations. Rigid bodies are polygonal or NURBS surfaces converted to unyielding shapes. Unlike conventional surfaces, rigid bodies collide rather than pass through each other during animation. To animate rigid body motion, you use fields, keys, expressions, rigid body constraints, or collisions with other rigid bodies or particles. In our case, the orb will be colliding with the boxes and the floor, all affected by a gravity field.*

**In this lesson you will learn the following:**

- How to create a Passive Rigid Body;

- How to create an Active Rigid Body;

- How to add a gravity field to rigid bodies;

- How to simulate your dynamics;

- How to set rigid body attributes;

- How to set rigid body keyframes;

- How to cache a dynamic simulation.

In animation, sometimes there are scenarios that just aren't worth spending the time keyframing. Collisions between objects, for example, might look much too complex to animate by hand. In that case it is better to use dynamic simulations.

## Active and Passive

Maya has two kinds of rigid bodies - active and passive. An Active Rigid Body reacts to dynamics - fields, collisions, and springs; not to keys. A Passive Rigid Body can have Active Rigid Bodies collide with it. You can key its translation and rotation attributes, but dynamics has no effect on it.

### 1 Test scene

- Select **File** → **New**.
- Create a polygonal cube and scale it so that it looks like a floor.
- Rename the cube *floor*.
- Create a polygonal sphere and another polygonal cube and place them side by side above the floor.

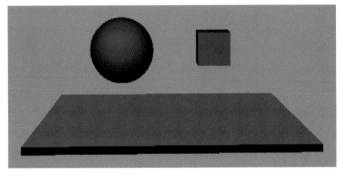

*The test scene*

### 2 Active Rigid Body

- Select the sphere.
- Press **F4** to display the **Dynamics** menu set.
- Select **Soft/Rigid Bodies** → **Create Active Rigid Body**.
- Playback the animation.

*Nothing is happening because there are no forces in the scene.*

**Note:** *When using dynamics, make sure the scene playback is set to* **Play Every Frame** *in the general preferences. If not, you might get unpredictable results.*

### 3  Gravity field

- Select the sphere.

- Select **Fields** → **Gravity**.

- Playback the animation.

*The sphere falls straight down.*

**Note:** *You may want to increase your playback range in the Time Slider.*

### 4  Passive Rigid Body

- Select the *floor*.

- Select **Soft/Rigid Bodies** → **Create Passive Rigid Body**.

- Playback the animation.

*The sphere falls and collides with the floor.*

### 5  Rotate the floor

- Select the *floor* and rotate it sideways.

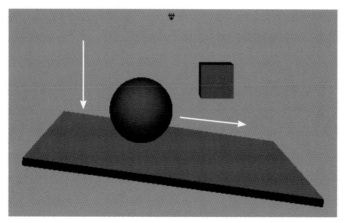

*Rotate the floor*

- Playback the animation.

*The sphere collides and rolls off the floor.*

**Note:** *It is very important to rewind to frame 1 before playing a dynamic simulation to see accurate results. Also, you should not scrub in the timeline.*

## 6 Set the cube as active

- Select the *cube*.

- Select **Soft/Rigid Bodies** → **Create Active Rigid Body**.

- Playback the animation.

*The cube does not fall with gravity since it was not connected.*

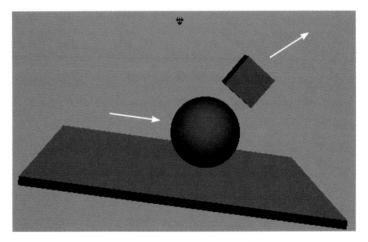

*The cube collides without gravity*

## 7 Assign gravity

- Select the *cube* and **Shift-select** the gravity field.

- Select **Fields** → **Affect Selected Object(s)**.

- Playback the animation.

*The cube falls on the floor like the sphere.*

## 8 Change dynamic attributes

- Select the *cube*.

- In the Channel Box, highlight the *rigidBody* input connection.

- Set the following:

  **Mass** to **2**;

  **Bounciness** to **0.1**;

  **Static Friction** to **0.5**;

  **Dynamic Friction** to **0.5**.

*Setting those attributes specifies that the cube is heavier and will react differently against other rigid bodies. It also doesn't bounce much and has more friction against other rigid bodies.*

- Playback the animation.

*The cube falls and stops on the floor. This is because you have reduced attributes like bounciness and increased friction.*

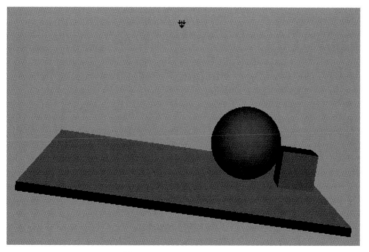

*The cube stops the sphere*

## 9  Center of mass

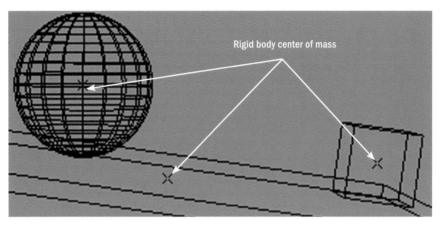

*The center of mass*

If you look closely at the rigid bodies, you will notice a small **x** which defines the rigid bodies' center of mass.

Not all objects have their center of mass exactly at their centers. For example, a toy punching bag stays straight even when it is pushed over.

- Select the sphere to change its center of mass.

- In the Channel Box, highlight the *rigidBody* input connection.

- Set the **Center Of Mass Y** to **-1**.

*The center of mass icon moved to the bottom of the sphere.*

- Playback the animation.

*The sphere falls and stops on the floor, bobbing from side to side.*

*The new center of mass*

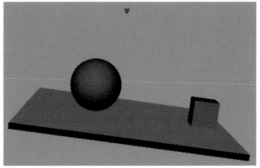

*The sphere is bobbing in place*

## Orb simulation

With your knowledge, you can now add a rigid body simulation to the orb scene. You will first set the Active and Passive Rigid Bodies. You will then keyframe the orb rigid body from passive to active, which will allow it to keep the path animation until the malfunction. Once the orb becomes an Active Rigid Body, it will crash into the box stack.

### 1 Open the orb scene

- Open the file *13-orbAnimation.ma*.

- Save the scene as *14-orbDynamics.ma*.

- Make the *roomLayer* selectable in the Layer Editor by toggling the **r** key.

### 2 Create the rigid bodies

- Select the *room* geometry by **RMB-clicking** over the *roomLayer* and choosing **Select Objects**.

- Select **Soft/Rigid Bodies** → **Create Passive Rigid Body**.

- Select all the *boxes* from the box stack.

- Select **Soft/Rigid Bodies** → **Create Active Rigid Body**.

**Note:** *Make sure that none of the boxes interpenetrate with each other or the floor. If this happens, translate them to produce a small gap between the boxes.*

### 3 Make the orb a rigid body

To make the orb a rigid body requires more attention. For the orb to continue following its animation, it needs to be made as a Passive Rigid Body first.

- Select the *orbGroup* node, which should be child of the *animLocator* and parent of all the orb geometry.

**Note:** *If you don't find the orbGroup, select the orb geometry and press* **Ctrl+g** *to group them under the animLocator. Select the new group and rename it orbGroup.*

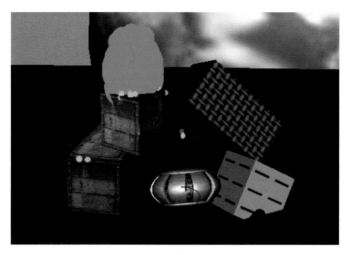

*The passive orb collides with the boxes*

- Go to frame **1**.

*It is important to be at frame 1 when creating a Passive Rigid Body on an animated object, or the dynamics might not simulate as expected.*

- Select **Soft/Rigid Bodies** → **Create Passive Rigid Body**.

- Playback the animation.

**Note:** *During a dynamic simulation, if two objects intersect, a warning is displayed in the Command Feedback line.*

## 4 Keyframe the rigid body

In order for the orb to crash into the boxes as an Active Rigid Body, you need to set a special type for keyframes which will change its state from passive to active.

- Go around frame **50** where the orb does not touch any other geometry.

- Select the *orbGroup* rigid body.

- Select **Soft/Rigid Bodies** → **Set Passive Key**.

- Go around frame **85**, where the orb still does not touch any other geometry.

- Select **Soft/Rigid Bodies** → **Set Active Key**.

- Set the end of the animation in the Time Slider to **200**.

- Go to frame **1**.

- Playback the animation.

## 5 Assign gravity

- Select all the rigid bodies in the scene (*room*, *boxes* and *orbGroup*).

- Select **Fields** → **Gravity**.

*A new gravity field with the default earth-like gravity appears at the origin.*

- Playback the animation.

*Now all the rigid bodies bounce off the floor.*

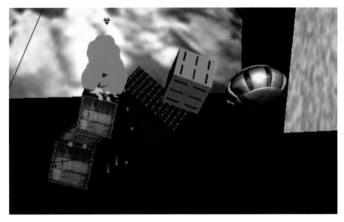

*The active orb collides with the boxes and bounces off*

## 6 Fine-tune the simulation

For a better simulation, the rigid bodies' attributes should be tweaked to give more realism to the scene. Following are some general steps that you should do, but it may vary from scene to scene.

- For the *boxes*, change the following:

  Move down the **Center Of Mass Y** of the bigger boxes.

  Change the **Mass** attributes between **0.2** and **1.5**, depending on the size of the boxes.

Lower their **Bounciness** attributes to **0.2**.

Increase their **Static Friction** and **Dynamic Friction** attributes to **0.5**.

- For the *floor*, change the following:

Lower the **Bounciness** attribute to **0.2**.

Increase the **Static Friction** and **Dynamic Friction** attributes to **0.5**.

- For the *orb*, change the following:

Lower its **Bounciness** attribute to **0.2**.

*The final simulation*

## Simulation cache

When you simulate rigid body dynamics, the rigid body solver recalculates the simulation every time you play through the Time Slider. You can speed up the playback of your scene by saving a rigid body cache in memory. A cache stores the positions of all the rigid bodies at every frame, letting you quickly preview the results without having to create a playblast. This offers many benefits, including scrubbing back and forth in the Time Slider.

If you want to tweak the objects' attributes to alter the simulation, you will not see the results until you delete the cache, so that the solver recalculates a new simulation.

### 1 Enable the cache

- Select **Solvers** → **Rigid Body Solver...**

*This will open the Attribute Editor for the rigid body solver in the scene.*

**Note:** *It is possible to have multiple rigid body solvers in a scene. This is useful when you have distinct systems that don't interact together.*

- Scroll to the **Rigid Solver States** section in the Attribute Editor.

- Turn **On** the **Cache Data** checkbox.

- Rewind and playback the entire scene so that the solver can create the cache.

*When it finishes playing the scene and writing the cache to memory, you should see a difference in the playback speed since it does not recalculate the simulation.*

**Note:** *The rigid body cache is saved in the RAM (Random Access Memory) and is not written to disk.*

### 2 Tweak the simulation

- Select the *orbGroup* and change its rigid body **Mass** attribute to **3**.

*You should not see any difference when you playback your scene since no recalculation is done.*

- Select **Solvers** → **Rigid Body Solver**...

- In the **Rigid Solver States** section, click the **Delete Cache** button.

*This will force the solver to recalculate the cache.*

- Rewind your scene and play it so that the solver can create a new cache.

- If you want to disable the solver's cache, simply turn **Off** the **Cache Data** checkbox.

## Conclusion

You have experienced the basics of the powerful dynamics tools found in Maya. You learned how to create Active and Passive Rigid Bodies, along with gravity fields. You also tweaked their attributes to add realism to your simulation.

You are now ready to delve into more advanced topics. In the next project, you will create a complete biped character ready for animation.

BLUEGALLERY

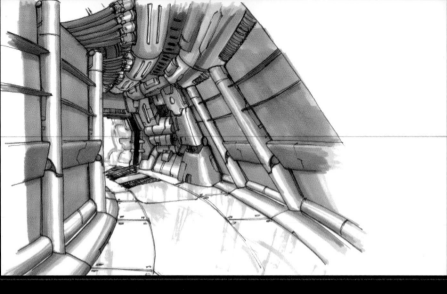

## *BLUE* - Transcription of Aaron Webster Interview

This is the first and last sketch I guess I did of the hallway and the ship. Basically, the hallway ended up looking exactly like I drew it. Lights going all the way through it and...and pretty much I started in 3D again just to get my perspective down. Although I know perspective, it's a real pain, especially with things. So, I mean it's just easier in 3D if you have that at your disposal, you might as well use it.

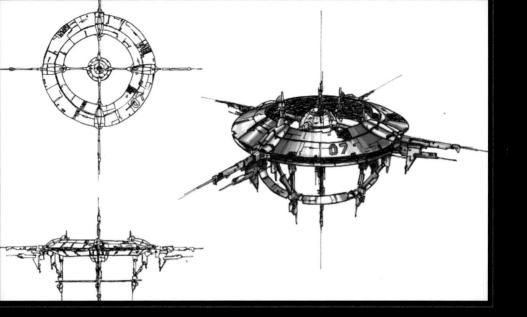

his was the final sketch of the exterior of the space station. I wanted kind of a *2001: Space Odyssey* with the big circle thing that's simulating gravity, but kind of turned it just to get that ring ook and it's got like a central core with, I guess where the power is…and it's got these sensor ays that I kind of was inspired by the *Sulaco* from *Aliens*. It's got that cool spiky sensor ray at the ront of the ship so I kind of ripped that off and threw that in there because I'm a big fan of that. nd basically again it was quickly modeled in 3D just to get the perspective down and take it from here with just some prisma color markers and some tech pens, black tech pens.

# Alias SketchBook Pro Storyboards

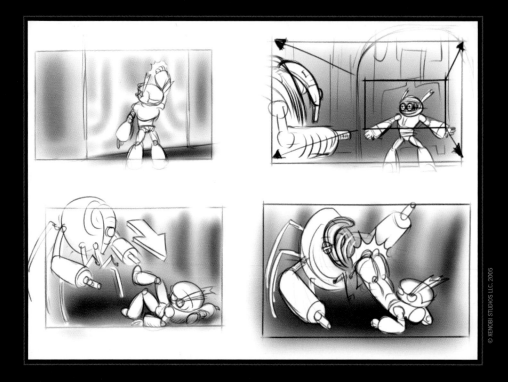

Storyboarding is an indispensable tool for movie-making and creating them in SketchBook Pro is a dynamic process. The ability to visualize a story allows for easy experimentation and helps sort out the logistics of a sequence. Drawing with layers is a quick format for arranging and changing elements. Modeling, animating and rendering a sequence is a time intensive process. With good planning you can be efficient, as you learn to work on only the story essentials.

*– Roark Andrade*

**BLUE GALLERY**

# Scenes from *Blue*

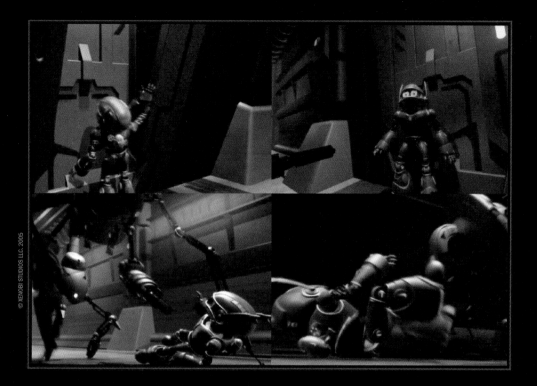

**Q. Tell us what a Lyca reel is.**

A. A Lyca reel is, basically, once you get all your storyboards you sew them all together and that's basically your movie. And as you go, as you progress through your movie, you replace these still images or sketches or whatever you have with your finished, or your works in progress. And eventually that Lyca reel will turn into your finished product.

**Like an animatic?**

Yeah, exactly. It's like an animated storyboard, you go through it, your timing is there, your camera shots are there – all the essential information you need to make your shots.

# Awoken Sentry-bot

© XENOBI STUDIOS LLC. 2005

his is one of my favorite images. This is when Blue realizes that his sigh  has awoken the evil

entry-bot, and he's about to get throttled. It's really dramatic -- he's got the glowing eyes staring

nto darkness and there's no light coming from the hallway and there's the depth of field in the

ackground, good sense of atmosphere, and you've got his little Tron-like decals just glowing there.

# Peering *Blue*

This is another cute one – he's peering out of the space where the door would normally go. This is probably my most hated render because it shows a really bad texture blemish on that side of the doorway I worked on. We did this without a Lyca reel so we didn't know what the camera shots were going to be, so basically everything was modeled and textured as if it was all going to be seen from the same kind of view and angle. And in this particular instance, it got a little bit too close to something that I didn't think would be in closeup and there's a big nasty looking corner of one of the details in the door. So. The rest of the image is great, though [Laughs].

# Five-o Wakes Up

This is where Five-o wakes up. Chris did a really good job animating that. He kind of wakes up, his eye starts up and starts moving around and his little T-Rex arms start twitching, you know, like they haven't been used in a little while. And Blue, he's curious, he doesn't know what this thing is yet -- he doesn't know whether to be afraid or just go up to him and hang out or try...again it's pretty moody. Blue's looking into this hall of darkness. There are no lights. Actually I think there might be one, it's flickering on and off to give you that feeling of foreboding .

## Colored Lighting

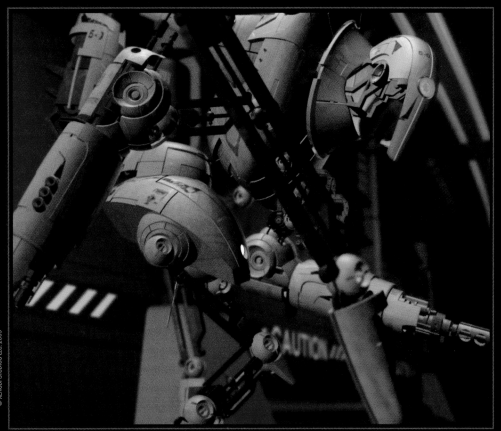

This is a good example of Chris' usage of colored lighting. This is Five-o (the Sentry-bot) after thinking he's

lost Blue – basically Blue woke him up walking around the halls and Five-o went looking for him. He couldn't

find him so he decided to, you know, just huff and puff and go back to where he was. Blue sighs and the

Sentry's like: "What? What was that?" and he turns around and the lights go red like emergency red and it

zooms in on Blue's face and it's a really good sequence. The mood is really Intense. [Laughs]

## Brawling Five-o

© XENOBI STUDIOS LLC. 2005

This is nearing the end of the film where Five-o finally pins down his prey; they're kind of brawling it out. Five-o's having a bit of a problem trying to ping him down and I think this is actually where he gets kicked in the head, falls over. Very good animation with the two interacting with each other and Chris did a good job of showing the weight of the robots.

# Blue Awakens

This is right at the beginning of the film. This is where Blue short circuits awake and

he gets up – it's like he's never been there before because he's conscious all of a

sudden. He's in this really grey looking, lifeless room and there's a big blue light com-

ing from the planet outside. It's really ethereal and it's causing a glow on everything.

You don't know if these are stills or sketches?

BLUE GALLERY

# X-ray Shader

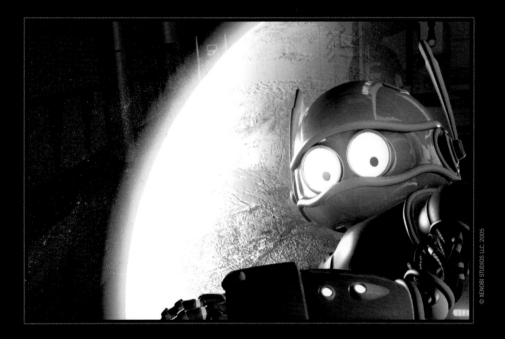

This is a frame where Blue realizes in the reflection of the window that there's a door in the background that's open - and eventually he goes out. It's got the planet in the background, which is actually animated, I believe. It's rotating very, very slowly. It's got several layers, one for clouds so they're moving at different rates, and it's got kind of an x-ray shader for the atmosphere around it, which is basically just a Sampler Info node driving a ramp texure in V and we just tweaked the values until it looked just the right thickness around the planet and became transparent, however foreign to the planet I wanted it to.

# Hallway Probe

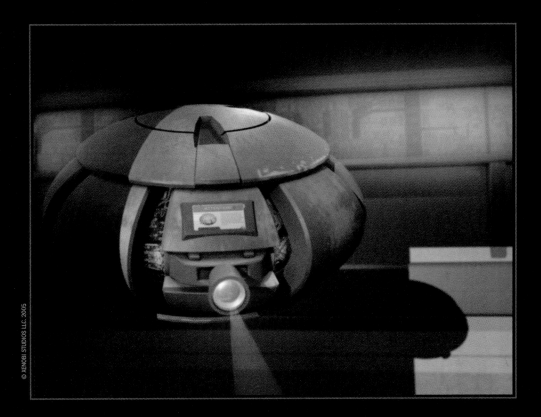

This is the hallway probe – I can't take any credit for that one. Sorry Chris, but it's a really mediocre design [laughs]. I see you used my paintbrushes on it, but you know, you can't polish a turd. This is Chris' hallway probe – it just flies around. Right after Blue gets the door open it comes around, looks at him, scans him and then goes on its way. It's got volumetric light to simulate the laser that he's scanning with. Pretty basic design. You just see some basic metal textures on there with some scrapes that were used using the brushes that I made with the metal scrapes and whatnot. And there's some incandescent wiring in there that he can see.

In this still, Blue has just started his exploration of the lab. Chris used some simple and

effective lighting techniques to create a sort of dead atmosphere in the room. The solitary

strip of 'moonlight' makes for a nice composition and leads the eye to the hologram

# Laboratory

This is an overall shot of the laboratory where Blue wakes up. It's got all the props and most of the main features that you see throughout the ship in here – cables on the ceiling, geometry on the walls that just give a little more life. Lots of incandescent decals just to bring more detail until otherwise pretty mundane geometry, especially at the back. Those kind of things, they can really bring out textures when there's nothing else going on in the room. You might notice that it's all curved and the station was actually modeled in several concentric rings and we eventually instanced maybe a three-and-a-half degree piece of pie

BLUE GALLERY

# Project Three

## Lessons

This project is similar to the last one, but pushes the level of difficulty. You will create an entire robot character ready for animation. First, you will model the biped character using NURBS surfaces. You will then texture, test-render and set up the robot to be animated.

Once the character rig is complete, you will generate a low resolution version of the robot that you will use to animate a walk and a jump cycle. Finally, you will integrate all the elements done so far to create a complete scene.

# Lesson 15  NURBS modeling

*This lesson will introduce you to modeling with NURBS (Non-Uniform Rational B-spline) surfaces. With NURBS you can create curves and surfaces to build up your models. In this lesson, you will build a robot character using primitives and tools such as revolve, loft and extrude. You will also learn the first steps of how to use existing geometry to help you build new geometry.*

### In this lesson you will learn the following:

- How to select NURBS CVs with hulls;

- How to project a curve on a surface;

- How to trim a surface;

- How to snap points to curves and isoparms;

- How to duplicate curves from a surface;

- How to cut and attach curves;

- How to use the loft, extrude, revolve and planar surface tools;

- How to mirror geometry.

# Set up your project

Since this is a new project, you must set a new directory as your project directory.

## 1  Set the project

- Go to the **File** menu and select **Project** → **Set...**

*A window opens that points you to the Maya projects directory.*

- Open the folder named *support_files*.
- Click on the folder named *project3* to select it, then click on the **OK** button.

## 2  Make a new scene

- Select **File** → **New Scene**.

# Building the foot

You will start building the foot of the robot using primitives, NURBS shapes and simple NURBS tools.

## 1  Build the toes

- Select **Create** → **NURBS Primitives** → **Sphere**.
- Enter **90** for the **Rotate Z** attribute to place the sphere sideways.
- In the Channel Box, set the *makeNurbSphere* construction history as follows:

  **End Sweep** to **90**;

  **Sections** to **4.**

- Translate the sphere on the **Z-axis** by **1** unit.
- Scale the sphere on the **Y-axis** to **0.75**.
- Rename the sphere as *toes*.

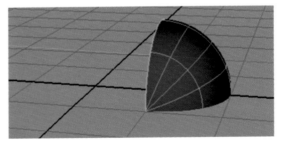

*The toes*

## 2 Build the calf

- Select **Create** → **NURBS Primitives** → **Cylinder**.

- Translate the cylinder up on the **Y-axis** by **1** unit to even it with the floor.

- Press **F8** to go in Component mode and enable the **Points** and **Hulls** buttons.

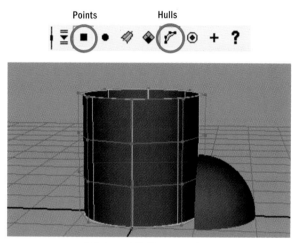

*Points and Hulls components*

**Tip:** *Clicking on a hull will select all the CVs connected to that hull.*

- Reshape the cylinder as follows:

*Basic shape of the calf*

- Press **F8** to go back in Object mode.

- Rename the cylinder *calf*.

## 3    Project a curve on NURBS

In order to create an opening for the toes, you will project a curve on the calf surface to be used with the **Trim Tool**.

- Select **Create** → **EP Curve**.

- From the side view, draw a curve that will be used to trim the calf surface.

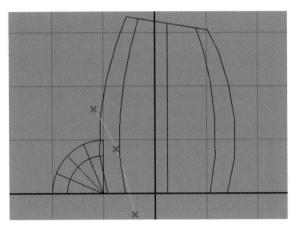

*The curve for the toes opening*

- Hit **Enter** to finish the curve.

- Select the *curve,* then **Shift-select** the *calf*.

- Still from the side view, go to the Modeling menu set and select **Edit NURBS** → **Project Curve on Surface**.

**Note:** *It is important to do this action from the side view since the projection of the curve is made from the active camera. You can change that behavior in the options of the **Project Curve on Surface Tool**.*

## 4    Trim Tool

The Trim Tool lets you choose one or more portions of a surface that was divided by curves on surface.

- Select the *calf* surface.

- Select **Edit NURBS** → **Trim Tool**.

- Click on the upper section of the *calf* that you want to keep. The other section will be deleted.

- Hit **Enter** to execute the tool.

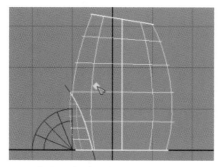
*Select the good portion to keep*

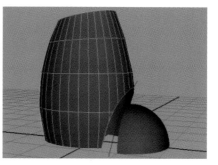
*The trimmed surface*

**Tip:** *You can still modify the original projection curve to dynamically update the trimmed surface.*

**Note:** *Trimming a surface does not delete or modify any NURBS components. The surface of the trimmed section is simply not drawn. To display a trimmed surface, select* **Edit NURBS** → **Untrim Surfaces**.

## Boot sole

You will build the boot sole starting from a curve extracted from the calf surface. You will then cut the curve and duplicate it to create the sole surface. This will introduce you to new curve and surface tools.

### 1   Sole curve

- **RMB-click** the *calf* surface and select **Isoparm** from the context menu.

*Notice the isoparms of the surface are highlighted in blue.*

- Click on the lowest horizontal isoparm of the *calf*.

**Note:** *When you click directly on an isoparm to select it, the isoparm gets highlighted with a continuous yellow line. If you* **click+drag** *on an isoparm, a dotted yellow line shows you the isoparm at the cursor's position.*

- With the isoparm selected, select **Edit Curves** → **Duplicate Surface Curves**.

- Due to the trimmed *calf*, you might not get a full curve when duplicating the surface curve. To correct this, highlight the *curveFromSurfaceIso* input node from the Channel Box and set both the **Min Value** and **Max Value** to **0**.

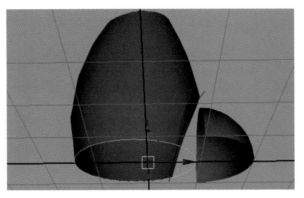

*The duplicated curve*

## 2   Second sole curve

- Select **Create** → **EP Curve**.

- Hold down the **c** hotkey to enable the snap on curve option. **Click+drag** on the left side of the trim edge of the *calf* to create the first curve point. Make sure to drag the curve point all the way down onto the trim edge.

- Now, hold down **c** again and click+drag on the right side of the trim edge of the *calf* to create the second curve point. Again, make sure to drag the curve point all the way down onto the trim edge.

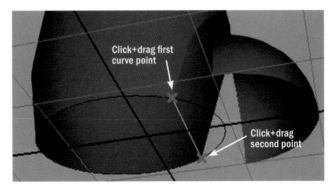

Click+drag first curve point

Click+drag second point

*The second sole curve*

- Press **Enter** to finish the curve.

## 3  Cut the curves

- **Select** the first curve, then **Shift-select** the second curve.

- Select **Edit Curves → Cut Curves**.

*This will cut the first curve so that you can delete the unnecessary front portion of the curve.*

- Delete the superfluous curve segment.

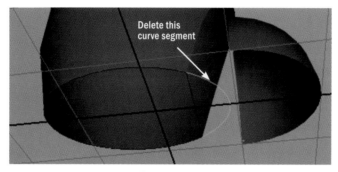

*The cut curves*

## 4  Attach the curves

Now that you have proper sole curves, you will notice that there are actually three curves forming the sole. The first curve was split into two parts because of the closing point of the cylinder used for the calf. So you will need to attach all three curves together before creating the sole surface.

- Select two of the sole curves.

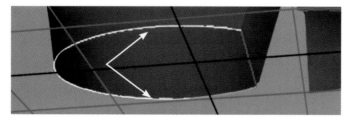

*Select two curves*

**Tip:**  *It will be easier to select the curves if you turn off the surface selection mask button located in the status bar when in Object mode.*

- Select **Edit Curves** → **Attach Curves** → ❑.

- Change the **Attach Method** to **Connect**.

*This will attach the curves with minimal smoothing.*

- Click the **Attach** button to execute the command.

*The two selected curves are now attached together.*

- With the new attached curve selected, select the remaining curve.

- Press the **g** hotkey to execute the last tool again.

*You should now have a single and complete sole curve.*

**Tip:** *If you find that your curves are not attaching like the image below, you may need to select the new curve and in it's Attribute Editor, turn **Reverse1** to **On**. This will reverse the direction of one of the curves so that they attach properly.*

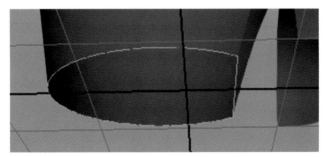

*The finished sole curve*

- Rename the curve *soleCurve*.

**Note:** *The Attach command kept the original curves for construction history. You will need to manually delete the unnecessary curves in order to keep your scene clean.*

## 5 Loft curves

The new curve will be used to create a loft surface that will look like the border of the sole. A loft is a surface generated from curves used as isoparms.

- Select the *soleCurve*.

- Select **Modify** → **Center Pivot** to center the pivot of the curve.

- Press **Ctrl+d** to duplicate the sole curve.

- Press **r** to show the **Scale Tool**.

- Scale the new curve in **X** and **Z** by holding down **Ctrl** and **click+dragging** on the **Y-axis** of the manipulator.

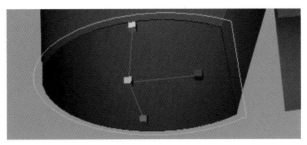

*The duplicated curve*

- Press **Ctrl+d** to duplicate the sole curve again.

- Move the new curve down on the **Y-axis**.

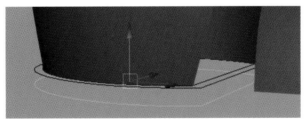

*Move the new curve down*

- Select all three curves in order.

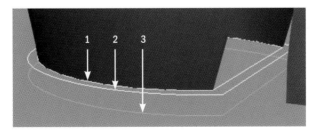

*Select the curves in the correct order*

- Select **Surfaces** → **Loft**.
- Rename the loft *soleEdge*.

*Lofted surface*

## 6    Planar

A planar surface is a surface created from a closed curve or isoparm. In order for a planar to be successfully computed, the CVs of the curve or isoparm defining it must be perfectly flat.

- Select the third *soleCurve*.
- To ensure the curve is perfectly flat, set its **Scale Y** to **0**.
- Select **Surfaces** → **Planar**.
- Rename the planar *sole*.

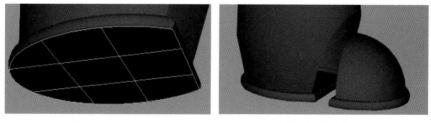

*Planar surface*                                    *The NURBS boot*

## 7    Second sole curve

- Redo steps **1** to **6** to create the toes' sole.

# Boot details

So far, the boot is missing an inner part that will fill the hole between the calf and toes' surfaces. It is also missing a nice border on the upper part of the calf. The Extrude Tool can be used to fill in these gaps. The next steps will show examples of how to use the Extrude Tool.

## 1  Inner foot extrusion

- Select **Create** → **EP Curve**.

- From the side view, hold down **c** to **snap on curve** and **click+drag** up on the *toes* isoparm. Make sure to drag the curve point all the way up onto the toes' edge.

- Create the remaining curve points as follows:

Using snap on curve, click+drag the first point on the isoparm then up

*The new inner foot curve*

- Press **Enter** to finish the curve.

- **RMB** on the *toes* and select isoparm.

- Select the *toes'* edge isoparm, then **Shift-select** the curve you just created.

- Select **Surface** → **Extrude**.

- In the Channel Box, highlight the *extrude* input node and set **Extrude Type** to **Flat**.

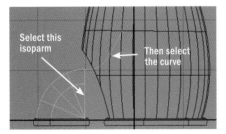

Select this isoparm

Then select the curve

*Prepare for the extrusion*

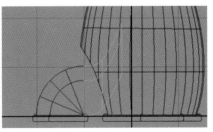

*The extruded surface*

- Go into Component mode and tweak the extrusion surface so it doesn't interpenetrate the calf geometry and so the space between the toes and the calf is flat.

- Rename the extrusion *innerFoot*.

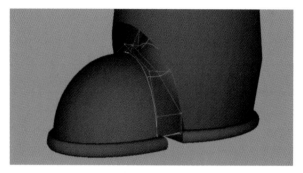

*Tweak the extrusion*

## 2   Calf border extrusion

- Select **Create** → **NURBS Primitives** → **Circle**.

- **RMB-click** on the calf surface and select **Isoparm**.

- With the new circle still selected, click on the calf's top isoparm.

- Select **Surface** → **Extrude** → **❑**.

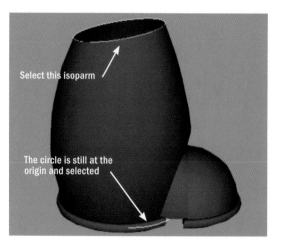

*Prepare the extrusion*

- Set the extrude options as follows:

    **Style** to **Tube**;

    **Result Position** to **At Path**;

    **Pivot** to **Component**;

    **Orientation** to **Path Direction**.

- Click the **Extrude** button.

*The extrusion does not seem correct because the circle used for the extrusion is too big and flat on the grid.*

*The new extrusion*

- Select the *circle* used for the extrusion.

- Rotate the circle by **90-degrees** on the **X-axis**.

*The finished border*

- Scale down the *circle* until the border looks appropriate.

- Rename the extrusion *calfBorder*.

## 3 Save your work

- Save your scene as *15-robotModel.ma*.

# Modeling the legs

Now that you have completed the boot and used several NURBS tools, you can complete the leg quite easily. First, you will create a hinge for the knee, then you will create the upper leg and finally you will make the hip articulation.

## 1   Knee

- Select **Create** → **NURBS Primitive** → **Cylinder** → ❑.

- In the options window, set **Caps** to **Both**, which will add end caps to the cylinder.

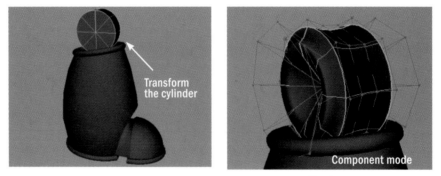

*The modified knee*                     *The knee*

- Click the **Create** button.

- Transform the *cylinder*.

- Press **F8** to go into Component mode and tweak the shape of the cylinder.

- Rename the cylinder *knee*.

## 2   Leg

- Select **Create** → **NURBS Primitive** → **Cylinder**, which will create another cylinder with end caps.

- In the construction history, change the **Spans** attribute of the *makeNurbCylinder* node to **3**.

- Move the cylinder in place and tweak its shape so that it looks like a thigh.

**Note:** *When moving components on the edges of the cylinder, make sure to also select the components of the adjacent cap to move them at the same time.*

- Rename the cylinder *leg*.

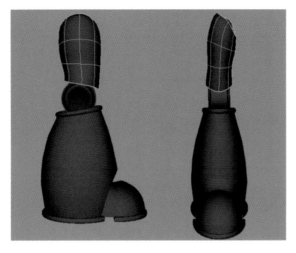

*The leg*

## 2   Leg extrusions and hip articulation

- Refine the leg by adding two extrusions around the *leg*'s hard edges, like you have done with the upper calf.

- Rename the extrusions *upperLegBorder* and *lowerLegBorder*.

The hip articulation will be made out of two objects. The first piece will be a basic NURBS sphere, but the second piece will be created from a revolved curve.

- Create a NURBS sphere and translate it up on the **Y-axis** above the leg.

- Rename the sphere *hip*.

- Select **Create** → **EP Curve**.

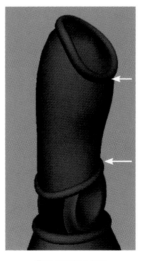

*The leg borders*

- From the front view, draw a curve as follows:

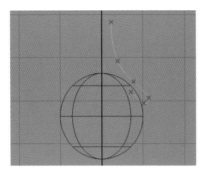

*The hip articulation curve*

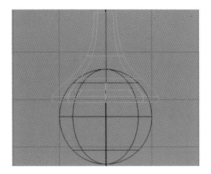

*The revolved curve*

- Select **Surfaces** → **Revolve**.
- Rename the revolved surface *hipArticulation*.

**Note:** *You can still tweak the curve components to change the shape of the revolved surface.*

## 4 Placing the hip articulation

Since both the *hip* and *hipArticulation* don't share the same pivot, if you want to scale, translate and rotate them, they will move according to their own pivot and not together. In order to transform both objects together, you need to group them first.

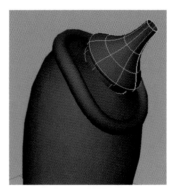

- Select both *hip* and *hipArticulation* and press **Ctrl+g** to group them together.

- Select **Modify** → **Center Pivot** to center the pivot of the group to its children.

*The proper position of the hip articulation*

- Place the group as shown to the right.

**Note:** *If you transform the curve and the revolved surface together, the revolved surface will change shape since construction history still connects them.*

## 5 Mirror the leg

- Select the entire leg geometry and press **Ctrl+g** to group it together.

- Rename the group *rightLeg*.

- Press **Ctrl+d** to duplicate the leg group.

- Change the **Scale X** of the new leg group to **-1**.

- Rename the new group *leftLeg*.

- Translate the *leftLeg* group on the **X-axis** to **-1** and translate the *rightLeg* group on the **X-axis** to **1**.

*Doing so will make it easier to model the body of the robot centered on the Y-axis.*

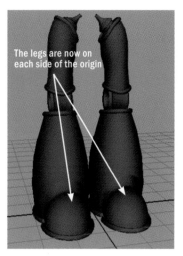

The legs are now on each side of the origin

*Both legs*

## 6 Clean up the scene

You have done quite a lot of modeling operation and there might be groups, curves and surfaces that are no longer needed in the scene. You should clean up your scene in order to keep it light and fast.

- Open the Outliner.

- Delete obsolete curves, groups and surfaces.

## 7 Save your work

# Modeling the body

You can now start modeling the robot's body. You will begin by creating the pelvis geometry, then building the chest up to the neck. The following steps are quite similar to what you have experienced already in this lesson, so the steps are less detailed.

## 1 Crotch

- Select **Create → NURBS Primitive → Torus.**

- Change the *torus* construction history to the following:

    **Radius** to **0.4**;

    **End Sweep** to **180**;

    **Sections** to **4**;

    **Height Ratio** to **0.2.**

- Transform the torus as shown in the robot's crotch image:

- Rename the torus *crotch*.

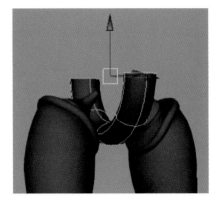

*The robot's crotch*

## 2 Pelvis

- Create a **Create → NURBS Primitive → Cylinder** with caps.

- Rename it *pelvis* and place it as shown to the right:

*The robot's pelvis*

## 3 Model half of the chest

To keep the chest section simple, you will model only half of the chest and then mirror the geometry and connect the two surfaces together.

- Create another **Create → NURBS Primitive → Cylinder,** but this time without the caps.

- Rename the *cylinder* to *chest*.

- Change the *chest* construction history **End Sweep** to **180** and place it as shown to the right:

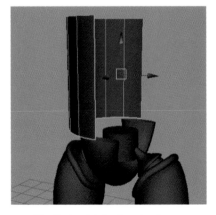

*Starting point for the chest*

- **RMB-click** on the *chest* and select **Isoparm** from the context menu.

- To select a new horizontal isoparm on the lower chest section, **click+hold** the **LMB** on the lowest isoparm and drag the mouse up until you see a red line. Let go of the mouse button and you should see a dotted yellow isoparm line.

*The selected isoparm*

- Select **Edit NURBS** → **Insert Isoparms**.

*The selected isoparm*

- Press **F8** to go in Component mode and scale the lowest row of CVs toward the inside to close the lower portion of the *chest*.

***Tip:*** *You can adjust the scaling pivot's position to get a proper scaling.*

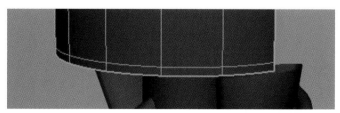

*The new isoparm*

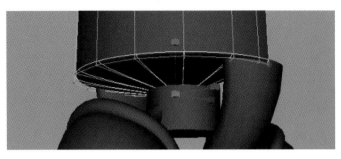

*The closed bottom*

**Tip:** *You don't need to go back and forth between Component and Object mode to select and insert isoparms. Stay in Component mode and toggle the isoparm mask button.*

- Repeat the previous actions in order to refine the *chest* geometry as follows:

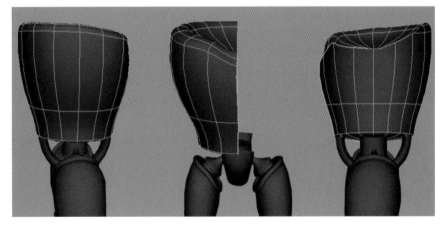

*The refined chest geometry*

## 4   Mirror the chest

- Go into Object mode and select the *chest* geometry.

- Press **Ctrl+d** and set the **Scale Z** of the *chest* to **-1**.

*You can now see the complete chest of the robot.*

## 5   Attach the chest pieces

- **RMB-click** on the *chest* surface and select **Isoparm** from the context menu.

- Click on the front vertical isoparm on the edge of the surface.

*A yellow line indicates the selection.*

- **RMB-click** on the other *chest* surface and select **Isoparm** again from the context menu.

- Hold down **Shift** and click on the front vertical isoparm on the edge of the surface.

*You should now have two edge isoparms selected, one on each surface.*

- Attach the two sufaces together by selecting **Edit NURBS** → **Align Surfaces** → ❐.

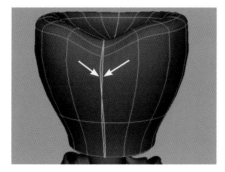

The two edge isoparms selected

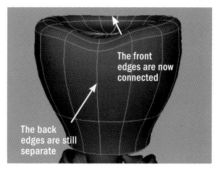

The attached chest

- In the options window, set the following:

    **Attach** to **On**;

    **Modify Position** to **Both.**

- Click on the **Align** button.

*The two surfaces should now be attached together, but the back edges are still separate.*

- To close the surface completely, select **Edit NURBS** → **Open/Close Surfaces** → ❐.

- In the options window, set the following:

  **Surface Direction** to **V**;

  **Shape** to **Blend**.

- Click on the **Open/Close** button.

*The chest surface is now completely closed.*

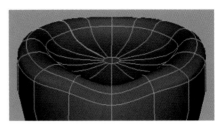

*The chest is now closed*

## 6  Neck

- Create a sphere.

- Rename it *neck* and place it as shown to the right:

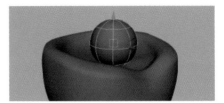

*The robot's neck*

## 7  Neck border

In order to create a neck border, you will use the intersect function.
This function will create a curve on surface at the exact intersection point between two surfaces, which you will use with an extrusion.

- Select the *neck*, then **Shift-select** the *chest* geometry.

- Select **Edit NURBS** → **Intersect Surfaces**.

*If you change the shading to wireframe, you will see the curves located at the exact intersection point between the two surfaces. There are actually two sets of curves, one of each intersecting surface.*

- Select **Edit Curves** → **Duplicate Surface Curves**.

*There should be two sets of curves in the Outliner. One set is not required.*

- Delete one of the obsolete sets of curves.

- Attach the two remaining curves by selecting **Edit Curves** → **Attach Curves**.

**Tip:**  Make sure the **Attach Method** *is set to* **Connect** *in the Attach Curves options.*

- **Extrude** a neck border like you have done before for the upper calf border.

- Rename the extrusion *neckBorder*.

*The robot's neck border*

## 8   Save your work

## 9   Rest of the body

If you want to skip modeling the rest of the character, you can open the file *15-robotModel.ma* from the support files. If you want to perfect your modeling skills, reproduce the following head and arm geometry using what you already know:

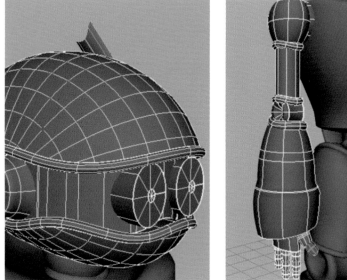

*The robot's head*

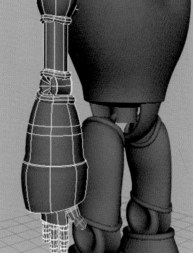

*The robot's arm*

**Tip:**   *Don't forget to mirror symmetrical geometry to speed up your work.*

## 10 Clean up the model

- Select **Edit** → **Delete All by Type** → **History**.

- Make sure to delete any obsolete nodes in the Outliner.

- Select all the geometry and groups, then select **Modify** → **Center Pivot**.

- Select all the geometry and groups, then select
**Modify** → **Freeze Transformations**.

- Group all the geometry under a single group called *robotGeo*.

- Create a new layer called *robotLayer* and add the *robotGeo* group to it.

**Tip:**   *Select the robotGeo group and press **1** to reduce the NURBS smoothness display if the display is too slow.*

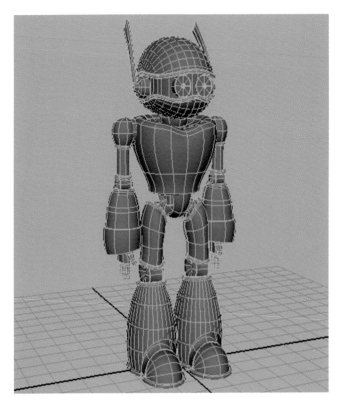

*The final robot geometry*

## Conclusion

You now have a good knowledge of working with curves and surfaces. You have seen how to change the shape of objects using their components. You have also experimented with curves and how they can be used to generate surfaces with the help of tools such as revolve, loft, planar and extrude. Finally, you have sped up your work by duplicating and mirroring geometry.

In the next lesson, you will experiment with NURBS texturing and the 3D Paint Tool.

# Lesson 16     NURBS texturing

*In this lesson, you will learn about NURBS texturing, 3D placement projections and the 3D Paint Tool. You will start by texturing the robot using the texture placement attributes and the Texture Placement Tool. You will then use the various texture projection types. Once you understand the basics of NURBS texturing, you will experiment with the 3D Paint Tool, using both regular and Paint Effects brushes to create your texture maps.*

## In this lesson you will learn the following:

- How to project a texture using a projection node;

- How to prevent texture sliding;

- How to convert a shading network to a file texture;

- How to place a texture using the placement node's attributes;

- How to place a texture using the Texture Placement Tool;

- How to assign and paint a texture using the 3D Paint Tool;

- How to remove unused shading groups.

# Texturing surfaces

Unlike polygonal geometry, UV mapping is not required on NURBS geometry since texture coordinates are determined by the U and V directions of the NURBS surface itself. You will see later in this lesson that the only way to map a texture differently is by using projection mapping.

## 1 Checker texture

In order to view the default UV maps, you will create both a Lambert and checker texture, and then assign them to the boot geometry.

- In the Hypershade, create a **Lambert** material.

- Map the **Color** of the new material with a **Checker** texture.

**Tip:**   *Make sure the create option at the top of the Create Render Node window is set to **Normal**.*

- Assign the new checker material to the boot surfaces and see how the texture is mapped.

*On fairly square surfaces (such as the unfolded calf cylinder), the checker texture won't appear to be too stretched, but on long and thin surfaces, such as the borders, the texture will look stretched. Also, when a NURBS surface has a pole, the texture will look pinched.*

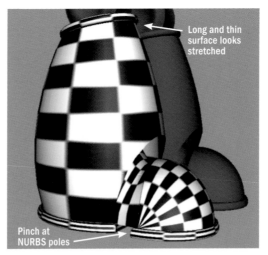

*NURBS texture mapping*

## 2   Assign a file texture

- Create a **Blinn** material.

- Map the **Color** of the new material with a **File** texture.

- Set the **Image Name** of the file texture to be *calfTexture.tif* from the *sourceimages* folder.

- Assign the new material to the *calf* surface.

*When the texture is seamless, you should not see any seam on the geometry.*

*Calf texture*

## 3   Assign another file texture

You will now map the toe's surface, but since you can clearly see the checker pinching, you will use a projected texture.

- Create another **Blinn** material and assign it to the toes.

- Click on the **Map** button for the **Color** of the new material.

- Change the **Create** option at the top of the **Create Render Node** window to **As Projection**.

- Now click on the **File** button to create the file texture along with its projection node.

- Set the **Image Name** of the file texture to be *blueMetal.tif* from the *sourceimages* folder.

- Assign the new material to the *toes* surface.

*The projection of the texture is determined by the 3D texture placement node located at the origin.*

- Select the placement node.

- In the Attribute Editor, click on the **Fit to group bbox** button.

*The node will move to fit the bounding box of the surfaces using this texture.*

Toes' texture placement node          The placement node set to fit the toes

## 4  Texture reference object

While the projected texture works well at this time, it might not when the surface is moved or deformed since the texture placement node does not move along with the surface, causing a sliding texture problem. You, therefore, need to set up a non-deformed reference object to lock the texture on the geometry.

- Select the *toes* surface.

- Under the Rendering menu set, select **Texturing** → **Create Texture Reference Object**.

*An unselectable object duplicate will appear as wireframe in the viewport. This object is only selectable through the Outliner or the Hypergraph.*

- Create a new layer called *textureReferences*.

- From the Outliner, select both the *place3dTexture* and the new *toes* reference object.

- **RMB** on the *textureReferences* layer and select **Add Selected Objects** from the context menu.

- Set the layer visibility to **Off**.

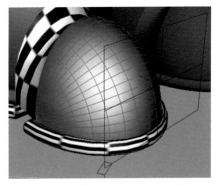

The template reference object

**Note:** *If the reference object would be made visible, it would not render. You are hiding it to keep the viewport clean.*

## 5   Finish the boot

- Create a Blinn material with a gray color and assign it to
  the *innerFoot* surface.

- Create another Blinn material with a dark gray color and assign it to the
  *sole* and *border* surfaces.

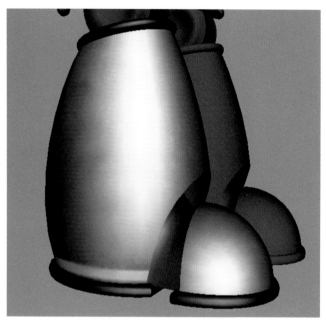

*The textured boot*

## 6   Other boot

- Assign the same materials onto the other boot.

- Create another reference object for the other *toes* surface and add it to
  the *textureReferences* layer.

*You should now have two identical boots. You will be altering their textures
later in this lesson using the 3D Paint Tool.*

## 7   Save your work

- Save your file as *16-textureModel.ma*.

# Convert to texture

You will now create a shading network to project a logo on the shoulder of the robot. Since it will be a complex shading network, you will convert the network as a single file texture, which will be much more efficient to render.

## 1   Create the logo shader

- In the Hypershade, create a **Blinn** material.

- Rename the material *logoBlinn*.

**Note:** *You can rename a node in the Hypershade by holding down the* **Ctrl** *key and* **double-clicking** *on its name.*

- Click on the **Color Map** button.

- Make sure the creation option is still set to **As Projection** and click on the **File** button.

- Set the **Image Name** of the file texture to be *01.tif* from the *sourceimages* folder.

- Rename the file texture *01.tif*.

## 2   Project logo texture

- Assign the shader to the right *shoulder* of the robot.

- Select the new *place3dTexture* and click the **Fit to group bbox** button in the Attribute Editor.

- Select *projection2* from the Hypershade.

- In the Attribute Editor, change the **Proj Type** to be **Spherical**.

*The default projection*

**Tip:**   *To raise the texture display quality, select the logoBlinn material and in the Attribute Editor, set the* **Texture Resolution** *from the* **Hardware Texturing** *section to* **Highest**.

- Use the manipulator to rotate, scale, and translate the projection as follows:

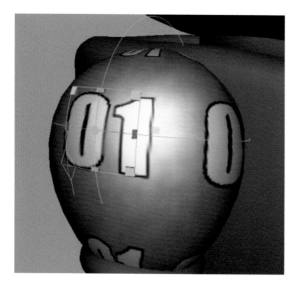

*The adequate projection*

## 3   Fix texture wrapping

- Select the *place2dTexture* of *logoTexture*.

- In the Attribute Editor, turn **Off** both **Wrap U** and **Wrap V**.

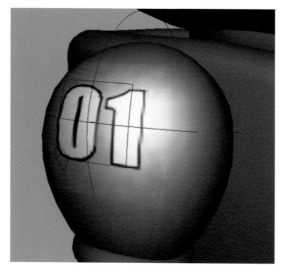

*No texture wrapping*

## 4    Change the default color

The texture is displayed correctly, but the default shader color is displayed outside the texture boundary.

- Select *logoTexture* and open the Attribute Editor.

- Scroll down to the **Color Balance** section and click on the **Map** button of **Default Color.** *The Default Color is the color underneath the texture which is revealed when the Coverage is less than 1.0.*

- Change the creation option to **Normal** and create a **File** texture.

- Click the browse button next to the **Image Name** and select *blueMetal.tif* from the *sourceimages* folder.

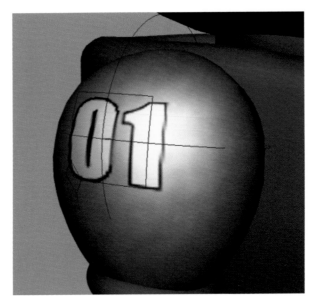

*The corrected logo*

## 5    Convert the shading network

The logo shading network is becoming fairly complex, but could be much simpler with a proper texture to fit the UV map of the shoulder geometry. Maya can convert a complex shading network into a single texture file. This simplifies the shader and will speed up the render time.

- Select *logoBlinn* shader and **Shift-select** the *shoulder* geometry.

- From the Hypergraph, select **Edit → Convert to File Texture (Maya Software) → ❑**.

- In the option window set the following:

    **UV Range** to **Entire Range**;

    **X Resolution** to **512**;

    **Y Resolution** to **512**;

    **Image Format** to **TIF**.

- Click the **Convert and Close** button.

*Maya will convert the network to a texture and will create and assign a new network using only a single texture. The new texture is automatically saved in the current project's sourceimages folder.*

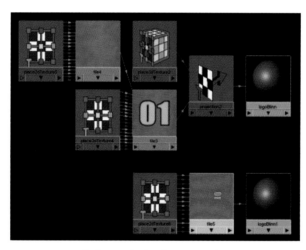

*Before and after the conversion*

**Note:** *By converting a shading network to a texture, you do not require a projection and a reference object. The texture fits the geometry perfectly.*

## 6   Duplicate the network for the other shoulder

- Select the new *logoBlinn1* shader.

- Select **Edit** → **Duplicate** → **Shading Network**.

- Assign the new *logoBlinn2* to the other shoulder.

*Notice the logo is inverted.*

- Select the file texture's *place2dTexture* node.

- In the Attribute Editor, set **Repeat UV** to be **1** and **-1**.

*This will cause the texture to be inverted on the V-axis.*

## 7   Interactive Placement Tool

- Still in the Attribute Editor with the file texture's *place2dTexture* node selected, click on the **Interactive Placement** button.

*Doing so will invoke the* **NURBS Texture Placement Tool***. This tool displays a red manipulator on the NURBS geometry which allows you to interactively place the texture in the viewport.*

**Note:** *You can also access the* **NURBS Texture Placement Tool** *via the* **Texturing** *menu when a NURBS surface is selected.*

- **MMB+drag** the red marker located in the middle of the texture placement manipulator to center the logo appropriately.

*Notice the value of the place2dTexture node update as you drag the manipulator. You could also set the place2dTexture values manually.*

## 8   Save your work

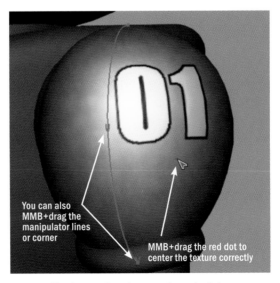

You can also
MMB+drag the
manipulator lines
or corner

MMB+drag the red dot to
center the texture correctly

*The interactive placement manipulator*

# 3D Paint Tool

Another great way to create custom texture is to paint a texture directly on a model in the viewport. The 3D Paint Tool allows you to paint using default paintbrushes or Paint Effects brushes. You can use the tool to outline painted details in separate software or to create a final texture directly in Maya.

## 1 Chest shader

- In the Hypershade, create a **Blinn** material.

- Rename the material *chestBlinn*.

- Map the **Color** attribute with a **File** texture, making sure the creation option is set to **Normal**.

- Browse and set the **Image Name** to be *blueMetal.tif* from the *sourceimages* folder.

- Assign the *chestBlinn* material to the *chest* geometry.

## 2 Set the 3D Paint Tool

- Select the *chest* geometry.

- Select **Texturing** → **3D Paint Tool** → ❑.

*This will open the tool's option window.*

- Scroll down to the **File Textures** section.

- Make sure **Attribute to Paint** is set to **Color**.

- Click the **Assign/Edit Textures** button.

*This should open the new texture creation options.*

- Set **Image Format** to **Tiff (tif)**.

- Set both the **Size X** and **Size Y** to **512**.

- Click the **Assign/Edit Textures** button.

Doing so will duplicate the currently assigned texture and save it in your project in the *3dpainttextures* folder. As you paint on the geometry, only this new texture will be updated and not the original file texture.

## 3 Set Erase Image

To make sure that you can erase your drawing and come back to the original texture, you need to set the erase image as the current texture.

- Scroll to the **Paint Operations** section and click on the **Set Erase Texture** button.

## 4  Paint on geometry

- Scroll back at the top of the 3D Paint Tool window and make sure the second **Artisan** brush is enabled in the **Brush** section.

- If the brush size is too big or too small for painting on the geometry, set its **Radius (U)** in the option window, or hold the **b** hotkey and drag the radius of the brush in the viewport.

- You can change the **Color** attribute to paint with another color.

- Start painting on the geometry.

*3D Paint Tool*                    *Erase the previous stroke*

## 5  Erase painting

- Scroll to the **Paint Operations** section and change the **Artisan** attribute to **Erase**.

- Paint to erase your drawing and then return to the original texture.

## 6  Paint using Paint Effects

- Scroll to the **Brush** section of the tool and enable the **Paint Effects** brush.

- To choose a template brush, click on the **Get Brush** button to invoke the Visor.

- In the Visor, scroll to the **Fun** directory and choose the last brush called *weird.mel*.

- Paint on the geometry.

*Get Brush button*

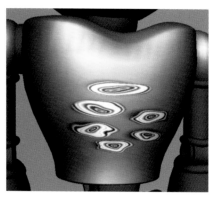

Paint with weird.mel brush

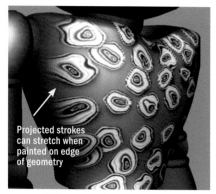

Projected strokes can stretch when painted on edge of geometry

Different angle after painting

## 7   Screen projection

When painting with a Paint Effects brush, you will notice that the brush icon in the viewport looks stretched. This is because the brush bases itself on the object's UVs, which are stretched. To correct the problem, you need to enable the screen projection option.

- Expand the **Stroke** section in the Paint Effects window.

- Turn **On** the **Screen Projection** attribute.

- Paint on geometry.

Stretched brush

**Note:** *When painting with Screen Projection, you are painting using the current camera view. This can be very useful in some cases, but can also create stretched textures when painting on geometry parallel to the view.*

## 8   Erase all drawing

- In the **Flood** section, click the **Flood Erase** button.

## 9   Reflection

- In the **Stroke** section, turn **Off** the **Screen Projection** checkbox.

- Turn **On** the **Reflection** checkbox and enable **X** as the **Reflection Axis**.

- In the **Brush** section, click the **Artisan** brush.

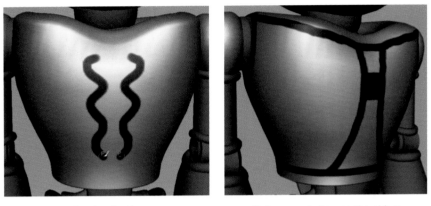

*Brush reflection*          *Reference strokes on the object*

## 10 Reference strokes

You might find it easier to draw only reference strokes in Maya and then use a paint program to refine the look of the texture. To do so, you will draw where you want to add texture details on the object, and then open the texture in a paint program. Once you are done with the texture, you will reload it in Maya.

- In the **Flood** section, click the **Flood Erase** button.

- Draw details, such as lines and logo position, as shown above in the image to the right.

## 11 Save textures

You have not yet saved the texture just drawn to disk, making it inaccessible to another program.

- To save the texture manually, click the **Save Textures** button in the **File Textures** section.

Or

- To save the texture automatically on each stroke, turn **On** the **Save Texture on Stroke** checkbox in the **File Textures** section.

## 12 Edit the texture

You can now edit your texture from the *3dpainttextures* directory in a paint program. When you are done modifying the texture, save the new image out.

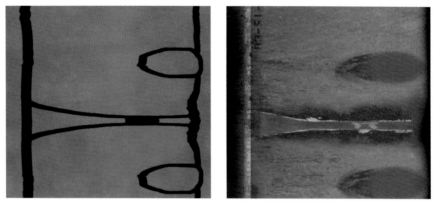

*The texture saved on disk*          *The final texture*

- Back in Maya, in the texture's Attribute Editor, click the **Reload File Texture** button to update the *chest* for the new version.

**Tip:** *If you saved the file under a different name or in a different location, browse to get the modified texture.*

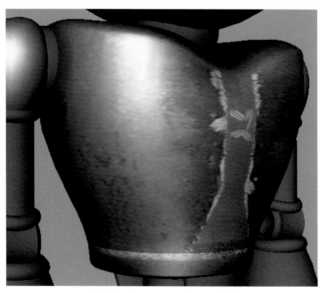

*The final texture on the model*

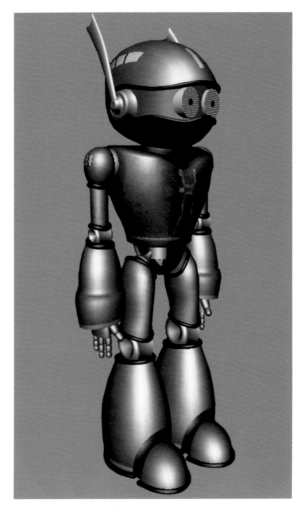

*The final robot*

## 13 Finish texturing the robot

- Using what you have learned in this lesson, texture the rest of the robot by yourself.

- You can also add bump maps and specular maps to improve the rendering quality of the robot.

## 14 Save your work

## Optimizing the scene

To maintain a good workflow, clean up your scene once texturing is complete.
For instance, you might want to delete all unused shading networks in the scene.

**1   Delete unused nodes**

- From the Hypershade window, select **Edit → Delete Unused Nodes**.

*Maya will go through the list of render nodes and delete anything that is not
assigned to a piece of geometry in the scene.*

**2   Optimize scene size**

- Select **File → Optimize Scene Size**.

*Maya will go through the entire scene and remove any unused nodes.*

**3   Save your work**

**4   Final robot**

The final *16-textureModel.ma* file can be found in the support files.


## Conclusion

You have garnered more experience texturing NURBS surfaces and learned
how to use projections and how to convert a projection into a texture. You also
learned how to paint directly on a surface and use the resulting texture file.
Finally, you cleaned your scene to remove any unused nodes, speeding up the
file loading and render time.

The next lesson will explore some other rendering engines available in Maya.

# Lesson 17    Maya Render types

In previous lessons you were introduced to Maya software and the Hardware Render Buffer to render your scenes. In Maya, there are three additional rendering types to choose from: Maya Hardware, Maya Vector, and mental ray for Maya. Each has its own strengths and you should determine which rendering engine to use on a per project basis depending on the final application.

You will now use a new robot scene as a basis for reviewing the three render types.

## In this lesson you will learn the following:

- How to change the current renderer;

- How to render with mental ray;

- How to render with Maya Vector;

- How to render with Maya Hardware.

# mental ray

Perhaps the most complex and powerful rendering type available in Maya is mental ray. It offers many solutions for the creation of photorealistic renders, such as Global Illumination, caustic reflections and refractions, support for High Dynamic Range Imaging, custom shaders, and motion blurred reflections and shadows.

In this exercise, you will open an existing scene that includes the robot you just textured, plus animation, reflection and lighting. Using mental ray, the shadows will have motion blur and the motion blur on the robot will be reflected into a mirror.

## 1   Open the robot scene to render

- Select **File** → **Open** and choose *renderTypes.ma*.

## 2   Open the Render Settings

- Select **Window** → **Render Editors** → **Render Settings...**

- In the **Render Settings** window, select **Render Using** → **mental ray**.

## 3   Set the rendering options

To render the animation, you must set up the scene's file extensions to indicate a rendered sequence. You must also set up the start and end frames.

- Click on the **Common** tab.

- From the **Image File Output** section, set the following:

    **File Name Prefix** to **mentalRay**.

*This sets the name of the animated sequence.*

**Frame/Animation Ext** *to:*

    **name.#.ext** (for Windows, Mac);

*This sets up Maya to render a numbered sequence of images.*

    **Start Frame** to **1**;

    **End Frame** to **20**;

    **By Frame** to **1**.

*This tells Maya to render every frame from 1 to 20.*

**4   Set up the mental ray render settings for motion blur**

- Under the **mental ray** tab, select **Quality** → **ProductionMotionblur**.

*This image quality preset automatically turns on high quality motion blur. It also sets up raytracing, as well as high quality anti-alias and texture sampling values for mental ray.*

**5   Set up the depth map shadows for mental ray**

- Select *pointLight1* from the **Light** tab in the Hypershade and open the Attribute Editor.

- Under the *spotLightShape1* tab, open the **mental ray** section.

- Enable the **Shadow Map** checkbox.

- Click on the **Take Setting From Maya** button.

*The resolution, samples and softness will be automatically updated.*

**6   Perform a test render**

- Go to frame **5**.

- Make the Perspective view active.

- Select **Render** → **Render Current Frame**...

*mental ray rendering*

**7   Batch render**

- Select **Render** → **Batch Render**.

**Tip:** *If your computer has multiple processors, it is recommended that you set* **Use all Available Processors** *to* **On** *in the batch render options, since the render can be time-consuming.*

- When the render is complete, select **Render** → **Show Batch Render...** This will invoke the fcheck utility to playback the animated sequence.

**Or**

- From the browser, select one of the frames of the animation, then click **Open**.

*Notice that the reflection and shadows in the scene have a motion blur.*

## Maya Vector

The Maya Vector renderer can output files in 2D vector format. It can also be used to create stylized flat renderings seen in illustrations and 2D animation.

Using the previous scene, you will set up a Maya Vector render.

### 1  Set up the depth map shadows

- Select *pointLight1* and open the Attribute Editor.
- Under the *spotLightShape1* tab, expand the **Shadows** section.
- Set **Use Depth Map Shadows** to **On**.
- Change the **Shadow Color** to a dark gray.

### 2  Open the Maya Vector Render Settings

- Select **Window** → **Rendering Editors** → **Render Settings** ...
- In the **Render Settings** window, select **Render Using** → **Maya Vector**.

### 3  Set up the Maya Vector options

- Select the **mental ray** tab.

- In the **Fill Options** section, set the following:

   **Fill Objects** to **On**;

   **Fill Style** to **Single Color**;

   **Show Back Faces** to **On**;

   **Shadows** to **On**;

   **Highlights** to **On**;

   **Reflections** to **On**.

- In the **Edge Options** section, select the following:

   **Include Edges** to **On**;

   **Edge Weight Preset** to **3.0 pt**;

   **Edge Style** to **Outlines**.

*Maya Vector rendering*

## 4  Perform a test render

- Make the Perspective view active.
- Select **Render** → **Render Current Frame...**

## 5  Batch render

- Repeat step 7 from the previous exercise in this lesson.

# Maya Hardware

Not to be confused with the Hardware Render Buffer introduced in the first project, the Maya Hardware renderer allows you to create broadcast resolution images faster than with the software renderer.

In many cases, the quality of the output will be high enough to go directly to broadcast but some advanced shadows, reflections and post-process effects cannot be produced with the Hardware renderer. The final image quality of Maya Hardware renderer is significantly higher than that of the Hardware Render Buffer.

## 1   Set up the depth map shadows

- Make sure the **Use Depth Map Shadows** attribute for the *pointLight1* is still **On** from the past exercise.

## 2   Open the Maya Hardware Render Settings

- Select **Window** → **Rendering Editors** → **Render Settings...**

- In the **Render Settings** window, select **Render Using** → **Maya Hardware**.

- Select the **Maya Hardware** tab.

- Under the **Quality** section, set **Presets** to **Production Quality**.

- Under the **Render Options** section, set **Motion Blur** to **On**.

## 3   Perform a test render

- Make the Perspective view active.

- Select **Render** → **Render Current Frame...**

*You cannot see a reflection in the mirror since the raytracing feature is unavailable with the Hardware renderer. However, the renderer is otherwise capable of fast high quality rendering, including texture mapped reflections, depth map shadows and motion blur.*

## 4   Batch render

Repeat step 7 from the first exercise in this lesson.

*Maya Hardware render*

## Conclusion

You have now completed this short introduction to the additional rendering types available in Maya. For more mental ray, Maya Vector, Maya Hardware and Maya Software rendering tutorials, see the online documentation for Maya.

# Lesson 18    Skeleton

*In this lesson you will create the skeleton hierarchy to be used to bind the geometry and to animate the robot character. In order to create a skeleton, you need to draw joints to match the surface of your character. The surfaces are then bound to the skeleton and deformations are applied.*

**In this lesson you will learn the following:**

- How to create skeleton joints;

- How to navigate around a joint hierarchy;

- How to edit joint pivots;

- How to mirror joints;

- How to reorient joints;

- How to edit the joint rotation axis.

# Drawing a skeleton chain

In this exercise, you will draw skeleton chains. Even if this operation appears to be simple, there are several things to be aware of as you create a joint chain.

## 1 Joint Tool

- Open a new scene and change the view to the *side* Orthographic view.

- From the Animation menu set, select **Skeleton** → **Joint Tool** → ❑.

*The tool's option window is displayed.*

- Change the **Orientation** attribute to **None**.

**Note:** *This attribute will be explained later in this exercise.*

- Click the **Close** button to close the tool window.

- In the side view, **LMB+click** two times to create a joint chain.

- Press **Enter** to exit the tool.

## 2 Joint hierarchy

- Open the Hypergraph.

*Notice the joint hierarchy, which is composed of two nodes.*

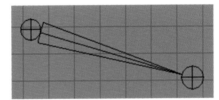

*A joint chain*

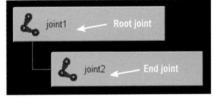

*Joint hierarchy*

## 3 Adding joints

- Click on the **Joint Tool** icon in the toolbox or press the **y** hotkey to invoke the last tool used.

- **LMB-click** on the end joint of your previous chain.

*The tool will highlight the end joint.*

▪ **LMB+click** two times to create a Z-like joint chain.

*The new joints are children of the joint selected in the previous step.*

▪ You can **MMB+drag** to change the last joint placement.

▪ Press **Enter** to exit the tool.

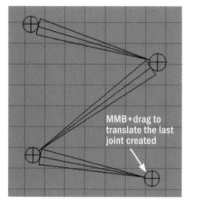

MMB+drag to
translate the last
joint created

*New joint chain*

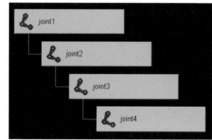

*Joint hierarchy*

## 4 Automatic joint orientation

When using the automatic orientation, all three joint axes are aligned
according to the right-hand rule. For example, if you select an orientation of
XYZ, the positive X-axis points into the joint's bone and towards the joint's
first child joint, the Y-axis points at right angles to the X-axis and Z-axis, and
the Z-axis points sideways from the joint and its bone.

**Note:** *If you look closely at the joints in the Perspective view, you can see these
axes and where they are pointing.*

▪ Double-click on the **Joint Tool** icon in the toolbox.

*The tool's option window is displayed.*

▪ Change the **Orientation** attribute to **XYZ**.

▪ **Close** the tool window.

- Create a second joint chain similar to the first one.

*Notice that as you draw the joints, they are automatically oriented toward their child.*

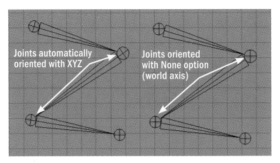

*Joint orientation*

## 5 Joint rotation axis

To better understand the effect of the joint orientation, you need to select the Rotation Tool in local mode and compare the two chains you have created.

- Double-click on the **Rotate Tool** icon in the toolbox.

*The tool's option window is displayed.*

- Select **Local** as the **Rotation Mode**.

*This will tell Maya that you want to rotate nodes based on their local orientation rather than using the global world axis.*

- **Close** the tool window.

- Select the second joint of both chains and see the difference between their rotation axes as you rotate them.

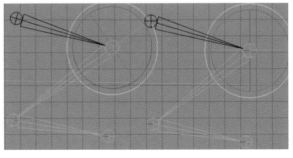

*Joint rotation axis*

*Notice that when the joint is properly oriented, it moves in a more natural way.*

# Complex joint chain

When you create a complex joint chain, you can use some Maya features intended to simplify your work. For instance, you can navigate in a hierarchy of joints as you create them. You can also use a command to reorient all the joints automatically.

### 1   Navigate in joint hierarchy

- Delete all the joint chains in your scene.

- Make the *top* view active.

- Press the **y** hotkey to invoke the **Joint Tool**.

**Note:** *Make sure the tool* **Orientation** *is set to* **XYZ**.

### 2   Draw the arm joints

- Draw three joints as follows:

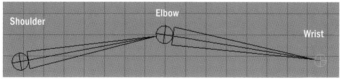

*Arm chain*

- Draw a thumb made of two joints.

- Press the **up arrow** twice on your keyboard to put the selection on the wrist joint.

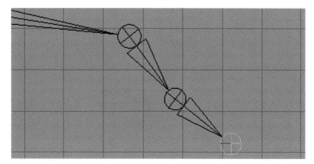

*Thumb joints*

*The arrows let you navigate in the hierarchy without exiting the Joint Tool.*

- Draw the index joints and press the up arrow again.

- Draw the remaining fingers as follows:

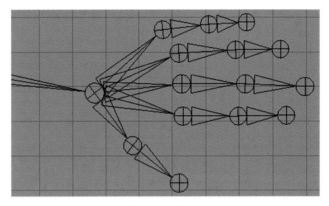

*Completed hand*

## 3   Snap to grid

- Press the **up arrow** until the selection is on the shoulder joint.

- Hold down the **x** hotkey to snap to grid and add a spine bone.

- Press **Enter** to exit the **Joint Tool**.

## 4   Reroot a skeleton

In the last step, you created a spine bone that is the child of the shoulder bone. This is not a proper hierarchy since the spine should be the parent of the shoulder. Maya has a command that allows you to quickly reroot a joint chain.

- Select the spine bone, which was the last joint created.

- Select **Skeleton → Reroot Skeleton**.

*The spine is now the root of the hierarchy.*

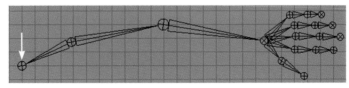

*Spine bone*

*Spine joint as root*

## 5    Mirror joints

*Another very useful feature is to have the ability to mirror a joint chain automatically.*

- Select the shoulder bone.

- Select **Skeleton** → **Mirror Joint** → ☐.

- In the option window, specify **Mirror Across** the **YZ** plane.

- Click the **Mirror** button.

*Both arms*

# Robot skeleton

You are now ready to create a skeleton for the robot from Lesson 16. To do so, you need to determine the proper placement of each joint. Once that is done, you will need to set a proper joint orientation so that when you rotate a joint, it rotates in an intuitive manner. If you do not take great care for placement and orientation, you will have difficulty later animating the character.

## 1    Open the robot scene

- Open the file *16-textureModel.ma*.

- Select **File** → **Save As** and save the file as *18-skeleton.ma*.

## 2    Character spine

In this step, you need to determine a good placement for the pelvis bone, which will be the root of the hierarchy. Once that is done, it will be easy to create the rest of the spine bones.

- Select **Skeleton** → **Joint Tool**.

- Make the *side* view active.

- **LMB+click** to create the *pelvis* joint, the *neck* and the *head* joint.

*It is recommended that the pelvis joint be aligned with the hips. The neck and head should also be centered to their geometry.*

**Note:** *A human spine would require many more bones, but that is not required in this example.*

- Add an *eye* joint for reference when you will be animating the character with the geometry hidden.

- Press **Enter** to exit the tool.

- Rename each joint properly.

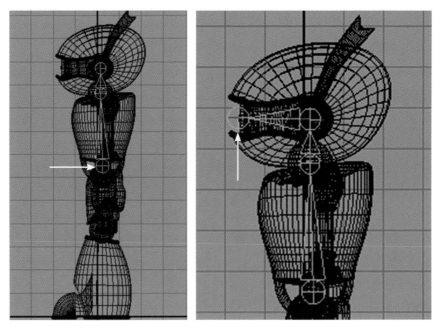

Pelvis, neck and head joints                    Eye joint

## 3   Create a leg

You now need to create the legs of the character. The new joint chain will be in a separate hierarchy, but you will connect it to the pelvis later on.

- Select **Skeleton** → **Joint Tool**.

- **Click+drag** the *hip* joint to its proper location.

*The hip joint should be centered on the hip articulation geometry.*

- Create the remaining *knee*, *ankle* and *toe's* joints, and create an extra joint on the tip of the foot, which should be called *toesEnd*.

- Press **Enter** to exit the tool.

- **Rename** all the joints appropriately.

**Note:** *You can do this by* **Ctrl+double-clicking** *on the joint name in the Hypergraph and typing a new name. Make sure to prefix the joints on the left side with* **l** *and the ones on the right side with* **r**. *For instance, if you name the left ankle, you may want to call it lAnkleJoint.*

- Change the current view to the *front* view.

*Notice that all the bones you created were drawn on the Y-axis. That was correct for the spine, but not for the leg.*

- Translate the *hip* and *knee* joint on the X-axis to fit the geometry as follows:

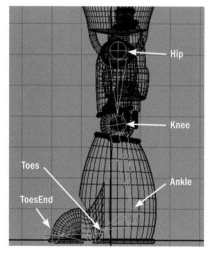

Leg joints                         Front view

## 4   Connect and mirror the leg

- Select the *hip* joint, then **Shift-select** the *pelvis* joint.

- Select **Skeleton** → **Connect Joint** → ❏.

- Change the **Mode** option to **Parent Joint**.

- Hit the **Connect** button.

*The leg is now connected to the pelvis.*

**Note:** *You could also parent using the* **p** *hotkey.*

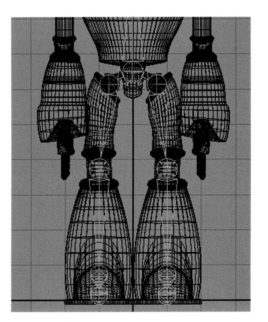

*Completed lower body*

- Select the *hip* joint.

- Select **Skeleton** → **Mirror Joint** → ❏.

- Make sure the **Mirror Across** option is set to **YZ**.

- Click on the **Mirror** button.

*If your character was modeled symmetrically, it should now have two legs properly placed.*

## 5   Arm and hand joints

- Change the current view to the *side* view.

- Select **Display** → **Joint Size** → **25%**.

*Doing so will reduce the display size of the joints in the viewport, making it easier to place joints close together, such as the finger joints.*

- Create the first character's arm and hand.

> **Tip:**   Don't forget to use the **up arrow** to navigate the joint hierarchy.

- Rename all the bones correctly.

## 6   Joint pivot

In some cases, you might want to adjust the position of a joint without moving all of its children. You can use the **Insert** key (**Home** key on Macintosh) to move a joint on its own.

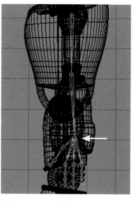

In the image to the right, you can clearly see that the angle defined by the shoulder, elbow and wrist joints is backwards, unlike a normal arm. You need to correct the problem by moving the wrist bone forward.

*The arm and hand joints*

- Select the wrist joint.

- Select the **Move Tool**.

- Press the **Insert** key (**Home** on Macintosh).

- Move the pivot of the *wrist* joint forward.

> **Tip:**   If you cannot achieve a proper arm angle with the wrist alone, move the elbow pivot slightly towards the back.

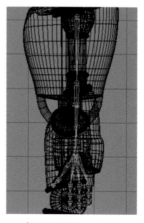

*Corrected arm angle*

## 7  Adjust the joint position

- Change the current view for the front view.

- While in **Smooth Shaded mode**, select **Shading** → **X-Ray** from the panel menu.

- Translate the arm joints on the X-axis to fit the arm geometry.

*The X-ray view*

**Tip:**  *It is a better workflow for joint placement to rotate the joints rather than translate them.*

- Turn off the X-ray view by selecting **Shading** → **X-Ray** again.

## 8  Connect and mirror the arm

- Repeat step **4** to connect the *shoulder* joint to the *pelvis* joint.

## 9   Last details

- Starting from the *head* joint, create new joints for the ears and translate and mirror them as follows:

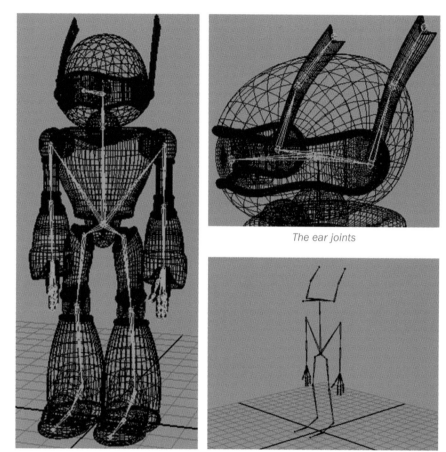

*The ear joints*

*Proper arms*                    *Complete skeleton*

## Joint orientation

Now that your robot has a skeleton, you need to double check all the joint orientations using the Rotate Tool. In this case, most of the joint orientations will be good by default, but there will be times when you will need to change some orientations to perfect your skeleton.

## 1   Hide the geometry

- From the *Perspective* view, select **Show** → **NURBS Surfaces** to hide them.

## 2  Default rotation values

It is recommended that all rotations of a joint hierarchy be zeroed out.
This means that when the skeleton is in the current default position, all the
joint rotations are zero.

- Select the *pelvis* joint.

- Select **Modify** → **Freeze Transformations**.

*If you rotated bones in previous steps, their rotations are now zeroed out.*

**Note:** *Unlike geometry, joint translations cannot be zeroed or else they would
all be at the origin.*

## 3  Reorient all joints

You can reorient all the joints in a hierarchy automatically to your preferred
orientation, such as XYZ.

- Select the *pelvis* joint.

- Select **Skeleton** → **Orient Joint** → ❑.

- Make sure the **Orientation** is set to **XYZ**, then click the **Orient** button.

*All the joints are now reoriented to have the X-axis pointing toward their children.*

## 4  Local rotation axes

The automatic orientation of the joints is not always perfect. Depending on how
your skeleton was built, it can flip certain local rotation axes and you need to
manually fix those pivots.

- Select the *pelvis* joint.

- Press **F8** to go in Component mode and enable the **?** mask button.

*Local rotation axes mask*

*All the local rotation axes are displayed in the viewport for the selected joints.*

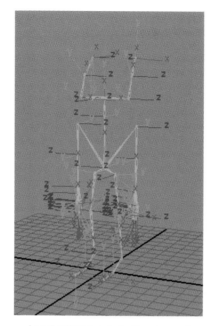

*Local rotation axes in the viewport*

## 5   Manually set the local rotation axes

It might seem confusing at the moment, but changing the local rotation axes
is quite easy. There is one axis per joint and if you dolly closer to a joint, you
will see that the axis respects the right-hand rule, where the X-axis points
toward the first child joint.

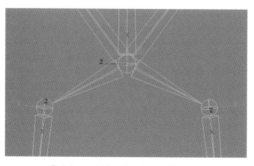

*Pelvis and hips local rotation axes*

In certain cases you will not want the automatic orientation setting.
The problems usually arise when you select multiple bones and rotate them
at the same time. For instance, if you select the head and neck joints you
would notice an odd rotation, since their rotation axes are not aligned.

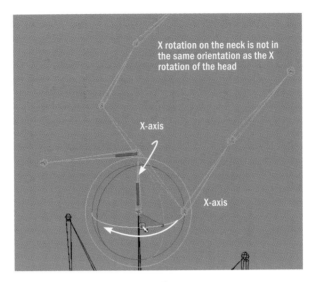

*Bad rotation axes*

To fix the problem, manually select an incorrect local rotation axis and rotate it into a good position.

- Still in Component mode with the local rotation axis displayed, select the *head* local rotation axis by clicking on it.

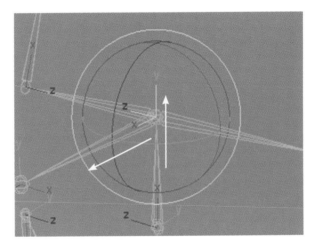

*The selected head rotation axis*

- Select the **Rotate Tool** by pressing the **e** hotkey.
- Rotate the **Z-axis** so that the red X-axis points up like the neck axis.

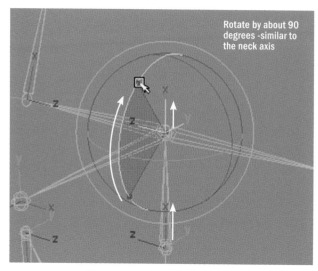

*The corrected head rotation axis*

- Go back in Object mode and try rotating the head and neck together.

*The problem seen earlier is now solved.*

## 6   Test the skeleton

You should now test your skeleton to see if everything is rotating as expected. If you notice incorrect local rotation axes, attempt to correct them manually by following the steps as outlined above.

## Conclusion

You now have greater experience creating skeleton chains and navigating skeleton hierarchies. You learned how to move and rotate joints, and how to use joint commands such as reroot, connect, mirror and orient. Finally, you manually changed local rotation axes, which is the key to creating a good skeleton.

In the next lesson, you will bind the robot geometry to the skeleton and explore different techniques and tools used for character rigging.

# Lesson 19    Skinning

To get surfaces to deform as you move joints, you must bind them to the skeleton. There are many skinning techniques in Maya to bind a surface. In this lesson, you will first experiment with basic examples, which will allow you to understand the various types of skinning. You will then use this understanding to bind the robot character.

**In this lesson you will learn the following:**

- How to bind using parenting;

- How to use rigid binding;

- How to use the Edit Membership Tool;

- How to edit rigid bind membership;

- How to use flexors;

- How to use lattice binding;

- How to use smooth binding;

- How to paint weights;

- How to set and assume a preferred angle;

- How to set joint degrees of freedom and limits.

# Parent binding

Perhaps the simplest type of binding is to parent geometry to joints. This type of binding is very fast and needs no tweaking, but requires the pieces of a model to be separate. For instance, an arm would need to be split in two parts: an upper arm and a lower arm. There are other scenarios where parenting is appropriate, for example, a ring on a finger or the eyes of a character.

## 1    Create a simple scene

- Open a new scene and change the view to the top Orthographic view.

- Draw three joints defining an arm.

- Change the view to the Perspective view.

- Create two polygonal cylinders and place them over the bones, as follows:

*Basic parenting setup*

## 2    Parent the geometry

- Select the *left cylinder*, then **Shift-select** the *left bone*.

- Press the **p** hotkey to **Parent** the cylinder to the bone.

- Repeat the last two steps to **Parent** the *right cylinder* to the right bone.

**Note:** *Notice that the geometry is now the child of the joints in the Outliner.*

## 3    Test joint rotations

- Select the bones and rotate them to see the result of the parenting.

**Note:** *Notice that when selecting, bones have a higher selection priority than geometry. To select a bone, simply make a bounding box selection over the bone and geometry.*

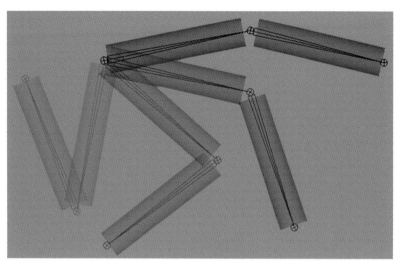

*Joints rotation*

# Rigid binding

Rigid binding works basically like the parenting method, except on the geometry's components. By rigid binding geometry on bones, the vertices closer to a certain bone will be instructed to follow that bone. This type of binding usually looks good on low resolution polygonal geometry or NURBS surfaces, but can cause cracking on dense geometry. Following are two examples using rigid binding:

## 1   Create a simple scene

- Open a new scene and change the view to the top Orthographic view.

- Draw three joints defining an arm.

- Select the first joint and press **Ctrl+d** to duplicate the joint chain.

- Move the joint chains side by side.

- From the Perspective view, create a *polygonal cylinder* and a *NURBS cylinder*.

- Place each cylinder to entirely cover a joint chain.

- Set the polygonal cylinder's **Subdivisions Height** to **10**.

- Set the NURBS cylinder's **Spans** to **10**.

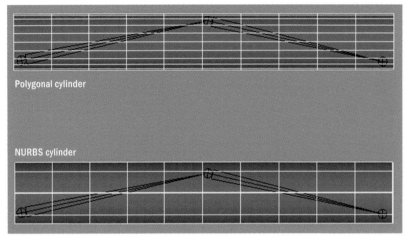

*Rigid binding*

## 2 Rigid bind

- Select the *first joint chain*, then **Shift-select** the *polygonal cylinder*.

- Select **Skin** → **Bind Skin** → **Rigid Bind**.

- Select the *second joint chain*, then **Shift-select** the *NURBS cylinder*.

- Select **Skin** → **Bind Skin** → **Rigid Bind**.

## 3 Test joint rotations

- Select the bones and rotate them to see the result of the rigid binding on both geometry types.

*The polygonal object appears to fold in on itself, since a vertex can only be assigned to one bone. The NURBS object seems much smoother because the curves of the surface are defined by the CVs, which are bound to the bones just like the polygonal object.*

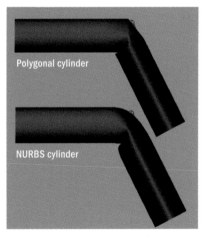

*Rigid binding*

**Note:** *Notice in the Outliner that the geometry is not parented. The binding connects the geometry's vertices to the joints.*

## 4   Edit Membership Tool

When using rigid bind, you might want to change the default binding so that certain points follow a different bone. The Edit Membership Tool allows you to specify the cluster of points affected by a certain bone.

- Select **Deform** → **Edit Membership Tool**.

- Click on the *middle bone* of the first joint chain.

*You should see all the vertices affected by that joint highlighted in yellow. Vertices affected by other bones are highlighted using different colors to distinguish them.*

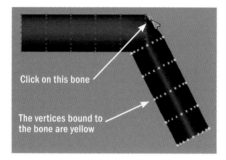

The Edit Membership Tool

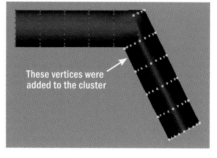

*Added polygon vertices*

- Using the same hotkeys as when you select objects in Maya, toggle points from the cluster using **Shift**, remove points from the cluster using **Ctrl** and add points to the cluster using **Shift+Ctrl**.

- Repeat the same steps for the NURBS geometry to achieve a better deformation.

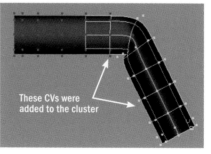

*Added NURBS vertices*

# Flexors

Flexors are a type of deformer designed to be used with rigid bound surfaces. By creating a flexor for a joint, you can smooth out the binding region between two bones, thus preventing geometry from cracking. Flexor points can also be driven by Set Driven Keys to modify their positions as the bone rotates. For instance, you can refine an elbow shape when the elbow is folded.

### 1   Creating flexors

- From the previous scene, reset the rotations of the bones to their default positions.

- Select the *middle joint* for the first joint chain.

- Select **Skin** → **Edit Rigid Skin** → **Create Flexor...**

*An option window is displayed.*

- Make sure the **Flexor Type** is set to **Lattice**.

- Turn **On** the **Position the Flexor** checkbox.

- Click the **Create** button.

*A flexor is created at the joint's position and is selected so that you can position it correctly.*

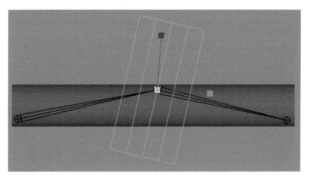

*The flexor deformer*

- **Translate** and **scale** the flexor to cover the bending region.

### 2   Test joint rotations

- Select the *middle bone* and rotate it to see the result of the flexor on the geometry.

*Notice that the bending area of the polygonal geometry is now much smoother.*

**Tip:** *If necessary, hide the flexor object by toggling* **Show** → **Deformers***, so you can see the deformations more clearly.*

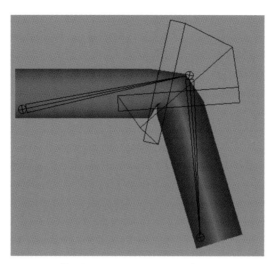

*The bent geometry using a flexor*

## 3  Set Driven Keys

- Zero the rotation of the bones.

- Select **Animate** → **Set Driven Key** → **Set** → ❑.

- In the **Driver** section, load the *middle joint* and select **Rotate Y** attribute.

- Select the *flexor* and press **F8** to display its points.

- Select all the flexor's lattice points and click the **Load Driven** button in the Set Driven Key window.

- Highlight all the driven objects in the **Driven** section and highlight the **XYZ values** on the right side.

- Click the **Key** button to set the normal position.

- Go back in Object mode and **rotate** the *middle joint* on the **Y-axis** by about **80-degrees**.

- Select the *flexor* and press **F8** to display its points.

- Move the flexor points to confer a nice elbow shape to the cylinder.

- Click the **Key** button to set the bent position.

**Note:** *The points on the flexor might not move exactly as expected since they are using the local space of the middle bone.*

## 4   Test joint rotations

- Select the *middle bone* and rotate it to see the result of the driven flexor on the geometry.

*Notice that you can achieve a much better crease by using a driven flexor.*

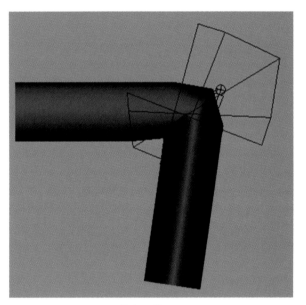

*Driven flexor*

## Lattice binding

Another way to achieve nice skinning using rigid bind is to create a lattice deformer on the geometry and rigid bind the lattice to the bones. This technique can achieve a very smooth binding, using the simplicity of the rigid binding to your advantage.

## 1   Detach a skin

- Select the *polygonal cylinder* from the previous exercise.

- Select **Skin** → **Detach Skin**.

*The geometry returns to the original shape and position it was in before being bound.*

- Select the *middle joint* and zero its rotation.

- Select the *flexor* and press **Delete** on your keyboard, as it is no longer required.

## 2 Create a lattice

- Select the *polygonal cylinder*, then select **Deform** → **Create Lattice**.

*A lattice is created and fits the geometry perfectly.*

- Increase the number of lattice subdivisions by going to the **Outputs** section in the Channel Box and setting its **T Divisions** attribute to **9**.

## 3 Rigid bind the lattice

- With the lattice still selected, **Shift-select** the *first bone* of the joint chain.

- Select **Skin** → **Bind Skin** → **Rigid Bind**.

## 4 Test joint rotations

- Select the *middle bone* and rotate it to see the result of the lattice on the geometry.

*At this time, the binding is not much different than a normal rigid binding.*

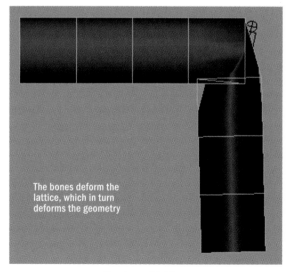

The bones deform the lattice, which in turn deforms the geometry

*The bound lattice*

## 5   Adjust the lattice

- Select the *lattice* object.

- In the **Outputs** section of the Channel Box, highlight the *ffd1* node.

- Set the following:

     **Local Influence S** to **4**;

     **Local Influence T** to **4**;

     **Local Influence U** to **4**.

*The deformation of the geometry is now much smoother.*

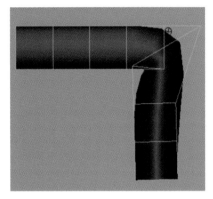

*The edited rigid bind membership*

## 6   Edit membership

It is now much easier to edit the membership of the lattice points rather than the dense geometry vertices.

## 7   Driven lattice

If the Edit Membership Tool does not provide enough control over the deformation of the geometry, you can use driven keys to achieve a much better deformation for the elbow and the elbow crease, just like in the previous flexor exercise. You can also use driven keys to bulge the bicep.

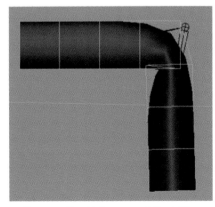

*The smoothed influences of the lattice*

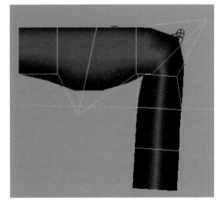

*Driven lattice*

# Smooth binding

The most advanced type of Maya skinning is called smooth binding. Smooth binding allows an object vertex or CV to be influenced by multiple bones, according to a certain percentage. For instance, a vertex's influence can follow at 100% a particular bone, or that influence can be spread across multiple bones in varying percentages, such as 50%-50% or 25%-75%. Doing so will move the vertex accordingly between all the influence bones.

## 1 Set up the scene

- Using the scene from the previous exercise, set the *middle joint* rotation to zero.

- Select **Edit** → **Delete All by Type** → **History** to remove the lattice object.

## 2 Smooth bind

- Select the *first joint*, then **Shift-select** the *polygonal cylinder*.

- Select **Skin** → **Bind Skin** → **Smooth Bind**.

## 3 Test joint rotations

- Select the *middle bone* and rotate it to see the result of the smooth binding on the geometry.

## 4 Edit smooth bind influence

Modifying the influences of each bone on each vertex can be a tedious task, but you can use the Maya Artisan Tool to actually paint the weights of the vertices directly in the viewport. The *Paint Skin Weight Tool* will display an influence of 100% as white, an influence of 0% as black and anything in between as grayscale. This makes it easier to visually edit the influence of bones on the geometry.

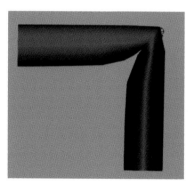

*Default smooth binding*

- Select *polyCylinder* and go to **Shading** → **Smooth Shade All**.

- Select **Skin** → **Edit Smooth Skin** → **Paint Skin Weights Tool** → ❐.

*The painting option window shows up and the geometry gets displayed in grayscale.*

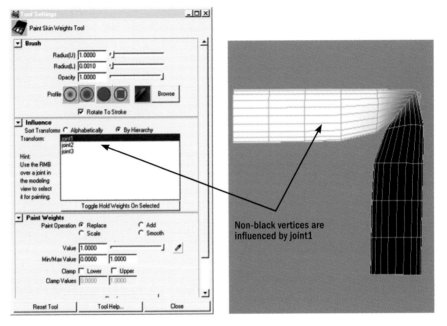

The Paint Skin Weights Tool and the weights on the geometry

Painting skin weights requires a solid understanding of bone influences. Since the tool is based on the Artisan Tool, you can edit the skin weighting on your own. Smooth binding, along with its various related tools, will be covered in greater detail in the intermediate *Learning Maya 7 | Modeling & Animation*.

# Binding the robot

Since the robot is mostly composed of mechanical objects, you will bind the bulk of its geometry using rigid binding. You could also use parenting, but it is an easier workflow to keep geometry in one hierarchy and the character setup in the other.

## 1  Open the last lesson scene

- Open the file *18-skeleton.ma*.

- Save the file as *19-binding.ma*.

## 2   Set Preferred Angle

When binding geometry on a skeleton, you need to test the binding by rotating the bones. By doing so, you should be able to replace the skeleton back to its default position quickly. Maya has two easily accessible commands called *Set Preferred Angle* and *Assume Preferred Angle*, that allow you to first define the default skeleton pose, and then return to that pose whenever you want.

**Note:** *The preferred angle also defines the bending angle for IK handles, which you will use in the next lesson.*

- Select the *pelvis* joint.
- In the viewport, **RMB-click** over the *pelvis* joint to pop the contextual marking menu.
- Select **Set Preferred Angle**.

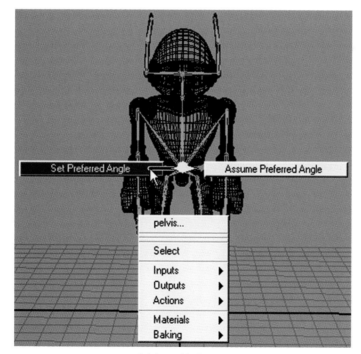

*Joint marking menu*

**Note:** *These commands are also available in the* **Skeleton** *menu.*

## 3   Assume Preferred Angle

- **Rotate** several joints to achieve a pose.

- Select the *pelvis* joint.

- In the viewport, **RMB-click** over the *pelvis* joint and select **Assume Preferred Angle**.

*The skeleton should return to its preferred angle set in the previous step.*

## 4   Bind the pelvis

- Select **Skin** → **Bind Skin** → **Rigid Bind** → ❑.

- In the rigid bind options, change **Bind To** to **Selected Joints**.

*This option will bind the geometry only to the selected joints, instead of to the entire joints hierarchy as done at the beginning of this lesson.*

- Select the *pelvis* joint, then **Shift-select** all the objects that should be moving with that bone.

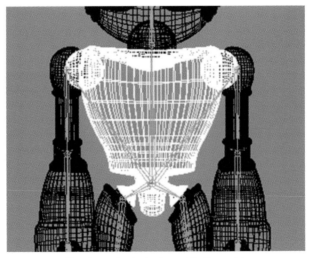

*The geometry to be bound to the pelvis*

- Click the **Bind Skin** button in the rigid bind option window.

*You will notice that the wireframe of the bound geometry is now purple, which is a visual cue to show the connection to the selected joint with history.*

- **Rotate** the *pelvis* joint to see if the geometry follows correctly.

## 5 Smooth bind the antennae

- Select **Skin** → **Bind Skin** → **Smooth Bind** → ❑.

- In the Smooth Bind options, change **Bind To** to **Selected Joints**.

- Select the *lAntenna1* and *lAntenna2* joints, then **Shift-select** the *lAntenna* geometry.

- Click the **Bind Skin** button in the Smooth Bind option window.

- Repeat the previous steps to bind the other antenna.

- **Rotate** the *antenna* joints to see if the geometry bends correctly.

## 6 Rigid bind the inner foot

- Select the *lAnkle* and *lToes* joints, then **Shift-select** the *innerFoot* geometry on the left foot.

- Select **Skin** → **Bind Skin** → **Rigid Bind**.

- Repeat the previous steps to bind the right inner foot.

- **Rotate** the *foot* joints to see if the geometry bends correctly.

**Note:** *Since the inner feet are NURBS geometry, rigid binding looks good.*

## 7 Rigid bind the rest of the robot

You can now rigid bind all the remaining geometry pieces on their respective bones.

- Select the *pelvis* joint, then select **Skeleton** → **Assume Preferred Angle**.

*Doing so will ensure all the skeleton rotations are set to their preferred values.*

**Note:** *Do not translate bones. The preferred angle command only keeps rotation values.*

- Rigid bind all the remaining geometry to the skeleton.

## 8  Ensure everything is bound

- To ensure all the geometry is bound, select the *pelvis* joint and translate it. You will notice if a piece is left behind.

- **Undo** the last movement to bring the skeleton back to its original position.

*The entirely bound character*

# Joint Degrees of Freedom and Limits

A character is usually unable to achieve every possible pose. In this case, the robot's mechanical articulation might not allow the joints to rotate a certain way or exceed certain rotation limits. Bending joints too much or in the wrong way might cause the geometry to interpenetrate or appear broken. Maya joints have many options to let you control how they are bent by the animator.

## 1    Degrees of Freedom

By default, all three rotation axes on a joint are free to rotate. If you need to, you can limit the degrees of freedom on a joint. In the case of the robot, the elbows and knees cannot bend in all three directions due to the structure of the model. Therefore, you need to limit these joints' rotations to a single axis, the Z-axis.

- Select the *lElbow* joint.

- Notice on which axis the joint should be allowed to bend.

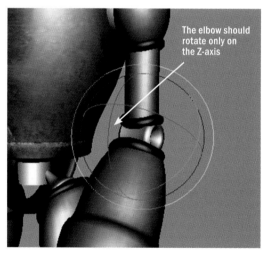

The elbow should rotate only on the Z-axis

*The elbow rotation axes*

**Tip:**    The **Rotate Tool** *must be in* **Local** *mode.*

- Open the Attribute Editor and scroll to the **Joint** section.

- Turn **Off** the **X** and **Y** checkboxes for the **Degrees of Freedom** attribute.

*Notice that the* **Rotate X** *and* **Rotate Y** *attributes in the Channel Box are now locked.*

## 2    Joint limits

A joint limit allows you to specify the minimum and maximum values allowed for a joint to rotate. In this case, the elbow joint needs to stop rotating before interpenetrating with the upper arm.

- Select the *lElbow* joint.

- **Rotate** the joint on the **Z-axis** and stop just before it interpenetrates with the upper arm.

- In the Attribute Editor, open the **Limit Information** section.

- In the **Rotate** section, turn **On** the **Rot Limit Z Max** attribute.

- Click on the **>** button to put the **Current** value in the **Max** field.

- **Rotate** the *lElbow* joint on the **Z-axis** the other way and stop when the arm is perfectly straight.

- Back in the Attribute Editor, turn **On** the **Rot Limit Z Min** attribute.

- Click on the **<** button to put the **Current** value in the **Min** field.

The lElbow rotation limits

## 3    Remainder of skeleton limits

You can now set the limitations on the robot skeleton as you would like them to be. The completed version of the bound robot can be found in the support files as *19-binding.ma*.

## 4    Save your work

## Conclusion

You have now explored the various skinning types required to bind a character to its skeleton. You also learned how to change joints' degrees of freedom and set limit information.

In the next lesson, you will refine your character setup by using IK handles, constraints and custom attributes. You will also create a reverse foot setup that will help maintain the robot's feet on the ground.

# Lesson 20    Ik handles

*In this lesson, you will add IK (inverse kinematics) handles and constraints to the existing robot skeleton in order to make the character easier to animate. You will also create a reverse foot setup, which simplifies floor contacts when animating, and hand manipulators, which will help lock hands upon contact with the environment.*

## In this lesson you will learn the following:

- How to add single chain Ik handles;

- How to add rotate plane Ik handles;

- How to create a reverse foot setup;

- How to use point, orient and parent constraints.

# IK handles

There are several types of Ik handles in Maya and you will experiment with two types in this lesson: the *single chain IK* and the *rotate plane IK*. The difference between the two Ik handle types is that the single chain Ik handle's end effector tries to reach the position and orientation of its Ik handle, whereas the rotate plane Ik handle's end effector only tries to reach the position of its Ik handle.

## Single chain IK

A single chain Ik handle uses the single chain solver to calculate the rotations of all joints in the IK chain. Also, the overall orientation of the joint chain is calculated directly by the single chain solver.

### 1    Open the last robot scene

- **Open** the file *19-binding.ma*.

- **Save** the file as *20-ik.ma*.

### 2    Joint rotation limits

For better results using IKs, it is not recommended to have rotation limits on joints that are part of an Ik handle. Limiting joint rotations will prevent the IK solver from finding good joint rotations and may cause it to behave unexpectedly.

- Remove rotation limits for the *shoulder*, *elbow* and *wrist* bones.

- Remove rotation limits for the *hip*, *knee*, *ankle* and *toes'* bones.

**Note:** *Rotation limits are especially useful on joints animated manually.*

### 3    Single chain IK

- Select **Skeleton** → **Ik handle Tool** → □.

*The tool's option window will be displayed.*

- Change the **Current Solver** for **ikSCsolver**.

- Click on the **Close** button.

- In the viewport, click on the *IShoulder* bone.

*The joint will be highlighted. This is the start joint.*

- Click on the *IWrist* bone.

*The Ik handle gets created, starting at the shoulder, going down to the wrist of the character.*

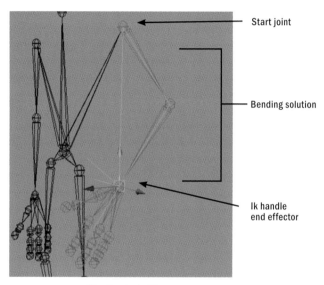

*Single chain IK*

In the Hypergraph, you can see the end effector connected into the hierarchy and the Ik handle to the side. The end effector and the Ik handle are connected along with the appropriate joints at the dependency node level. When you control the handle, you control the whole IK chain.

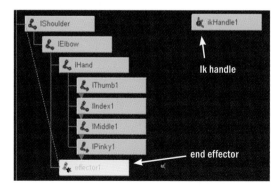

*Node in Hypergraph*

## 4   Experiment with the Ik handle

- Press **w** to enter the **Translate Tool**.

- **Translate** the Ik handle and notice the resulting bending of the arm.

**Tip:**   *If the Ik handle does not bend the arm or if it bends it the wrong way, it is because the angle in the arm joint chain was not appropriate. To remedy the situation, delete the Ik handle, bend the arm appropriately, and then recreate the IK.*

- Press **e** to enter the **Rotate Tool**.

- **Rotate** the Ik handle and notice the resulting bending of the arm.

*Rotating the Ik handle will change the bending solution, but will not affect the wrist's rotation. You will create a hand setup in a later exercise.*

- **Rename** the Ik handle *lArmIk*.

## 5   Preferred angle

- With the IK selected, **RMB** in the viewport and select **Assume Preferred Angle**.

*The arm joints and the Ik handle will move back to the preferred angle set in the previous lesson.*

## 6   Right arm IK

- Create another single chain IK for the right arm and rename it *rArmIk*.

**Tip:**   *Ik handles have a higher selection priority than joints and geometry. To pick an Ik handle, simply make a selection bounding box over the Ik handle.*

# Rotate plane IK

A rotate plane Ik handle uses the rotate plane solver to calculate the rotations of all joints in its IK chain, but not the joint chain's overall orientation. Instead, the IK rotate plane handle gives you direct control over the joint chain's orientation via the pole vector and twist disc, rather than having the orientation calculated by the IK solver.

**Note:** *The twist disc is a visual representation showing the vector defining the chain's overall orientation. You will experiment with the twist disk in the following steps.*

## 1   Rotate plane IK

- Select **Skeleton** → **Ik handle Tool** → ☐.

- Change the **Current Solver** for **ikRPsolver**.

- Click on the **Close** button.

- In the viewport, click on the *lhip* bone.

- Click on the *lAnkle* bone.

*The Ik handle gets created, starting at the hip, going down to the ankle of the character.*

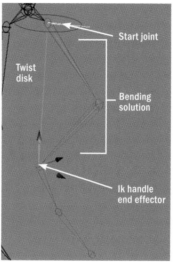

*Rotate plane IK*

## 2   Experiment with the Ik handle

One differentiating feature of this type of Ik handle is the ability to control the twist of the solution using the *twist* and *pole vector* attributes.

- Move the Ik handle up.

- Press **t** to show the Ik handle manipulators.

- Move the pole vector manipulator located next to the twist disk.

*This manipulator affects the pointing direction of the IK chain.*

- Highlight the **Twist** attribute in the Channel Box and **MMB+drag** in the viewport.

*This attribute also affects the pointing direction of the IK chain, but overrides the pole vector attributes.*

- Rename the Ik handle *lAnkleIk*.

**3  Reset the Ik handle's position**

- Undo the last step to bring the Ik handle back to its default position.

**4  Right leg IK**

- Create another rotate plane IK for the right leg.

- Rename the Ik handle *rAnkleIk*.

**5  Save your work**

## Reverse foot

When you animate a walking character, you need the character's foot to plant itself while the other foot is lifted into position. In the time it is planted, the foot needs to roll from heel to toe. A reverse foot skeleton is the ideal technique for creating these conditions.

**1  Draw the reverse foot skeleton**

- Change the viewport for a *four view* layout.

- Dolly on the feet of the robot in all views.

- Select **Skeleton** → **Joint Tool**.

*The **Orientation** of the tool should be set to **XYZ**.*

- In the *side* view, create the first joint on the heel of the robot's boot geometry.

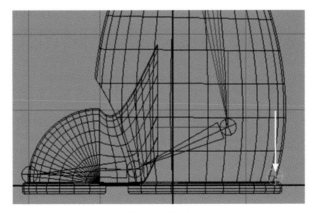

*The heel joint*

- In the *front* view, **MMB+drag** the new joint to align it with the rest of the foot joints.

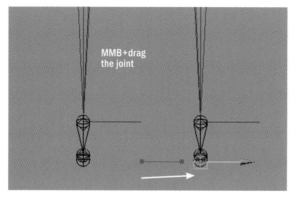

*Move the heel joint*

- In the *Perspective* view, turn **Off** the NURBS surface display by selecting **Show → NURBS Surfaces**.
- Hold down the **v** hotkey to enable **Snap to Point**.
- Draw three other bones, snapping them to the *toesEnd*, *toes* and *ankle* joints respectively.

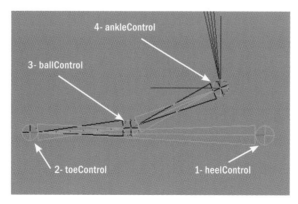

*The complete reverse foot*

- Press **Enter** to exit the tool.

**2    Rename the joints**

- Rename the joints as shown adding left and right prefixes:

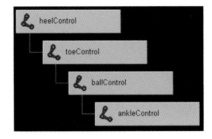

*Renamed joints*

## Set up the reverse foot

To control the foot and have a proper heel to toe rotation, you will now constrain the Ik handle, ankle and toes' joints, to the reverse foot chain. This will allow you to use the reverse foot chain to control the foot and leg.

**1    Point constrain the Ik handle**

- Select the *ankleControl* joint on the reverse foot chain.
- **Shift-select** the Ik handle.
- Select **Constrain** → **Point**.

*The point constraint forces an object to follow the position of a source object. The Ik handle is now positioned over the reverse foot's ankleControl joint.*

**Tip:** *You may want to use the Hypergraph panel to help you select the joints.*

**2    Test the reverse foot chain**

- Select the *heelControl* joint.
- Move the joint to test the foot setup so far.

*The ankle moves with the reverse foot chain but the joints do not stay properly aligned.*

**3    Orient constrain the toes**

To align the rest of the foot, you will orient constrain the *toes* joint to the reverse foot.

- Select the *toesControl* joint on the reverse foot chain.

- **Shift-select** the *toes* joint from the leg chain.

- Select **Constrain → Orient**.

*The orient constraint forces an object to follow the rotation of a source object.*

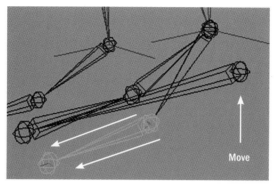

*Orient constrained toes joint*

## 4  Orient Constrain the ankle joint

You will now repeat these steps for the *ankle* joint.

- Select the *ballControl* joint on the reverse foot chain.

- **Shift-select** the *ankle* joint from the leg chain.

- Select **Constrain → Orient**.

*Now the foot joints and reverse foot joints are aligned.*

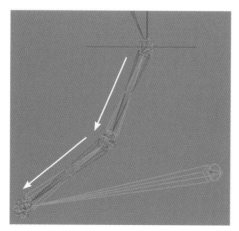

*Orient constrained ankle joint*

## 5   Test the movement of the reverse foot

- Select the *heelControl* joint.

- Move the joint to test the motion.

*If you pull the reverse foot further than the leg chain will allow, the leg will pull away from the reverse foot. This is the desired effect.*

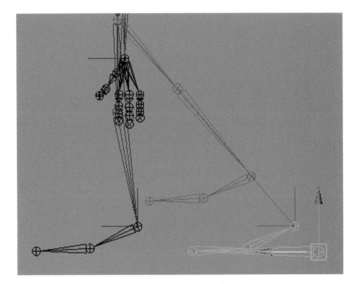

*Moving the reverse foot chain*

- **Undo** the last movement to bring the *heelControl* joint back to its original position.

## Creating the heel to toe motion

You can now control the rotation of the foot by rotating the various control joints on the reverse foot. Instead of requiring the rotation of several joints to achieve a heel to toe motion, you will use Set Driven Key to control the roll using a single attribute on the *heelControl* joint.

## 1   Add a Roll attribute

- Select the *heelControl* joint.

- Select **Modify** → **Add Attribute**.

- Set the following values in the **Add Attribute** window:

  **Attribute Name** to **roll**;

  **Data Type** to **Float**;

  **Minimum** to **-5**;

  **Maximum** to **10**;

  **Default** to **0**.

- Click **OK** to add the attribute.

*You can now see this attribute in the Channel Box. The minimum and maximum values give reasonable boundary values for the roll.*

| heelControl | |
|---|---|
| Translate X | 1 |
| Translate Y | 0.112 |
| Translate Z | -1.396 |
| Rotate X | 0 |
| Rotate Y | 0 |
| Rotate Z | 0 |
| Scale X | 1 |
| Scale Y | 1 |
| Scale Z | 1 |
| Visibility | on |
| Roll | 0 |

*The roll attribute in the Channel Box*

## 2    Prepare the Set Driven Key window

- Select **Animate** → **Set Driven Key** → **Set** → ☐.

- Select the *heelControl* joint and click **Load Driver**.

- In the **Driver** section, highlight the **Roll** attribute.

- Select the *heelControl, ballControl* and *toeControl* joints and click **Load Driven**.

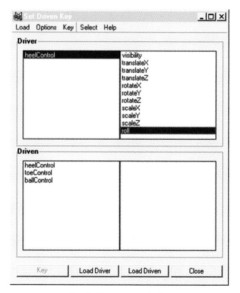

*Set Driven Key window*

## 3    Key the heel rotation

- In the **Driven** section, highlight **heelControl** and the **rotate Z** attribute.

- Click on the **Key** button to set the starting rotation.

- In the Channel Box, set the **Roll** value to **-5**.

- Set the **Rotate Z** to **20**.

- Again, click on the **Key** button.

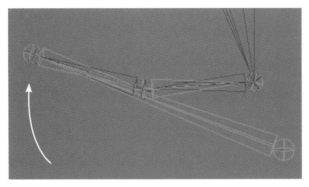

*Foot rotated back on heel*

- You can now test the **Roll** attribute by clicking on its name in the Channel Box and **MMB+dragging** in the viewport. You can see that the foot rolls from the heel to a flat position.

- Set the **Roll** attribute to **0**.

## 4    Key the ball rotation

- In the **Driven** section, click on **ballControl** and then on **rotate Z**.

- Click on the **Key** button to set the starting rotation.

- Click on **heelControl** in the **Driver** section and set the **Roll** value to **10**.

- Click on **ballControl** and set the **Rotate Z** to **30**.

- Again, click on the **Key** button in the Set Driven Key window.

- Click on **heelControl** and set the **Roll** value back to **0**.

**Tip:**    *When working with Set Driven Key, always set the value of the driver before setting the driven. If you set the driver second, it will reset your driven value because of earlier keys.*

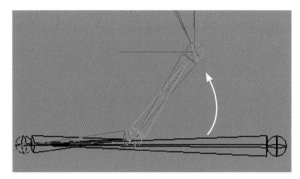

*Foot rotated forward on ball*

## 5 Key the toe rotation

- In the **Driven** section, click on **toeControl** and then on **rotate Z**.
- Click on the **Key** button to set the starting rotation.
- Click on **heelControl** and set the **Roll** value to **10**.
- Click on **toeControl** and set the **Rotate Z** to **30**.
- Again, click on the **Key** button.

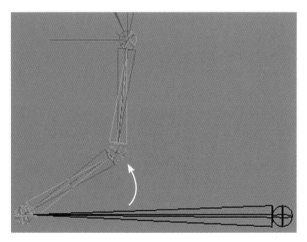

*Foot rotated forward on toe*

## 6 Test the foot roll

- Select the *heelControl* joint.
- Click on the **Roll** attribute name in the Channel Box and **MMB+drag** in the viewport to test the roll.

- Set the **Roll** back to **0**.

- Click the **Close** button in the Set Driven Key window.

## 7   Right foot setup

Create another reverse foot setup for the right leg.

## 8   Test the setup

- Select the *pelvis* joint.

- Move and rotate the pelvis to see the effect of the constrained Ik handles.

- Undo the last step to bring back the pelvis to its original position.

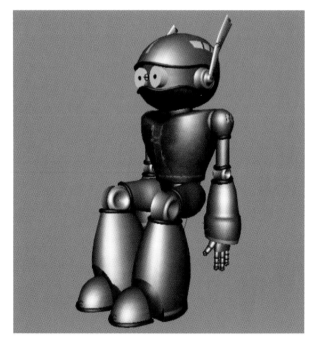

*Moving the pelvis joint*

## 9   Save your work

## Hand setup

It is good to be able to plant the feet of your character, but it would also be good to control the hand rotations. In this exercise, you will create a basic hand setup that will allow you to control the hand rotations.

**1    Change the arm IK type**

Single plane IKs are best used when you don't need to bother with the hands rotation. This means that they are not ideal for the type of control you are looking for. You will need to delete the ones you have on the arms and create new rotate plane IKs.

- Select the two arm Ik handles.

- Press **Delete** on your keyboard.

- Select **Skeleton** → **Ik handle Tool**.

*The IK type should already be set to ikRPsolver.*

- Create Ik handles for both arms.

**2    Create a hand manipulator**

- Select **Show** → **NURBS Surfaces** to hide all the NURBS surfaces in the viewport.

- Select **Create** → **NURBS Primitives** → **Circle**.

- Rename the circle *handManip*.

- Press **w** to enter the **Translate Tool**.

- Hold down the **v** hotkey and snap the *circle* to the *lWrist* of the skeleton.

**3    Constrain the Ik handle**

- With the *circle* still selected, **Shift-select** the *left arm Ik handle*.

- Select **Constrain** → **Parent**.

*The parent constraint forces an object to follow a source object just as it would be parented to it.*

**4    Constrain the wrist**

- Select the *circle*, then **Shift-select** the *lWrist* joint.

- Select **Constrain** → **Orient**.

**5    Test the wrist manipulator**

- Move and rotate the *handManip* to see how it affects the arm and hand.

- Move and rotate the *pelvis* joint to see how it affects the arm and hand.

*Notice the hand stays planted wherever it is. This is exactly the behavior you are looking for.*

- Undo the last steps to place the *pelvis* and *handManip* in their original locations.

## 6    Create a pole vector constraint

- Select **Create** → **Locator**.

- Hold down **v** to enable **Snap to Point**, then snap the locator on the *lElbow* joint.

- **Move** the *locator* back on the **Z-axis** by about **2 units**.

- With the *locator* selected, **Shift-select** the *left arm Ik handle*.

- Select **Constrain** → **Pole Vector**.

*The pole vector constraint will connect the locator's position into the Ik handle's* **Pole Vector** *attribute. By doing this, you can now control the rotation of the arm using a visual indicator.*

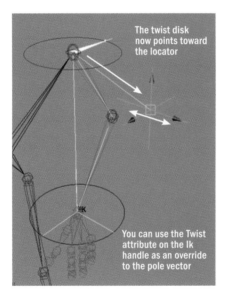

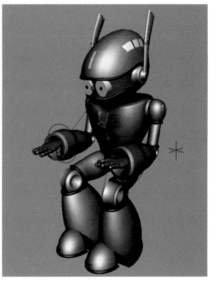

A pole vector locator                    The completed IK setup

## 7    Right hand manipulator

- Create the same type of manipulator on the other hand.

## 8    Save your work

## Conclusion

In this lesson, you learned the basics of how to use Ik handles in a custom setup. You experimented with some of the most popular tricks, such as the reverse foot setup and manipulators. You also used the twist attribute and pole vector constraints, which are required for any good Ik handle animation. Keep in mind that there are many more ways to take advantage of the various Maya IK types and it is up to you to experiment with them.

In the next lesson, you will refine the current character setup even more. Steps will include locking and hiding non-required attributes, and then adding and connecting custom attributes. Doing so will make your character rig easier to use, limiting manipulation errors that could potentially break it. Lastly, you will generate a low resolution version of the geometry for a faster playback when animating the character.

# Lesson 21  Rigging

*Character rigging requires a thorough knowledge of objects in Maya and lots of experimentation. The more you experiment with creating and animating character rigs, the better you will become at producing first-rate setups.*

*In this lesson, you will finalize the robot rig by making it animator friendly. This means that you will make the various useful attributes easy to find, as well as hiding unnecessary ones. You will also create a low-resolution polygonal version of the robot, in order to get faster playback and visualization when animating.*

## In this lesson you will learn the following:

- How to organize the rig's hierarchy;

- How to create selection sets;

- How to strategically place attributes;

- How to lock and hide nodes and attributes;

- How to convert NURBS to polygons;

- How to create a character node for keyframing.

# Rig hierarchy

When you look in the Outliner, your character's hierarchy should be clean, well named and simple to understand. For instance, all the setup nodes should be parented together under a master node. You could then use that master node for the global placement of the character in a scene.

## 1 Open the last setup scene

- Open the file *20-ik.ma*.

- Save the scene as *21-rigging.ma*.

## 2 Create a master node

- Change the current view for the *top* view.

- Select **Create → EP Curve → ❑**.

- Change the **Curve Degree** for **1 Linear**.

- Click the **Close** button.

- Hold down **x** and draw a four-arrows shape as follows:

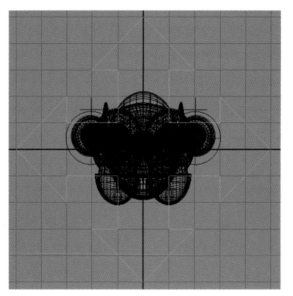

*The master node curve*

- Hit **Enter** to complete the curve.

- Rename the curve *master*.

**3  Hierarchy**

- Select **Panels** → **Saved Layouts** → **Persp/Outliner**.

- In the Outliner, select all character setup nodes and **Parent** them to the master node.

MMB+drag the selected nodes on the master node

*Parent setup nodes to master*

**Note:** *Do not parent bound geometry or the geometry group to the master node.*

**4  Node names**

- Make sure all nodes are named correctly.

**5  Character rig layer**

- In the Layer Editor, click on the **Create new layer** button.

- Rename the new layer *setupLayer*.

- Select the *master* node in the *Perspective* view, then **RMB** on the *setupLayer* and select **Add Selected Objects**.

*All the character rig nodes can now be hidden by hiding the setupLayer.*

# Selection sets

Selection sets are meant to simplify the selection process of multiple objects. In the robot setup, it would be nice to select all the finger joints at once in order to be able to open or close the hand easily.

## 1   Select the fingers

- Select the *IHand* joint.

- Select **Edit** → **Select Hierarchy**.

*This will select all the joints child of the IHand joint.*

- **Ctrl+click** on the *IHand* bone to deselect it.

- Put the cursor over the Outliner and press **f** to frame the selected objects.

*You should see that all the fingers and the IHand_orientConstraint are selected.*

- **Ctrl+click** on the *IHand_orientConstraint* to deselect it.

## 2   Create a set

- Select **Create** → **Sets** → **Quick Select Set...**

- In the Create Quick Select Set window, enter the name *IHandSet*.

- Click the **OK** button.

*The new set*

*If you scroll down in the Outliner, there will be a set called IHandSet.*

## 3   Use the selection set

- Select *IHandSet* in the Outliner.

- **RMB** to pop a contextual menu and select **Select Set Members**.

*All the objects in the set are selected.*

- Press **e** to enter the **Rotate Tool**.

- **Rotate** all the joints simultaneously.

**Tip:**   *If you notice that some joint local rotation axes are not aligned to close the fingers correctly, you can go into Component mode and adjust them.*

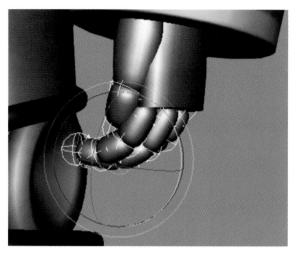

*Rotate all fingers simultaneously*

## 4   Edit a selection set

- Undo the last rotation.

- Select **Window** → **Relationship Editors** → **Sets**.

- On the left side of the Relationship Editor, click on the **+** sign next to the *lHandSet* to expand it.

*All the objects in that set are displayed.*

- Still in the left side of the Relationship Editor, highlight the *lThumb1* joint member *lHandSet*.

- Select **Edit** → **Remove Highlighted for Set**.

**Note:** *When you highlight a set in the Relationship Editor, its members are highlighted on the right side of the panel. Toggle objects on the right side to add or remove them to the current set.*

- **Close** the Relationship Editor.

## 5   Try the selection set again

- Select *lHandSet* in the Outliner.

- **RMB** and select **Select Set Members**.

- Rotate all the joints at once.

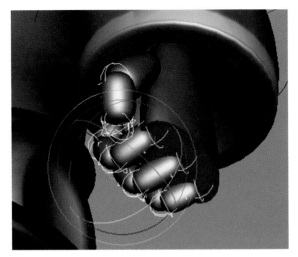

*Test the member's rotations again*

- Undo the last rotation.

## 6   Create a set for the right hand

## 7   Save your work

## Custom attributes

As you will notice by working in the current rig, some attributes are not easy to access. You should place useful attributes on strategic nodes for easy access.

Since you control the arms and legs' IK handles using custom setups, it is a good idea to place useful IK attributes on the hands manipulator and the reverse foot bones.

### 1   Add new attributes

- Select the *lHandManip*, the *rHandManip*, the *lHeelControl* and the *rHeelControl*.

- Select **Modify → Add Attribute**.

- Set the following:

    **Attribute Name** to **twist**;

    **Data Type** to **Float**;

    **Default** to **0**.

- Click the **Add** button.

*This will add the **Twist** attribute to all selected nodes. The Add Attribute window will remain open for further attribute additions.*

- Set the following:

 **Attribute Name** to **ikBlend**;

 **Data Type** to **Integer**;

 **Minimum** to **0**;

 **Maximum** to **1**;

 **Default** to **1**.

- Click the **OK** button.

## 2  **Connect the new attributes**

- Select **Window** → **General Editors** → **Connection Editor**.

- Select the *lHandManip*.

- In the Connection Editor, click on the **Reload Left** button.

- Scroll down and highlight the **Twist** attribute.

- Select the *lArmIkHandle*.

- In the Connection Editor, click on the **Reload Right** button.

- Scroll down and highlight the **Twist** attribute.

*You have just connected the **Twist** attribute of the hand manipulator to the left arm IK handle **Twist** attribute.*

- Highlight the **ikBlend** attribute on the left side of the editor.

- Highlight the **ikBlend** attribute on the right side of the editor.

*The **ikBlend** attribute of the hand manipulator is now connected to the left arm IK handle **ikBlend** attribute.*

## 3  **Repeat step 2**

- Repeat the previous steps in order to connect the remaining *rHandManip*, *lHeelControl* and *rHeelControl* attributes to their respective IK handles.

- Click the **Close** button to close the Connection Editor.

## 4  **Hide the IK handles**

Since you have connected the *Twist* and *IK Blend* attributes of the IK handles to their manipulators, the IK handles can now be hidden since they are no longer required to be visible or selected.

- Select the *lArmIkHandle*, the *rArmIkHandle*, the *lLegIkHandle* and the *rLegIkHandle*.

- Set the **Visibility** attribute in the Channel Box to **Off** by typing in **0** in the Channel Box

*All the IK handles are now hidden.*

- Highlight the **Visibility** attribute's name.

- **RMB** in the Channel Box and select **Lock Selected**.

*Doing so will prevent the IK handles from being displayed, even when using the* **Display** → **Show** → **All** *command*

## Selection handles

There are several nodes that you will need to select when animating the character. Unfortunately, those nodes can be hidden under geometry or difficult to pick in the viewport. This is where a selection handle becomes helpful.

### 1 Show selection handles

- Select the *lHeelControl*, the *rHeelControl* and the *pelvis* joints.

- Select **Display** → **Component Display** → **Selection Handles**.

- Clear the current selection.

- **Click+drag** a selection box over the entire character in the viewport.

*Since selection handles have a very high selection priority, only the three selection handles get selected.*

### 2 Move selection handles

- Go into Component mode.

- Make sure only the **Selection Handle** mask is enabled.

- Select the selection handles for the *lHeelControl*, the *rHeelControl* and the *pelvis* joints.

*The selection handle mask*

- Press **w** to enable the **Translate Tool**.
- Translate the selection handles towards the back on the **Z-axis** until they are outside the geometry.
- Go back in Object mode.

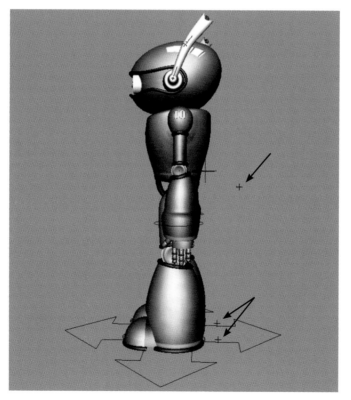

*The selection handle outside the geometry*

## 3 Save your work

# Hide and lock nodes and attributes

Many nodes and attributes in the character rig are not supposed to be animated or changed. It is recommended that you double-check each node and attribute to see if the animator requires them. If they are not required, you can hide and lock them.

The Channel Control window allows you to quickly set which attributes are displayed in the Channel Box and which ones are locked.

## 1   Lock geometry groups

Since all the geometry is bound to the skeleton, it must not be moved. All the geometry attributes should therefore be locked.

- Select **Window** → **Hypergraph**.

- Make sure all nodes are visible in the Hypergraph by setting
  **Options** → **Display** → **Hidden Nodes** to **On**.

- Select all the geometry groups.

- In the Channel Box, highlight the **Translate**, **Rotate** and **Scale**
  attribute names.

- **RMB** in the Channel Box and select **Lock Selected**.

- Select **Window** → **General Editors** → **Channel Control**.

- In the **Keyable** tab, highlight all the translation, rotation and scale attributes.

- Click on the **Move** button.

*This will move all the highlighted attributes in the **Nonkeyable** column. Notice that only the Visibility attribute is still visible in the Channel Box.*

- Select the **Locked** tab.

*Notice that all the attributes that you locked through the Channel Box are listed in the **Locked** column.*

## 2   Lock geometry

Lock and hide the **Translate**, **Rotate** and **Scale** attributes for all the geometry in the scene. Leave the **Visibility** attribute since you might want to hide parts of the model.

**Tip:**   *Try using* **Edit** → **Select All by Type** → **NURBS Surface**.

## 3 Lock joints

Joints can usually rotate, but should not be translated or scaled. There are exceptions, such as *joint* roots, that usually need to be able to translate.

Lock and hide the **Translate**, **Scale** and **Visibility** attributes for all the joints in the scene, except for *pelvis*, *lHeelControl* and *rHeelControl,* which requires translation.

**Tip:**   *Try using* **Edit** → **Select All by Type** → **Joints***.*

## 4 Hide end joints

End joints are usually not animated. Lock and hide all the end joints on your skeleton.

**Tip:**   *When all the joints are selected, press the* **down arrow** *repetitively until all the end joints are selected.*

## 5 Rest of setup

You should spend some time checking each node in your character rig hierarchy to lock and hide unwanted attributes or nodes. When you don't know what an attribute does, you should at least set it to non-keyable, so that it doesn't appear in the Channel Box. This will prevent it from being keyframed accidentally.

## 6 Master scale

You should make sure to set the *master*'s scaling attributes to non-keyable, but you should not lock these attributes. By doing so, you can be sure no keyframes will be made on the global scaling of the character, but you will still be able to change the robot's scaling to fit its environment.

## 7 Save your work

# Low resolution model

When animating a character, it is good to have the choice of displaying either the high resolution or low resolution model. In some cases, you must have a low resolution model since a model can become very heavy on your system.

Luckily, the robot model is made out of NURBS surfaces, which will greatly simplify the low resolution creation. If the model was made out of polygons, you might be required to completely model a low resolution model.

## 1   Convert NURBS to polygons

- Select **Edit → Select All by Type → NURBS Surfaces**.

- Select **Modify → Convert → NURBS to Polygons → ❏**.

*The Convert option window will be displayed.*

- Set the **Tessellation Method** attribute to **Control Points**.

- Click on the **Tessellate** button to execute the command.

*A low resolution polygon mesh will be created for each NURBS surface.*

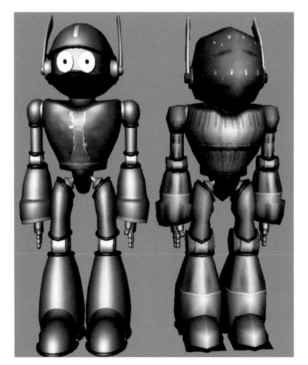

*The converted low resolution geometry*

## 2   Layer

- Press **Ctrl+g** to **Group** all the low resolution meshes.

- Rename the new group *robotLowGeo*.

- Click the **Create a new layer** button in the **Layer Editor**.

- Rename the layer *robotLowLayer*.

- Add the *robotLowGeo* group to the new *robotLowLayer*.

*The layers will allow you to quickly toggle between the low and high resolution models.*

## 3   Work on the low resolution model

Spend some time refining the low resolution geometry so that it better fits the high resolution model.

- Delete all objects that are not necessary for the general shape of the model.

- Tweak the shape of the polygonal objects to better fit the high resolution model.

**Tip:**   *Template the robotLayer so that you can work with it as a reference model.*

- Assign a simple blue Lambert shader.

- Rename the objects accordingly.

## 4   Bind the low resolution model

- Select the *robotLowGeo* group.

- Select **Edit** → **Select Hierarchy**.

- Select **Edit** → **Delete by Type** → **History**.

- Rigid bind every object to its respective joint.

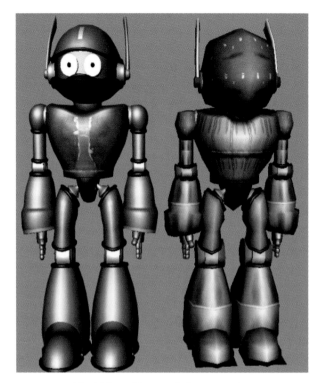

*The high and low resolution geometry*

## Creating character nodes

In the next lesson, you will use keyframing techniques to make the robot walk. To organize all animation channels needed for keyframing, you can create character nodes. These nodes let you collect attributes into a single node that can then be efficiently keyed and edited as a group.

### 1   Create a main character node

- Select the *master* node.

- Select **Edit** → **Select Hierarchy**.

- Select **Character** → **Create Character Set** → ❑.

- Set the **Name** to *robot*.

- Click **Create Character Set**.

*This character is now active and visible next to the Range Slider. It was created with all the keyframable attributes for the entire master hierarchy.*

## 2    Remove unnecessary attributes from the character

- Select the *robot* character node
  from the Outliner.

*All the character attributes are listed
in the Channel Box.*

*You will notice that lWrist and rWrist rotations are already connected.
They are being driven by orient constraints, therefore, they are not
needed in the character.*

*The character node*

| robot | |
| --- | --- |
| master.tx | 0 |
| master.ty | 0 |
| master.tz | 0 |
| master.rx | 0 |
| master.ry | 0 |
| master.rz | 0 |
| pelvis.tx | 0 |
| pelvis.ty | 6.497 |
| pelvis.tz | -0.241 |
| pelvis.rx | 0 |
| pelvis.ry | 0 |
| pelvis.rz | 0 |
| neck.rx | 0 |
| neck.ry | 0 |
| neck.rz | 0 |
| head.rx | 0 |
| head.ry | 0 |
| head.rz | 0 |
| rAntenna1.rz | 0 |
| rAntenna2.rz | 0 |
| lAntenna1.rz | 0 |
| lAntenna2.rz | 0 |
| lHip.rx | -0 |
| lHip.ry | 0 |
| lHip.rz | 0 |
| lKnee.rz | 0 |
| rHip.rx | 0 |
| rHip.ry | 0.001 |

*Character menu*

- Use the **Ctrl** key to highlight the
  following in the Channel Box:

  *lWrist.rx*;

  *lWrist.ry*;

  *lWrist.rz*;

  *rWrist.rx*;

  *rWrist.ry*;

  *rWrist.rz.*

- Select **Character** → **Remove
  from Character Set**.

*Character attributes
for robot*

# Conclusion

You now have a biped character all hooked up and ready for a stroll. You made
your character rig simpler for an animator to use and virtually unbreakable. You
also created a low resolution model, which will be very useful for animation.

In the next lesson, you will animate the robot using the character rig and
character node. It will test both your rig and your animation skills.

# Lesson 22    Animation

*The character you built is
now ready to be animated.
To create a walk cycle, you
will build up the motion one
part at a time. Starting with
the sliding of the feet, you will
then lift the feet, use the roll
attribute, and set the twist of
the pelvis. When that is done,
you will animate the upper
body accordingly. You will also
create another animation of
the robot jumping forward.*

*These separate animated
sequences will later be
brought into the Trax Editor
to be manipulated.*

## In this lesson, you will learn the following:

- How to reference a scene;

- How to animate the character's legs and arms;

- How to animate the roll of the foot;

- How to animate the twist of the pelvis;

- How to create a cycle using the Graph Editor;

- How to bake animation channels;

- How to create a Trax clip.

- How to export a Trax clip.

# Reference

Instead of working with the file from the last lesson, you will reference the robot. A reference refers to another scene file that is set to read-only. It allows you to animate the character, leaving the rig file untouched.

## 1 Create a reference

- Select **File → New**.
- Select **File → Create Reference → □**.

*Doing so will open the **Create Reference** options.*

- Set **Resolve all nodes with this string**: *robot*.

*This will prefix all the reference nodes with the string robot.*

**Note:** *For simplicity reasons, the robot prefix will not be cited.*

- Click on the **Reference** button.
- In the browse dialog that appears, select the file *21-rigging.ma*, then click **Reference**.

*The file will load into the current one.*

*Notice the small **r** in the Outliner and the red names in the Hypergraph. This means that the robot nodes are loaded from a reference file as read-only.*

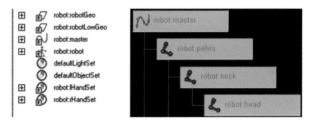

*Referenced nodes in the Outliner and Hypergraph*

**Note:** *If you need to bring changes in the character setup from the last lesson, you will need to open the rig file, make your changes, then save the file. Once that is done, you will need to open the animation file again to reload the new referenced rig. Be careful; if you remove nodes or attributes that are animated in the animation file, their animation will be lost.*

## 2 Layers

- Turn the visibility **Off** for the *robotLayer*.

- Turn the visibility **On** for the *robotLowLayer* and *setupLayer*.

*You should now see only the low resolution model along with its rig.*

## 3 Change the view panels

- Select **Panels** → **Layouts** → **Two Panes Stacked**.

- Change the top panel to a *side* view and the bottom panel to a *Perspective* view.

- For the *side* view, select **View** → **Predefined Bookmarks** → **Left Side**.

- In the *side* view, turn **Off** both **Show** → **NURBS Surfaces** and **Show** → **Polygons**.

*This panel will be used to watch the movements of the rig.*

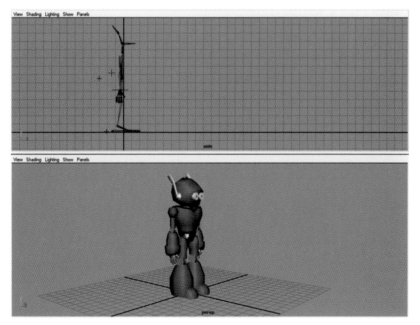

*View panel layout*

# ANIMATING A WALK CYCLE

To create a walk, you will start with a single cycle. To create a cycle, you will need the start position and end position to be the same. There are several controls that need to be keyed, including the position of the feet, the roll of the feet, and the rotation of the pelvis.

## Animate the feet sliding

You will now key the horizontal positions of the feet to establish their forward movement. This will result in a sliding motion of the feet.

### 1    Set your time range

- Set the **Start Time** and **Playback Start Time** to **1**.

- Set the **End Time** and **Playback End Time** to **20**.

*This will give you a smaller time range to work with as you build the cycle.*

### 2    Make the robot character active

- In the **Current Character** menu next to the Range Slider, select *robot*.

*Active Character menu*

*Now any keys you set will be set on all the attributes of this character node.*

### 3    Position and key the lower body start pose

You will key the starting position of the character in the position of a full stride.

- Go to frame **1**.

- Select the *lHeelControl* selection handle and **translate Z** to **4** units.

- Select the *rHeelControl* selection handle and **translate Z** to **0** units.

*Tip:*    *Make sure the Translate Tool is set to be in World coordinates.*

- Set the *pelvis* **translate Z** to **3.5** units.

- Move the *pelvis* down until the knees bend.

**Note:** Leave the arms behind for now. Later, you will add secondary animation.

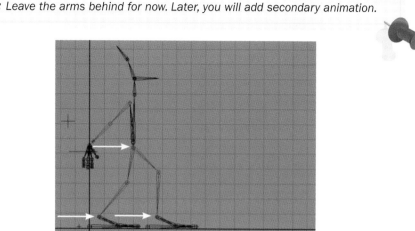

*Lower body position*

- Press **s** to set a key on all the channels of the *robot* character.

## 4   Position and key the right foot

- Go to frame **10**.

- Set the *rHeelControl* **translate Z** to **8** units.

*This value is exactly double the value of the initial left foot key. This is important to ensure that the two feet cycle together later.*

- Set the *pelvis* **translate Z** to **7.5** units.

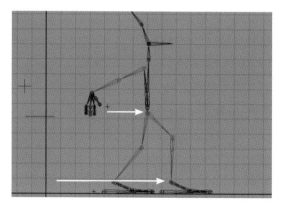

*Right leg position*

- Press **s** to set a key on all the channels of the *robot* character.

## 5   Position and key the left foot

You will move the left foot into a position that is similar to the
starting position.

- Go to frame **20**.

- Set the *lHeelControl* **translate Z** to **12** units.

*Again, the value is set using units of 4. This will ensure a connection
between cycles later.*

- Set the *pelvis* **translate Z** to **11.5** units.

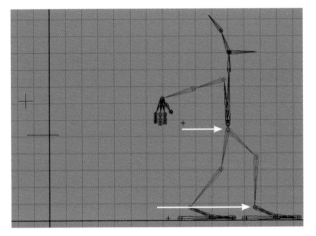

*Left leg position*

- Press **s** to set a key on all the channels of the *robot* character.

## Edit the animation curves

To refine the in-between motion of the feet, you can use the animation curves to
view and change the tangent options for the feet.

## 1   View the curves in the Graph Editor

You will edit the animation curves produced by the keys in the Graph Editor.

- Clear the selection.

- Select **Window → Animation Editor → Graph Editor**.

- In the Graph Editor, highlight the *robot* character.

- Select **View → Frame All**.

- Press the **Ctrl** key to select *lHeelControl.TranslateZ* and *rHeelControl. TranslateZ* in the Outliner section of this window.

- Select **View** → **Frame Selection**.

*The pattern of the animation curves you have created should look as follows:*

*Animation curves in Graph Editor*

- Playback the animation to see the motion.

**Note:** *If you open the Graph Editor when the feet are selected, you will see an animation channel with keys set in the negative direction. This is the animation curve connecting the Rotate Z of the foot to the Roll attribute.*

## 2   Edit the curve tangents on the feet

The curve tangent type should be changed so that the steps cycle smoothly. The default tangent type is clamped.

- Select the two animation curves for *lHeelControl.TranslateZ* and *rHeelControl.TranslateZ*.

- Select **Tangents** → **Flat**.

*The visual difference between clamped and flat tangents in the Graph Editor is subtle. Look at the beginning and end keyframes on the curves. The flat tangents will create a smooth hook-up for the cycle between the start frame and end frame.*

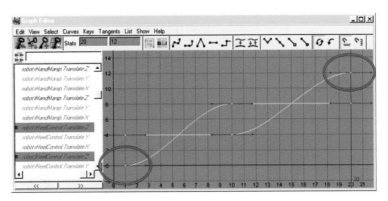

*Flat tangents*

## Animate the feet up and down

You will now key the vertical raising and lowering of the feet to establish the stepping action.

### 1 Turn on Auto Key

You will now use **Auto Key** to help with the raising of the feet.

- Click on the **Auto Keyframe** button in the right side of the Time Slider to turn it **On**.

- Open the **Animation Preferences** window, using the button just to the right of the **Auto Keyframe** button.

- Click on the **Animation** category and set the following under the **Tangents** section:

  **Default In Tangent** to **Flat**;

  **Default Out Tangent** to **Flat**.

*This will set all future tangents to flat.*

- Click on the **Save** button.

### 2 Raise the right foot at midstep

Key the high point of the raised foot at the appropriate frame.

- Go to frame **5**.

- Select the *rHeelControl*.

- Translate the foot about **0.5** units up along the **Y-axis**.

*This sets a new key for the Y-axis channel of the foot using Auto Key.*

## 3 Raise the left foot at midstep

- Go to frame **15**.

- Select the *lHeelControl*.

- Move the foot about **0.5** units up along the **Y-axis**.

*Again, a key is automatically set.*

- Playback the results.

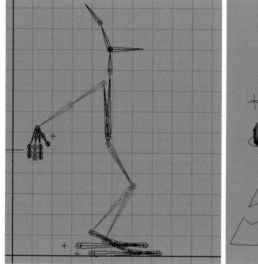
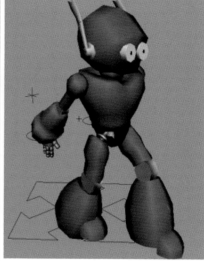

*Raised step for right foot*          *The character is walking*

## 4 Save your work

**Tip:** *Leave Auto Key set to On.*

# Animate the pelvic rotations

To create a more realistic action, the pelvis' position and rotation will be set to work with each step. You will again set keys for the translation and rotation of the pelvis using Auto Key.

## 1 Select the pelvis Y rotation

You will now animate the pelvis rotation to give the walk a little more motion.

- Go to frame **1**.
- Select the *pelvis* node using its selection handle.

## 2 Rotate the pelvis

- In the *top* view, **Rotate** the *pelvis* using the rotation handle in a clockwise direction.

*This points the left hip towards the left foot and the right hip towards the right foot.*

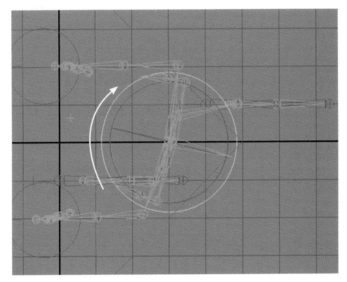

*Rotate pelvis toward left foot*

## 3 Rotate in the opposite direction

- Go to frame **10**.
- Rotate the pelvis in the opposite direction.

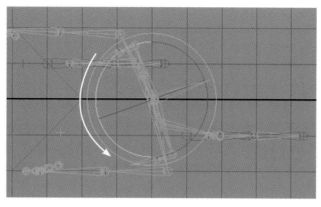

*Rotate pelvis toward right foot*

## 4   Copy the first Y rotation

- Go to frame **1**.

- In the Time Slider, **MMB+drag** the current time to frame **20**.

*The display has not changed, but the time has changed.*

- With the *pelvis* still selected, highlight the **Rotate X** attribute in the
  Channel Box, then **RMB** and select **Key Selected**.

*By doing so, you have manually set a keyframe on the rotateX value of the
pelvis from frame 1 to frame 20.*

- Refresh the Time Slider by dragging anywhere in the time indicator.

*Notice that the pelvis' rotateX attribute has the exact same value at frame 20
that it does at frame 1.*

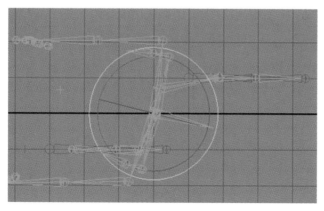

*Copied rotation value at frame 20*

## 5   Pelvis in front view

- Go to frame **5**.

- In the *front* view, **Rotate** the *pelvis* so that the right hip is raising with the right leg.

- **Translate** the *pelvis* on the X-axis so that the weight of the robot is on the left leg.

- Go to frame **15**.

- **Rotate** the *pelvis* in the opposite direction as the left foot raises.

- **Translate** the *pelvis* on the X-axis so that the weight of the robot is on the right leg.

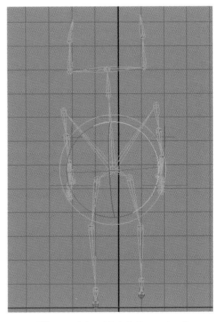

*Offset pelvis with right foot raised*          *Offset pelvis with left foot raised*

## 6   Edit the keys

To prepare the file for creating cycles later, you will need to ensure that the rotations match at the start and end of the cycle.

- Clear the selection.

- In the Graph Editor, press the **Ctrl** key and highlight the **Translate X**, **Rotate X** and **Rotate Y** channels for the *pelvis*.

- Select **View** → **Frame All**.

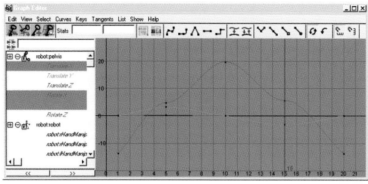

*Pelvis curves*

Since you copied frame 1 of the pelvis' X rotation onto frame 20 in Step 4, the start and end values of the animation curve are a perfect match. If they were different, you could have fixed the curve in the Graph Editor so that the cycled motion is smooth.

## Add a bounce to the walk

To create a bouncing motion for the walk, you will add keyframes to the Y translation of the *pelvis* node.

### 1   Edit the pelvis height

- In the Graph Editor, highlight the *pelvis.TranslateY* channel.

### 2   Insert keys

- Select the **Insert Keys Tool** found in the Graph Editor.

- Select the **translateY** curve, then with your **MMB** insert a key at frame **5** and frame **15**.

### 3   Edit the Y translation value of the keys

- Press **w** to select the **Move Key Tool**.

- Select the new keys at frame **5** and frame **15**.

- **Click+drag** with the **MMB** to move these keys to a value of about **6.2** to add some bounce to the walk.

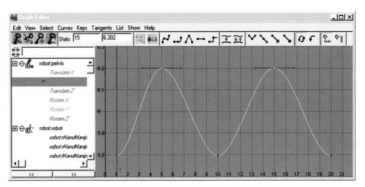

*Pelvis Y Translate channel*

## Animate the heel rotation

When you created the reverse foot setup, you spent a great deal of time preparing the foot for the *heel to toe* motion that occurs when walking. You are now going to keyframe the foot rotations to take advantage of this work.

### 1  Set a key on the right foot's roll

- Go to frame **1**.
- Select the *rHeelControl* using its selection handle.
- Set the *rHeelControl*'s **Roll** attribute to **5**.

*Foot rotated forward for frame 1*

### 2  Set a second roll key

- Go to frame **10**.
- Set the *rHeelControl*'s **Roll** attribute to **-5**.

*Foot rotated backward for frame 10*

## 3 Set a third key on the right foot's roll

- Go to frame **20**.

- Set the *rHeelControl*'s **Roll** attribute to **5**.

*Foot rotated forward for frame 20*

## 4 Set an in-between key on the right foot's roll

- Go to frame **13**.

- Set the *rHeelControl*'s **Roll** attribute to **0**.

**5   Set a key on the left foot's roll**

- Use the same technique to set the *lHeelControl*'s **Roll** attribute as follows:

    At frame **1**, set **Roll** to **-5**;

    At frame **3**, set **Roll** to **0**;

    At frame **10**, set **Roll** to **5**;

    At frame **20**, set **Roll** to **-5**.

**6   Playback the results**

**7   Save your work**

## Animate the arm swing

The character needs some motion in his arms. To do this, you will animate the translation of the arm manipulators to create an animation that can be cycled.

To add some secondary motion, you will also set keyframes on the rotation of the head.

**1   Set keys for the start position**

- Go to frame **1**.

- Move the *lHandManip* behind the body and low down.

- Rotate the *lHandManip* back on the **X-axis**.

- Move the *rHandManip* in front of the body and up.

- Rotate the *rHandManip* forward on the **X-axis**.

*Now the arms are opposite to how the feet are set up. This makes the swinging motion work with the feet.*

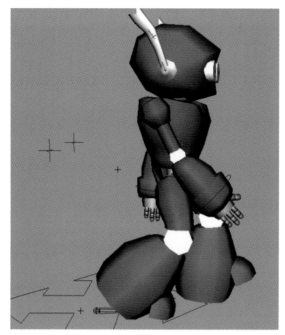

*Arm positions*

- Select the *head* joint and rotate it around the **X-axis** by around **15-degrees**.

*This has the head and hips moving in opposite directions.*

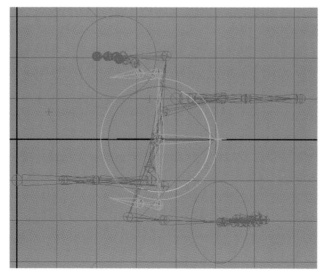

*Top view of head rotation*

## 2   Copy keys for the end position

In order to create a smooth transition for the arm cycle, you must have matching values at the start and end of the cycle.

- Select the *lHandManip* and *rHandManip* nodes.

- In the timeline, **MMB+drag** and move the Time Slider to frame **20**.

*The character will not move when you scrub along the timeline with the MMB depressed.*

- Highlight the translation and rotation attributes in the Channel Box.

- **RMB** and select **Key Selected** from the pop-up menu.

*This sets keyframes only on the attributes you have selected in the Channel Box.*

*Because you also have the rHandManip node selected, you can see three dots after the lHandManip name in the Channel Box. This indicates that the rHandManip node is active, and has also received the keyframes.*

- Refresh the **Time Slider** at frame **20**.

*You will see that you have set keyframes at the current position on the manipulators, but they are not following the robot.*

- Translate the *lHandManip* and *rHandManip* nodes on the **Z-axis** by exactly **8** units.

*Two simple ways of doing this are either by adding 8 to the current **Translate Z** attribute value or by entering \* \* **8** in the **Numeric Input Relative** field.*

**Note:** *You can also use the Dope Sheet to copy and paste selected keyframes, or you can cut and paste keyframe values from the Graph Editor.*

## 3   Set keys for the head

Use the method outlined in Step 2 to set the last keyframe for the head rotation.

- Select the *head*.

- **MMB+drag** the Time Slider from frame **1** to frame **20**.

- **LMB** over the *head* **Rotate X** attribute in the Channel Box to highlight it.

- **RMB** and select **Key Selected** from the pop-up menu.

**4   Set keys for the middle position**

- Go to frame **10**.

- Move the arm manipulators opposite to the *legs*.

- Rotate the head joint opposite to the *hips*.

*Arm positions at frame 10*

**5   Keyframe the in between**

- Make sure to set a good position for the arms at frames **5** and **15**.

**6   Fix the arm manipulator curves**

- In the Graph Editor, select the arm manipulators' **Translate** and **Rotate** attributes.

- Select all keyframes between frame **5** and **15**.

- Select **Tangents** → **Spline**.

**7   Delete the static channels**

If a curve is flat its whole length, the value of the attribute it represents isn't changing. Thus, this attribute is a static channel. Static channels slow Maya processing, so it's beneficial to remove them.

- Select the *robot* character from the Outliner.

- Select **Edit** → **Delete All By Type** → **Static Channels**.

**8   Turn off Auto Key**

**9   Save your work**

# Cycle the animation

So far, you have animated one full step for the walk cycle. Next, you will use the Graph Editor to complete the cycle.

## 1   Set your time range

- Set the **Start Time** and **Playback Start Time** to **1**.

- Set the **End Time** and **Playback End Time** to **300**.

## 2   View all curves in the Graph Editor

- Select *robot* from the Outliner.

- Select **Window** → **Animation Editor** → **Graph Editor** to see all the animation curves for the character.

## 3   View the cycle

In order to check if the cycle works smoothly, you can display the curves' infinity and set it to cycle.

- In the Graph Editor, select **View** → **Infinity**.

- Select all the animation curves.

- Select **Curves** → **Pre Infinity** → **Cycle with Offset**.

- Select **Curves** → **Post Infinity** → **Cycle with Offset**.

*Cycle with Offset appends the cycled curve's last key's value to the value of the first key's original curve. You can now see what the curves are like when cycled.*

- Play the animation.

## 4   Adjust the curves

- Zoom on the curves and adjust the tangents so they are without dents.

**Tip:**   *Pay close attention to the tangents at frame 20. The connection between the curves and cycle should be smooth.*

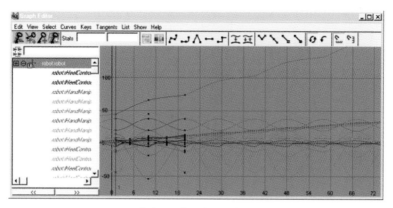

*Robot animation cycles*

## Bake the keyframes

Ultimately, you will use this animation inside the Trax Editor, so you will bake the keyframes of the post infinity onto the curves. The Trax Editor cannot use post infinity curves from the Graph Editor so we will create the actual keyframes by baking them.

### 1   Select the robot character

- In the Graph Editor, select *robot*.

### 2   Bake the keyframes

- In the Graph Editor, select **Curves → Bake Channel → ❑**.

- Set the following options:

  **Time Range** to **Start/End**;

  **Start Time** to **1**;

  **End Time** to **115**;

  **Sample** by **5**;

  **Keep Unbaked Keys** to **On**;

  **Sparse Curve Bake** to **On**.

- Click the **Bake** button.

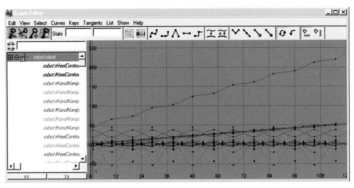

*Baked curves*

**3   Save your work**

## Create a Trax clip file

The animation is done, but because in the next lesson you will be working with
the Trax Editor, you will now create a Trax clip file and export it for later use.

**1   Open the Trax Editor window**

- Select **Window** → **Animation Editor** → **Trax Editor**.

**2   Create a clip**

- From the Trax Editor, select **Create** → **Clip** → ❑.

   Set the following options:

   **Name** to *walk;*

   **Leave Keys in Timeline** to **Off**;

   **Clip** to **Put Clip in Trax Editor and Visor**;

   **Time Range** to **Animation Curve**;

   **Include Subcharacters in Clip** to **Off**;

   **Create Time Warp Curve** to **Off**;

   **Include Hierarchy** to **On**.

- Click the **Create Clip** button.

- Press **a** in the Trax Editor to frame all.

*A clip is created and placed in the Trax timeline. A corresponding clip source file called walkSource is also placed in the Visor.*

*Until you export the clip, it can only be accessed through this scene file.*

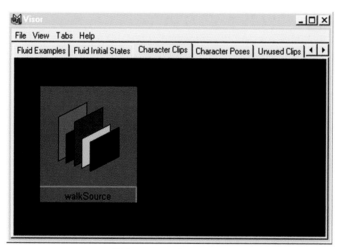

Walk clip in Trax Editor

## 3    Export the clip

- Select **File** → **Visor...**

- Select the **Character Clips** tab to see the clip source.

Walk source clip in Visor

- Select the *walkSource* clip.

- **RMB** on the clip and select **Export.**

*A pop-up menu will browse to the clips directory of your current project.*

▪ Save the clip as *walkExport*.

*Now you can import this clip into another scene.*

▪ Close the Visor.

# ANIMATING A JUMP CYCLE

Now that the walk cycle has been completed, you will animate one more sequence. The new sequence will be saved as another Trax clip.

Using the outlined methods, you will animate the robot jumping forward.

## Animate the jump

**1   Activate the robot character**

▪ In the **Active Character** menu, next to the Range Slider, ensure that the *robot* character is selected.

**2   Set your time range**

▪ Set the **Start Time** and **Playback Start Time** to **1**.

▪ Set the **End Time** and **Playback End Time** to **30**.

**3   Go to Frame 1**

▪ Move the Time Slider to Frame **1**.

**4   Clear the Trax Editor**

The walking clip is not required to build a new animation. It will be reapplied in the Trax Editor later in the lesson.

▪ Click on the *walk* clip in the Trax Editor to highlight it.

▪ Press the **Delete** key to remove it.

*All the animation has now been removed, but the character has kept its initial step position, which is the start pose of your jump cycle.*

**5   Keyframe the start pose**

▪ Press the **s** hotkey to keyframe the entire robot character.

▪ Turn **Auto Key On**.

## 6   Set keys for the anticipation

- Go to frame **5**.

- Bring the *rHeelControl* forward, next to the *lHeelControl*.

- Place the character as shown in the image to the right:

- Press the **s** key to set a key on the robot character at this new position.

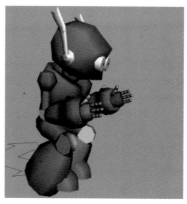

*Anticipation pose*

## 7   Set keys for the pushing motion

- Go to frame **10**.

- Place the character as shown in the image to the right:

- Press the **s** key to set a key on the robot character at this new position.

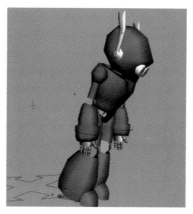

*Pushing pose*

## 8   Set keys for the jump pose

- Go to frame **15**.

- Place the character as shown in the image to the right:

- Press the **s** key to set a key on the robot character at this new position.

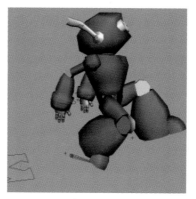

*Jump pose*

## 9   Fix jump pose tangents

- **RMB** in the Time Slider and select **Tangents** → **Spline**.

## 10  Set keys for the landing anticipation pose

- Go to frame **20**.

- Place the character as follows:

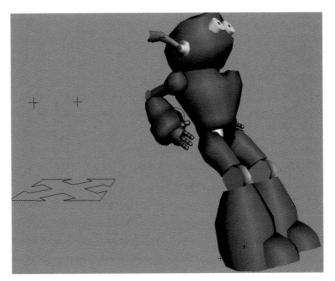

*Landing anticipation*

> **Note:** *Make sure that when the feet land, only the translate Z moves forward. All the other translation and rotation axes should be the same as the starting pose.*

- Press the **s** key to set a key on the robot character at this new position.

## 11  Set keys for the landing pose

- Go to frame **25**.

- Place the character as shown on the following page:

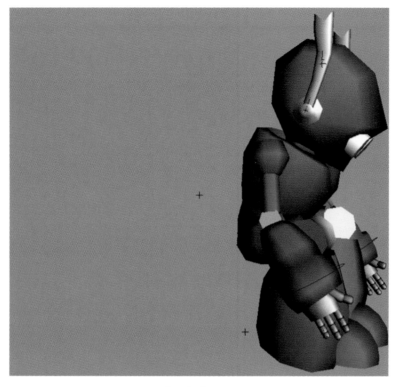

*Landing pose*

- Press the **s** key to set a key on the robot character at this new position.

## 12 Set keys for the end pose

The end pose should be the same as the starting pose, but with an offset on the Z-axis. You will need to copy the start pose, and paste it on the last frame. Then you will have to manually offset the robot on the Z-axis.

- Go to frame **1**.
- **RMB** in the Time Slider and select **Copy** from the pop-up menu.
- Go to frame **30**.
- **RMB** in the Time Slider and select **Paste** → **Paste** from the pop-up menu.

*The end pose is now exactly like the start pose, but you need to manually offset the character.*

## 13 Offset the character

- Select all the nodes intended for translation:

  *lHeelControl*;

  *rHeelControl*;

  *pelvis*;

  *lHandManip*;

  *rHandManip*.

**Note:** *You can also select the arms' pole vector locators.*

- Select the **Translate Tool** and offset the nodes on the **Z-axis**.

- Move the current time indicator between frame **25** and **30** and make sure the *rHeelControl* stays in place at frame **30**.

- Press the **s** key to set a key on the robot character at this new position.

## 14 Playback the animation

## 15 Save your work

## Jump curves

Using the method described, create a jump cycle for the robot and make sure the animation is smooth.

## 1  Delete the static channels

- Select the *robot* character from the Outliner.

- Select **Edit** → **Delete All By Type** → **Static Channels.**

**2    View all curves in the Graph Editor**

- Select **Window** → **Animation Editor** → **Graph Editor** to see all the animation curves for the character.

**3    Extend the animation curve view**

- Make sure **View** → **Infinity** is turned **On**.

**4    Cycle the jump**

- Select all the animation curves.

- Select **Curves** → **Pre Infinity** → **Cycle with Offset**.

- Select **Curves** → **Post Infinity** → **Cycle with Offset**.

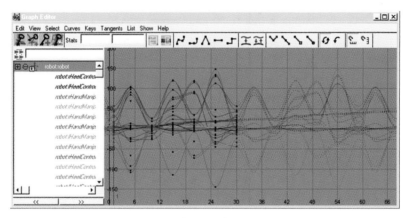

*Jump cycle*

**5    Set your time range**

- Set the **Start Time** and **Playback Start Time** to **1**.

- Set the **End Time** and **Playback End Time** to **300**.

**6    Test your animation**

**7    Save your work**

# Create a Trax clip for the jump

The animation is done so you will now create a Trax clip file from the animated jump cycle.

## 1   Open the Trax Editor window

- Select **Window** → **Animation Editor** → **Trax Editor**.

## 2   Create a clip

- From the Trax Editor select **Create** → **Clip** → ❑.

    Set the following options:

    **Name** to *jump*;

    **Leave Keys in Timeline** to **Off**;

    **Clip** to **Put Clip in Trax Editor and Visor**;

    **Time Range** to **Animation Curve**;

    **Include Subcharacters in Clip** to **Off**;

    **Create Time Warp Curve** to **Off**;

    **Include Hierarchy** to **On**.

- Click on the **Create Clip** button.

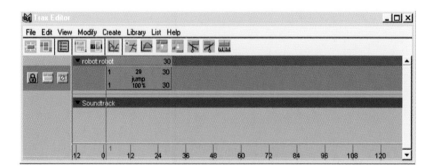

*Jump clip in Trax Editor*

## 3  Export the clip

- Select **File** → **Visor...**

- Select the **Character Clips** tab to see the clip source.

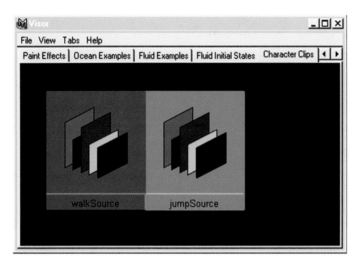

*Jump source clip in Visor*

- Select the *jumpSource* clip.

- **RMB** on the clip and select **Export.**

- Save the clip as *jumpExport.*

- Close the Visor.

## 4  Save your work

## Conclusion

Congratulations, you have completed a walk and jump cycle! You learned how to reference a file, and then you animated the robot using the character node. You also produced perfect cycles, and created and exported Trax clips.

In the next lesson you will use the Trax Editor to combine the two clips and create a new animated sequence.

# Lesson 23    The Trax Editor

*In the last lesson, you animated the robot by setting keyframes and you created two Trax clips from the animated sequences. In this lesson, you will create a more complex motion by joining the walk clip with the jump clip in the Maya Trax Editor.*

*The advantage of working with the Traxnon-linear animation lies in the ability to move, edit, connect, and reuse multiple clips freely, without having to edit multiple time curves. You can also add numerous sound files to the scene using Trax.*

## In this lesson, you will learn the following:

- How to work with relative and absolute clips;

- How to clip, split, blend and merge clips;

- How to layer non-destructive keys over clips;

- How to use sound in Trax;

- How to animate a two-node camera.

## Initial set up

### 1  Open file

- If you are not continuing from the previous lesson directly, either open the file you saved at the end of the last lesson, or select the pre-existing file, *22-animation.ma.*

### 2  Import space warehouse into scene

To make visualization easier for the clip transitions, import the last file from the previous project into the scene.

- Select **File** → **Import** → ⬜.
- Set **Group** to **On**.
- Set **File Type** to **mayaAscii**.
- Click the **Import** button.
- Select *14-dynamics.ma* from *project2*'s *scenes* folder.
- Once the scene is imported, **rename** the room group to *warehouseGroup*.

### 3  Save the scene

- Save the scene as *23-trax.ma.*

### 4  Make the robot to scale

As you can see, the robot does not have a proper scale compared to the room. Since it is not beneficial to scale the dynamics of the orb, you will have to scale the robot.

- From the Outliner, select the robot *master*.
- Press **r** to select the **Scale Tool** and scale the *master* uniformly to **0.2**.

**Note:** *If the master's scale attributes are non-keyable and unlocked, they will not show in the Channel Box, but the Scale Tool will still work. Alternatively, you can access the scale attributes in the Attribute Editor. If the scale attributes of the master are locked, you need to unlock them in the referenced file, which is 21-rigging.ma, then open 23-trax.ma again.*

**5    Set up the work area**

- Set the **Playback Frame Range** to go from **1** to **140**.

- From the menus in any modeling window, select **Panels → Saved Layouts → Persp/Trax/Outliner**.

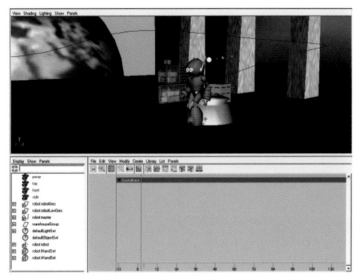

*Persp/Trax/Outliner window layout*

## Generate the animation

The following exercise uses several Trax commands that will establish the animation of the robot. The animation you want to achieve in the scene goes like this:

*The robot walks quietly in the room when the orb comes in. As he jumps over a wire, he surprises the orb, who loses control. The orb crashes into the pile of boxes and the robot stops to look at the scene. The robot then realizes he could be in trouble, so he quickly leaves the room.*

**1    Load the first two clips**

- Select *robot* from the Outliner.

*The Trax Editor will get updated, showing the jump cycle from the last lesson.*

- Select **Library → Insert Clip → walkSource**.

*Both the walk and jump clips are now in the Trax Editor.*

▪ **Click+drag** each clip in the Trax Editor so that the *walk* clip starts at frame **1** and the *jump* clip starts at frame **115**.

*Walk and jump clips*

## 2 Trim the walk clip

▪ Scrub to frame **58** in the timeline.

*This is a good place to match the jump clip, since it is a pose similar to the start pose.*

▪ Select the *walk* clip.

▪ Select the **Trim After** icon from the **Trax** menu to **Trim** the clip after frame **58**.

*Trim the walk clip after frame 58*

▪ Move the *jump* clip to its new starting position at frame **58**.

## 3 View the clips with absolute offset

▪ Play the animation.

*As the walk clip switches to the jump clip during playback, you will see the*

*robot jump back to the original keyframed values of the jump animation,
or absolute offset.*

## 4  Change the jump clip to relative offset

- Select the *jump* clip, then press **Ctrl+a** to open its Attribute Editor.

- Scroll to the **Channel Offsets** section and click the **All Relative** button.

- Play the animation.

*Now, as the walk clip switches to the jump clip during playback, you will see
that the robot keeps walking forward and then jumps. This is because the clip's
animation is relative to the end position of the clip preceeding it.*

## 5  Add another walk clip

- Go to frame **87**, which is the end of the jump clip.

- Select **Library** → **Insert Clip** → **walkSource**.

- Select the new *walk* clip.

- In the Attribute Editor, scroll to the **Channel Offsets** section and click the
  **All Relative** button.

*The robot will now continue walking after the jump.*

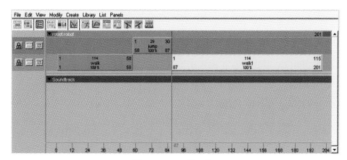

*The new walk clip*

## 6  Split the second walk clip

- Go to frame **98**.

- Select the second *walk* clip.

- Select **Edit** → **Split**.

*The walk clip will be split at the current frame and each section is placed on
a different track.*

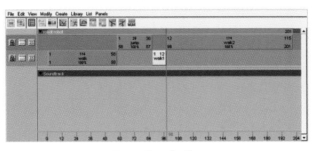

*The split walk clip*

## 7 Offset the last section of the walk clip

- Select the last *walk* clip section.

- **Click+drag** the clip so that its first frame becomes **110**.

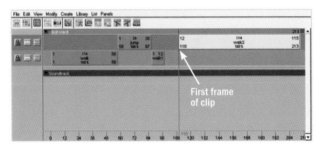

*Offset the second walk clip*

## 8 Speed up the last section of the walk clip

- **Double-click** on the clip's scale field, located just under the name of the clip.

- Enter **40**, then press **Enter**.

| 12 | 114 | 115 |
|---|---|---|
| | walk2 | |
| 110 | 40 ← | 213 |

*The scale value of the clip*

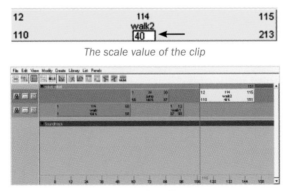

*The scaled clip*

## 9  Blend between the last two clips

- Select the *walk1* clip, then **Shift-select** the *walk2* clip.

- Select **Create** → **Blend** → ❏.

- In the option window, set **Initial Weight Curve** to **Ease In Out**.

- Click the **Create Blend** button.

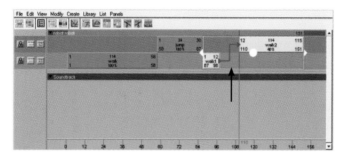

*The newly created blend*

## 10  Ease in the walk2 clip

- Select the *walk2* clip.

- **RMB** on the clip and select **Create Weight Curve**.

*A weight curve sets how the blend is interpolated at the beginning, middle, and end of the clip.*

- **RMB** on the clip again and select **Graph Weight**.

*The Graph Editor will be displayed, showing you the weight curve.*

- Select the first keyframe and set its **Value** to **0**.

*Notice the weight curve is displayed in the clip in the Trax Editor.*

*The weight curve displayed on the clip*

- Select the last keyframe and set its **Time** to **113**.

- If you scrub in the Time Slider, you will notice that the robot's faster walk starts smoothly rather than abruptly.

## 11 Offset all the animation

In order to match the jump of the robot with the orb's malfunction, you will offset all the animation.

- **Click+drag** a selection box in the Trax Editor to select all the clips.

*A manipulator will appear, which can be used to offset the selected clips.*

- **Click+drag** the round manipulator and offset the clips so that the first clip is at frame **-6**.

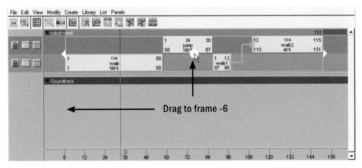

*The selected clip manipulator*

## 12 Trim the first clip

- Go to frame **1** in the Time Slider.

- Select the first *walk* clip.

- Select **Edit → Trim Before**.

## 13 Merge all the clips

- Go to frame **140**.

- Select all the clips in the Trax Editor.

- Select **Edit → Merge → ❏**.

- In the **Merge** option window, set the following:

    **Name** to *robotAnim*;

    **Merged Clip** to **Add to Trax**.

- Click the **Merge Clip** button.

*The new merged clip is now in the Trax Editor, and has replaced all the previous clips.*

## 14 Save your work

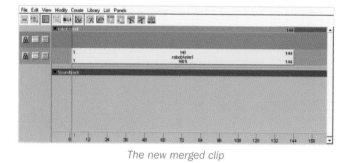

*The new merged clip*

# Orient the animation

Next, you will change the position and rotation of the robot's master node, so that it fits the scene and is able to surprise the orb.

## 1 Change the animation orientation

- Go to frame **1**.

- Select the robot's *master* node.

- Set the following:

    **Translate X** to **-4**;

    **Translate Y** to **0**;

    **Translate Z** to **9**;

    **Rotate X** to **0**;

    **Rotate Y** to **145**;

    **Rotate Z** to **0**.

- Highlight the previous attributes, then **RMB** and select **Key Selected**.

*Doing so will change the orientation of the whole animation.*

The animation of the robot is now well placed and if you play the scene, you will see that the robot is jumping right in front of the orb.

## 2 Place the wire

The robot needs to jump over something. Place the wire on the floor so the robot will jump over it.

- Go to frame **65**.

- Select the *wire* object and place it under the robot.

*The properly placed wire*

# Non-destructive keys

You have already experienced the flexibility of working with non-linear animation clips. To further refine the motion, you will add some non-destructive keys to the animation.

## 1 Add a start and end key on the head joint

When setting keyframes over a Trax clip, you need to set default keys before and after the region where you want to alter the animation. If you don't set those keys, the offset you keyframe will remain throughout the animation.

- Select the *head* joint.

- Go to frame **75**.

- Press the **Shift+e** hotkey to keyframe the rotation of the head.

- Go to frame **120**.

- Press the **Shift+e** hotkey again to keyframe the rotation of the head.

*You will notice some new keys being placed in the timeline.*

## 2 Add keys to modify the head rotation

- Go to frame **85** and rotate the *head* joint so the robot looks at the orb.
- Press the **Shift+e** to keyframe the head.

**Note:** *If Auto Key is On, you don't have to manually key the rotation.*

- In the Time Slider, **RMB** and select **Tangents** → **Spline** to set the tangents of the current keyframe.
- Go to frame **100** and rotate the *head* joint so the robot looks at the box stack.
- Press the **Shift+e** to keyframe the head.
- In the Time Slider, **RMB** and select **Copy** to copy the current keyframe.
- Go to frame **110**, **RMB** and select **Paste** → **Paste** to paste the keyframe.
- Playback the results.

*Now the robot's head is deviating from his original clip-based animation.*

**Note:** *These keys are not altering the clips in any way. In fact, these keys can be deleted or moved around and the clip-based animation will remain intact. You could also create another clip from these new keyframes.*

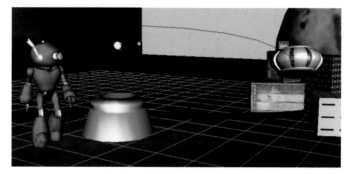

*The robot now looks at the orb*

## 3  Create a clip

- Select **Create** → **Clip** → □.

- Set the following options:

  **Name** to *animModifier*;

  **Leave Keys in Timeline** to **Off**;

  **Clip** to **Put Clip in Trax Editor and Visor**;

  **Time Range** to **Animation Curve**;

  **Subcharacters** to **Off**;

  **Time Warp** to **Off**;

  **Include Hierarchy** to **On**.

- Click on the **Create Clip** button.

*A new clip is added to the Trax Editor. The keyframes of this new clip are added to the existing animation clip.*

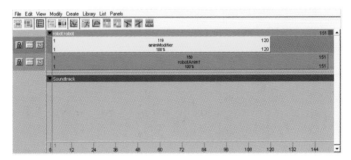

*The two clips in Trax*

## 4  Save your work

# Adding sound to Trax

An added feature in Maya is the ability to import sound files into the Trax Editor.

You can import **.wav** or **.aiff** sound files into Trax to synchronize motion and audio. More than one audio clip can be imported into the soundtrack, but you will be able to hear only one file at a time upon playback. The audio file at the top of the soundtrack display will take precedence over those below.

You will now import some pre-created sound files into your scene.

## 1   Set playback preferences

- Select **Window** → **Settings/Preferences** → **Preferences...**

- In the **Timeline** category under the **Playback** section, make sure **Playback speed** is set to **Real-time [24 fps]**.

## 2   Add a sound file

- From **Trax** select **File** → **Import Audio...**

- From the *sound* directory, select *blip.wav*.

## 3   See and hear the sound file

- **RMB** in the Time Slider.

- From the pop-up menu select **Sounds** → **Use Trax Sounds**.

*A green indicator bar will appear on the global timeline and the clips will display an audio waveform.*

## 4   Move the clip

- Select the sound clip and move it to frame **60**.

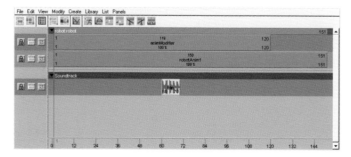

*Sound clip in Trax*

## 5   Import a second sound file

- Select **File** → **Import Audio...**

- From the *sound* directory, select *crash.wav*.

## 6   Sync the sound to the animation

- Play the animation with the sound.

*Notice that the top-most audio clip takes precedence as the scene is playing.*

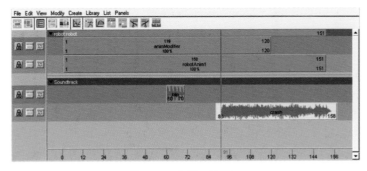

*Two sound clips in Trax*

- Move the crash sound clip so that the crash sound syncs up to the orb crash.

# Animating a camera and aim

You will now add a new camera to the scene and animate it so that you can follow the robot as he walks.

A camera can be created on its own or with additional nodes that provide control over the *aim point* and *up direction*. Most cameras only need one node that lets you key the camera's position and rotation. You will create a camera with aim to control both the *camera point* and the *view point*. Both these nodes can be keyed individually.

## 1   Set up your panel display

- Select a **Two Panes Stacked** view layout.

- In the Perspective view, make sure **Show → Cameras** and **Show → Pivots** are **On**.

*You will need to see these in order to work with the camera.*

## 2   Create a two-node camera

- Select **Create → Cameras → Camera and Aim**.

- Instead of the *front* view, select **Panels → Perspective → camera1**.

- Press **6** to view the textures in the *camera1* view.

*You can position the camera using either the Perspective or camera1 view.*

- In the *camera1* view, select **View → Camera Settings → Resolution Gate.**

- Still in the *camera1* view, select **View → Camera Attribute Editor.**

- Change **Fit Resolution Gate** to **Vertical.**

## 3   Position the camera

- Select the **Show Manipulator Tool.**

- In the Perspective view, position the *camera* and *view point* handles in front of the character.

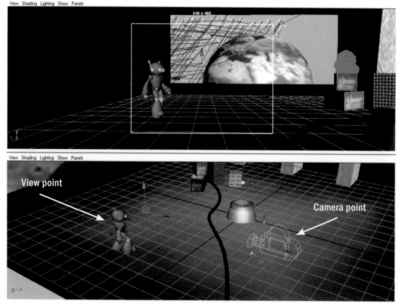

*Camera manipulator handles*

## 4   Set keys on the camera

You will now set keys on the camera point to follow the character from frame **1** to **60**.

- Go to frame **1**.

- Select *camera1*.

- Press **Shift+w** to keyframe the position of the camera point.

- Go to frame **60**.

- Move *camera1* so that it is again in front of the character, framing both the robot and the orb.

- Press **Shift+w** to keyframe the position of the view point.

*View at frame 60*

## 5  Set keys on the view point

The camera animation now frames the first portion of the animation correctly, but the second part of the animation could be better. You can set keys on the view point node to fix this.

- Select the *camera1_aim* node by clicking on the camera point icon.

- Go to frame **60**.

- Press **Shift+w** to set keys on the translation channels of the *camera1_aim* node.

- Go to frame **85**.

- Move the *camera1_aim* node from the Perspective view to the front of the box stack to frame both the crash and the robot.

- Press **Shift+w** to set keys on the translation channels of the *camera1_aim* node.

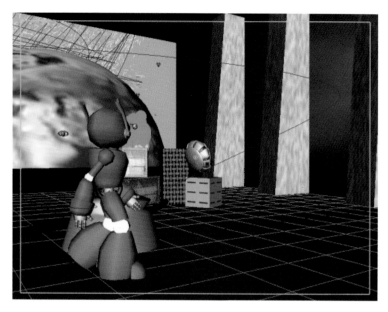

*View at frame 85*

If you don't like the framing in the in-between frames, you can reposition the camera and set new keys. Repeat this until you get the camera movement you want.

**6   Playback the results**

**7   Save your work**

## Testing the motion

You can now playblast the scene to test the motion. This will give you the chance to confirm the camera animation.

Make sure you maximize the camera view and display only NURBS surfaces, polygons and dynamics. Also make sure to display the high resolution character.

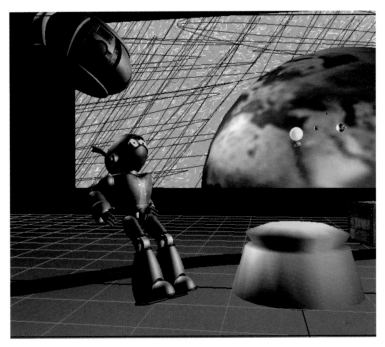

*Playblast of the animation*

# RENDERING THE ANIMATION

You can now render the scene using the Maya Software rendering.

**Note:** *You might also want to try one of the other render engines available in Maya shown in Lesson 17.*

To render, you should consider the various options outlined throughout this book. You need to set attributes on the surfaces themselves and in the Render Settings. Listed is a checklist of some of the considerations you should keep in mind when rendering. Test them out when you render the robot scene.

**Note:** *You will have encountered most of these issues in earlier Learning Maya projects. This checklist offers a compiled list of those issues and some new ones.*

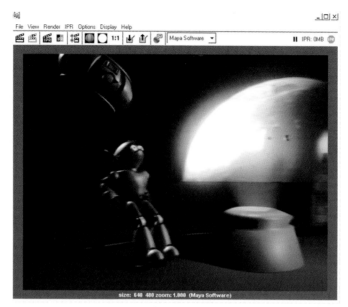

*Maya Software render*

## Object issues

Some render attributes need to be set for your objects' *shape* nodes. You can set these attributes in the **Rendering Flags** window, in the *shape* node's **Render** section in the Attribute Editor, or in the **Attribute Spread Sheet** window. Below are some of the attributes you should consider when you render:

### Surface Tessellation

Set a NURBS surface tessellation that is appropriate to the scene. Larger and more prominent objects will require a larger tessellation than background elements.

It is very important that you do not over-tessellate.

You can also use the default tessellation settings or choose **Explicit Tessellation** and refine even further.

### Motion blur

When you turn on motion blur in the Render Settings, you can also decide which objects will or will not use motion blur. If you have objects that are motionless or barely moving, turn motion blur off to speed up rendering.

You must also choose between 2D and 3D motion blur. The 2D motion blur is faster.

**Lights and shadows**

Limit the number of lights casting shadows in your scene. If possible, use depth maps shadows which are a little faster. If you want to add a lot of lights to a scene, consider linking some of the lights to only those objects that need the illumination.

## Render Setting issues

### Turn animation on!

If you want to render an animation, you must choose a Frame/Animation Ext. in the Render Settings that supports animation. It is very easy to forget this and send off what you think is a long night of rendering frames, only to come in the next day to see just a single frame.

### Renderable camera

Do you have the right camera set up for rendering? Do not leave the default *persp* camera as *renderable* when you want to render another camera.

### Masks and depth masks

If you plan to composite your renderings later, you may want to use these settings to create a matte layer (mask) to assist in the compositing process. You might also choose to use the **Render to Layer** settings found in Maya to support the compositing process.

### Render resolution

What is the render size that you want? Be sure that if you change the pixel size, you use the *Resolution Gate* in your view panel to make sure that the framing of your scene is preserved.

### Raytrace

Do you want to raytrace some of your objects? Remember that Maya has a selective raytracer and only objects that require reflections, refractions, or shadows will be raytraced.

Therefore, if you limit your reflective and refractive materials to key objects, you can raytrace them knowing that other objects in the scene are using the A-buffer.

If you are raytracing, try to limit the number of reflections set in the globals. A setting of 1 will look good in most animations unless, for example, you have a chrome character looking into a mirror.

**Render quality**

You may want to use the *Anti-aliasing Quality presets* pop-up to suggest render quality options until you are familiar with the individual settings.

## Other rendering considerations

### Test render, test render, test render

Do not start a major rendering unless you have test rendered at various levels. Render the whole animation at a low resolution with low quality settings to test the motion. Render random full-size single frames to confirm that materials, lights, and objects are rendering properly.

The more you test render, the less time you spend redoing renderings that didn't work out the way you wanted.

### Command Line rendering

You have learned how to batch render from within Maya. You can also render from the MS-DOS® Command Line. Here is the basic workflow for a Maya Software Command Line render:

- Set up your Render Settings.

- Save your scene file.

- Type `Render -help` for a list of all the Command Line options.

- Type `chdir` or `cd` into the directory with your file.

- Enter the `Render` command along with any flags followed by the file name, such as the start and end frames for the rendering as shown in the following:

    ```
    Render -s 1 - e 150 walkTest.mb
    ```

## Conclusion

Congratulations! You have now completed your first non-linear animation using Maya Trax.

The next project gathers many small lessons covering topics not explored so far. Those lessons will take you through more complex examples, such as organic modeling, Maya Paint Effects™, MEL™ scripting and some Alias SketchBook™ Pro concepts.

## Lessons

This project covers several topics that you absolutely need to know about. You will experiment with tools that seem basic, but in fact they go very deep into the heart of Maya, which will leave room for you to experiment.

You will be introduced to several new tools such as polygonal proxies, subdivision surfaces, deformers, spline IKs and MEL scripts. You will also learn more about Paint Effects, constraints, and cameras and so on.

# Organic modeling

In this lesson, you will create an alien tree-like model by using the Smooth Proxy Polygon Tool. Smooth Proxy enhances polygonal modeling by using low-resolution models, called proxies, which define higher resolution smoothed models.

**In this lesson, you will learn the following:**

- How to model using Smooth Proxy;

- How to wedge polygonal faces;

- How to extrude polygonal faces along a curve;

- How to use selection constraints;

- How to use the Mirror Cut Tool;

- How to smooth polygons.

## Initial set up

**1   Set the current project**

- Select **File** → **Project** → **Set...**

- Select the *project4* directory.

**Note:** *If project4 cannot be found, copy it from the support files.*

**2   Create a new scene**

- Select **File** → **New Scene**.

## Modeling a tree

You will start modeling a tree from a polygonal cube primitive. You will then assign a Smooth Proxy to this cube and use the various polygonal tools to achieve a tree-like shape.

**1   Create a cube and assign a Smooth Proxy**

- Select **Create** → **Polygon Primitives** → **Cube**.

- Scale the cube to **2** in all directions and move it above the ground plane.

- Rename the cube *tree*.

- Change the *Perspective* view to **Smooth Shaded**.

- With the cube still selected, select **Polygon** → **Smooth Proxy**.

*If you look in the Outliner, you will notice the tree object was duplicated and grouped under a node called treeSmoothProxyGroup.*

- In the *Perspective* view, select **Shading** → **Wireframe on Shaded** to see the wireframe structure of the smooth object.

**Note:** *The proxy object and the smooth object are separate and can be moved independently if needed.*

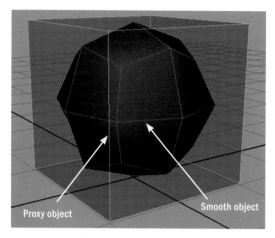

*The smooth proxy cube*

## 2   Extrude a face

- **RMB** on the *tree* proxy object and select **Faces** from the marking menu.
- Select the top face, then select **Edit Polygons** → **Extrude Face**.
- Move the face up.

## 3   Wedge a face

- Select a side face from the newly extruded polygons.
- **RMB** on the proxy and select **Edges** from the marking menu.
- **Shift-select** the top horizontal edge of the current face.
- Select **Edit Polygons** → **Wedge Face**.

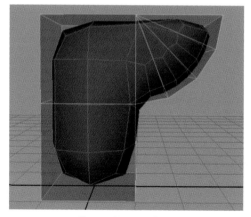

*The wedged surface*

## 4  Extrude along a curve

- Select a *side* Orthographic view.

- Select **Create** → **EP Curve Tool** and draw a curve as shown to the right:

- Press **Enter** to complete the curve.

- In Object mode, select the new *curve*.

- **RMB** on the proxy and select **Face**.

- **Shift-select** the top wedge face.

- Select **Edit Polygons** → **Extrude Face**.

*The polygonal face will be extruded along the curve.*

## 5  Refine the extrusion

- With the proxy object selected, highlight the *polyExtrudeFace,* which is listed first in the **Inputs** section of the Channel Box.

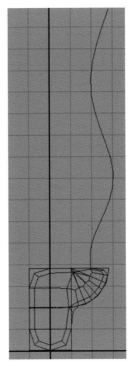

*A curve for extrusion*

- Highlight the **Division** attribute and **MMB+drag** in the *Perspective* view to increase the number of divisions of the last extrusion to **10**.

*You should see the extrusion update as you enter higher values.*

- Highlight the **Taper** attribute and **MMB+drag** in the *Perspective* view to decrease its value to **0.2**.

- Highlight the **Twist** attribute and **MMB+drag** in the *Perspective* view to increase its value to **180**.

- Press **Ctrl+a** to pop-up the Attribute Editor.

- Select the same *polyExtrudeFace* as in the Channel Box to display its values.

*The Taper Curve ramp*

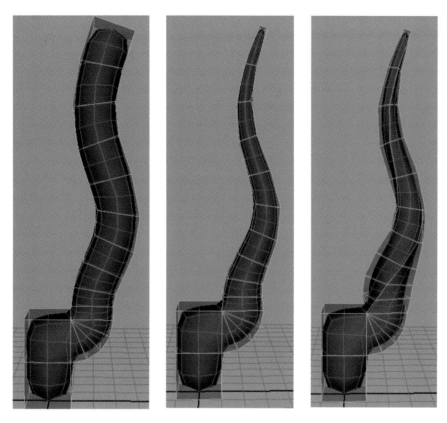

| *The refined extrusion* | *Effect of Taper attribute* | *Effect of Twist attribute* |

- **Click+drag** in the **Taper Curve** ramp to insert and change new values.

*As you change the* **Taper Curve** *values, the extrusion gets updated in the viewport to reflect the changes.*

## 6   Create a tree base

- Select the bottom face at the roots of the tree.

- Select **Edit Polygons** → **Extrude Face**.

- **Scale** the face bigger to create a base for the tree.

- Press the **Delete** key to remove the face.

*The smooth object will snap to the edges of the deleted face. This is because the smooth object is set to keep the edges of the proxy object.*

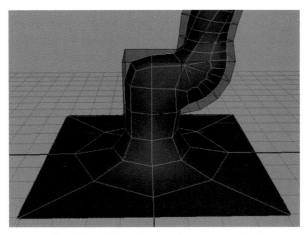

*The deleted face effect on the smooth object*

## 7    Change the Smooth Proxy option

- Highlight the *polySmoothProxy* node in the **Outputs** section of the Channel Box.

- Set the following:

  **Keep Border** to **Off**;

  **Exponential Level** to **2**.

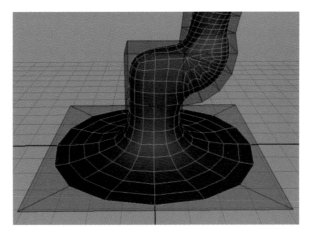

*The updated smooth object*

**Note:** As long as you keep the construction history, you will be able to edit the curve used to extrude the polygonal faces.

**8   Save your work**

- Save your scene under the name *24-organicModel.ma*.

# Refine the tree artwork

Many other tools can be used when modeling with polygons. The following example will extrude random branches and mirror the tree.

**1   Selection constraints**

- Select the proxy object.

- Press **F11** to display the faces.

- Select **Edit Polygons** → **Selection** → **Selection Constraints**.

*The Selection Constraints options are displayed.*

- Set **Constrain** to **Next Selection**.

- In the **Random** section, set the following:

    **Activate** to **On**;

    **Ratio** to **0.4**;

- **Click+drag** a selection box over the branch section of the tree.

*Since the selection of the faces is constrained by the options set earlier, a random set of faces gets selected.*

- Click the **Close and Reset** button in the **Selection Contraints** window.

**2   Extrude random faces**

- Set the **Polygons** → **Tool Options** → **Keep Faces Together** to **Off**.

- Select **Edit Polygons** → **Extrude Faces**.

- **Move** the new faces on their **Z-axes** and **scale** them down.

- Select **Edit Polygons** → **Extrude Faces** again.

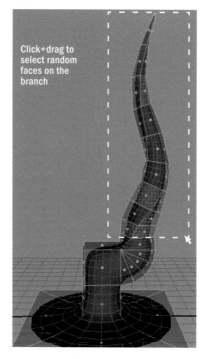

Click+drag to select random faces on the branch

*The updated smooth object*

- Move the new faces on their **Z-axes** and **scale** them down.

- Press the **w** hotkey to change the manipulator to world coordinates.

- **Translate** the faces up.

## Manipulating the geometry

Now that you have used the Smooth Proxy Tool to visualize the smooth object, you might wonder what you should do with it. Since the smooth object is only a smoothed copy of the proxy object, you can delete it, continue modeling with other polygonal tools, and then recreate the smooth object later.

### 1 Delete the smooth object

- From the Outliner, select the smooth object called *tree1*.

- Press **Delete** on your keyboard.

### 2 Reset the shading of the proxy object

- **RMB** on the tree object and select **Materials → Assign Existing Material → lambert1**.

### 3 Use the Mirror Cut Tool

- Select the *tree* geometry.

- Select **Polygons → Mirror Cut**.

*A plane manipulator will appear over your model. This manipulator defines the plane to use to mirror the geometry.*

- **Rotate** the plane on the **Y-axis** by **180-degrees**.

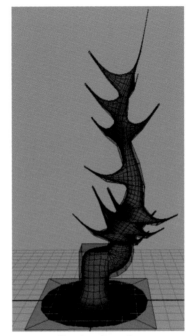

*Random branches*

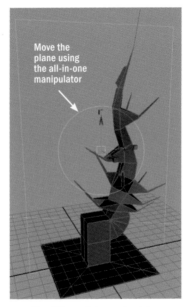

Move the plane using the all-in-one manipulator

*The Mirror Cut manipulator*

**4    New tree object**

A new geometry object was created as the result of the Mirror Cut Tool.

- Rename the new tree geometry as *lowTree*.

**5    Clean up the scene**

So far, all the steps have been recorded in the construction history. If you are finished making changes on the geometry, it is a good idea to delete the history and clean the scene.

- Select **Edit** → **Delete All by Type** → **History**.

- **Delete** the *mirrorCutPlane1* and *curve1* since they are no longer required.

**6    Save your work**

# Finishing the tree

You can now texture the low resolution tree. You will use a 3D texture to simplify the texturing process of the tree. Once that is done, you will smooth the low resolution geometry.

**1    Layout UVs**

- Select *lowTree*.

- Select **Edit Polygons** → **Textures** → **Automatic Mapping**.

**Note:** *You can review the automatic mapping in the UV Texture Editor.*

**2    Texture the tree**

- Open the Hypershade.

- Create a new Lambert and assign it to the *lowTree* geometry.

- Double-click on the new *lambert* to open the Attribute Editor.

- Click the **Map** button next to the **Color** attribute.

- In the **3D Textures** section, select a **Solid Fractal** texture.

**3 Adjust the texture**

- Select the *solidFractal*'s *place3dTexture* placement node.
- In the Attribute Editor, click on the **Fit to group bbox** button.
- Select the *solidFractal* node.
- In the Attribute Editor, change the **Color Gain** to **orange**.

**4 Hide the texture placement manipulator**

- Select *place3dTexture1* and add it to a new layer called *refLayer*.
- Turn **Off** the **Visibility** of *refLayer*.

**5 Smooth the geometry**

You can now smooth the tree geometry to regain the same aspect of the smooth object seen in the previous exercise. When using this tool, the UVs of the tree will be maintained on the smoothed model.

- Select *lowTree*.
- Select **Polygons** → **Smooth**.
- Highlight the *polySmoothFace* input in the Channel Box.
- Set the following:

    **Divisions** to **2**;

    **Keep Border** to **Off**.

**6 Reset the smooth node**

- Set the *polySmoothFace* **Divisions** to **1**.

> **Tip:** It is a good idea to keep the polySmooth construction history since you can keep the model at its lowest resolution, then boost up the resolution when needed.

**7 Save your work**

*The final tree geometry*

## Conclusion

You have now gained experience modeling with polygonal smooth proxies.
You also used many new polygonal tools, like Mirror Cut Tool, which helped you
create organic looking surfaces.

In the next lesson, you will experiment with the various Maya deformers.

# Lesson 25    Deformers

*The tree you modeled in the last lesson looks kind of strange, but would improve greatly if you twirled and twisted it. In this lesson, you will be introduced to various Maya deformers to experiment with. These deformers will help create an organic feel to your geometry. They can even be animated, as you will learn.*

## In this lesson, you will learn the following:

- How to use wire deformers;

- How to use point on curve deformers;

- How to use clusters;

- How to use the Soft Modification Tool;

- How to use nonlinear deformers.

- How to change the deformation order.

# Wire deformer

To begin, you will modify the tree from the last lesson using a wire deformer.
A *wire deformer is* used to deform a surface based on a NURBS curve. You will
use that type of deformer for one of the tree branches.

> **Tip:** It is recommended to display the tree in its unsmoothed state.
> Showing the lowest possible geometry resolution will make your
> Maya interaction faster.

## 1   Open the previous scene

- Open the last lesson file called *24-organicModel.ma*.

- Save the scene as *25-deformers.ma*.

## 2   Draw a curve

- Select **Create** → **EP Curve Tool**.

- From a *side* view, draw a curve along a branch, then press **Enter**.

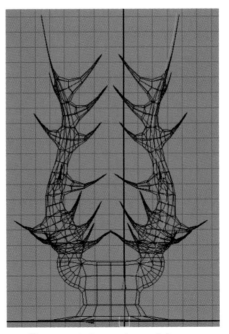

*The curve to be used as a deformer*

**3   Create the wire deformer**

- Select **Deform** → **Wire Tool**.

*The Wire Tool requires two steps. First, you must select the deformable surfaces, then you must select the NURBS curve to be the deformer.*

- Select the tree geometry and press **Enter**.

- Select the NURBS curve and press **Enter**.

*The wire deformer is created.*

**4   Edit the shape of the curve**

- With the *curve* selected, press **F8** to go in Component mode.

- Select some CVs and move them to see their effect on the geometry.

*The deformation does not look very smooth.*

*The default wire deformer effect*

**5   Edit the deformer attribute**

Just like any other deformers, the attributes of the wire deformer can be changed through the Channel Box.

- In the Channel Box, select the *wire1* history node.

- Highlight the **Dropoff Distance** attribute and **MMB+drag** in the viewport to increase it to **5**.

*The effect of the wire deformer will be smoother across the geometry.*

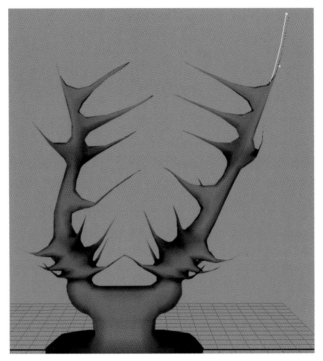

*Deformer with more dropoff*

## 6    Edit the deformer membership

The dropoff has a nice effect, but the deformer starts affecting the other branch of the tree. You can correct that by defining the membership of the geometry to the deformer.

- Select **Deform** → **Edit Membership Tool**.

- Select the *curve* to define the vertices affected by it.

*All the vertices of the tree geometry will be highlighted yellow.*

- Hold the **Ctrl** key and **deselect** the vertices of the base and left branch.

*All the vertices that are no longer deformed will move back to their original positions.*

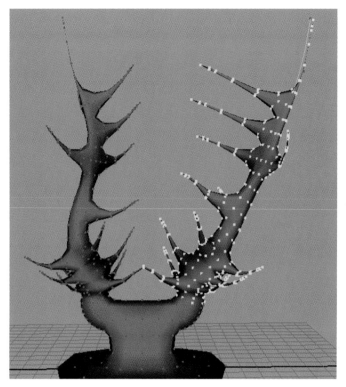

*The deformer's membership*

***Tip:*** *You can also use* **Deform** → **Paint Set Membership Tool** *to define the membership of the tree's vertices.*

### 7 Finalize the deformer's effect

Now that the deformer no longer affects the other branch, you can set its dropoff to a higher value.

- Press **q** to exit the **Edit Membership Tool** and enable the **Pick Tool**.

- Select the *curve* and set the **Dropoff Distance** to **10** in the Channel Box.

- Experiment moving the *curve*'s CVs to see the effect of the deformer.

### 8 Save your work

# Point on Curve and Cluster Deformer

The wire deformer is working well to deform the tree, but is not practical to deform the curve. Several other types of deformers can be used to deform the curve itself. Here you will experiment with the *Point on Curve* deformer and the *Cluster* deformer.

## 1  Point on Curve deformer

The Point on Curve deformer will create a locator linked to a curve edit point.

- **RMB** on the *NURBS curve* and select **Edit Point**.

*Unlike CVs, edit points are located directly on the curve.*

- Select the edit point located at the top of the branch.

- Select **Deform** → **Point on Curve**.

*A locator is created at the edit point's position.*

- Select **Modify** → **Center Pivot** to center the pivot of the *locator*.

- Move the locator to see its effect on the curve.

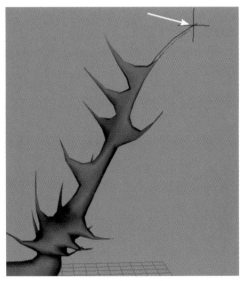

*The Point on Curve deformer*

**Note:** *Rotating a Point on Curve deformer has no effect on the curve.*

## 2   Cluster deformer

The Point on Curve works well, but has its limitations. For instance, it can only control one edit point at a time and it cannot be used for rotation. The Cluster deformer will create a handle that controls one or more vertices. When a cluster has multiple vertices in it, it can also be rotated.

- **RMB** on the *NURBS curve* and select **Control Vertex**.

- Select the two CVs down to the Point on Curve deformer.

**Tip:**   *It might be easier to locate the CVs by also displaying hulls.*

- Select **Deform** → **Create Cluster**.

*A cluster handle is displayed with a* **C** *in the viewport.*

- *Move and rotate* the *cluster handle* to see its effect on the curve and branch.

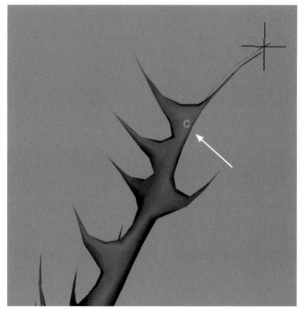

*The cluster handle*

**Note:** *Both the Point on Curve locator and cluster handle can be animated.*

# Soft Modification Tool

The *Soft Modification Tool* lets you push and pull geometry as a sculptor would push and pull a piece of clay. By default, the amount of deformation is greatest at the center of the deformer, and gradually falls off moving outward. However, you can control the falloff of the deformation to create various types of effects.

## 1 Create the deformer

- **RMB** on the *tree* surface and select **Vertex**.

- Select some vertices at the base of the tree.

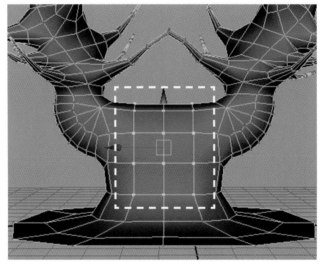

*The cluster handle*

- Click on the **Soft Modification Tool** in the toolbar, or select **Deform → Soft Modification**.

*An **S** handle similar to the cluster handle will be created. The tool's manipulator will also be displayed.*

## 2 Edit the deformer

- Move, rotate and scale the deformer to see its effect on the geometry.

- Click on the manipulator's option icon to change the behavior of the manipulator.

*The new manipulator allows you to edit the falloff center and falloff radius.*

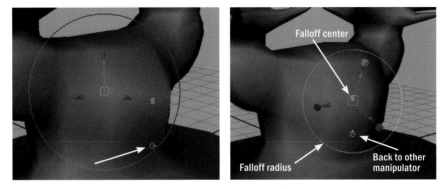

The Soft Modification manipulator                    The Soft Modification manipulator

## 3    Edit the falloff

- Press **Ctrl+a** to open the Attribute Editor for the deformer.

*The various deformer options can be edited here, such as the Falloff Curve.*

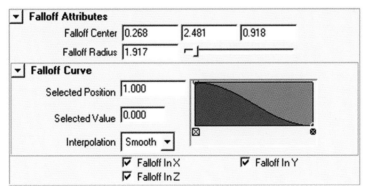

Soft Modification options

**Note:** *The Soft Modification effect can be seen well on high resolution models.*

**4   Modeling with Soft Modification Tool**

When modeling a high resolution model, such as a character's face, you can create multiple Soft Modification deformers to achieve a final shape. The deformers can even overlap.

**5   Delete Soft Modification deformers**

If you want to delete the deformer, simply select its **s** handle and delete it. If you want to keep the shape of the geometry but remove the deformers, you must delete the model's history.

**Alias**   *Be open-minded. Maya is always evolving and there's no reason not to evolve*
**Tip:**   *with it. By doing so, you might find better and more efficient workflows.*

*Tim Wong | Product Specialist*

## Nonlinear deformers

Maya has several *Nonlinear deformers*. Nonlinear deformers can affect one surface, multiple surfaces or parts of a surface, and are very simple to use. In this exercise, you will experiment with all the nonlinear deformers.

**1   Bend deformer**

- Select the *tree* geometry, then select **Deform** → **Create Nonlinear** → **Bend**.

*The Bend handle is created and selected.*

- In the Attribute Editor, highlight the *bend1* input.

*All the attributes for this deformer type are listed.*

*Experiment and combine the different attributes to see their effect on the geometry.*

**Tip:**   *Most of the attributes have visual feedback on the deformer's handle in the viewport. You can also use the **Show Manipulator Tool** to interact with the deformer in the viewport.*

- Moving, rotating and scaling the handle will also affect the location of the deformation.

- When you finish experimenting, select the deformer and delete it.

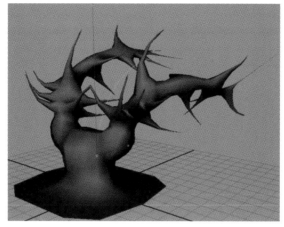

*Bend deformer*

## 2   Flare deformer

- Select the *tree* geometry, then select **Deform** → **Create Nonlinear** → **Flare**.

*The Flare handle is created and selected.*

- In the Attribute Editor, highlight the *flare1* input.

*Experiment by moving, rotating, scaling and combining the different attributes to see their effect on the geometry.*

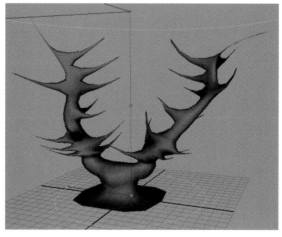

*Flare deformer*

- When you finish experimenting, select the deformer and delete it.

## 3   Sine deformer

- Select the *tree* geometry, then select **Deform** → **Create Nonlinear** → **Sine**.

  *The Sine handle is created and selected.*

- In the Attribute Editor, highlight the *sine1* input.

- Experiment by moving, rotating, scaling and combining the different attributes to see their effect on the geometry.

- When you finish experimenting, select the deformer and delete it.

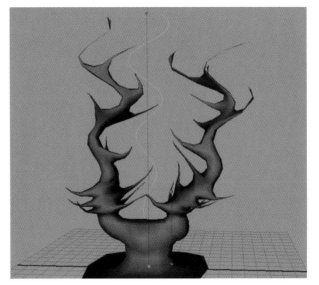

*Sine deformer*

## 4   Squash deformer

- Select the *tree* geometry, then select **Deform** → **Create Nonlinear** → **Squash**.

  *The Squash handle is created and selected.*

- In the Attribute Editor, highlight the *squash1* input.

- Experiment by moving, rotating, scaling and combining the different attributes to see their effect on the geometry.

- When you finish experimenting, select the deformer and delete it.

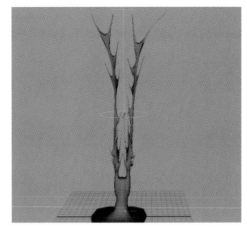

*Squash deformer*

## 5   Twist deformer

- Select the *tree* geometry, then select **Deform** →
  **Create Nonlinear** → **Twist**.

*The Twist handle is created and selected.*

- In the Attribute Editor, highlight the *twist1* input.

- Experiment by moving, rotating, scaling and combining the different
  attributes to see their effect on the geometry.

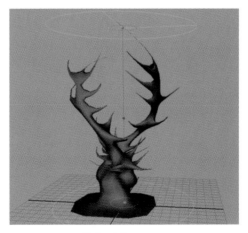

*Twist deformer*

- When you finish experimenting, select the deformer and delete it.

## 6   Wave deformer

- Select the *tree* geometry, then select **Deform** → **Create Nonlinear** → **Wave**.

*The Wave handle is created and selected.*

- In the Attribute Editor, highlight the *wave1* input.

- Experiment by moving, rotating, scaling and combining the different attributes to see their effect on the geometry.

*Wave deformer*

- When you finish experimenting, select the deformer and delete it.

## 7   Finalize the tree

Spend some time deforming the tree as you would like. To animate the scene later in this project, consider keeping the deformers in the scene.

Once you are finished, add the deformer handles to a new layer for easy access.

## 8   Save your work

# Deformation order

The deformation order of a surface is very important to take into consideration. For instance, if you apply a *sine* deformer and then a *bend* deformer, the results are different than if you apply a *bend* deformer and then a *sine* deformer.

But, the deformation order does not only apply to nonlinear deformers. For instance, a rigid binding and a polygonal smooth will have a different effect than a polygonal smooth and a rigid bind.

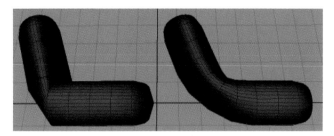

*Smooth/Rigid bind vs Rigid bind/Smooth*

**Note:** *To elaborate on the previous statement, a rigid bind followed by a smooth would evaluate much faster and give better results than a smooth followed by a rigid bind, since the rigid binding would have to skin a higher resolution model.*

## 1 New Scene

- Select **File** → **New**.

## 2 Create a cylinder

- Select **Create** → **Polygon Primitives** → **Cylinder**.

- Edit the *cylinder* as shown in the image on the right:

## 3 Apply deformers

- Select the *cylinder*, then select **Deform** → **Nonlinear** → **Bend**.

- Select the *cylinder*, then select **Deform** → **Nonlinear** → **Sine**.

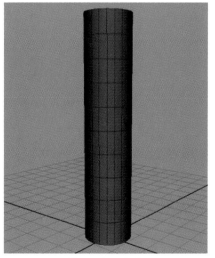

*Example cylinder*

## 4   Edit the bend deformer

- Select the *cylinder*.

- In the Channel Box, highlight the *bend1* deformer.

- Set the **Curvature** attribute to **2**.

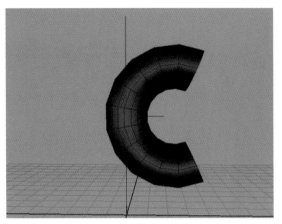

*Bend deformer effect*

## 5   Edit the sine deformer

- Select the *cylinder*.

- In the Channel Box, highlight the *sine1* deformer.

- Set the **Amplitude** attribute to **0.1**.

- Set the **Wavelength** attribute to **0.35**.

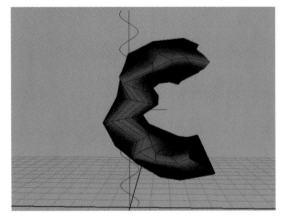

*Sine and bend deformer effect*

## 6 List input for the cylinder

- **RMB** on the *cylinder*.

- Select **Inputs** → **All Inputs...**

*Doing so will display a window
with all the history nodes
affecting the cylinder.*

*List of input for cylinder and re-ordering
the deformation effect*

## 7 Change the order of deformation

- In the Input window, **MMB+drag** the *Non Linear(sine1)* item over the
*Non Linear(bend1)* item to change their order.

## 8 Result of the new order of deformation

*New deformation order effect*

## Conclusion

You should now be comfortable using basic deformers. Being aware of the
results created by the deformation order will allow you to reorder them if needed.

In the next lesson, you will experiment with one of the most powerful tools found
in Maya: Paint Effects. You were introduced to this tool in Lesson 6, but now we
will explore it's great potential more in-depth.

# Lesson 26    Paint Effects

In the last two lessons, you
created an organic tree model.
Even though the learning
experience was a good one
and you can apply this new
knowledge to an endless variety
of scenarios, there are much
faster ways to create content
for your scene. The Maya Paint
Effects Tool gives you access to
lots of preset brushes, ranging
from grasses to trees or
buildings to lightning bolts, but
they can also be customized for
your own scenarios.

In this lesson, you will use
several Paint Effects' brushes
and test render your scene.

## In this lesson, you will learn the following:

- How to paint on canvas;

- How to set an image plane;

- How to share, blend and customize brushes;

- How to save brush presets;

- How to auto paint a surface;

- How to convert Paint Effects to polygons.

# Create a scene

In order to test various Paint Effects' brushes, you will create an outer space scene with multiple planets. First, you will need a background space image to establish the mood for the rest of the lesson.

## 1 Create a new scene

- Select **File** → **New**.
- Save the scene as *26-paintEffects.ma*.

## 2 Paint in the Paint Effects window

- Press **8** to display the **Maya Paint Effects** preview window.
- Select **Paint** → **Paint Canvas**.

*This will set the canvas to a 2D paint mode.*

- In the Paint Effects window, select **Brush** → **Get Brush**.

*The Visor will open, letting you browse through the various template Paint Effects' brushes.*

- Open any brush folder, select a brush and paint on the canvas.

*You can now experiment with different brushes.*

**Note:** *Hold down* **b** *and* **LMB+drag** *to change the size of the current brush.*

- Select **Canvas** → **Clear**.

## 3 Change the background color

- Select **Canvas** → **Clear** → ❐.
- Set the **Clear Color** to black, then press the **Clear** button.

**Note:** *You can also import an image as a starting point by selecting* **Canvas** → **Open Image**.

## 4  Paint your image

- In the Visor window, open the *galactic* folder.

- Select the *galaxy* brush and paint some space onto your image.

- Continue painting space elements to your image using the different preset brushes.

- If you make a mistake you can **undo** the last brush stroke by selecting **Canvas → Canvas Undo**.

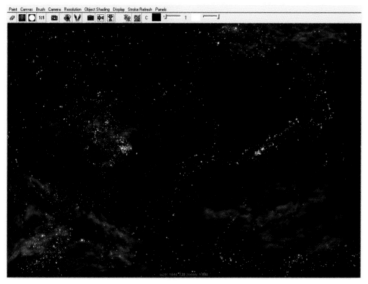

*Background image*

## 5  Save the image

- When you are finished with your image, select **Canvas → Save As → ❑**.

- In the **Option** window, make sure that **Save Alpha** is turned **Off**.

- Click on **Save Image** and name your image as *background*.

## Setting up the image plane

You are now going to import the background image and set it as a camera image plane. This plane will be used behind the rest of the scene to help compose the final shot.

## 1  Create a new camera

You will create a new camera to hold the image plane.

- Select **Create** → **Cameras** → **Camera**.

*This places a camera at the origin.*

- **Translate** the new camera backwards on the **Z-axis**.

## 2  Set up your panels

- In a four view layout, select one of the *Orthographic* views and select **Panels** → **Perspective** → **camera1**.

- Press **6** to shade the *camera1* panel.

- From the *camera1* view panel, select **View** → **Camera Settings** → **Resolution Gate**.

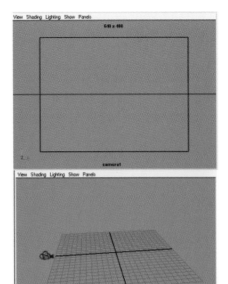

*Current layout*

## 3  Add the image plane

- From the *camera1* view panel, select **View** → **Image Plane** → **Import Image**.

- Choose the *background.iff* image file from the *sourceimages* directory.

*Your background image is loaded as the image plane of camera1.*

## 4  Set up the image plane

- Select the *camera1*.

- Press **Ctrl+a** to open the Attribute Editor, then select the *imagePlane1* tab.

- Scroll down to the **Placement** section.

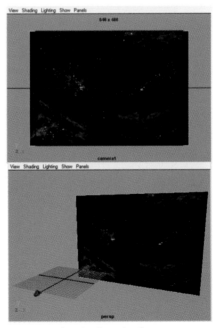

*Image plane in place*

- Set the **Fit** attribute to **To Size**, then click the **Fit to Resolution Gate** button.

*This will place the image to fit the Resolution Gate.*

- Select the *cameraShape1* tab and scroll down to the **Display Options** section.

- Set the **Overscan** attribute to **1.1**.

*This will reduce the gap around the Resolution Gate.*

**5  Save your work**

*The camera1 view*

# Paint Effects' strokes

You drew a Paint Effects stroke back in Lesson 6, but the lesson was not greatly detailed. Now you will learn how strokes can share the same brush, as well as how to scale Paint Effects.

**1  Paint a city on a small planet**

- Select **Create → NURBS Primitives → Sphere**.

- Place the new *sphere* in the top left corner of *camera1* and rename it *cityPlanet*.

- In the *Perspective* view, press **f** to frame the *cityPlanet*.

- With *cityPlanet* selected, select **Paint Effects → Make Paintable**.

*Doing so will allow you to paint directly on the sphere.*

- Select **Paint Effects → Get Brush...**

- In the Visor, select the *cityMesh* directory, then click on the **skyscraper** brush preset.

- Paint directly on the *cityPlanet* skyscrapers.

**Tip:**   *Don't forget to tumble around the planet to paint all the sides equally.*

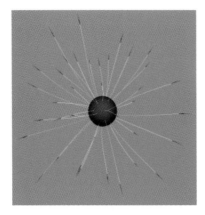
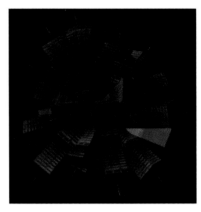

*The cityPlanet in the viewport*      *The rendered cityPlanet*

## 2   Test render the planet

- Select **Render** → **Render Current Frame**.

---

**Alias Tip:** *Paint FX is still the coolest thing going for me. It continues to blow my mind that I can create such realistic looking natural scenes with so little effort (and artistic talent, but that's another story). I saw the beginnings of this demo'd long before it found its way into the product, and it was something that made me think, "Now \*this\* is why I got into computer graphics.*

*Kevin Picott | Principal Engineer*

---

## 3   Share one brush

It would be good to scale the brush down to minimize interpenetration of the buildings.

- Open the Outliner.

*You should see all the different strokes you have drawn on the planet.*

At the moment, all of these strokes are using a different brush, letting you customize each one individually. The method for scaling down the buildings simultaneously is to tell all the similar strokes to share the same brush.

- Select all the *strokeSkyscraper* strokes.

- Select **Paint Effects** → **Share One Brush**.

*Now all the strokes use the same brush. Modifying this brush will change all the buildings at the same time.*

## 4   Scale down the buildings

- Press **Ctrl+a** to open the Attribute Editor for any of the selected strokes.

- Select the *skyscraper* tab.

*This is the brush shared among all the strokes.*

- Set the **Global Scale** attribute to **2**.

**Note:** *The scale of the brush is relative to how far you placed the planet from the camera.*

## 5   Test render the scene

- Select *cityPlanet*.

- Select **Lighting/Shading** → **Assign New Material** → **Lambert**.

- In the Attribute Editor, change the **Color** of the planet to a dark brown.

- Render *camera1*.

**Note:** *If you move or animate the planet, the strokes will follow accordingly.*

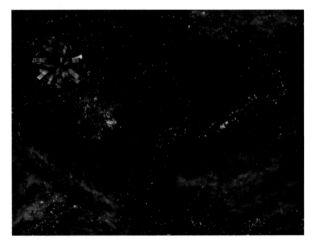

*A camera1 render*

## 6   Save your work

## Customize brushes

In this exercise, you will blend brushes together and customize your own brushes. You will also save your custom brush presets on your shelf for later use.

### 1 Create another small planet

- Select **Create** → **NURBS Primitives** → **Sphere**.

- Place the new *sphere* on the right side of *camera1* and rename it *plantPlanet*.

- With *plantPlanet* selected, select **Paint Effects** → **Make Paintable**.

### 2 Blending brushes

- Select **Paint Effects** → **Get Brush...**

- In the Visor, select the *plantMesh* directory, then click on the **cortinarius** brush preset.

- Still in the Visor, select the *fun* directory, then **RMB** on the **jumpingSpring** brush preset.

*This will display a menu letting you blend the current brush with the new one.*

- Select **Blend Brush 20%**.

*This will blend part of the spring brush onto the mushroom brush, giving a twirled mushroom type.*

- **RMB** again on the **jumpingSpring** brush preset and select **Blend Shading 5%**.

*This will blend the mushroom shading with the spring shading and generate a twirled multi-color mushroom type.*

*The new mushroom brush*

**3   Test render the new brush**

- Paint one stroke of the new brush on *plantPlanet*.

- Test render the planet.

**4   Customizing brushes**

- In the Attribute Editor, select the **jumpingSprings** tab.

*Doing so will display all the Paint Effects' attributes for the current brush and the current stroke.*

- Try changing some of the values to see their results on the current stroke. Following are some examples:

  **Global Scale** to **1**;

  **Tubes** → **Creation** → **Tubes Per Step** to **0.2**;

  **Tubes** → **Creation** → **Tubes Width1** to **0.2**;

  **Tubes** → **Creation** → **Tubes Width2** to **0**;

  **Growth** → **Flowers** → **Petal Length** to **0.5**;

  **Behavior** → **Displacement** → **Curl** to **0.1**;

  **Behavior** → **Displacement** → **Curl Frequency** to **3**;

  **Behavior** → **Forces** → **Gravity** to **0**;

**Tip:**   *You may have to test render the stroke in order to see changes.*

- Reduce the quality of the brush to speed up rendering time:

  **Tubes** → **Creation** → **Segments** to **25**;

  **Growth** → **Flowers** → **Petal Segments** to **5**.

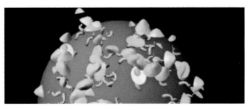

*The customized brush*

## 5 Get brush settings from stroke

In order to draw more customized mushrooms, you need to update the current template brush with the settings of the stroke you just modified.

- With the stroke selected, select **Paint Effects** → **Get Settings from Selected Stroke**.

*This will set the customized mushroom brush as the current template brush.*

## 6 Save custom brushes

You can save the current template brush for later use. The brush can be saved either to your shelf or the Visor.

- Select **Paint Effects** → **Save Brush Preset...**

- Set the following in the **Save Brush Preset** window to save to current shelf:

  **Label** to *Custom Mushrooms*;

  **Overlay Label** to *mushrooms*;

  **Save Preset** to **To Shelf**.

**Or**

- Set the following in the **Save Brush Preset** window to a *Visor* directory:

  **Label** to *Custom Mushrooms*;

  **Overlay Label** to *mushrooms*;

  **Save Preset** to **To Visor**;

  **Visor Directory** to *brushes* from your *prefs* directory.

- Click the **Save Brush Preset** button.

**Note:** *You can obtain an image for your new brush only through the Paint Effects Canvas panel.*

## 7 Automatically paint a surface

- Delete the stroke you painted on the *plantPlanet*.

- Select *plantPlanet*.

- Select **Paint Effects** → **Auto Paint** → **Paint Grid** → ☐.

- In the **Paint Grid** options, set the following:

  **Spans U** to **8**;

  **Spans V** to **8**;

  **Curve Degree** to **3**;

  **Sample Density** to **10**;

  **Share One Brush** to **On**.

- Click on the **Paint Strokes** button to automatically paint the selected surface.

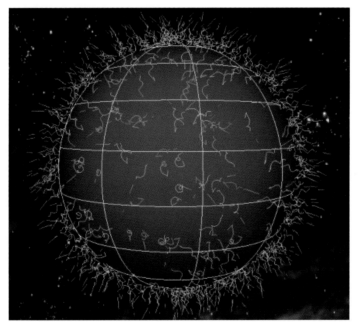

*Automatically painted strokes*

## 8   Test render the scene

- Select *plantPlanet*.

- Select **Lighting/Shading** → **Assign New Material** → **Lambert**.

- In the Attribute Editor, change the **Color** of the planet to a light brown.

- Render *camera1*.

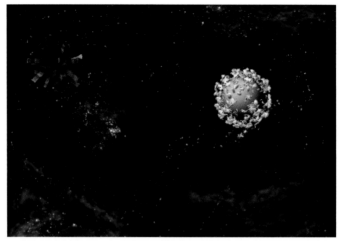

*A camera1 render*

> **Alias Tip:** *I love painting plants and greenery with Paint Effects. Even a developer can make something that looks good :-)*
>
> *Mike Taylor | Software Architect*

## 9  Scene set up

- Open the Outliner and **group** the strokes and planets together under *cityGroup* and *plantGroup*.

- Create a new layer called *planetLayer* and add *cityGroup* and *plantGroup* to it.

> **Tip:** To speed up the rest of the lesson, you can hide the planetLayer.

## 10  Save your work

## Finalize the scene

In order to finish the scene, you will create a third planet closer to the camera, import the tree from the last lesson and add some more Paint Effects' strokes.

## 1    Create a big planet closer to the camera

- Select **Create** → **NURBS Primitives** → **Sphere**.

- Set the following:

   **Rotate X** to **-90**;

   **Scale XYZ** to **50**;

   **End Sweep** to **180**.

- Move the planet close to *camera1* and rename it *mainPlanet*.

## 2    Import the tree

- Select **File** → **Import** and select the file *25-deformers.ma*.

---

**Tip:**    *You should have the **Group** option enabled in the **Import** options. This will allow you to move the group and keep the deformers in place for animation.*

---

- Place the tree as follows:

*The scene is taking shape*

*Lots of Paint Effects*

## 3    More Paint Effects

Add some Paint Effects on the ground surface of the *mainPlanet*. You can add grass, flowers and trees, and customize them for the proper look and scale. Make sure to leave a spot for the character that you will model in the next lesson.

**Tip:**    *Reduce the* **Display Percent** *attribute on a stroke to reduce the amount of reference lines in the viewport. Select multiple strokes to reduce them simultaneously. Doing so will considerably speed up the interaction with Maya.*

## 4    Save your work

# Paint Effects to polygons

There are several advantages to converting Paint Effects to polygons.
Following is a list of things you can do with converted Paint Effects' strokes:

- Instead of looking at the reference lines, you can clearly see the geometry in your scene.

- A renderer that does not support Paint Effects, such as the Vector renderer, will render polygons.

- Polygonal Paint Effects will conserve its construction history, so you will still be able to customize and animate the brushes.

- Polygonal meshes can be used as a starting point for organic modeling.

## 1   Open a new scene

## 2   Draw some Paint Effects

- Select **Paint Effects** → **Get Brush**.

- In the **funMesh** directory, select the *feedingCreature* brush.

- **Draw** a stroke in the viewport.

**Note:** *All the Paint Effects' strokes can be converted to polygons.*

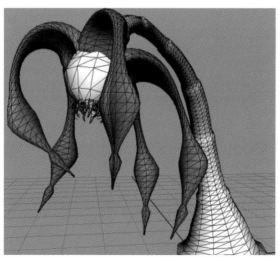
*Converted Paint Effects*

## 3 Convert Paint Effects

- Select the Paint Effects stroke.

- Select **Modify → Convert → Paint Effects to Polygons**.

- In the Attribute Editor, change any of the brush attributes.

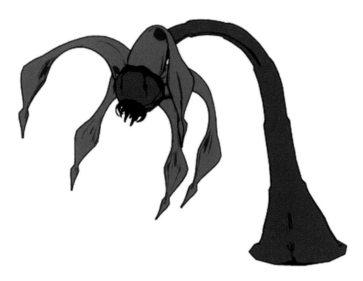

*Animated Paint Effects
rendered with Maya Vector*

## 4 View the results

- Press **6** to display the geometry with textures.

- Playback the scene.

*Since the Paint Effects brush was animated, the construction history is also animating the geometry.*

## Conclusion

You have garnered more experience with Maya Paint Effects, but have only scratched the surface of the power available in the Paint Effects Tool. Learning how to use the Paint Effects canvas, how to customize your brushes and how to convert Paint Effects to polygons will serve you well as you become more and more familiar with the tool.

In the next lesson, you will continue modeling organic geometry using subdivision surfaces.

# Lesson 27 — Subdivision Surfaces

*In this lesson, you will work with subdivision surfaces (SubDs) to create an organic-looking space creature.*

*Subdivision surfaces exhibit characteristics of both polygon and NURBS surfaces, allowing you to model smooth forms using comparatively few control vertices. They will enable you to create levels of detail exactly where you want.*

*As a prerequisite to modeling with SubDs. It is essential to complete the Polygonal orb and Organic modeling lessons.*

## In this lesson, you will learn the following:

- How to model using subdivision surfaces' Poly Proxy and Standard Modes;

- How to split polygons;

- How to extrude polygons along a curve;

- How to create finer levels of detail;

- How to work with creases;

- How to import shaders.

## Initial set up

Start a new file within the *project4* directory copied onto your system.

### 1  Create a new scene

- Select **File** → **New Scene**.

### 2  Set up the modeling panels

- Switch to the modeling module by pressing the **F3** hotkey.

- From the **Tool Box,** select the **Persp/Outliner** layout configuration.

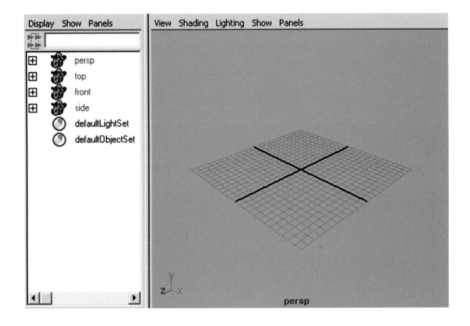

*Persp/Outliner window configuration*

# Modeling the space creature

The creature will be modeled starting with a subdivision surface primitive.
Its basic form will be constructed using the *Subdivision Surfaces' Poly Proxy Mode*.

Poly Proxy Mode creates an unshaded polygonal cage around the subdivision surface similar to the one used by the Smooth Proxy polygonal tool. This cage can be edited using the same set of tools as a regular polygon. The subdivision surface will remain smooth and maintain the history of edits made on the proxy object.

## 1   Position a primitive sphere

- Select **Create** → **Subdiv Primitives** → **Sphere**.

- Set each modeling view to **Shading** → **Smooth Shade All**.

- Press the **3** hotkey for a smooth display of the surface.

- **Rename** the surface *creature.*

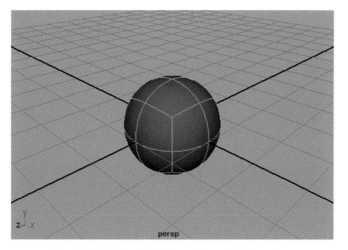

*Smooth shaded subdivision surface primitive sphere*

## 2   Poly Proxy Mode

- Select **Subdiv Surfaces** → **Poly Proxy Mode**.

- In the **Outliner**, set **Display** → **Shapes** to **On**.

- Click the **+** sign next to *creature* to display the shape nodes beneath.

*A new node called creatureShapeHistPoly has been created and grouped underneath the creature node. This is the proxy node that you will edit using the polygon toolset.*

### 3 Translate and scale the subdivision surface

- Select the *creature* object.

- Translate the surface by approximately **8** units on the **Y-axis**.

- Scale the surface uniformly to **2.5** in all directions.

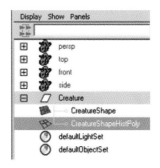

*Outliner with the proxy object selected*

### 4 Extrude a Poly Proxy Face

The marking menu of subdivision surfaces allows quick selection of subdivision tools and will be used extensively throughout this lesson.

- **RMB** over the *creature* node.

- Select **Face** from the marking menu.

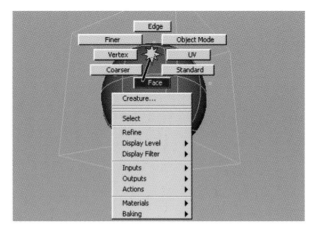

*Marking menu display*

- Select the bottom face of the proxy object.

- Select **Edit Polygons** → **Extrude Face**.

- **Click+drag** to extrude the face downwards by approximately **1** unit.

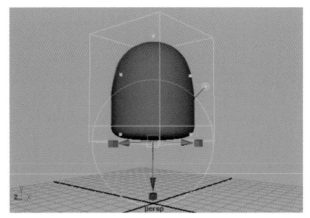

*Proxy face extruded downward*

**Note:** *The global translation of this face is in the negative Y direction. However, its local translation value in Z comes from the local space of the extruded face.*

## 5 Scale the extruded face

- Click on any scale cubes on the manipulator to invoke the extrusion **Scale Tool**.

- **Scale** the face to a value of approximately **0.7**.

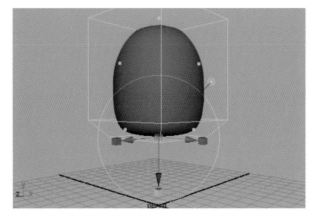

*Scaled proxy face*

> **Note:** *The scale and translation values suggested can be checked and edited in the Channel Box or under the Local Scale and Translation X, Y and Z fields.*

## 6   Repeat Extrude Face and scale

- Make sure the bottom face is still selected.
- Select the **g** key to reactivate **Edit Polygons** → **Extrude Face**.
- **Click+drag** to extrude the face downwards.
- Translate the new face along its local **Z-axis** approximately **1** unit.
- Scale the face to approximately **1.1**.

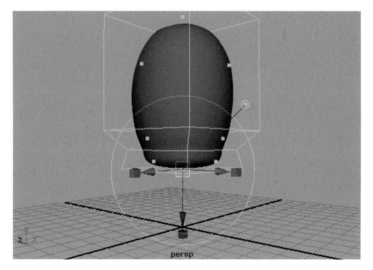

*Extruded and scaled face*

## 7   Blocking out the creature's body

Continue to rough in the creature's body by repeating the steps above until you reach the shape shown in the image at the top of the next page.

## 8   Save your work

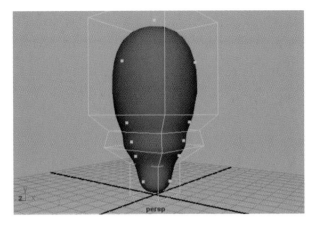

*Creature's body blocked out*

## The creature's head

The body is roughed in now, but the head needs more work. Before leaving Poly Proxy Mode, the cranium should be larger and the forehead needs further definition. To do this, you will be using the Move and Scale Tools, as well as the Split Poly Tool.

### 1 Lengthen the head

- Select the back face of the head.
- Translate the face back on the **Z-axis**.
- Rotate the face on the **X-axis**.

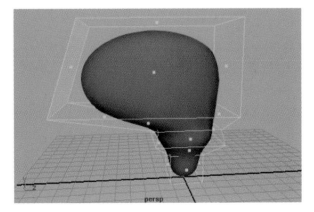

*Rear face moved and rotated*

## 2   Widen the head

- Select the face on the side of the head.

- **Shift-select** the same face on the other side of the head.

- **Scale** the **X-axis** to enlarge the sides of the head.

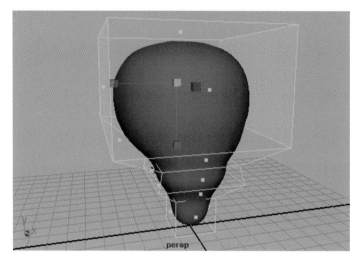

*Enlarged cranium*

## 3   Define the forehead region

- Go in Object mode.

- Select the proxy object if it is not already selected.

- Select **Edit Polygons → Split Poly → □**.

- Set the following options:

    **Subdivisions** to **1**;

    **Snap to Edge** to **On**;

    **Snap to Magnets** to **On**;

    **Number of Magnets** to **3**;

    **Magnet Tolerance** to **100**.

- **Split** the front face of the creature's head into two faces.

- Press **Enter** to finish the poly split.

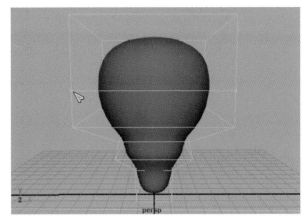

*Split the front face*

## 4   Move the new edge

- **RMB** over the *creature* and select **Edge** from the marking menu.

- Select the new split edge.

- Move the edge forward and up.

- Select the edge at the front top of the head.

- Move the edge even more forward and up.

## 5   Enlarge the base of the head

- Select the bottom back edge of the head.

- Scale the edge along the **X-axis** to create a wider skull base.

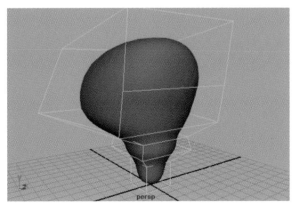

*Defined forehead and enlarged skull base*

## The eye

The alien creature needs an eyeball and an eye socket. The socket will be created with a few more polygon face extrusions. The eyeball will be a simple polygon sphere.

### 1   Define the eye socket area

- **RMB** and select **Face** from the marking menu.
- Select the front face below the forehead.
- Select **Edit Polygons** → **Extrude Face**.
- Scale the face down.

### 2   Indent the eye socket

- Press the **g** key to re-invoke **Edit Polygons** → **Extrude Face**.
- Move the face back along the **Z-axis** to define the eye socket.

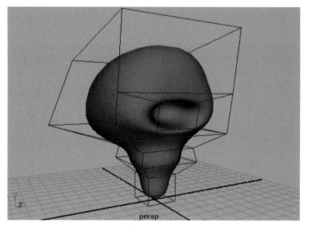

*Eye socket*

### 3   Create the eyeball

- Select **Create** → **Polygon Primitives** → **Sphere** → ❐.
- Rename the sphere *eyeball*.
- Rotate the eyeball by **-80-degrees** around the **X-axis**.
- Move and Scale the sphere to fit inside the eye socket.

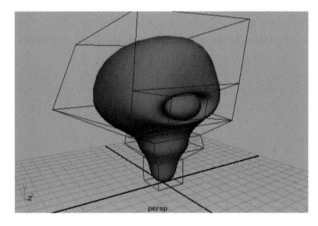

*Eyeball of creature*

### 4   Group the geometry together

- Select the *eyeball*, then **Shift-select** the *creature*.

- Press **Ctrl+g** to **Group** the objects.

- Rename the new group *creatureGroup*.

## The arms

To create three arms on the creature, you will extrude polygon faces along a NURBS curve. With very few polygon faces, the subdivision surface created will be smooth and organic-looking.

### 1   Draw a NURBS curve

- Select **Create → CP Curve Tool**.

- In the *front* view, place six CVs as follows:

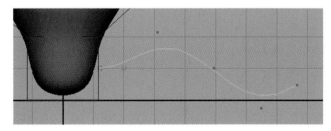

*NURBS curve for extrusion*

- Press **Enter** to complete the curve.

## 2   Edit the shape of the curve

- **RMB** over the curve and select **Control Vertex** from the marking menu.

- Select and **move** the CVs if necessary.

- Rotate the curve by **-30-degrees** around the **Y-axis** to form the wire basis of the arm extrusion.

## 3   Extrude the arms

- Select the curve.

- **RMB** over the creature and select **Face** from the marking menu.

- **Shift-select** the polygon face closest to the curve.

- Select **Edit Polygons** → **Extrude Face** → ❒.

- Set the following options:

  **Use Selected Curve for Extrusion** to **On**;

  **Taper** to **0.3**;

  **Divisions** to **5**.

- Click the **Extrude Face** button.

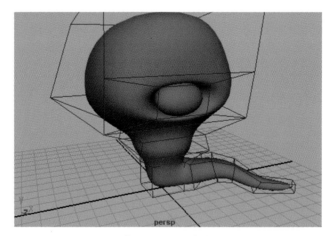

*One arm extruded*

## 4   Duplicate curve for the two other arms

- Select the curve and press **Ctrl+d** to duplicate it.

- Rotate the duplicated curve into place for the opposite arm.

- Press **g** to re-invoke **Edit** → **Duplicate**.

- Rotate the duplicated curve into place for the back arm.

- Move the CVs for the back arm to make it longer than the others.

## 5    Create the remaining arms

- Repeat step **3** for the remaining arms.

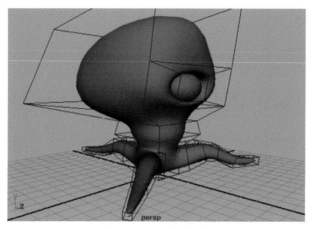

*Three arms extruded*

## 6    Save your work

> **Note:** Since the model has construction history, you can continue to edit
> the inputs to the creature and adjust the values in the Channel Box,
> through the Attribute Editor, or by enabling the Show Manipulator Tool.
> You can also continue to adjust the original NURBS curve for the arms.
> The subdivision surface will be updated to match the edits as long as
> its construction history remains intact.

# Entering Standard Mode

So far, you have been using Poly Proxy Mode to create a smooth subdivision
surface, by editing a few faces and edges on a simple polygon mesh.
The polygonal cage surrounding the subdivision surface has provided enough
detail to this point.

Now you will leave Poly Proxy Mode and edit the rest of the model with subdivision surfaces using Standard Mode. In Standard Mode, you can edit vertices, faces and edges, plus you can achieve a greater level of detail using the hierarchical levels of refinement available with subdivision surfaces.

## Standard Mode editing

### 1   Leave Poly Proxy Mode

- Select the *creature*.

- Select **Subdiv Surfaces** → **Standard Mode**.

*This eliminates the Poly Proxy Mode geometry. The proxy can be regenerated and edited by invoking* **Subdiv Surfaces** → **Poly Proxy Mode** *again if necessary, but the construction history will not be rebuilt.*

### 2   Display subdivision surface vertices

- **RMB** over the subdivision surface and select **Vertex** from the marking menu.

*This displays vertices at the same coordinates as the proxy vertices and refers to the roughest level of subdivision surface refinement.*

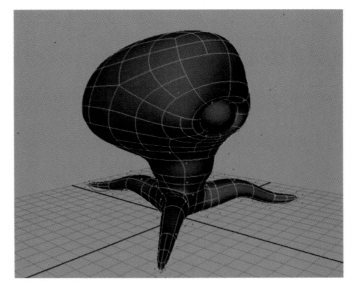

*Subdivision surface vertices*

# Model brow ridges

To enhance the brow area, you will need to edit finer levels of the subdivision surface vertices.

## 1 Display finer levels of detail

- Select **Subdiv Surfaces** → **Component Display Level** → **Finer**.

- Select the finer vertices and move them forward to produce brow definition as indicated in the following image:

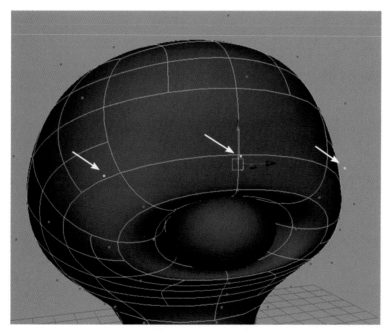

*Finer vertices moved forward*

## 2 Create more detail in the area by refining selected vertices

- Keep the same three vertices selected.

- Select **Subdiv Surfaces** → **Refine Selected Components**.

*This will refine the area and display new vertices.*

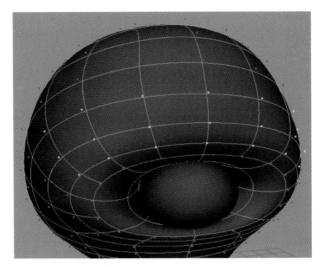

*Refined vertices*

### 3    Create a furrowed brow

- **RMB** and select **Edges** from the marking menu.

*Edges of subdivision surfaces look similar to NURBS hulls and can help realize the shape defining the surface. They can also be selected individually, just like polygonal edges.*

- Select and move edges forward to create a furrowed brow.

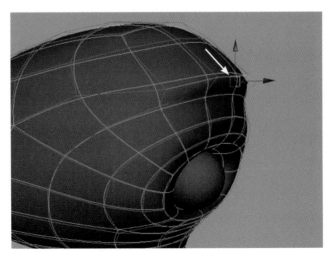

*Selected edges moved forward*

## 4   Emphasize the facial expression

- Using the **Move Tool**, edit the edges and vertices around the eye area to create a facial expression.

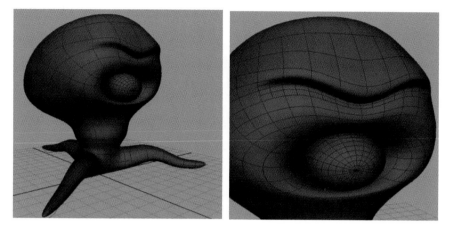

*Vertices and edges edited to create facial expression*

*Partial edge crease in brow*

## 5   Create a partial crease between the furrows

- **RMB** and select **Edges** from the marking menu.

- Select the edges in-between the furrows on the brow.

- Select **Subdiv Surfaces** → **Partial Crease Edge/Vertex**.

*A partial crease will define and sharpen the surface outlined by the selected edges or vertices.*

# Pointed horns

In addition to defining brow ridges, you can use the full crease option to create sharp points on your model without adding unnecessary control vertices.

## 1   Model the horns

- **RMB** and select **Vertex** from the marking menu.

- Select every other vertex along the middle of the head.

- Select **Modify** → **Transformation Tool** → **Move Tool** → ❑.

- Switch the **Move** settings to **Normal**. This will allow you to translate the vertices using the surface normal.

- Using the **N-axis** of the manipulator, **move** all the vertices out from the surface of the head simultaneously.

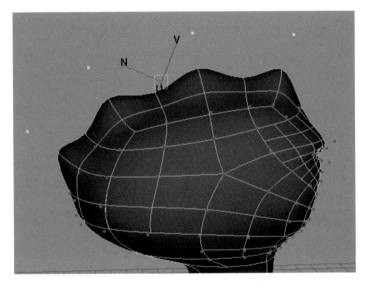

*Vertices edited with Move Tool set to Normal*

## 2  Create the pointed ends for the horns

Making a subdivision surface vertex *Full Crease* will create hard points on the ends of the horns.

- With the vertices at the tips of each bump still selected, **RMB** and select **Refine Selected** from the marking menu.

- Select the refined vertices at the tips of the bump.

- **Move** these vertices even further away from the head and give the horns a bit of a curve.

- To further define the tips of the horns, repeat the above process to define even finer vertices.

*The refined horns*

- Select the vertices at the tips of the horns.

- Select **Subdiv Surfaces** → **Full Crease Edge/Vertex.**

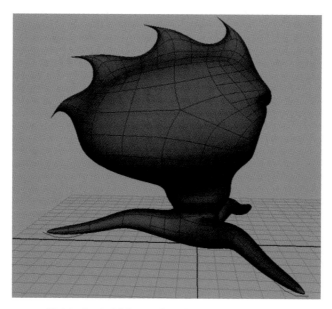

*Finished subdivision surfaces' space creature model*

**3   Save your work**

# Texture the space creature

Texturing subdivision surfaces is very similar to polygon UV mapping techniques learned in Lesson 10. To map the creature, you will import pre-created procedural texture to the model and convert this procedural texture to a file. This is one way to stop a 3D texture from sliding on a deformed surface.

## 1   Import the procedural shader

- Switch to the **Hypershade/Persp** layout from the **Tool Box**.

- Inside the Hypershade window, select **File** → **Import** and choose the file *skinShader.ma* from the *shader* folder.

- **MMB+drag** the shader onto the *creature*.

- Press **6** to see the texture.

## 2   Create the UV maps

- Select the *creature*.

- Select **Subdiv Surfaces** → **Texture** → **Automatic Mapping** → ❐.

- In the option window set the following:

    **Planes** to **12**;

    **Optimize** to **Less Distortion**;

    **Layout** to **Into Square**;

    **Scale** to **Uniform**.

- Click on the **Project** button.

## 3   Convert the procedural texture

- Select the *creature*, then **Shift-select** the *SkinShader_phong* material.

- Inside the Hypershade window, select **Edit** → **Convert to File Texture (Maya Software)** → ❐.

- Set the following options:

    **Anti-alias** to **On**;

    **Background Mode** to **Extend Edge Color**;

    **Fill Texture Seams** to **On**;

    **X** and **Y Resolution** to **512**;

    **File Format** to **TIF**.

- Select **Convert and Close**.

*The new shader will be automatically applied to the creature.*

---

**Tip:** *You can change the skin shader's* **Texture Resolution** *to* **Highest** *to better see the texture in the viewport.*

---

## 4   Check UV placement and new texture file in Texture Editor

- Select the *creature*.

- Select **Window** → **UV Texture Editor**.

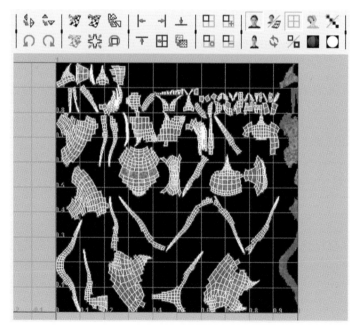

*UV Texture Editor displaying file texture*

*Notice how* **Automatic UV Mapping** *has placed the projections, and how* **Convert to File Texture** *created a file texture to fit into the UV space.*

## 5   Adjust the bump depth

Since file textures manage bumps slightly differently than procedural textures, the bump depth on the new shader needs adjusting.

- Select the new material called *SkinShader_phong1*.

- **Double-click** the shader to display its Attribute Editor.

- Under the **bump2d** tab, set **Bump Depth** to **0.2**.

## 6   Import and assign the eyeball shader

- Inside the Hypershade window, select **File** → **Import** and select *eyeballShader.ma* from the *shader* folder.

- **RMB** over the *eyeball*.

- From the marking menu, select **Materials** → **Assign Existing Material** → **EyeballBlinn**.

## 7   Convert the eyeball shader

- Select the *eyeball*, then **Shift-select** the *EyeShader_phong* material.

- Inside the Hypershade window, select **Edit** → **Convert to File Texture (Maya Software)**.

## 8   Optimize scene size

- In order to remove unused nodes and shaders, select **File** → **Optimize Scene Size**.

> **Alias Tip:** *Scene files get mysteriously filled with clutter, just like my house. It really helps to clean up regularly, so that you're not tripping over unused locators or invalid NURBS curves. File → **Optimize Scene Size** eliminates some of the possible causes for problems, making it easier to troubleshoot the actual cause. And Mom can be proud because you're always wearing clean data.*
>
> *Chris Carden | Technical Consultant*

## 9   Set appropriate Render Settings

**10 Test render the scene**

- Select the *Perspective* view.

- Select **Render** → **Render Current Frame**.

**11 Save your work**

## Conclusion

You have now gone through the process of modeling organic forms with subdivision surfaces. You also converted the subdivision surface into polygons and applied a converted file texture to the model.

In the next lesson, you will explore some more rigging techniques, in order to animate the space creature.

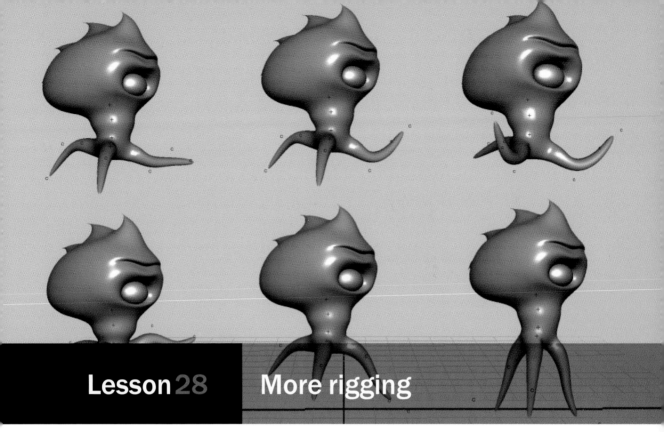

# Lesson 28    More rigging

*Since some of the following rigging tasks are similar to what you learned rigging the robot in the last project, make sure you understand the concepts of Project Three before continuing.*

*In this lesson, you will create a rig for the creature model. You will start by building a skeleton, binding the geometry and setting up spline IKs. Once that is complete, you will create a setup for the eye so that it can blink and look around. You will also use Sculpt and Jiggle deformers to deform the creature's brain.*

**In this lesson, you will learn the following:**

- How to bind subdivision surfaces;

- How to create spline IKs;

- How to use the aim constraint;

- How to create Sculpt deformers;

- How to create a MEL expression;

- How to use Jiggle deformers.

## Building the skeleton

You will start by creating a skeleton for the creature. Before drawing joints, you must visualize where the joints will go and how they will deform the geometry. Also, understand before beginning that the creature's long legs will require many joints to bend smoothly.

### 1  Delete all history

- Select **Edit** → **Delete All by Type** → **History**.

### 2  Draw the spine joints

- Select **Skeleton** → **Joint Tool**.

- From the *side* view, define a *pelvis*, then go up to draw the *spine*, *neck* and *head* joints.

---

**Note:** *The entire head will be bound only to one joint.*

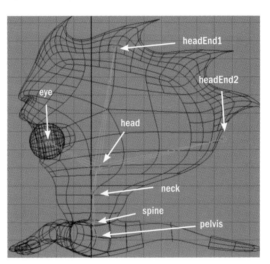

*Spine joints*

### 3  Draw the rear leg joints

- Select **Skeleton** → **Joint Tool**.
- Select the *pelvis* joint.

- From the *side* view, draw several bones along the rear leg as follows:

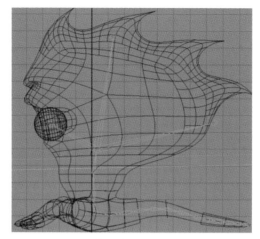

*Rear leg joints*

## 4   Draw the right leg joints

- Select **Skeleton** → **Joint Tool**.

- Select the *pelvis* joint.

- From the *front* view, draw several bones along the right leg as follows:

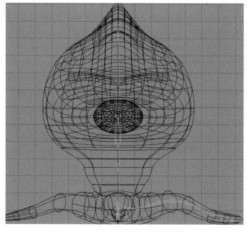

*Right leg joints*

- From the *Perspective* view, make sure to place all the bones accordingly within the leg geometry.

## 5  Mirror the leg joints

- Select **Skeleton** → **Mirror Joint** to mirror the joints for the left leg.

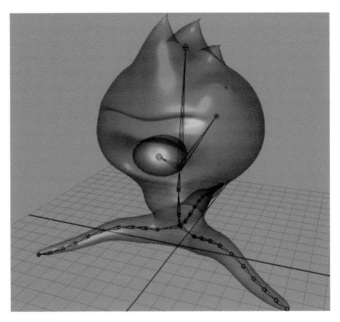

*Completed skeleton*

## 6  Reorient and freeze the joint chain

- Select the *pelvis* joint.

- Select **Skeleton** → **Orient Joint** to reorient all the joints correctly.

- With the pelvis still selected, select **Modify** → **Freeze Transformations** to reset any transformations you could have made on the joints.

## 7  Set Preferred Angle

- **RMB** over the *pelvis* joint and select **Set Preferred Angle**.

## Bind the geometry

You will use rigid binding to bind the creature on the skeleton. With rigid binding subdivision surfaces, you bind the lowest level of resolution of the model. This allows you to use the Edit Membership Tool to refine the binding of the geometry very easily.

## 1 Rigid binding

- Select the *creature* geometry, then **Shift-select** the *pelvis* joint.

- Select **Skin** → **Bind Skin** → **Rigid Bind** → ❏.

- Make sure to set the **Bind To** option to **Complete Skeleton**.

- Click the **Bind Skin** button.

**Note:** *The eye geometry will be attached to the skeleton later in the lesson.*

## 2 Edit rigid binding

- Select **Deform** → **Edit Membership Tool**.

- Select the various bones and correct any vertices membership if needed.

- Test the rotations of the skeleton and make corrections if needed.

- **RMB** over the *pelvis* joint and select **Assume Preferred Angle** to go back to the original position.

## 3 Save your work

# Create spline IKs

A spline IK handle lets you pose a joint chain using a NURBS curve. When you manipulate the curve, the handle's spline IK solver rotates the joints in the chain accordingly. You can use spline IK to pose and animate long, sinuous joint chains such as those for a tail, a tentacle, a snake and so on. This is the perfect solution for the creature's legs.

## 1 Create spline IKs

- Select **Skeleton** → **Spline IK Handle Tool** → ❏.

- Set the **Number of Spans** attribute to **3**.

*This attribute defines the amount of detail in the NURBS curve.*

- Turn **Off** the **Auto Parent Curve** option.

*This attribute specifies that you don't want the curve to be automatically parented to the parent joint of the spline IK.*

- Select the first joint in the rear leg joint chain, then select the last joint.

*The spline IK handle is created.*

- Create two other spline IKs for the front legs of the creature.

## 2 Create clusters

Since the spline IK handle needs its defining curve to be deformed in order to move the bones, you will need an easy way to deform the NURBS CVs in Object mode. To do this, you will define cluster deformers.

- Through the Outliner, select the *rear leg curve*.

- Go in Component mode.

- With the curve CVs selected as in the following image, select **Deform → Create Cluster**.

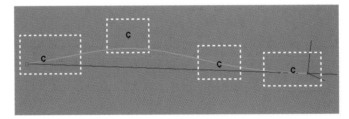

*The spline IK curve's clusters*

**Tip:** *It is important to have the clusters at the beginning and end of the curves for two member CVs to get rotations.*

- Repeat the previous step to define the same clusters for the front legs.

## 3 Rename the clusters

- Rename all the clusters accordingly.

## 4 Set up the legs

Now that you have clusters to control the spline IK curves, you need to set up the legs for animation. At the moment, if you move the pelvis joint, none of the legs will move. Since this is not what you want, you will parent the start cluster of each curve to the pelvis.

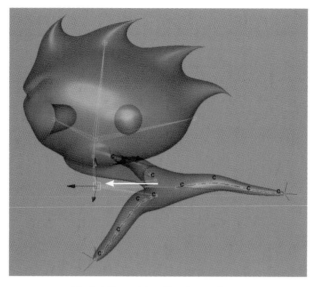

*Moving the pelvis without any clusters*

- Select the three *clusters* closest to the *pelvis* joint.

- **Shift-select** the *pelvis* joint.

- Press **p** to parent the *clusters* to the *pelvis*.

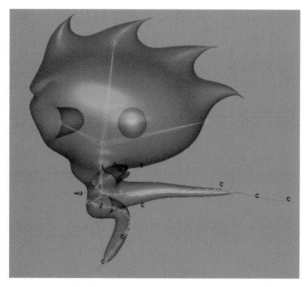

*Moving the pelvis with the clusters*

**Note:** *When parenting clusters into a hierarchy, Maya automatically groups the clusters to preserve their transformations.*

## 5    Hide unnecessary nodes

- Select the *legs' joints*, *IK handles* and *curves*, then press **Ctrl+h** to hide them.

## 6    Create a master node

- Draw a four-pointed arrow curve like in Lesson 21, and rename it *master*.

- Parent the *pelvis*, all the *clusters* and all the *IK handles* to the *master* node.

## 7    Group curves in a separate hierarchy

You cannot parent the curves to the *master* node since it would cause double transformations when moving the *master* node. *Double transformation* is caused when two or more objects define the position of the same object. For instance, if both the curve and the clusters define the same curve and they have the same parent, when you move the parent, the curve will move, then the clusters will move, causing a double transformation.

- Select all the *curves*.

- Press **Ctrl+g** to group them and **rename** the new group *IKcurves*.

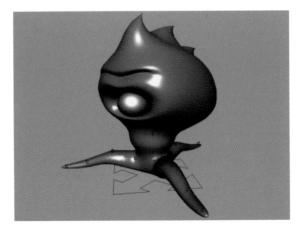

*The creature rig with selection handles*

**8   Selection handles**

- Select the *pelvis*, *spine*, *neck* and *head* joints.

- Select **Display** → **Component Display** → **Selection Handles**.

# Eye setup

The eye of the creature needs to be able to look around freely. To do so, you will create an aim constraint, which forces an object to aim at another object. You will also need to define a new attribute for blinking.

**1   Eye setup**

At the moment, the eye is scaled on the X-axis to give it an oval shape. With the eye set up like this, the eye rotation would look correct only when the creature looks up or down. You would achieve a better result if you group the eye and scale the group, so that the eye inherits the scaling and still rotates correctly.

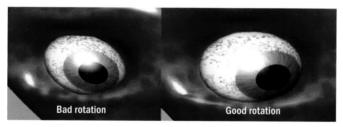

*The eye rotations*

- Select the *eyeball* and set its **Scale X** attribute to **1**.

- Press **Ctrl+g** to group the *eyeball* and rename it *eyeballGroup*.

- Set the **Scale X** attribute of the *eyeballGroup* to **1.5**.

*Now if you rotate the eyeball, it will rotate appropriately.*

**2   LookAt locator**

A locator will be used to specify a point in space where the eye will be looking.

- Select **Create** → **Locator** and **rename** it *lookAt*.

- Move the locator in front of the *creature*.

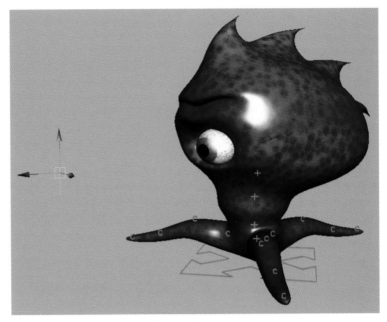

*The lookAt locator*

> **Tip:** The lookAt locator can be outside of all hierarchy so that its animation is separate from the creature.

## 3 Aim constraint

- Select *lookAt,* then **Shift-select** the *eyeball*.

- Select **Constrain** → **Aim** → ❑.

- Turn **On** the **Maintain Offset** checkbox, then click the **Add** button.

## 4 Experiment with lookAt

- Select the *lookAt* locator and **move** it around to see how the *eyeball* reacts.

**5  Parent constraint the eyeballGroup**

Now that the eye setup is working, you need to make the *eyeballGroup* follow the head joint so that it stays in its socket.

▪ Select the *eye* joint, then **Shift-select** the *eyeballGroup*.

▪ Select **Constrain → Parent**.

▪ Select the *head* joint and **rotate** it to see the results.

*The eyeballGroup will now follow the creature's head correctly, conserving the eye's aim constraint effect.*

**6  Assume Preferred Angle**

▪ **RMB** over the *pelvis* joint and select **Assume Preferred Angle**.

**7  Eye blink**

It would be good to have a *Blink* attribute on the locator, to make it easy to blink the creature's eye.

▪ Select the *lookAt* locator and select **Modify → Add Attribute…**

▪ Set the following in the new attribute window:

> **Attribute Name** to *blink*;
>
> **Data Type** to **Float**;
>
> **Minimum** to **0.1**;
>
> **Maximum** to **1**;
>
> **Default** to **1**.

▪ Click the **OK** button to add the new attribute.

▪ Open the **Window → General Editor → Connection Editor**.

▪ Load the *lookAt* node on the left side and the *eyeballGroup* on the right side.

▪ Connect the **Blink** attribute to the **Scale Y** attribute of the *eyeballGroup*.

▪ Test the **Blink** attribute.

**8  Save your work**

# Bulging brain

You can achieve a nice bulging effect on the creature's brain by using *Sculpt* deformers. A *sculpt* deforms geometry with a sphere influence object. As you move the sphere, the geometry will stretch around the sphere.

## 1  Deforming subdivision surfaces

In order to deform subvision surfaces, you need to select the appropriate vertices and then create the deformer.

- Select the *creature* surface, then go in Component mode.

- **RMB** on the *creature* and select **Display Level** → **2**.

- From the *side* view, select all the creature's brain area vertices.

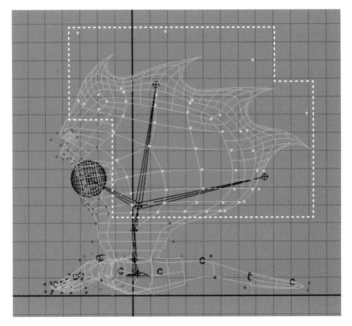

*The brain vertices*

- Select **Deform** → **Create Sculpt Deformer** → ❑.

- Turn **On** the **Grouping** attribute to group the sculptor with its locator.

- Press the **Create** button.

*The deformer is created within the head geometry.*

**2   Place the sculpt deformer**

- Go into Object mode.

- Select the *sculptGroup1* and select **Modify** → **Center Pivot**.

- Parent the *sculptGroup1* object to the *head* joint.

- Place the *sculptGroup1* object as follows:

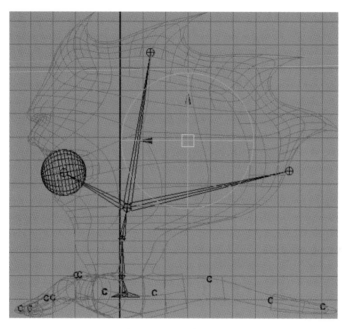

*The sculpt deformer*

**3   Create a MEL expression**

In order to automatically generate animation for the bulging brain, you will create a simple MEL expression that will control the scaling of the Sculpt deformer.

- Select the *sculptor1* node.

- Highlight the **Scale X** attribute in the Channel Box, then **RMB** and select **Expressions**...

*The Expression Editor will be displayed.*

- In the Expression Editor, enter *bulgeExpression* in the **Expression Name** field.

- In the Expression field at the bottom of the editor, enter the following MEL expression:

```
sculptor1.scaleX = (sin(time*5) / 5) + 1;
```

- Click the **Create** button, then the **Close** button.

*The expression will be created.*

- Playback the scene to see the effect of the expression over time.

## Jiggle deformer

Another nice deformer is the *Jiggle* deformer. The *Jiggle deformer* will make vertices jiggle as the geometry is moving. You will use a jiggle deformer on the back of the creature's brain so that it wobbles as the creature is walking.

### 1  Create a jiggle deformer

- **RMB** on the *creature* geometry and select **Display Level** → **0**.

- Go in Component mode and select the vertices defining the back of the head from a *side* view.

- Select **Deform** → **Create Jiggle** → ❏.

- In the option window, set the following:

> **Ignore Transform** to **On**;
>
> **Stiffness** to **0.2**;
>
> **Damping** to **0.2**.

- Click the **Create** button.

### 2  Test the Jiggle deformer

In order to test the Jiggle deformer, keyframe some rough animation and playback the scene. The attributes of the Jiggle deformer can be found in the Channel Box, when the creature geometry is selected.

Once testing is over, remove the animation and make sure all the joints are at their preferred angle.

### 3  Save your work

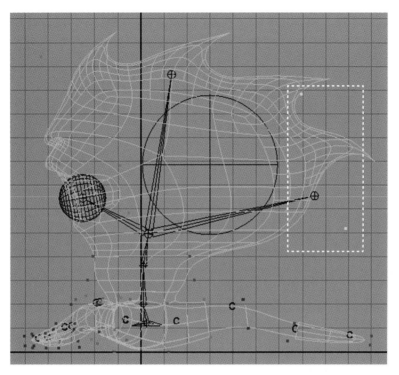

*The vertices to be used with the Jiggle deformer*

## Finalize the rig

Before you can call the rig final, you must go through your setup and make sure everything will work well for animation. You already did this in Lesson 21, but following is a checklist of things to review:

**1  Node names**

- Make sure all the nodes are correctly named.

**2  Hard to find attributes**

- Add strategically placed attributes and connect them to attributes that are hard to find. This will greatly simplify the animation process.

## 3   Objects and attributes

- Go over every node in your scene and lock/hide every attribute not intended for animation to prevent it from breaking.

*Tip:*   Do not lock the scaling of the master node.

- Lock and hide objects that are not needed in the viewport.

## 4   Layers

- Create one layer for the geometry and another layer for the rig.

*The final rig*

*Tip:*   *If the geometry is too heavy for animation, you can create a low resolution model by converting the subdivision surfaces to polygons.*

## 5   Save your work

## Conclusion

You have now experienced the spline IK handle, the aim constraint and two new kinds of deformer: Sculpt and Jiggle. You have also written a basic MEL expression, which opens the door for custom expressions and scripts.

In the next lesson, you will explore the MEL scripting language as you set up custom controls for blinking the creature's eye.

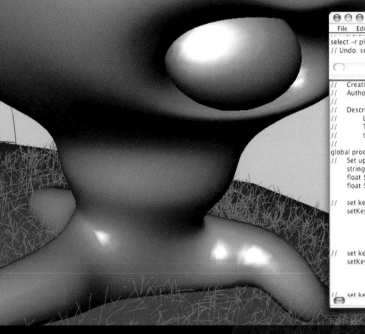

```
select -r planets:mainPlanet ;
// Undo: select -r planets:mainPlanet


//   Creation Date:  02/03/05
//   Author:       Mark Andre
//
//   Description:
//       Learning Maya tutorial script
//       This script builds a procedure for animating
//       the creature's lookAt.blink attribute
//
global proc blink (float $blinkDelay){
//   Set up variables that will be used in the script
     string $blink = "lookAt.blink";
     float $time = `currentTime -query `;
     float $blinkCurrent = `getAttr $blink`;

//   set key for the blink attribute at the current time
     setKeyframe    -value $blinkCurrent
                    -time $time
                    -attribute $blink
                    $blink;

//   set key for a blink of 0 half way through the blink
     setKeyframe    -value 0
                    -time ($time + $blinkDelay/2)
                    -attribute $blink
                    $blink;
//   set key for the original blink value at the
```

# Lesson 29    Blinking using MEL

*In this lesson, you will set keys on the Blink attribute that you created on the lookAt node in Lesson 28. To help with this task, you will create a MEL (Maya Embedded Language) script that will help you animate the blink.*

*MEL is a powerful scripting language that can be used by both technical directors and animators. Animators can take advantage of simple macro-like scripts to enhance their workflows, while technical directors can use more advanced MEL commands to rig up characters, add special visual effects, or set up customized controls.*

## In this lesson you will learn the following:

- How to recognize and enter MEL commands;

- How to create a MEL script procedure;

- How to use this procedure within the existing UI;

- How to build a custom UI element for the procedure;

- How to animate the creature's blinking using the procedure.

If you know nothing about programming and scripts, this lesson will, at first, seem foreign to your world of graphics and animation. While you can certainly be successful with Maya without relying on the use of MEL, this lesson offers a good chance to get your feet wet and see the possibilities. If you do learn how to use MEL, you might be quite surprised how a simple script can be used to enhance your work.

## Starting a new file

Rather than working in the creature scene file, you will practice using MEL in a new file. Once your scripts have been written and saved, you will return to the creature scene and use the custom UI tools in context.

**1  Start a new file**

- Select **File** → **New Scene**.

- Set up a single *Perspective* view panel.

- Make sure the Command Line, the Help line and the Channel Box are all visible.

# WHAT IS MEL?

MEL stands for Maya Embedded Language. It is built on top of the Maya based architecture and is used to execute commands used to build scenes and create user interface elements. In fact, every time you click on a tool, you are executing one or more MEL commands.

## Typing commands

A MEL command is a text string that tells Maya to complete a particular action. As a user, it is possible to skip the graphical user interface and use these commands directly. Generally, animators will choose the user interface instead – but it is still a good idea to know what MEL can do at a command level.

## The Command Line

You will now use the Command Line found in Maya to create and edit some primitive objects. The goal at this point is to explore how simple commands work.

**1  Create a cone using the Command Line**

- Click in the Command Line to give it focus.

*The Command Line can be found at the bottom left, just above the Help line.*

- Enter the following:

```
cone
Show Manipulator Tool: Select an object.
```

*Entering a MEL command*

- After you finish, press the **Enter** key on the numeric keypad section of your keyboard.

---

**Tip:** *The keyboard has two* **Enter** *keys that each work a little differently with the Command Line. The* **Enter** *key associated with the numeric keypad keeps your focus on the Command Line, while the* **Enter** *key associated with the alpha-numeric keyboard switches your focus back to the view panels.*

---

## 2 Rotate and move the cone with commands

The next step is to transform the cone using MEL commands.

- Enter the following:

```
rotate 0 0 90 < Enter >

move 5 0 0 < Enter >
```

*You now have a cone sitting on the ground surface, five units along the X-axis. You entered the commands by first entering the command, then adding the desired values.*

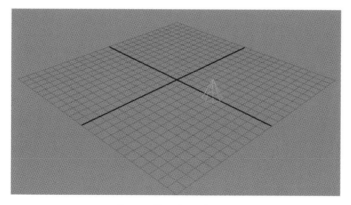

*Perspective view of cone*

## 3 Rename the cone

You can also rename objects from the Command Line.

- Enter the following:

```
rename nurbsCone1 myCone < Enter >
```

| Channels  Object | | |
|---|---|---|
| **myCone** | | |
| | Translate X | 5 |
| | Translate Y | 0 |
| | Translate Z | 0 |

*Look in the Channel Box to confirm that the object has been renamed.*

*Channel Box with cone's name*

## 4    Execute two commands at once

If you want to quickly enter more than one command without pressing the Enter key along the way, you can place a semicolon between the commands.

- Enter the following:

```
sphere; move 0 0 6; scale 4 1 1 < Enter >
```

*Using the semicolon(;), you executed three commands in a row. First, you created a sphere, then you moved it, then you scaled it. The semicolon will become more important later when you write scripts.*

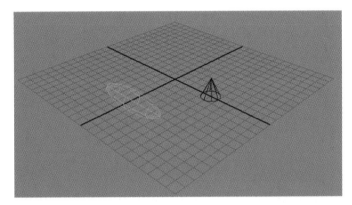

*Perspective view of new sphere*

## 5    Execute a command on an unselected object

If you want to execute a command on an object that is not selected, you simply add the name of the node that you want to affect. The node will follow the command without requiring the cone to be selected.

- Enter the following:

```
move -5 0 0 mycone < Enter >
```

*Oops! You got an error message saying that Maya cannot find the* mycone
*object. This is because the object name has a capital C for the word 'Cone'.*
*MEL is case sensitive, which means you should be especially aware of how*
*you spell and capitalize any names or commands.*

- Enter the following:

```
move -5 0 0 myCone < Enter >

scale 5 1 1 myCone < Enter >
```

*Always remember the importance of getting the spelling of commands*
*correct. Later, when you write scripts, correct spelling will be essential.*

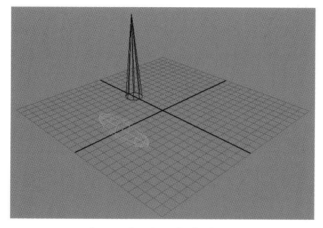

*Perspective view of edited cone*

## 6  Use command flags

Another important MEL capability is the command flag. You can use
these flags to be more specific about how you want the commands to be
executed. The command flags can have short or long names. Flags are
indicated with a hyphen in your script. Shown below are examples of both
kinds of flags.

- Enter the following using long names for flags:

```
cylinder -name bar -axis 0 1 0 -pivot 0 0
-3 < Enter >
```

- Enter the following using short names for flags:

```
cylinder -n bar2 -ax 0 1 0 -p 0 0 -6
-hr 10 < Enter >
```

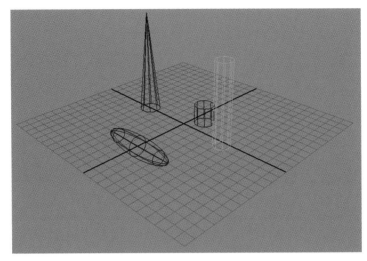

*Perspective view of cylinders*

*The short flag names represent the following:*

-n      name

-ax     axis

-p      pivot

-hr     height ratio

**Tip:** *You will notice that long flag names can create a command that is easy to read but hard to type in – short names are harder to decipher but easy to type. Generally, entering in the Command Line is a good place for short flags while long flags should be used in scripts to aid in readability.*

## 7   Delete all objects

- Enter the following:

```
select -all; delete < Enter >
```

# The Script Editor window

You may have noticed that the Command Line is a small space to work in and only one line of feedback. The Script Editor is a special user interface element that will make entering commands easier.

Up until now, you have been entering random commands in order to learn about their syntax and how they work. You will now use the Script Editor to build a sphere and a locator that will mimic the *eyeball/lookAt* relationship that you set in Lesson 28. The ultimate goal is to set up a Blink attribute that will control the blinking of the creature's eye.

## 1   Open the Script Editor window

- Click on the **Script Editor** button in the lower right of the workspace or select **Window → General Editors → Script Editor**.

*The window opens to show all of the commands you just entered.*

- From the Script Editor, select **Edit → Clear History**.

## 2   Create a primitive sphere

- Select **Create → Polygon Primitives → Sphere**.

*In the Script Editor, you can see the MEL command that was used to create the sphere. Also included are the flags with default settings presented in their short form.*

Script Editor

- In the lower portion of the Script Editor, type the following:

```
delete
```

- Press the numeric keypad **Enter** key to execute the command.

> **Tip:** *In the Script Editor, the numeric keypad's **Enter** key executes an action while the alpha-numeric keypad's **Enter** key returns to the next line.*

## 3   Copy and edit the sphere commands

Now that the sphere command is in the Script Editor's history, you can use this command as a start point to write your own command.

- In the Script Editor, select the parts of the Command Line up to the `-r 1` flag.

- Copy the text into the lower portion of the Script Editor.

- Edit the first part of the command to read as follows:

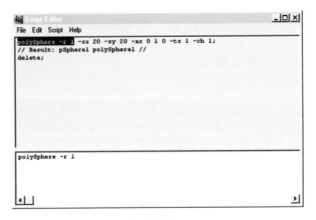

*Script Editor*

```
polySphere -r 2 -ax 1 0 0 -name eyeball
```

- Press the **Enter** key on your numeric keypad.

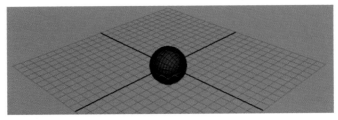

*The eyeball*

## 4    Create a locator

- Select **Create** → **Locator**.

*In the Script Editor, you will see a corresponding MEL command.*

- Enter undo to go back one step.

## 5    Echo all commands

- In the Script Editor, select **Script** → **Echo All Commands**.

- Select **Create** → **Locator**.

*In the Script Editor, you can now see a MEL command that you can use to create a locator:* createPrimitive nullObject;

**Note:** *This command is surrounded by other commands that belong to Maya. You only need to focus on the locator command.*

- In the Script Editor, select **Script** → **Echo All Commands** to turn this option **Off**.

## 6    Rename and move the locator

You will now name the locator as *lookAt*. This object will be used as a substitute for the control node you built earlier in the creature scene.

- Enter the following:

```
rename locator1 lookAt;

move 10 0 0 lookAt < Enter >
```

## 7    Add an attribute to the locator

You will now add a Blink attribute. This command is the same as using **Modify** → **Add Attribute** from the UI.

- Enter the following:

```
addAttr -ln blink -at "float" -min 0.1 -max 1 -dv 1 lookAt
< Enter >
```

*The short flag names represent the following;*

| | |
|---|---|
| -ln | long name of the new attribute |
| -at | attribute type |
| -min/max | minimum/maximum values for the attribute |
| -dv | default value for the attribute |

## 8   Make the attribute keyable on the Blink attribute

- Enter the following:

```
setAttr -keyable true lookAt.blink < Enter >
```

## 9   Set up your Perspective view panel

- Set up your view panel to see the eyeball object and locator.

- Press **5** to turn on hardware shading.

- Select **Display** → **Grid** to turn **Off** the grid.

- Select **Shading** → **Wireframe on Shaded.**

*Eyeball and locator*

## Learning more about commands

You now know how to use a few of the many Maya commands. To learn more about the commands, refer to the online documentation where you will find a complete list of all the commands available in MEL. Each command is listed with descriptions of the various flags.

# Expressions

When you write an expression in the Expression Editor, it can be written as a MEL script. You can also use MEL to create the expressions from within the Script Editor.

You will create an expression to control the *scale Y* of the *eyeball* node. In Lesson 28, you used a connection. Now you can compare the use of expressions and connections.

**1    Add an expression to the eyeball**

This expression will ensure that the Blink attribute scales the eyeball on the Y-axis.

- Enter the following:

```
expression -n blinkExpression -s "eyeball.
sy = lookAt.blink"< Enter >
```

**2    Test the Blink attribute**

- Enter the following:

```
setAttr "lookAt.blink" 0.1 < Enter >
```

**3    Set keys on the Blink attribute**

- Enter the following:

```
setKeyframe -at blink -t 1 -v 1 lookAt;

setKeyframe -at blink -t 5 -v 0.1 lookAt;

setKeyframe -at blink -t 10 -v 1 lookAt < Enter >
```

*The short flag names represent the following:*

| | |
|---|---|
| -at | attribute that is being keyed |
| -t | time at which you want the key set |
| -v | value of the attribute you want to key |

- Playback the results.

*Keys have been set on three frames so the eye is closing and opening.*

# Building a blink procedure

You are now going to create a blink procedure that you will save as a MEL script. The next few steps outline every part of the MEL script with some tips on how to enter and execute it. At the end of this lesson, you will find the script without descriptive text. You can enter the script later, in case you want to read over this section first.

## Writing the script

You will write the blink procedure, not in the Script Editor, but in a Text Editor. A Text Editor is an application that lets you work quickly with text and then save in a generic text format.

### 1   Open a Text Editor

- Open a Text Editor such as *Notepad, WordPad* or *TextEdit*.

### 2   Type comments to create header information

Every script should start with a header that contains important information for other people who might read your script later. Below is an example header. The // placed in front of these lines indicates that they are comments and therefore will be ignored when you later execute the script.

- Type the following:

```
//

//    Creation Date:   Today's date

//    Author:          Your name here

//

//    Description:

//          Learning Maya tutorial script

//          This script builds a procedure for animating

//          the creature's lookAt.blink attribute

//
```

> **Tip:**  Don't underestimate the importance of commenting on your scripts. Down the line, someone will need to read what you have done and the comments are much easier to follow than the actual script.

## 3   Declare the procedure

The first thing you enter is designed to declare the procedure. This line loads the procedure into the Maya memory so that it can be executed later.

▪ Type the following:

```
global proc blink (float $blinkDelay){
```

This line defines a procedure named *blink*. The required argument resides within the round brackets. This tells Maya what the script requires to execute. In this case, the length of the blink action is required. This is defined as a floating value called `$blinkDelay`. Because this value is not yet determined, it is known as a variable. The $ sign defines it as a variable. The open bracket – the { symbol – is added to the end of the declaration to let you start inputting MEL statements.

## 4   Set up variables

Within your script, you will use variables to represent values that may need to change later. At the beginning of the script, you need to set up the variables and set their value. In some cases, you may set their value with an actual number. But, for this script, you will use attribute names and values instead.

▪ Type the following:

```
//    Set up variables that will be
      used in the script

      string $blink = "lookAt.blink";

      float $time = `currentTime -query`;

      float $blinkCurrent = `getAttr $blink`;
```

The first variable set defines `$blink` as the Blink attribute found on the *lookAt* node. The second variable queries Maya for the current time. The third attribute gets the actual value of the `lookAt.blink` at the queried time.

> **Note:** *To generate the quotation marks for the float* $time *and float* $blinkCurrent *in the above lines, use the* ` *quotation mark located to the left of the number 1 key on most keyboards.*

## 5   Set keys on the blink

Next, you want to set keys on the Blink attribute at the beginning, middle and end of the blink. The length of the blink will be defined by the *blinkDelay* variable that was set as the main argument of the procedure. Notice that while other variables were set at the beginning of the script, the *blinkDelay* is used as an argument so that you can set it when the script is executed later. As you enter the keyframe commands, notice how you use the normal setup of command/flag/node name.

- Type the following:

```
// set key for the blink attribute at the current time

setKeyframe    -value $blinkCurrent

               -time $time

               -attribute $blink

               $blink;


// set key for a blink of 0 half way through the blink

setKeyframe    -value 0

               -time ($time + $blinkDelay/2)

               -attribute $blink

               $blink;


// set key for the original blink value at
   the end of the blink

setKeyframe    -value $blinkCurrent

               -time ($time + $blinkDelay)

               -attribute $blink

               $blink;

    }
```

In this part of the script, you have set keys using the *setKeyframe* command. The keys set at the beginning and end of the blink use the queried value of the Blink attribute, while the key set in the middle uses a value of zero. At the end, a closed bracket – the } symbol – is used to declare the statement complete.

## 6 Save your script

You can now save your script into your Maya *scripts* directory. This will ensure that the procedure is easily available within Maya any time you need it.

- In your Text Editor, save the script using the following path:

      \[drive]:\maya\scripts\blink.mel

**Note:** *Because the procedure is named blink, it is important to save the file as blink.mel. This makes it easier for Maya to find the function.*

## 7 Loading the script

Because you named the file *blink.mel* and placed it in your *maya\scripts* directory, the script will be loaded automatically the next time you launch Maya. For now, you need to load the script manually.

- In the Script Editor, select **File** → **Source Script**...

- Browse for the script you saved in the last step.

*The script is loaded and you now have access to it.*

## 8 Testing the script

If you enter `blink` with a value for the blink delay, Maya will look in the scripts directory for a procedure called *blink.mel*.

- Set the Time Slider to frame **40**.

- Enter the following:

      blink 10 < Enter >

- Scrub in the Time Slider to test the results.

*If this works, you can congratulate yourself on completing your first MEL script and move on to the next section. Nice work!*

*If it doesn't, you must have typed something incorrectly. Open the Script Editor to review its feedback to find your mistake.*

### 9 Debugging your script

To debug your script, you need to find out which line is causing the error, and then go back and check your spelling and syntax. Did you use the correct symbols? Did you name your nodes correctly? Is your capitalization correct?

▪ To display line numbers in the Script Editor, select **Script** → **Show Line Numbers**.

## Adding the function to the UI

Now that you have created your own function, you will want to have easy access to it. Below are three methods for adding your function to the default UI, which you can easily set up using interactive methods.

### 1 Creating a shelf button

▪ In the Script Editor, select the text `blink 10`.

▪ Click on the selected text with the **MMB** and drag up to the shelf.

*It is placed on the shelf with a MEL icon. You can now move the Time Slider to a new position and test it. You could also drag up different blinkDelay settings to offer different blink settings. Or, you could set up a marking menu as outlined below.*

### 2 Creating a blink marking menu set

▪ Select **Window** → **Settings/Preferences** → **Marking Menus...**

▪ Click on the **Create Marking Menu** button.

▪ Click on the top middle square with your right mouse button and select **Edit Menu item...** from the pop-up menu.

▪ In the Edit North window, type *Blink 10* in the **Label** field.

▪ In the **Command(s)**: field, type `blink 10`.

▪ Click **Save** and **Close**.

- Repeat for the other quadrants to set up blink commands that use a *blinkDelay* of 20, 30, and 40.

- In the **Menu Name** field, enter: `blinking`.

- Click the **Save** button, then **Close**.

## 3   Prepare the blink marking menu for a hotkey

The blink marking menu now needs to be set up.

- In the marking menu customize window, set the following:

     **Use Marking Menu in** to **Hotkey Editor**.

*Now the marking menu can be set up in the Hotkey Editor so that it can be invoked using a hotkey.*

- Click the **Apply Settings** button, then **Close**.

## 4   Assign the blink marking menu to a hotkey

- Select **Window** → **Settings/Preferences** → **Hotkeys...**

- Scroll to the bottom of the **Categories** list and click on the **User Marking Menus**.

- In the **Commands** window, click on the **blinking_Press** listing.

- In the **Assign New HotKey** section, set the following;

     **Key** to **F7**;

     **Direction** to **Press**.

**Note:** *Use the pulldown menu next to the key field when assigning a function key as a hotkey.*

*A message will appear stating whether or not a particular key has been assigned or not. In this case, F7 is not assigned.*

- Press the **Assign** key.

*A message should appear stating that the hotkey will not work properly unless the release is also set. Maya will ask if you want the release key set for you.*

- Click **Yes**.

- Click on **Save** in the Hotkey Editor window and then **Close**.

## 5    Use the new marking menu

- Go to frame **80**.

- Press and hold **F7**, **LMB** click, then pick one of the blinking options from the marking menu.

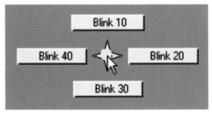

*Blink marking menu*

## Building a custom UI script

In the next section, you will write a second script that will build a custom user interface window that includes a slider for the *blinkDelay* variable and a button that executes the blink procedure you scripted earlier. In Maya, you have the ability to use MEL to build custom user interface elements.

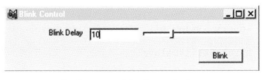

*Custom user interface window*

## 1    Start a new text file

## 2    Adding the opening comments

Start the script with a commented header that helps others read your work. While this was taught earlier, it can never be emphasized enough.

- Type the following:

```
//

//    Creation Date:   Today's date

//    Author:          Your name here

//

//    Description:

//          Learning Maya tutorial script

//          This script builds a custom user interface

//          for executing the blink procedure

//          and for setting the blink delay

//
```

## 3   Declare a get info procedure

You are now going to create a procedure called *blinkGetInfo* that will be used to get the *blinkDelay* value from a slider, which you will build later in the script. Since the value set in the slider is meant to be the chosen value for the blink, this procedure queries the slider to set the *blinkDelay*, and then adds that value next to the blink command.

- Type the following:

```
global proc blinkGetInfo() {

        // get necessary information from Maya

        float $blinkDelay = 'intSliderGrp

        -query -value blinkWindow|columnLayout|delaySlider';

        blink $blinkDelay;

}
```

## 4   Declare a second user interface procedure

You are now going to declare a procedure that will build a floating window. This window will look and act like any other window in Maya but will be designed to help you put a blink to the creature's eye.

- Type the following:

```
global proc blinkWindow() {
```

## 5  Remove any existing blink windows

As you start a user interface script, it is a good idea to check if the same UI element already exists in the scene and, if so, to delete it. This ensures that your new element is the only one recognized by Maya at any one time.

- Type the following:

```
// clean up any existing blinkWindows

if ( `window -ex blinkWindow`) == true ) deleteUI
blinkWindow;
```

## 6  Build the window called blinkWindow

The next part of the script is designed to build a window that is 400 pixels wide and 75 pixels tall. You will call it *Blink Control* in its title bar but Maya will know of it as *blinkWindow*.

- Type the following:

```
window

        -width 400

        -height 100

        -title "Blink Control"

blinkWindow;
```

## 7  Form a column layout

Within the window, you need to organize your user interface elements. One method of organization is a *columnLayout*. This sets up a column with a particular spacing in relation to the window.

- Type the following:

```
columnLayout

        -columnAttach "right" 5

        -rowSpacing 10

        -columnWidth 375

columnLayout;
```

## 8    Create a slider group

Within the layout, you want to build a slider that lets you set the *blinkDelay* value. MEL offers you preset *kits* using special group commands that build several UI types in one go. The *intSliderGrp* builds a slider along with a field for seeing the resulting value and for entering the value yourself. This slider is set to integer values since frames are generally set in whole numbers. The flags let you set the various values for the minimum and maximum settings of the slider.

- Type the following:

```
intSliderGrp

        -label "Blink Delay"

        -field true

        -minValue 2

        -maxValue 30

        -fieldMinValue 0

        -fieldMaxValue 100

        -value 10

delaySlider;
```

## 9    Create a button

The next part of the script builds a button that you will be using to execute the *blinkGetInfo* procedure, which in turn uses the *blinkDelay* value from the slider to execute the  *blink* command. At the end, you will enter *setparent* to link the button to the*columnlayout*.

- Type the following:

```
button

        -label "Blink"

        -width 70

        -command "blinkGetInfo"

button;

setParent ..;
```

## 10 Show the window

You are almost finished! Now you must tell Maya to show the window.

- Type the following:

```
showWindow blinkWindow;
```

## 11 Finish the script

Finally, you must complete the procedure and make one final declaration of the *blinkWindow* procedure name.

- Type the following:

```
}

blinkWindow;
```

## 12 Saving the script

You can now save your script into your *Maya scripts* directory.

- In your Text Editor, save the script using the following path:

```
\[drive]:\maya\scripts\blinkWindow.mel
```

## 13 Test your script

- In the Script Editor, select **File** → **Source Script** and browse to the script you just saved.

- In the Command Line or the Script Editor, type the following:

```
blinkWindow < Enter >
```

*The window should open. You can now set the Time Slider to a new time, and then set the blink delay using the slider; pressing the button will key the blink.*

# Keyframing the creature's blink

Congratulations! You now have your own custom user interface element built and ready to go. You can open your creature file from the last lesson and use this script to make it blink.

This will only work if you named your *lookAt* node correctly and created a **Blink** attribute as outlined.

# THE SCRIPTS

Here are the two scripts listed in their entirety for you to review:

## blink.mel

```
//

//    Creation Date:   Today's date

//    Author:          Your name here

//

//    Description:

//            Learning Maya tutorial script

//            This script builds a procedure for animating

//            the creature's lookAt.blink attribute

//

global proc blink (float $blinkDelay){

//    Set up variables that will be used in the script

      string $blink = "lookAt.blink";

      float $time = `currentTime -query`;

      float $blinkCurrent = `getAttr $blink`;


//    set key for the blink attribute at the current time

      setKeyframe     -value $blinkCurrent

                      -time $time

                      -attribute $blink

                      $blink;


//    set key for a blink of 0 half way through the blink

      setKeyframe     -value 0

                      -time ($time + $blinkDelay/2)

                      -attribute $blink

                      $blink;
```

```
//     set key for the original blink value at the
       end of the blink

       setKeyframe     -value $blinkCurrent

                       -time ($time + $blinkDelay)

                       -attribute $blink

                       $blink;

}
```

# blinkWindow.mel

```
//

//     Creation Date:  Today's date

//     Author:         Your name here

//

//     Description:

//             Learning Maya tutorial script

//             This script builds a custom user interface

//             for executing the blink procedure

//             and for setting the blink delay

//

global proc blinkGetInfo() {

       // get necessary information from Maya

       float $blinkDelay = `intSliderGrp -query -value
       blinkWindow|columnLayout|delaySlider`;

       blink $blinkDelay;

}

global proc blinkWindow() {

       // clean up any existing blinkWindows

       if ( (`window -ex blinkWindow`) == true )
       deleteUI blinkWindow;
```

```
window

        -width 400

        -height 100

        -title "Blink Control"

blinkWindow;

columnLayout

        -columnAttach "right" 5

        -rowSpacing 10

        -columnWidth 375

columnLayout;

intSliderGrp

        -label "Blink Delay"

        -field true

        -minValue 2

        -maxValue 30

        -fieldMinValue 0

        -fieldMaxValue 100

        -value 10

delaySlider;

button

        -label "Blink"

        -width 70

        -command "blinkGetInfo"

button;

        setParent ..;

showWindow blinkWindow;

}

blinkWindow;
```

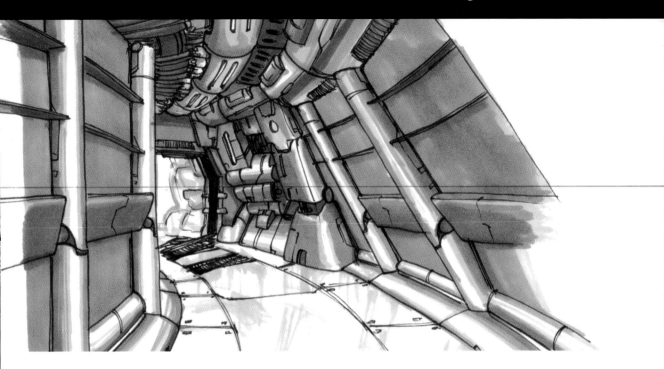

## Lessons

Alias SketchBook Pro software allows you to create, annotate and present images with incredibly agile drawing tools. You can use the pre-set brushes or customize an array of brushes, each with their own particular 'feel'.

# Lesson 30    Intro: Alias® SketchBook™ Pro

*SketchBook Pro features an ultra efficient gesture-based UI (user interface) and set of paint and drawing tools designed to be used with various computer drawing tablets.*

**In this section, you will learn the following:**

- How to use the UI;

- How to use the tool sets;

- How to customize preferences;

- How to distinguish between using different pen tablets

# User interface

As soon as SketchBook Pro loads up you can put the stylus to the surface and start drawing with the default 2B pencil. To change brushes, go to the bottom corner of the UI (the tool palette), press on the tooljar icon, and flick in the direction of the brush you want to use. As you become familiar with the degree positions of the tools you will develop 'muscle memory, allowing you to flick around quickly without waiting for the other icons to appear.

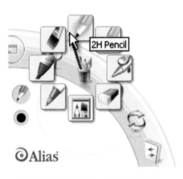

*Flicking to choose a pencil in a marking menu*

This Marking Menu™ (radial menu) technology is the heart of SketchBook Pro's fast tool selection functionality. At the top of the interface is a standard menu bar with the **File**, **Edit**, **Image** and **Help** menus. Although some of these are redundant over the Tool Palette, there is some functionality you must access from here, such as user preferences and image rotation, mirroring and cropping.

**Note:** *Although the barrel button on the stylus is not used in SketchBook Pro, the reverse end of many stylus' act as a default eraser.*

# Tool Palette

You will be regularly accessing the toolsets within the tool palette. Explore each of the main icons by pressing and holding on them. Further explore each of the marking menus in the lagoon by hovering over them to see the tool tip that appears.

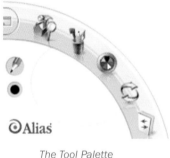

*The Tool Palette*

# Interface Controls menu

The tools in the interface controls menu let you reposition and hide the interface.

## Tools and Views menu

The Tools and Views menu houses the zoom and move puck, the selection and layer tools, the **Use Last Brush Tool** and the different canvas views. You will use these tools frequently.

*The Tools and Views marking menu*

## Brushes menu

The Brushes menu is where you choose your brushes. The Brush Palette, which lets you create custom brushes, is also accessed here.

*The Brushes marking menu*

## Colors menu

The Colors menu contains your palette of colors. The **Colors** window lets you choose a finer range of color.

*The Colors marking menu*

**Note:** *Some of these tools also have keyboard shortcuts known as hotkeys listed with the tool tips. A list of keyboard shortcuts is contained in the SketchBook Pro's Help section.*

## Edit menu

The **Edit** marking menu includes undo and redo. The hotkey for undo is **Ctrl+z**. Also contained in this menu is the **Clear Layer Tool**. From here you can continually expand the size of your canvas.

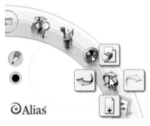

*The Edit marking menu*

## Files menu

The Files menu contains the **Open**, **Save** and **Create New Sketch** functions. The page icons with flipped corners let you flip back and forth between sketches.

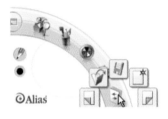

*The Files marking menu*

## Current Tool

The **Current Tool** icon displays the current tool you are using. If you are using a brush, clicking on it brings up the **Brush Palette**.

*The Current Tool icon*

## Current Color

This icon displays the current color you are using. Clicking on it brings up the **Colors** window.

*The Current Color icon*

# SETTINGS AND PREFERENCES

Two common preferences you will want to change are canvas size and undos. Depending on the final output of your work (i.e. screen or print), you may increase your canvas size up to 8000 X 8000 pixels.

Increasing the canvas to very large sizes is processor demanding and can effect performance. If you intend to print examples of artwork, make test prints from various resolutions.

For example, a multi-layered drawing created in SketchBook Pro at 3000 X 2400 pixels would result in detail for print, yet would not be overly processor demanding on a powerful computer. As you increase the size of your work you may wish to lower the number of undos.

Under the **Edit** menu you can also adjust your pen responsiveness.

*Accessing Preferences*

*Undo and Canvas Size settings*

*Pen Responsiveness slider*

**Note:** *For information on changing a Tablet PC's settings use the SketchBook Pro* **Help** *and go to* **Welcome** → **Select a Tool** *and scroll down to* **Adjust Tablet PC settings**.

# TABLETS

There are a few different types of drawing tablets that Alias SketchBook Pro has been designed to work with. The most common is the standard pen tablet that hooks up to a desktop or laptop PC. Another drawing tablet is the Wacom® Cintiq® , and more recently, the Tablet PC.

## Pen tablet

The standard pen tablet is the most common. Recent models connect via a USB port and Bluetooth® wireless. These drawing tablets come in the widest variety of sizes from 4x5 inches to 12x18 inches. The clearest difference in drawing with this kind of tablet is that you do not see your work on the surface you are drawing upon. In this unique drawing experience, your hand and pen are never blocking the view of the artwork.

*Wacom pen tablet*

## Cintiq tablet

This drawing tablet, manufactured by Wacom, is a precursor to the Tablet PC in that it allows the user to draw directly on the screen. This functionality brings the computer drawing and painting experience that much closer to reality. These units are favored by those in design and illustration. They come in two sizes: 17 inch and 21 inch. Like the pen tablet, one must connect this device to a PC. One feature that makes the Cintiq stand out from the rest is an innovative tilt-able and rotating easel that allows the artist to adjust the drawing surface with stability.

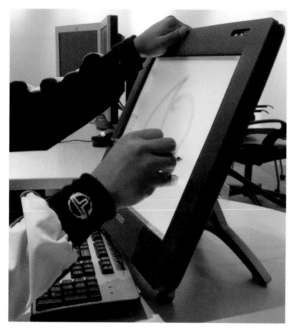

*Wacom Cintiq tablet*

## Tablet PC

As the name implies, this device is both a drawing tablet and a PC. It allows the user to draw directly on the screen like the Wacom Cintiq, but has the bonus of being a computer. One great advantage of this machine is its portability.

*Tablet PC*

Alias Sketchbook Pro software liberates the artist with an almost unending supply of ink and paper. You can create an assortment of brushes with strokes set to your own specifications.

A brushes stroke is made up of a series of stamps; adjusting the stamp settings produces different types of brushes. We will demonstrate how to create some custom brushes and then use them for the development of a simplified character design of the Blue robot referenced throughout this book.

## In this lesson you will learn the following:

- How to create custom brushes;

- How to draw a character design as image reference for modeling in Maya;

- How to use the color wheel;

# Brush Palette

The Brush Palette holds all the presets and custom brushes. It is accessed by flicking down in the **Brush Jar** icon or by clicking on the **Current tool** icon when using a brush. You can copy any of the presets to the **Custom** tab. When you copy a preset brush to the custom tab the Brush Editor pops up for you to adjust the settings of your new brush.

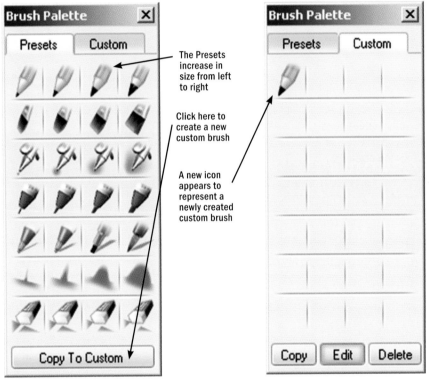

The Presets increase in size from left to right

Click here to create a new custom brush

A new icon appears to represent a newly created custom brush

*Presets tab in Brush Palette*                    *Custom tab in Brush Palette*

> **Tip:** When you are working on a complex drawing that you may return to later and you want to remember a unique custom brush, take a screen grab with the SketchBook Snapshot utility of the brush settings and some sample strokes for later reference. When you build up a full roster of brushes it can become difficult to remember which brush you used on a particular drawing.

# Brush Editor

The Brush Editor holds the controls that allow you to tweak your brushes. To understand the attributes of the various brushes, copy them to the **Custom** tab one by one and take time to sketch with them. Experiment with the attribute sliders to see how they affect your brush stroke.

You can keep the Brush Editor open while sketching and still use all other functionality such as erasing, zoom and move, etc. Take notice of which brushes you enjoy using and compare their settings to assess how they differ from each other. While exploring some favorable brush settings save them to the custom tab by clicking the **Done** button.

# Colors window

In Alias SketchBook Pro you can quickly access several default colors from the colors Marking Menu or select the **Colors** window, which gives you access to a full color spectrum.You can also bring up the color window by clicking on the **Current Color** icon.

Use the color picker to absorb a color from any pixel on your display.

Select a hue in the color wheel

Select saturation and value in the SV triangle

Select gray value from 11-step grayscale

Numerical RGB display

Color swatch updates with user selection

Eye dropper for color picking

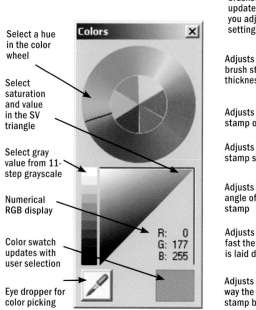

*Color selection attributes*

Sample brushstroke updates as you adjust settings

Adjusts the brush stamp thickness

Adjusts the stamp opacity

Adjusts the stamp shape

Adjusts the angle of the stamp

Adjusts how fast the stamp is laid down

Adjusts the way the stamp bleeds

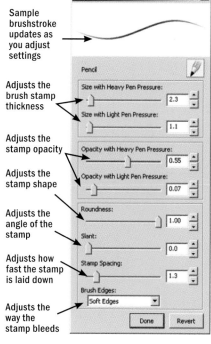

*Default brush settings for a 2B pencil*

> **Tip:** *Use SketchBook to take a screen grab of an image with a color scheme you like to source it as a color palette.*

# CREATE A CUSTOM PENCIL AND ERASER

By adjusting increments of the various brush settings you can customize a wide range of delicate to extreme brushes. You will now create a custom pencil and eraser to use for developing an example of a character design. We will adjust a few attributes to give them a slightly more organic variation on the presets.

## Custom Pencil

For the custom pencil you will **Copy To Custom** the default 2B pencil and adjust the roundness, slant and stamp spacing with the values indicated in the Brush Editor to the right.

Notice the sample brush stroke at the top of the editor update as you adjust the settings. This will apply a subtle uneven quality to the stroke. You may continue to adjust the custom pencil settings further to your liking. Use this custom pencil to draw out the robot character design.

Copy this preset pencil to the Custom tab

*Preset 2B pencil*

Squashes brush stamp slightly

Angles brush stamp slightly

Speeds up brush response slightly

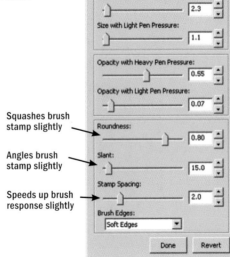

*Tweaked pencil settings*

*Sample of original, squashed & slanted pencil stamp*

**Note:** *When creating custom brushes, the size of your brush is important in relation to your canvas size. If you are working on a very large canvas you will want to increase your custom brush sizes accordingly.*

# Custom Eraser

You will create a custom eraser that will complement your custom pencil. The preset erasers have a hard edge and are good for sharp erasing, but may be too sharp for working on our character design.

For the custom eraser you will **Copy To Custom** a medium preset eraser and then lower the opacity and soften its edges. These settings will simulate a responsive eraser that allows for subtle clean up while drawing the character design.

Copy this preset eraser to the Custom tab

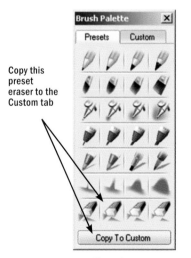

*Preset eraser*

Moderate range in opacity with pressure

Wide range in opacity with pressure

Soft edges give a gentle bleed

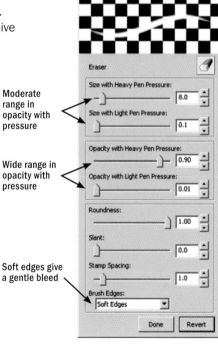

*Tweaked eraser settings*

# CHARACTER DESIGN

You will now go through the process of drawing a front and side view character design of the *Blue* robot. These drawings can be imported into front and side view cameras in Maya and used as reference planes for the 3D modeling of the character. You will first create some simple forms to establish proportions for the character. Then you will continue refining the shape of the character's head, torso and limbs. We will demonstrate the **rotate** and **mirror** functions and the use of color. Some of the steps in this process can be done with layers that will be introduced in the next section.

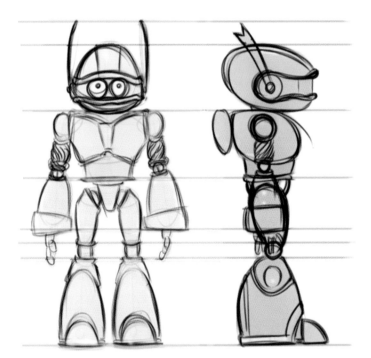

*Sample front and side view of the robot Blue*

## Sketching the front view

The following illustrations show from the initial sketching of *Blue's* proportions through to a refined front view. Use the custom pencil and eraser you created for these steps.

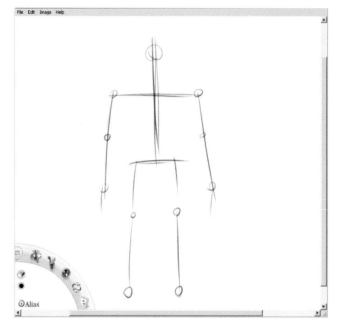

*Stick figure for basic shape*

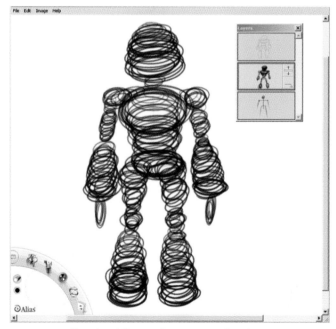

*Rough swirling marks to gesture in volume*

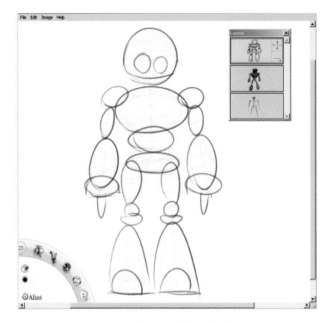

*Circles and ovals to clarify body elements*

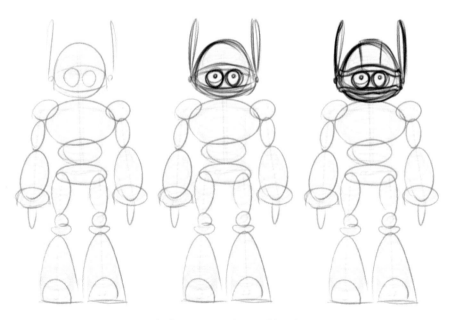

*Refinements to shape of head*

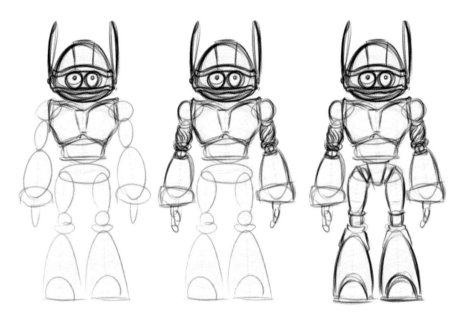

*Refinements to shape of torso and limbs*

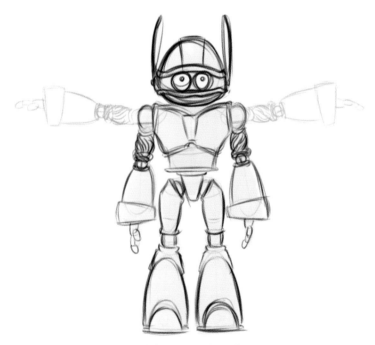

*Raised arms drawn in*

When you are finished drawing the front view save it out as a new duplicate drawing before continuing to the next stage. Use the **Edit** marking menu save function and save the file as *Robot_frontview.tiff*. The saved drawing can serve as a backup file in case you need to rework the drawing.

**Tip:** *Remember to save your file continually while drawing.*

## Drawing the side view

In this stage you will draw guidelines that can be followed to match *Blue* in a side view. Using a ruler on the tablet, you will draw a series of lines along key points of the robot. Then you will continue drawing the robot in a side view.

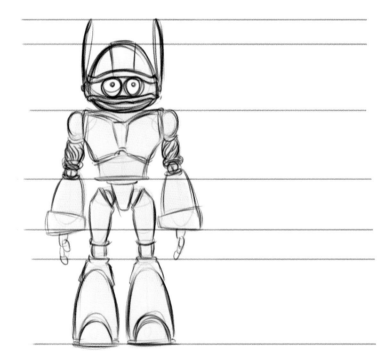

*Front view with corresponding guidelines*

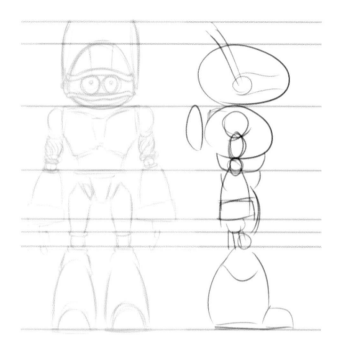

*Basic shapes for side view*

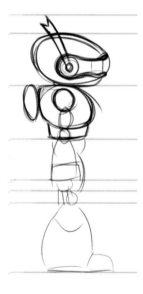

*Refinement of shapes in side view*

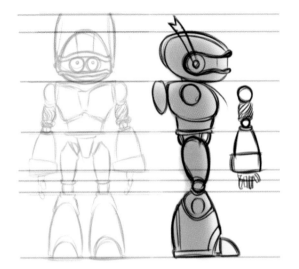

*Displaced arm shows unobstructed side view*

When this drawing is completed select around the side view and use the crop function under **Image → Crop to selection**. Save this drawing as *Robot_side_view.tiff*.

## Symmetry

One way to ensure a symmetrical drawing for the front view is to use the SketchBook Pro mirror function. Using the original front view, select and copy (**Ctrl+c**) the left half of the body as close as possible to the center.

Use the **Mirror** function from the top menu under **Image → Mirror** to refect the image. Once the image is mirrored, paste back down the unreflected left side.

Save the new symmetrical drawing as *Robot_front_sym.tiff*. You can now import the front and side view drawings into Maya as image planes. You can use the images for reference while modeling in 3D.

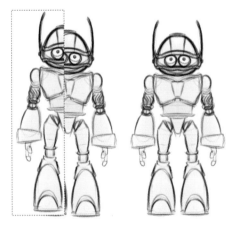

*Pasting and moving original half to match mirrored body*

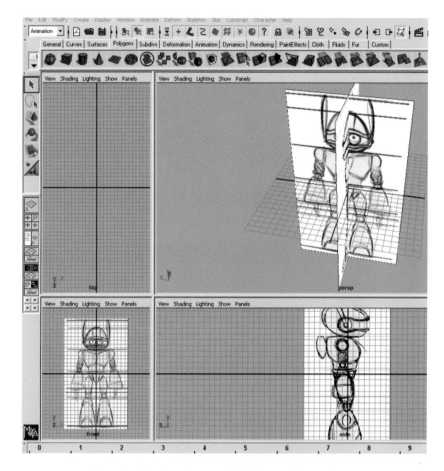

*Character drawings imported into Maya as image planes*

You have seen how to draw a front and side view character design that you can use to assist in your 3D modeling process. In addition to the front and side views, it is helpful to draw the top and bottom views for extra modeling references. Other helpful reference images would be larger detailed drawings of elements such as the hands, or any other intricate parts.

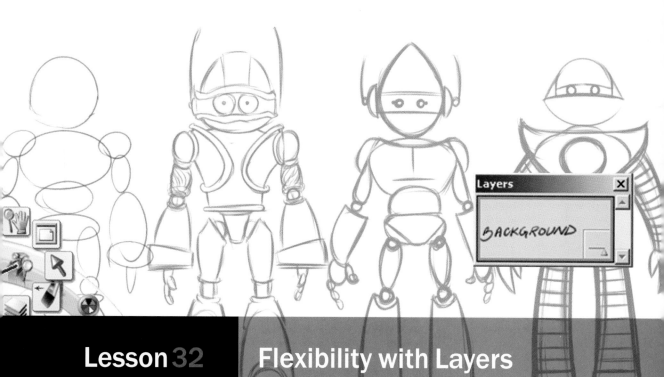

# Lesson 32  Flexibility with Layers

*Layers bring aspects from traditional printmaking and cel animation to the art of digital drawing. Layers in Alias SketchBook Pro software allow for fast and fine adjustment in drawing, painting and ideation. A layer becomes an extension of the canvas like a sheet of digital acetate, each with its own separate editing access. You will also see how you can vary iterations on a drawing by elaborating on the example of a character design.*

**In this lesson you will learn the following:**

- How to work with layers;

- How to use layers for ideation, and working with character design;

- How to use layers for story boarding;

## Layers window

When you flick down in the Toolbox marking menu to pick the **Layers Tool**, a layer window pops up. In this window press down to bring up the layers marking menu. Hover over each of the tools to see their tool tip info. These tools let you quickly add, delete, duplicate, hide, rename and lock layers. They also let you merge or completely flatten layers.

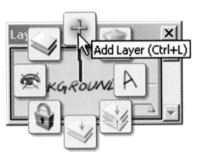

*Layers marking menu*

## Layer Opacity

In the bottom right of the layer is an icon of a line and pointer. Click on this to bring up the **Opacity** window. Move the slider to change the opacity of that layer. When you close the layer its level of opacity is reflected in the icon.

*Opacity icon*

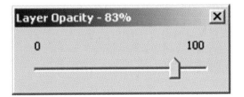

*Opacity slider*

## Layer handles

When you create more than one layer, a handle icon appears in the top right of the layer window. Grab and move this handle up or down to reposition the order in which layers are stacked upon each other.

*Layer handle*

Project Five

## Further layer control

There are more ways to subtly affect each layer. Within the tools and views marking menu you can use the **Move Tool** to move around the entire contents of a layer. You can also use the **Select Tool** to describe a portion of a layer that can be moved, copied or pasted. While the **Clear Tool** within the Edit marking menu will affect only the active layer, the **Expand Canvas Tool** expands all layers.

**Note:** *Use multiple layers liberally. SketchBook Pro maintains high performance even when creating artwork on dozens of layers.*

## Ideation

Another powerful way to use layers is for developing ideas on a design. Continuing with the example of a character design, you will examine methods to create multiple design variations on separate layers. Building upon a base layer of the original simple circle and oval shapes, you will add several layers for the head, torso, arms and legs. Using layers in this way allows you to quickly compare elements with each other.

*Multiple robot design variations*

Create several layers and name them as separate body elements. Drawing the corresponding body parts on their separate layers allows for clear editing on design variations.

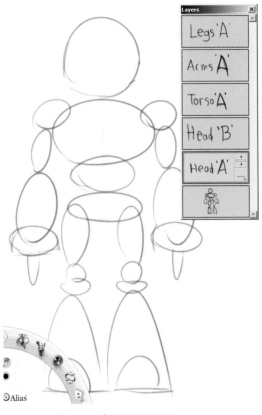

*Layer structure*

In the example on the following page, there are variations of the robots torso on different layers. Using the show and hide layer functions, you can quickly swap between variations.

Once a design is further developed you can also experiment with design motifs such as texture, decaling and color iterations by quickly showing and hiding layers.

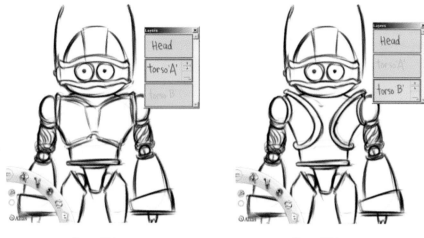

Torso 'A' layer                    Torso 'B' layer

# STORYBOARDS

The Alias SketchBook Pro layer functionality makes storyboarding a dynamic process. Creating storyboard panels on individual layers allows for easy sequence shuffling. You can also finely adjust your camera composition by drawing the storyboard frames on separate layers. By drawing the character and set elements on separate layers you can also reposition them as necessary. You will examine the following *Blue* storyboard examples to demonstrate these concepts. These storyboards were drawn in SketchBook Pro with the custom pencil and eraser made in the previous chapter, as well as the preset airbrushes.

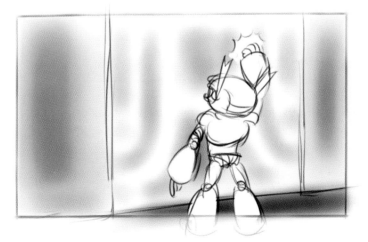

*Storyboard panels of Blue being hunted*

**Project Five**

*Storyboard panels of Blue being hunted*

*Blue being attacked and fending off villain robot*

# Resequencing a Storyboard

You can shuffle the sequence of your storyboard panels by drawing them on discreet layers. This allows for flexibility in storytelling.

Using the **Show**, **Hide** and **Move Layer Tools**, you can quickly rearrange the sequence of the frames.

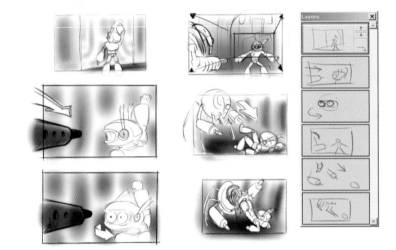

*Storyboard frames in layers*

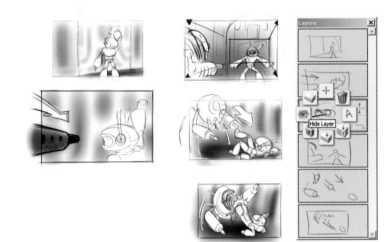

*Using hide layer function in layer window*

**Project Five**

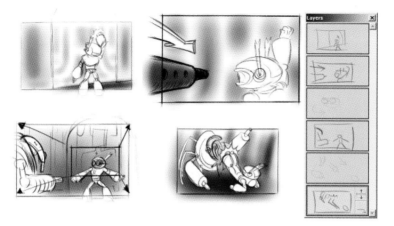

*New sequence after frames hidden and moved*

## Repositioning elements in a frame

Similar to shuffling the sequence of a storyboard, you can move around the contents of a frame. By having the elements (such as the character or frame itself) on separate layers, you have the freedom to quickly reposition them with the **Move Tool**. In the example frame below, the background, character, weapon and rectangular frames are drawn on separate layers.

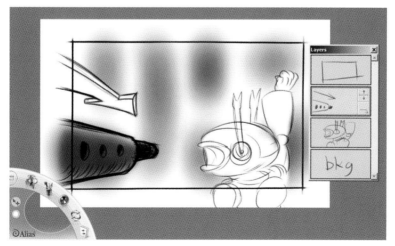

*Frame elements in layers*

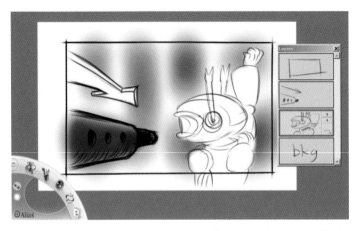

*Weapon and character moved closer into frame with Move Layer Tool*

**Note:** *Since layers in SketchBook Pro are transparent when on top of each other, you may want to paint a white or flat color underneath elements that you wish to move around. This will give those elements an opaque quality to delineate the characters from the background.*

After reaching a final composition and sequence of storyboards, you can merge the layers to reduce file size and resave it as a new file. This allows you to go back to the original layered files for further changes if necessary. You can also save out the frames individually and use them to create an animatic (animated storyboard) that can be edited into a video format to work with audio and pacing. Once your storyboards and animatics are complete, you have a reference upon which you can build your animation in Maya software.

## ANNOTATION AND PRESENTATION

Alias SketchBook Pro software is especially useful for image-based presentations in which you would want to mark over existing figures or illustrations. Using layers, one can make notes upon an image without overwriting the original file. You can minimize the interface and flip through a sequence of images in a folder as you would in a real sketchbook. Additionally, there is a sample of free downloadable background templates available from the Alias product page under SketchBook Pro (www.alias.com). Some of these drawing templates consist of perspective guides, storyboard layouts, TV and film aspect ratios that can assist you in the development of a computer animation project.

# Annotation

To annotate an existing image file, open it in SketchBook Pro and create a mark-up layer for comments or notes. You can rename the file in order to not overwrite it, or if the recipient of the file is also using SketchBook Pro for viewing the image, save it as a .TIFF file to preserve the layers.

This form of image annotation allows those giving and receiving project input to explicitly 'show' and 'tell' their concepts. Using layers in this way, artists can work collaboratively on an art piece, such as the pencil and ink drawings in the comic book format.

*Sample image markup*

# Presentation

Set up images within a folder in alpha-numeric order for a planned presentation. You can then easily flip back and forth between images or use the **Open File** command to jump to another image.

For meetings or instructional purposes, you can also make use of SketchBook Pro as a digital whiteboard by having your computer connected to a projector. Finally, you can print and email images directly from SketchBook Pro within the **File** menu.

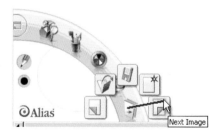

*Flipping through an image sequence*

> **Tip:** During presentations take advantage of the zoom and move puck to focus attention on particular areas of an image. Also, experiment with setting up an array of images together in one large resolution image file, and use the zoom and move puck to navigate through the multi-faceted image.

# Lesson 33  Painting a Texture Map

You can use Alias SketchBook Pro to paint textures that can stand as a form of art, on their own, or be used as an element in other areas of art such as collage, graphic design or 3D computer graphics. In this section we will examine the process of creating an image, known as a texture map, that can be used in Maya.

**In this lesson you will learn the following:**

- How to paint a planet texture map;

In Maya, any 2D image file can be used as a texture map and be projected or wrapped in a variety of ways around a 3D modeled object. This texture map conforms itself around the object, becoming the skin of that object. You can paint a texture map to represent anything from dust and scratches on panels of a wall or furniture, markings and blemishes on a characters skin, or even a fully executed landscape backdrop.

## Painting a planet texture

You will now create a planet texture using several brushes and functions. The swirling gas effect will be created using various sizes of the pre-set smear brushes. We will examine the work in stages and see how functions such as the smear brush and selection tools are used in this process. This texture map will be wrapped around a sphere in Maya to create a planet in 3D space.

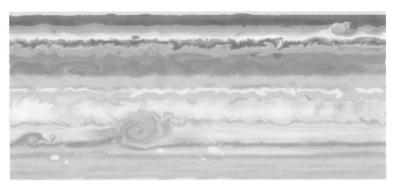

*Jupiter-like planet texture*

## Creating the texture in stages

To begin creating this texture, a palette of colors is laid down on a reference layer and then a main background color is used to fill out the canvas. On a few new layers, thick horizontal strips of color are applied to represent the main cloud bands that wind around the planet. This is done using a ruler on the drawing tablet. With the strips on separate layers, there is greater flexibility in changing the composition.

*Initial wider bands of color*

In the next stage, adding the smaller strips is done by sampling from the larger bands. Thin rectangular selections are made from the larger bands of color, then copied and pasted onto other areas to create several more bands.

*Composition with several thinner bands*

At this point, the smear brush can be used to experiment with creating a turbulence effect. Since the smear brush only works with color on the active layer, all the layers need to be flattened into one. Depending on how large a swirling effect is desired, different sizes of pre-set smear brushes can be used.

*Smaller smear brush presets used for initial swirling effect*

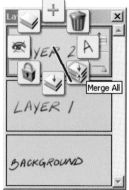

*Merge All function*

To give more smokey depth to the texture, some airbrush strokes are dragged and spotted along the bands.

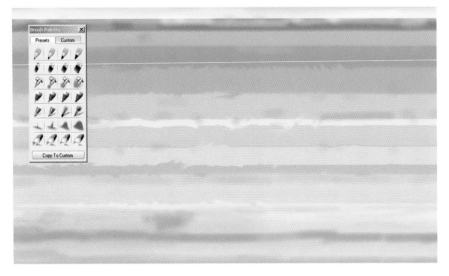

*Light airbrush strokes added*

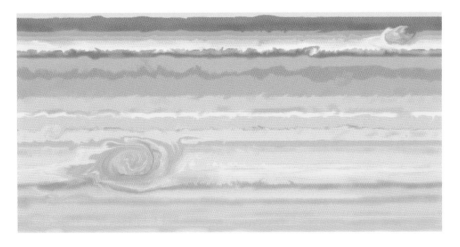

*More swirling added with splotches of color dabbed in*

*Thickness of bands changed with larger smear brush*

**Tip:**    Create a very low-opacity smear brush that can be used for subtle
blending. This kind of custom brush is effective for softening harsh
transitions or lines.

*Large and small dabs of color swirled in with airbrush, pencil and smear brush*

Once the painting is completed to the desired level of detail, copy it into the
*textures* folder of a new Maya project. The texture is then mapped onto a sphere
in Maya to create a planet in 3D space.

**Note:** The closer a camera comes to a textured object in Maya dictates how much detail and resolution you should add to your painting. If the object is far out in the frame, it may not require extreme detail. Optionally, if you wish to have the object be seen closer in the frame for a static shot you can create a second image based on the zoomed-in portion of the original texture. For example, if the giant swirling storm in the final painting were to be used in a full frame, it could be redrawn as a new high-resolution texture.

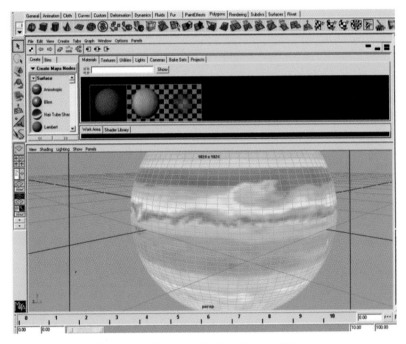

*Texture map being applied to sphere in Maya*

You have seen how a texture can be created with various layer and brush techniques. Besides painting a texture from scratch you can open a photographic image in SketchBook Pro and use that as a base to paint upon. A more complex way to implement textures in 3D is to layer them on top of each other in Maya. Using the planet example, you can draw additional cloud and swirling gas layers, then project them onto the sphere in separate layers. This 3D layering would simulate the textures being on different atmospheric levels.

*Final rendering in Maya*

## Conclusion

You are now familiar with the Alias SketchBook Pro interface and have seen
examples of how it can be used as a design and planning tool for a computer
animated movie like *Blue*. You have seen the advantages of using SketchBook
Pro software for character design, storyboarding and painting texture maps.
Digital drawing in this way brings an unprecedented ability for an artist and
designer to edit and evolve their artwork and drawing process. Regardless of
your ability you can use SketchBook Pro to enhance your paint and drawing
skills. In addition to the software, Alias Sketchbook Pro discussions are a
valuable resource, accessible through technical support at www.alias.com.

# Index

*Notes*

![EVE - Online © CCP2005]

# GET MORE OUT OF MAYA®
## with the Maya Silver Membership program!

**A**s award-winning software, Maya® is the most comprehensive 3D and 2D graphics and animation solution on the market. And whether you're using Maya Personal Learning edition to learn more about computer graphics and animation, or you have a full Maya license that you're using to produce professional content, the Maya Silver Membership program helps you take your Maya skill to the next level.

## What is Maya Silver Membership?

Your Maya Silver Membership program gives you quick, online access to a wide range of Maya learning resources. These educational tools – in-depth tutorials; real-life, project-based learning materials; the Maya Mentor learning environment plug-in; Weblogs from experienced Maya users – are available for a fixed monthly, or cost-saving annual, subscription fee.

Silver Membership also keeps you abreast of the latest computer graphics industry developments and puts you in touch with other Maya users and industry experts. Plus, you get 30 days of personal help to orient you around the site.

## Key Benefits

- **Unbeatable Value**
- **Faster Learning**
- **Competitive Advantage**
- **Industry Contacts**

© Grey Advertising 2005

# Silver Membership Features

### Downloadable Learning Tools
Silver members now have access to selected Learning Tools, at no charge.

### Project-based Learning Materials
A wide range of up-to-date, online learning materials takes you through sample projects. Step-by-step new projects are published each month!

### Maya Mentor
Maya Silver members can download this unique Maya plug-in that provides real-time, visual tutoring directly within the Maya user interface.

### Tutorials Database
This extensive, sort-able database provides access to over 100 Maya tutorials created by Alias Product Specialists and industry experts.

### Concierge Program
Silver membership entitles you to 30 days of personal, one-on-one access to a site attendant who will help you learn how to best use the online resources of the Silver Membership program.

### Duncan's Corner
You can now learn from Alias' own Principal Scientist – Duncan Brinsmead. This Silver-exclusive Weblog will feature workflow tips as well as demo files and example files from the man behind such important Maya innovations as Maya Paint Effects™ and Maya Fluid Effects™.

### Alias® Weblogs
Interact with industry leaders or Product Specialist to discuss how they created a particular work using Maya.

### Industry Knowledge Articles
These articles include interviews and stories on industry-related topics.

### Textures & Shaders Database
Silver members will have access to a new collection of extremely high-resolution (2048 x 2048), tile-able textures and shaders that are ready for use in production or on any Maya project.

### Discussion Forums
Join in a Silver Membership discussion forum, hosted by an experienced 3D artist or instructor, and get answers on questions related to the learning materials.

### Personal Gallery Page
Annual subscribers are also entitled to post a personal gallery page on the alias.com site that lets them share personal information and Maya images they've created with other members of the Maya community.

### *Bonus Offers*
*As a Silver member you receive bonus magazine subscriptions with your membership. Plus all members who take out an annual membership receive, in addition to their magazine subscription, a bonus Maya Learning Tool.*

For pricing and other information regarding the Maya Silver Membership program: **www.alias.com/silver**

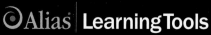

changing the face of 3D

# New Old School

## The natural way to draw, the modern way to work.

**A**lias® SketchBook™ Pro, the high quality paint and drawing tool for use with tablet PC's and digitized tablets, has a fast, simple and natural interface that has the tactile feel of drawing with a pencil and paper and all the benefits of a digital format.

Artist friendly, the gesture-based user interface of SketchBook Pro is easy enough for the casual user to master, yet has all the features that experts demand. But don't take our word for it. We've included a free, permanent license of SketchBook Pro 1.1 in *Learning Maya 7 | Foundation* ($199.99 Value). Master the features included here, then download a full-featured trial version of SketchBook Pro 2 for Mac® or Windows® at www.alias.com/sketchbookpro.

**Upgrade to Alias SketchBook Pro 2 & Save $100**

### Alias
# SketchBook Pro

DOWNLOAD UPGRADE
Alias
SketchBook
Pro 2
FOR ONLY $79

○Alias | www.alias.com